Classics of
Science Fiction and Fantasy
Literature

Classics of Science Fiction and Fantasy Literature

Volume 2
The Man in the High Castle — Zothique
343 – 698
Indexes

edited by
Fiona Kelleghan
University of Miami

SALEM PRESS, INC.
Pasadena, California   Hackensack, New Jersey

Library of Congress Cataloging-in-Publication Data
Classics of science fiction and fantasy literature / edited by Fiona Kelleghan.
    p. cm. — (Magill's choice)
"Plot summaries and analyses of 180 major books and series in the fields of science fiction and fantasy . . . all but eight of the essays in these volumes are taken directly from Salem Press's four-volume Magill's guide to science fiction and fantasy literature, which was published in 1996"—Publisher's note.
    Includes bibliographical references (p.) and index.
    ISBN 1-58765-050-9 (set : alk. paper) — ISBN 1-58765-051-7 (v. 1 : alk. paper) — ISBN 1-58765-052-5 (v. 2 : alk. paper)
    1. Science fiction—Stories, plots, etc. 2. Fantasy fiction—Stories, plots, etc. I. Kelleghan, Fiona, 1965-   II. Magill's guide to science fiction and fantasy literature. III. Series.

PN3433.4 .C565 2002
809.3'876—dc21

2002001113

PRINTED IN THE UNITED STATES OF AMERICA

Contents

Contents

Classics of
Science Fiction and Fantasy
Literature

The Man in the High Castle

Political intrigue and the struggles of daily life in a conquered America after Germany and Japan win World War II

Author: Philip K. Dick (1928-1982)
Genre: Science fiction—alternative history
Type of work: Novel
Time of plot: Shortly after World War II
Location: San Francisco, California, and elsewhere in the western United States
First published: 1962

The Story

The Man in the High Castle is probably the finest and certainly the most influential alternative history novel ever written, evidenced by its Hugo Award for best novel of 1962 and allusions to it in subsequent alternative histories. It is set shortly after an Axis victory in World War II, which led to partitioning of the United States into the German-controlled eastern region, the Japanese-occupied West Coast, and a buffer zone in the Rocky Mountain states. In contrast to the brutal Nazi regime, Japanese control is more cultural and economic in nature than military or political. Japanese bureaucrats eagerly consume the cultural treasures of the country while Americans study the I Ching and artificially darken their skin.

The novel opens with a telephone call from Nobusuke Tagomi, a bureaucrat in the Japanese occupation government, to Robert Childan, an American antiques dealer. Tagomi wishes to purchase a gift for a visiting Swedish official. This official is in reality Rudolf Wegener, a German agent. Wegener's mission is to prevent a surprise nuclear attack on the Japanese home islands by enlisting covert Japanese support for Reinhard Heydrich, the head of the Gestapo.

A second strand in the narrative web of the novel begins when Childan is told that one of his antiques is counterfeit. The informer is Frank Frink, a Jewish refugee from the east and a former employee of the Wyndam-Matson Corporation, a manufacturer of counterfeit antiques. His visit to Childan's store is part of a scheme to start a jewelry-making business by extorting money from his former employer. After an outraged Childan complains to his supplier, Wyndam-Matson gives two thousand dollars to Frink and his partner but asks the police to investigate them.

An important element in the background of these characters' lives is *The Grasshopper Lies Heavy*, a novel depicting the world as it might have been following an Allied victory. Most affected by the novel is Frink's estranged wife, Juliana, who works as a judo instructor in Colorado. She is introduced to the book by her new lover, a truck driver named Joe Cinnadella, with whom she undertakes a journey to visit the book's author, Hawthorne Abendsen, at his home in Wyoming.

Childan, disturbed at the possibility that his antiques may not be authentic, agrees to carry Frink's jewelry in his shop. Paul Kasoura, a young Japanese man whose friendship Childan seeks, tells Childan that the jewelry exhibits *wu*, the Daoist virtue of wisdom or comprehension, and that one of his associates is interested in mass-producing copies for sale in South America. Childan summons enough pride in himself and the work of his countrymen to refuse the offer.

Tagomi, deeply distressed after killing two German agents who were attacking Wegener and a Japanese admiral, visits

Philip K. Dick.
(Courtesy of the Philip K. Dick Society)

Childan's store, where he is given one of Frink's ornamental pins. After meditating on the object he finds himself briefly in what appears to be the reader's world, complete with traffic, smog, and disrespectful Americans. After his vision, Tagomi returns to his office to find a request for the extradition of Frink. Enraged by the German attack on his office, Tagomi instead orders Frink's release; he then suffers a heart attack, his recovery from which is left in doubt.

In Wyoming, Juliana discovers that Cinnadella is actually a German agent sent to murder Abendsen. She kills Cinnadella and proceeds to the author's house alone, where she learns that Abendsen—like Philip K. Dick himself—wrote his novel in consultation with the I Ching. A question to the ancient book of oracular wisdom reveals that *The Grasshopper Lies Heavy* signifies "Inner Truth," a response that prompts Juliana to abandon her own reality as illusion and to embrace the truth of the novel's utopian vision.

Analysis

The Man in the High Castle is among the most highly regarded of Dick's works. It strays from the standard formula of the dystopia, one that culminates in the overthrow of a corrupt social order, to a more complex narrative form in which the dystopia is both less corrupt and more powerfully entrenched. Because the dystopia is not overthrown, there is no single central action that unites all the novel's characters; the narrative structure is therefore more complex. The absence of an organized resistance frustrates the reader's desire for a rectification of history, a desire that fuels the conventional novel of alternative history. The reader's desire for resistance is frustrated and transformed by the novel into an acknowledgment of alien values. The only character to openly defy the German authorities is not an American but a Japanese; nevertheless, when Tagomi refuses to sign Frink's extradition papers, American readers are likely to cheer the act of defiance.

The Man in the High Castle further undermines the dystopian formula by establishing a sharp contrast between the mere rigidity of Japanese rule and the horrors of Nazism. Like the German Mars landing that serves as a recurring background motif throughout the novel, Nazi violence and oppression occur almost exclusively offstage. This is partly a result of the genocidal scale of the Nazi holocaust, which encompasses the entire African continent. In contrast to what Childan refers to as "the difficulty in Africa," the Japanese exploitation of South America consists chiefly of "erecting eight-floor clay apartment houses for ex-headhunters."

The novel's thematic concerns are not limited to the political sphere; they extend into the realm of aesthetics through such artifacts as Frink's jewelry. The conflict within the novel between historical and artistic authenticity ultimately is self-referential in nature. Frink's jewelry is described as "a new thing on the face of the world," in contrast to the merchandise in Childan's store, the value of which is derived solely from its supposed historicity. In the same manner as the duplication of historic artifacts undermines their authenticity, so the proposed reproduction of Frink's jewelry would strip from it the *wu* that it possesses. The relevance of this for *The Man in the High Castle* and alternative history in general lies in the fact that, like Frink's jewelry, the alternative history novel is not dependent on historical authenticity or verisimilitude for its artistic value. It does not attempt to duplicate the superficial aspects of historical reality but instead allows readers to see more deeply into reality than the mere imitation of history permits.

—*Edgar V. McKnight, Jr.*

The Man Who Folded Himself

> A time traveler encounters and interacts with past and future alternative versions of himself, ultimately becoming his own father and mother, only to have his child begin the process again

Author: David Gerrold (Jerrold David Friedman, 1944-   )
Genre: Science fiction—time travel
Type of work: Novel
Time of plot: From prehistory to the far future
Location: Primarily Earth, with references to travel in outer space
First published: 1973

The Story

A young man named Daniel Jamieson Eakins inherits a time-traveling belt device from his "Uncle Jim." He decides to go one day into the future, get that day's newspaper, and then bounce back to the present and go to the races. The newspaper will allow him to place winning bets on horses. When he does so, he encounters his future "self," who proposes that they go together to the races. They do so and win a large sum of money, then go out to celebrate afterward. Daniel becomes his future self, waiting for his past self to pop into the future. He repeats the experience of attending the races with his earlier self.

Curious about whether he can alter the past, he changes the size of the bets placed and is about to attempt to turn what was a $57,600 five-horse parlay into a $1.5 million eight-horse parlay. Another future version of himself appears to warn him that such an action will lead to unpleasant consequences, such as massive publicity and an investigation.

Daniel engages in a wide range of activities in the past, present, and future, always certain that, should anything unpleasant or harmful be about to occur, one of his future "selves" will appear to warn him in time to alter his behavior. Through the use of the time-travel device, apparently endless numbers of alternative versions of himself are able to simultaneously visit the same time, resulting in such recreations as poker games with a room full of his alternative selves and homosexual experimentation with the ultimate narcissistic love objects, his own past and future selves.

Daniel concludes that each time he makes different decisions, he is actually creating a parallel universe in which his life is different. He experiments in changing the past, doing things such as eliminating certain political assassins or historical figures such as Jesus Christ and Adolf Hitler. Ultimately, he determines that some of these changes must themselves be undone; eliminating Christianity, it turns out, creates a present that is too "alien" for him to live in.

At one point, he evidently has changed things enough that the various alternative versions of himself stop appearing. Lonely and confused, he flees to the distant past, before there are humans on Earth. There he encounters "Diana Jane Eakins," a female version of himself, the woman he would have been had he been born female. She is from yet another parallel time-universe. A torrid love affair results in the birth of a child. Daniel wishes the child to be a boy, Diana wishes it to be a girl, and each of them uses advanced scientific techniques to turn wish into reality. Each ultimately takes a version of the child they have created to their own futures.

Daniel and Diana fight and break up. Daniel now realizes that he is his Uncle Jim, and he proceeds to raise the child as Daniel Jamieson Eakins, his younger self. He also travels to a time and place where various older versions of himself gather to witness the heart attack that ultimately ends his life as he arrives there from his travels through time.

At the end, the child has grown, Uncle Jim has died, and Daniel now again inherits the time-travel belt, although this time with a manuscript that is Uncle Jim's diary, which describes all that has gone before, so that Daniel can avoid past mistakes. Although shocked at some of the things Uncle Jim's diary says he has done, Daniel decides to put on the time belt and explore all the experiences that await.

Analysis

Although attacked by some critics for its short, choppy sentences, this is a lively, inventive, and entertaining time-travel story. Its basic premise, that of a time traveler encountering other versions of himself, is certainly derivative of two short stories by Robert A. Heinlein. In Heinlein's "By His Bootstraps" (first published under the name Anson MacDonald in the October, 1941, *Astounding Science-Fiction*), the protagonist interacts with various past and future versions of himself, ultimately becoming the person who first recruited him to visit the future, and in "All You Zombies—" (*The Magazine of Fantasy and Science Fiction*, March, 1959), the protagonist is recruited into a corps of time travelers and through a convoluted plot device also becomes his/her own mother and father.

Aside from a couple of "stick figure" characters such as the protagonist's landlady and the (nameless) lawyer who informs Daniel that his Uncle Jim is dead, all the characters in the novel are ultimately the same person, albeit alternative versions of him. The weakness of the book is the lack of true character development. Because all the protagonist's interactions are with other versions of himself, his motivations and actions are necessarily self-serving and require no justification other than his own pleasure. A revised version of the book published in 1991 eliminates some positive references in the original to marijuana use and drug culture but also seems to make some of the text, which is written as first-person internal reflection, seem less spontaneous and more contrived.

David Gerrold's career began with writing the *Star Trek* episode "The Trouble with Tribbles" (1967). He is also the author of *When Harlie Was One* (1972), concerning an intelligent computer. The promise of Gerrold's early works, including *The Man Who Folded Himself*, is realized in the author's ongoing War Against the Chtorr series of novels, including *A Matter for Men* (1983), *A Day for Damnation* (1984), *A Rage for Revenge* (1989), and *A Season for Slaughter* (1992). In these more mature works, the inventiveness of the author's ideas is combined with depth of character development.

—*Bernard J. Farber*

The Mars Trilogy

Humanity colonizes Mars, and the colonists declare their independence from Earth

Author: Kim Stanley Robinson (1952-   )
Genre: Science fiction—future history
Type of work: Novels
Time of work: 2027 to the twenty-third century
Location: Mars
First published: *Red Mars* (1992), *Green Mars* (1993), and *Blue Mars*
(1996)

The Story

Red Mars is a sweeping saga of humanity's colonization of Mars. It is told
primarily from the viewpoint of the First Hundred, the initial Martian
colonists. The novel begins with the death of John Boone, the first man to
set foot on Mars and one of the leaders of the colony. Boone's death was
plotted by his best friend, Frank Chalmers, his rival in politics and romance. The story then flashes back to the flight to Mars, as the colonists
endure alternating bouts of boredom and intense preparation for their
landing. The creation of the colony and a manned base on the moon
Phoebus goes smoothly, marred only by a debate over the pace and
methods of terraforming Mars. The Reds, led by geologist Ann Clayborne, want to retain Mars in its natural state for study. The Greens,
led by Saxifrage Russell, believe in adapting the Martian environment
through biological and industrial processes so that people may one day
walk the Martian surface without need of artificial breathing devices.

As the First Hundred develop Mars, additional colonists arrive. Development on Mars is nominally under the control of the United Nations, but the growth of transnational corporations on Earth leads to a
growing corporate presence on Mars. As conditions on Earth decline,
immigration to Mars and access to its resources increasingly are seen as
rights on Earth, even as the Martian colonists begin to develop a sense of
independence. Chalmers, the leader of the American delegation, deals
with Earth officials and Martian factions to maintain a fragile balance of
power. This balance begins to break down as an asteroid is maneuvered
into orbit to be used as raw material and the base for a space elevator, a

cable connecting the asteroid and Mars to provide low-cost transportation from Mars's gravity well.

Martian medical personnel discover a way to slow the aging process dramatically. This precipitates a crisis on Earth, as differences widen between the haves and the have-nots. This pressure spills over to Mars, as increased immigration and worsening living conditions lead colonists to disappear into the wild. Hiroko Ao, head of the first farm colony on Mars, leads her team and psychologist Michel Duval into the southern hemisphere, and other colonists join them.

In 2061, a violent revolution breaks out. Town barriers are breached, and the revolutionaries are slaughtered. The space elevator is destroyed, and Phoebus is blown up because of fears of invasion from space. The Earth forces reassert control, and Chalmers is killed as the survivors of the First Hundred flee to the southern hemisphere for sanctuary.

Green Mars begins twenty years after the failed revolution. Mars is rebuilding slowly after the revolution, and refugees are beginning to reenter Martian society, using false identification. Ao also has begun to produce children, using artificial wombs. Life in the sanctuaries is detailed through the eyes of one of these children, Nirgal, a grandson of members of the First Hundred. Much of the action, on both Mars and Earth, deals with a discussion of what type of society should be established to sustain development.

Megacorporations have developed on Earth and taken over Third World countries. They openly flout the authority of the United Nations on Mars, establishing their own police forces. Parallel to this repression, the underground society develops an alternative lifestyle in which differences in social, political, and religious beliefs are tolerated. They also develop an economy based on the barter system and the exchange of hydrogen, an extremely rare element on Mars. Thanks to the antiaging drug, the First Hundred who survived the revolution are still active members of society, even though they are more than one hundred years old.

The Martian independence movement grows again, led by Nadia Cherneshevsky and Maya Toitovana, members of the First Hundred, and Nirgal and Jackie Boone from the younger generation. This movement is more tempered, governed by political opportunity rather than rash actions. The various factions gather to debate the formation of the postindependence government, writing the Dorsa Brevia declaration, which widely divergent groups agree will govern their life in the postrevolutionary environment. Cherneshevsky and Toitovana work tirelessly to keep the movement in check while waiting for a catastrophic event on Earth that will divert attention from Mars.

The opportunity for revolution occurs when part of Earth's Antarctic continent breaks off and threatens to flood major coastal cities as it drifts north and melts. As the novel ends, the new Martian revolution, less violent than the first, appears to have been a success.

Blue Mars begins with the formation of a Martian government, with strict provisions for protection of the environment, including establishment of a primitive zone where the landscape forever will remain as it was before settlement. The First Hundred remain prominent in society, and Cherneshevsky is elected as the first Martian president. Relationships are developed not only with Earth, which receives a delegation consisting of Nirgal Boone, Maya Toitovana, and Michel Duval, but with the new colonies developing around the solar system as well. Tensions between the Green and Red movements and between the older and younger settlers develop as they debate the number of immigrants the Martian ecosystem is able to absorb. A practical method of travel beyond the solar system is found, and Jackie Boone becomes one of the first colonists to the stars.

Members of the First Hundred, now more than two hundred years old, begin to experience memory problems. By the end of the novel, they have begun dying of natural causes. Longtime enemies Ann Clayborne and Sax Russell have developed an understanding of each other's viewpoints, mirroring the Martian society as a whole.

Analysis

These are novels of development, in both political and technological senses. In them, Kim Stanley Robinson shows an encyclopedic knowledge of research on the potential for colonization of Mars and on its landscape. He extends and develops this knowledge into what might happen in the future. This detail consumes a large part of the trilogy, and in sections it slows the narrative, as in the extensive descriptions of the new landscape as the colonists begin to terraform Mars. One critic described the novels as "reading NASA tech manuals" and thought that the level of detail interrupted the story's flow. Robinson chooses to provide a level of detail that allows the reader to become a part of the society, and his descriptions of everyday activities, such as Martian jogging and theater, provide a convincing level of depth to his portrait of Martian society.

Parallel with the technological details (and certainly in the forefront in *Green Mars* and *Blue Mars*) is the development of Martian society. The society contains a number of segments, some based on elements from Earth's society, such as nationality or religion, and some more specific to

Mars, such as the ecological divide between the Reds and the Greens on issues concerning terraforming. The resulting discussions, especially the Dorsa Brevia conference in *Green Mars*, shows Robinson's belief that positive change still can be accomplished through people gathering in organizations.

The continued development of the Martian government and the reform of Earth's governments in response to ecological catastrophe in *Blue Mars* shows a positive view of the future. Each side's point of view is presented at length and is examined objectively. There are no easy answers to the difficulties Mars faces as the crisis on Earth lowers living standards on both planets, but decisions are made for the good of the whole instead of narrow interests. The novels have large casts of characters, with many appearing in all three books. These large casts allow Robinson to examine different places and viewpoints but mean that characters often disappear into the background just as the reader gets involved with their part of the story. Female characters are particularly strong in *Green Mars* and *Blue Mars*. Cherneshevsky and Toitovana, along with Jackie Boone, lead the political underground and the Martian government, and Ao develops the ecological underground movements. Robinson consistently has used strong women as central characters in his fiction.

Robinson wrote several novels before beginning the Mars trilogy. His first novel, *The Wild Shore* (1984), was an Ace special, a series of first novels selected by noted science-fiction editor Terry Carr. It describes the development of a postcatastrophe culture after the United States has lost a war. *The Gold Coast* (1988) deals with Orange County, California, about thirty years in the future, showing the results of unfettered technology. *Pacific Edge* (1990) shows yet another view, that of a utopia with environmental and population controls that allow everyone to lead a good life. Those three novels are referred to as the Orange County trilogy.

Robinson also is a noted writer of short fiction and won a Nebula in 1987 for his novella "The Blind Geometer." Although Robinson was an established author before the publication of *Red Mars*, this novel and its sequels moved him to the ranks of the major writers of the 1990's. *Red Mars* won several awards, including a 1994 Nebula and 1993 British Science Fiction Association Award. *Green Mars* won the 1994 Hugo and the 1994 Locus Award

—*Catherine Doyle*

The Martian Chronicles

Americans attempt to colonize Mars in the twenty-first century

Author: Ray Bradbury (1920-   )
Genre: Science fiction—alien civilization
Type of work: Stories
Time of plot: 1999 to 2026
Location: Mars and Earth
First published: 1950 (revised version published in England as *The Silver Locusts*, 1951)

The Story

In January, 1999, the first manned rocket to Mars is launched from Ohio. So begins Ray Bradbury's *The Martian Chronicles*, a book composed of fourteen stories and twelve sketches that are thematically connected and chronologically arranged. All but the last three stories take place between 1999 and 2005, during which time Mars is quickly settled and then, even more quickly, abandoned. People want to relocate on Mars primarily to escape tightening government controls and impending atomic war, but the Martians use their telepathic abilities to deceive and destroy the crews of the first three exploratory expeditions.

The fourth expedition succeeds because the Martians have been decimated by a plague of chicken pox inadvertently carried to Mars on a previous rocket. A crewman named Spender fears that people will come to Mars only for crass commercial and military purposes, not respecting and ultimately destroying what remains of a high Martian culture. Spender's fears appear justified after Benjamin Driscoll ("The Green Morning") discovers a quick way to make the Martian atmosphere more breathable. Human "locusts" now arrive in stages Bradbury likens to the development of the American West. In June of 2003, African Americans come in their own rockets ("Way in the Middle of the Air").

"Night Meeting," balancing quietly at the book's center, records the first friendly meeting between a human (Tomás Gomez) and a Martian (Muhe Ca). Prior to meeting Ca (who appears to be from either the past or the future), Gomez is told by an old man to approach Mars as if it were a "kaleidoscope"—that is, "Enjoy it. Don't ask it to be nothing else but what it is."

"The Martian" returns to what already has developed into a major thematic strand woven throughout the book. Contrary to the wise advice offered in "Night Meeting," people mistakenly persist in trying to combat loneliness and homesickness by molding Mars into something it is not—a twin to Earth. When war breaks out on Earth in November, 2005, virtually everyone returns "home."

The final three stories take place twenty-one years later (in 2026), the traditional span between birth and adulthood. Has the human race matured enough to embrace the beauty and desirability of cultural and racial diversity? "The Long Years" reunites on Mars two members of the fourth expedition. When Hathaway dies and Captain Wilder leaves, the process they originally had set in motion is finished. The next story ("There Will Come Soft Rains"), set on Earth, provides no evidence of human survival. Attention centers on the "death" of a completely automated house, its family having been killed by an atomic blast. In the last story ("The Million-Year Picnic"), a family has escaped to Mars in a "Family" rocket. Perhaps a few other families will follow. With all the wisdom of the old man in "Night Meeting," they decide to adapt to Mars and not try to make it into a second Earth. They will be the first of a new race of Martians. Perhaps Muhe Ca was indeed from the future, perhaps even a descendant of this very family. The book ends on this subdued but firm note of hope.

Analysis

Bradbury's second book, *The Martian Chronicles*, remains a major literary contribution to the "myth of Mars"—the notion of technologically advanced Martians confronting survival on a dying desert world—that began in 1877, when Giovanni Schiaparelli reported *canali* (mistranslated into English as "canals") on Mars. Developed mainly by Percival Lowell and embellished fictionally by writers such as H. G. Wells, Edgar Rice Burroughs, and C. S. Lewis, the myth grew.

When, in the last half of 1949, Bradbury put together the pieces of his first thematically unified book, he included twelve previously published Mars stories, added two new stories ("Night Meeting" and "The Green Morning"), and composed twelve bridging sketches. Bradbury did an admirable if imperfect job of choosing, revising, and arranging. Readers who notice that *The Martian Chronicles* is not sufficiently self-contained should consult "The Fire Balloons" in Bradbury's *The Illustrated Man* (1951).

Sherwood Anderson's *Winesburg, Ohio* (1919), Ernest Hemingway's *In Our Time* (1925), and the frontier thesis of historian Frederick Jackson

Turner guided Bradbury in organizing his grand mosaic of *The Martian Chronicles*. That he arranged some pieces as a series of waves roughly equivalent to stages in the settling of the American frontier has been noted. Not often noted is how Bradbury structured *The Martian Chronicles* like a Shakespearean tragedy, humanity's tragic flaw being an emotional immaturity that disallows the acceptance of diversity.

The diversity theme, found in many of his works, stems from the fact that Bradbury was conceived not long after older brother Samuel, twin to Leonard, died at the age of two. Bradbury grew up suspecting that he was supposed to replace the dead twin. He tried to escape such pressures by developing his own ego, yet he felt ambivalent about not meeting parental expectations. Bradbury came to perceive himself as an outsider, a family freak. In a poem written later in life, he wondered if his parents had been "incredulous" at the "humpbacked . . . Martian son" they had produced.

It is no surprise, then, that an important, self-reflective theme, universalized in *The Martian Chronicles*, involves the need to accept and cherish diversity—whether of individuals, racial groups, places, or cultures. "The Martian," with a main character whose name means "twin," is a key story illustrating the dangers involved in molding people or places into what they are not. Indeed, efforts to transform Mars into a twin to Earth prove abortive. Bradbury's message, rather, is to celebrate diversity: "Enjoy" Mars. "Don't ask it to be nothing else but what it is."

Although many mainstream critics praised the collection for its literary merits, some hard-core science-fiction readers were dismayed by its lack of scientific plausibility and seemingly antiscientific stance. When teachers discovered the book's appeal to high school and college students, its success was ensured. The theme of accepting diversity while fighting pressures to conform has continuing relevance; the book has never been out of print.

The Martian Chronicles remains a kaleidoscopic, lyrical work of many colors, meanings, and mythic possibilities. Sometimes poetic, sometimes satiric, and often moralistic, it is Bradbury's most accomplished, complex, and rewarding work, an imaginative blending of science fiction and fantasy that can justly claim the status of a classic.

—*Marvin E. Mengeling*

Martian Time-Slip

The strongman of a Martian colony tries to use the latent extrasensory powers of an autistic child to profit in land speculation

Author: Philip K. Dick (1928-1982)
Genre: Science fiction—extrasensory powers
Type of work: Novel
Time of plot: The near future
Location: Mars
First published: 1964 (serial form, "All We Marsmen," *Worlds of Tomorrow*, 1963)

The Story

Jack Bohlen is an immigrant to Mars living there with his family and working as a repairman for the Yee Company. He is assigned to do a small job for Arnie Kott, Supreme Goodmember of the Water Workers Local, Fourth Planet Branch. This assignment places Jack in the middle of a power struggle over a parcel of apparently worthless land that is to be developed by the United Nations.

Unlike Bohlen, Supreme Goodmember Kott is ruthlessly committed to the acquisition of power and material wealth at any cost. He uses people without hesitation or shame. He uses Dr. Glaub, a psychiatrist at the local camp for mentally disturbed children, to learn about a contemporary school of Swiss psychotherapists and their recently developed theory. They believe that autism and other forms of schizophrenia are caused by a discrepancy in the time sense of the sufferers. They believe that autistics and schizophrenics experience the world as running either much faster or much slower than do others. If their time is much faster, they would speed ahead into the future and get stuck there, isolated from the rest of humanity. From this vantage point, though imprisoned in their own heads, they might have special knowledge of the future. Establishing communication with such a person could be a profitable means of obtaining information.

Kott comes to believe that one particular autistic child, Manfred Steiner, not only is able to perceive time in this expanded fashion but also has the power to control it. Kott kidnaps the strange boy and takes him to Dirty Knobby, a Martian mountain that holds great religious significance for the indigenous population, called Bleekmen. Using an ancient visionary prescription from the Bleekmen and Manfred's extrasensory powers, Kott attempts to travel back in time and stake his claim to the land in question before its value skyrockets.

Kott's plan fails. He is incapable of navigating the insane time-travel tunnel that he believes will lead to success in his claim-jumping scheme. The innate compassion of the Bleekmen and Bohlen prevail. It appears that Bohlen had a bout with schizophrenia back on Earth and feels sympathy for young Manfred. Similarly, Doreen Anderton, Kott's mistress and feminine agent, had a schizophrenic brother and therefore sympathizes with schizophrenics. Her sympathy swings to Manfred's side and against her boss.

Most instrumental in the downfall of the Supreme Goodmember, however, is the accumulated enmity of other people he has mistreated. In a dispute arising from a tangentially related matter, Kott is assassinated out of revenge by a business rival whom he had previously destroyed with hardly a second thought.

Bohlen returns to a life of domestic harmony, and Manfred Steiner is able to avoid the fate of institutionalized horror he had foreseen in his own future. He makes one last, memorable appearance during the denouement, as a time-traveling cyborg.

Analysis

Martian Time-Slip is vintage Philip K. Dick, published only two years after his Hugo Award-winning *The Man in the High Castle* (1962). One of the wildest imaginations of the twentieth century explodes into full flower here, with no sign of the occasional loss of control that sometimes subverted its full effects. The thread of the plot unwinds intricately through the lives of more than a dozen characters. Their hopes, dreams, torments, and insanities are always well ordered against the backdrop of the basic conflict over land development.

As usual, the characters in this Dick novel are ordinary folks who attain noble stature in their struggles with extraordinary circumstances. Even the antagonist, Kott, earns some sympathy in his ability to accept the terms of life on Mars and his unabashed dedication to making the best of things. The amoral contagion of his energy sweeps the other characters, the plot, and the reader through the story from start to finish. The inner struggles and strength of Bohlen, the protagonist, contrast effectively with Kott. Jack's profoundly human sensibility is emphasized at the end of the book, when he actually mourns Kott's death.

The minor characters are drawn with a fine distinction. Kott's estranged wife, Anne Esterhazy, is seen through his eyes as a stereotypical idealist until she pulls a Machiavellian political coup against Dr. Glaub. Later, it seems appropriate that Anne and the ineffectual psychiatrist form a last-ditch alliance and attempt to rescue Manfred. His father, Norbert Steiner, is convincing in the opening pages of the novel as he falls victim, tragically, to suicidal impulses. Likewise, the development of Kott's assistant, Otto Zitte, from a superficial seducer of lonely housewives to Kott's assassin is entirely believable.

Thematically, *Martian Time-Slip* is a fascinating investigation of the relationship between schizophrenia and the human experience of time. The idea that mentally disturbed people run at a different speed from the rest of society is a typically entertaining science-fiction concept. Hypersensitivity to or obsession with the ultimate consequences of time, however, is one of the great themes of literature.

Death and decay await everyone at some point in the future, and thinking about it too much is not good for mental health. Communication, the main problem for schizophrenic people, is useless or impossible under the domination of this perspective on time. Language is reduced to gibberish, or "gubbish" as it is called in this novel. A lover's beauty and a child's innocence crumble to dust under the pressure of time's inevitable passage. The rewards of worldly success evaporate in the breeze of the calendar's fanning pages. Ironically, however, Dick demonstrates in *Martian Time-Slip* that this awareness of the crushing futility of life marks the beginning of true wisdom.

—*Steven Lehman*

The Merlin Trilogy

Merlin uses his powers as a magician and prophet to unify Britain
against Saxon attack by creating and then protecting King Arthur

Author: Mary Stewart (1916-   )
Genre: Fantasy—mythological
Type of work: Novels
Time of plot: The late fifth century C.E.
Location: Great Britain
First published: *The Crystal Cave* (1970), *The Hollow Hills* (1973), and *The Last Enchantment* (1979)

The Story

The Merlin trilogy tells the King Arthur story from the viewpoint of
Merlin, Arthur's protector, teacher, and adviser. *The Crystal Cave* focuses
on Merlin's childhood and youth as he struggles to find his father and
develop the gift of the Sight, the ability to see visions of events elsewhere
or in the future. The novel begins by introducing Merlin as the illegitimate son of Niniane, daughter of a Welsh king. She has refused to tell
anyone the name of the man who fathered her child.

Merlin is an outsider at his grandfather's court because of his birth
and strange ways; he is not interested in the war games that preoccupy
the other boys and instead studies healing and magic with Galapas, a
local wise man. When Merlin's grandfather dies, the boy flees from his
uncle Camlach, who sees Merlin as a threat and wishes to kill him.
Through a series of coincidences he attributes to the god who guides
him, Merlin discovers that his father is Ambrosius, the exiled rightful
king of Britain. Merlin uses his gift of prophecy to help his father regain
his throne, which then passes to his uncle Uther when Ambrosius dies.
Foreseeing that Uther's first son will be the king Britain needs to shield it
against Saxon invasion, Merlin agrees to help when King Uther falls in
love with Ygraine, wife of his chief ally Duke Gorlois of Cornwall. Dis-
guising Uther as Gorlois, Merlin takes him to Ygraine so that Arthur will
be conceived during their passion that night. Gorlois dies in a separate
attack that same night, and Uther rejects Merlin afterward for his failure
to foresee that Uther would be able marry Ygraine honorably one day
later.

The Hollow Hills is the story of Merlin's guardianship of his young cousin Arthur. Still at odds with Uther over the events at Tintagel, Merlin makes peace with the king in order to gain custody of Arthur upon his birth. Uther, fearing that his enemies may try to harm his son, asks Merlin to conceal the boy until he has grown. While Arthur is reared in a noble household, ignorant of his true position as heir to the kingdom, Merlin embarks on a quest to locate the great sword Caliburn for Arthur to find when he comes of age. When Arthur is ten years old, Merlin becomes his teacher; when the boy is

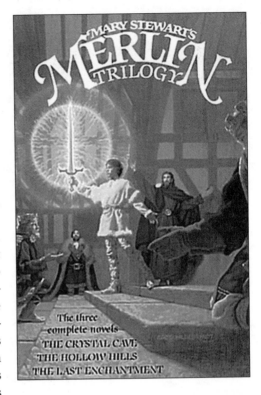

fourteen, Merlin takes him to his father, the dying King Uther. The night before his father's death, Arthur sleeps with Morgause, not knowing that she is his half-sister. She deliberately seduces him in a play for power. Arthur proves himself fit to fight and lead the kingdom in battle. Through the help of Merlin's magic, Arthur raises the sword from the stone where Merlin has hidden it and is proclaimed High King.

The Last Enchantment covers Merlin's service to the young king. The magic Merlin used when Arthur raised the sword has burned out his power, and he must adjust to living without it. He spies on Morgause, who uses her pregnancy with Arthur's incestuous bastard son, Mordred, to plot against her brother. Because of Merlin's prophecy that Mordred will eventually kill his father, Arthur wishes Merlin to kill the baby, but Merlin refuses. He attempts instead to find Mordred, but he fails because he now lacks the Sight to show him where Morgause has hidden her son.

Merlin eventually returns to Arthur to build the new fortress of Camelot. Still lacking his power, Merlin is unable to fend off Morgause's attempt on his life. She poisons him, leaving him mad for almost a year and prematurely aged. When he returns to the king's service, however, Merlin regains his powers of Sight and prophecy, which allow him first to save Arthur's queen, Guinevere, from an assault and then to acquire an assistant, Nimuë, to whom he passes on his arts. When Merlin apparently dies and is buried in Bryn Myrddin, the cave that has been his home, he has prepared Nimuë to take over his role as Arthur's adviser. Merlin awakes from his illness trapped in the cave and stripped of all his power, the fate he long ago foresaw for himself, but he escapes after several weeks. He refuses to return to public life, though, and the novel ends with his reunion with Arthur and Nimuë and his retirement back to Bryn Myrddin.

Analysis

Mary Stewart is well known for the gothic romances that occupied the first half of her writing career, but she changed to the genre of historical fiction when writing the Merlin trilogy. Most writers who have retold the "matter of Britain" (the Arthurian legends) set their stories in a pseudo-medieval England based on the great medieval sources of the legends: Geoffrey of Monmouth, Chrétien de Troyes, and Sir Thomas Malory. Although Stewart also uses these romances as sources for her plots, she opts to set her version of the story in late fifth century Britain, the time of the real though shadowy historical figure on whom the legends are based. This choice of setting profoundly affects the telling of her tale. Approaching the subject as historical fiction rather than romance, she strives for realism and as much historical accuracy as research allows her. Her Merlin claims to tell the "factual" events on which the legends are based.

Stewart deals with the fantasy component of the Merlin Trilogy in a manner in keeping with her vision of the historical period. She borrows the ancient Welsh legend of the Sight as the basis for Merlin's visionary ability. In a story set when the practices of pagan and Christian religions crisscrossed, Merlin naturally sees his power as coming from the gods. It sets him apart from other men because he experiences a spiritually dynamic universe in which the gods intervene in human affairs. Merlin's role is like that of a biblical prophet: When he works magic, he is serving as a channel through which the god speaks or acts. The supernatural thus directs the action of the books, although Stewart depicts events as realistically as she can.

By using Merlin as her narrator, Stewart emphasizes the ironic limitations of his power. Readers see that although both great and ordinary people stand in awe of his ability to work magic and kings request his help, Merlin himself knows that he does not so much command his power as it commands him. Nor is foreknowledge a simple matter, and Merlin is well aware that his gods are cryptic. Although he can see results, he often cannot see the means by which they are achieved or the price that must be paid. Furthermore, the deterministic universe that Stewart creates traps Merlin as much as it does ordinary people. Knowing that Arthur will be the savior of Britain, Merlin bends all of his efforts in the first two books toward making what the Sight has shown him come true; however, he is also helpless before the future when he foresees that Mordred will destroy the kingdom Arthur has created and protected. Some critics see the guilt that Merlin feels over his helplessness as self-pity or anticlimactic inaction, but his emotions fit the nature of the universe Stewart envisions.

Stewart deliberately parallels the story of Merlin's childhood and rise to power in *The Crystal Cave* with Arthur's own youth in *The Hollow Hills*. Both Merlin and Arthur live hidden childhoods as bastard boys searching for their fathers; they are then acknowledged as royal and brought into public life in their early teens. Each boy's search for his father is clearly a search for identity and power.

Stewart repeats this theme in *The Wicked Day* (1983), a coda to the trilogy that tells Mordred's story. As Arthur's bastard son by incest, he is brought up in ignorance of his parentage until his teens, when Arthur finds and acknowledges him. He learns to love his father and becomes one of Arthur's faithful Companions. Mordred is the traditional villain of the Arthurian legend, but Stewart tells his story with some sympathy, as a man who resents and resists the fate ordained for him as a parricide in a deterministic universe. This novel is less engaging than the trilogy, perhaps partially because the use of omniscient third-person narration instead of first-person narration creates a sense of distance between the reader and Mordred not present between the reader and Merlin. The book nevertheless gives a coherent account of the tragic events that bring an end to Arthur's reign, in keeping with the world Stewart portrays in the Merlin trilogy.

—*Kara K. Keeling*

Mission of Gravity and Star Light

A story of planetary exploration in which conditions radically different from those of Earth require humans to depend on alien Mesklinites to move across planets

Author: Hal Clement (Harry Clement Stubbs, 1922-   )
Genre: Science fiction—alien civilization
Type of work: Novels
Time of plot: The distant future
Location: Within twenty light years of Earth in the direction of the constellation Cygnus
First published: *Mission of Gravity* (1954; serial form, *Astounding Science-Fiction*, April-July, 1953) and *Star Light* (1971; serial form, *Analog*, June-September, 1970)

The Story

Hal Clement creates, in *Mission of Gravity*, a fictional planet called Mesklin in the double-star system known to astronomers as 61 Cygni. In the sequel, he moves to the gigantic Dhrawn, a few light years away and still in the known universe. In both stories of adventure and exploration, two motivations drive the Mesklinite aliens, who are clearly more interesting characters to Clement than their human handlers and explorer counterparts. First, the tiny Mesklinites are hardy explorers and astronauts who want to carry on their explorations. In the time between the two novels, they establish a College of Mesklin. The Mesklinites are also shrewd bargainers who exploit their human visitors in order to acquire more scientific knowledge than the dominant humans seem to want to give. Conversely, even though they are on major missions, the humans seem less eager and shrewd than their tiny partners. The younger humans are more eager, and in the sequel, Clement makes good use of this trait, as he does in his fiction for young adults and juveniles.

Mesklinites resemble fifteen-inch caterpillars, though they have an immensely tough exoskeleton. They are the most intelligent of the many species on Mesklin, which has variable gravity ranging from three Earth gravities at the equator to nearly seven hundred Earth gravities at each pole. The environmental details of the planet, and of Dhrawn in the sequel, along with Clement's ideas of what may cause such conditions, are as interesting as characterization and plot. A further conjecture by Clement concerns how planetary conditions affect the evolved life-forms—small, hard-shelled creatures evolve in high gravity. The entire mix is extremely detailed to fascinate readers interested in hard science. The human characters themselves, however, resemble science-fiction readers or scientists. Their main activity in both books is to discuss how to manage in the variable conditions of Mesklin and Dhrawn, as well as how to learn more about planetary conditions.

In the first novel, human astronauts accidentally land a research rocket at the South Pole of Mesklin and cannot retrieve it because of the immense gravity there. Charles Lackland has been on the surface at the equator for several Earth months and has taught the clever Mesklinite leader and ship captain, Barlennan, enough English to plan a rescue mission. The Mesklinites agree to undertake the difficult journey to the South Pole in their ship *Bree*. Near the novel's conclusion, they hold the humans hostage until they are taught the principles of flight, which is an incredible accomplishment for their species.

In the sequel, Barlennan cleverly invents a fiction about possible alien life on Dhrawn, knowing that humans are always looking for new life-forms. He manipulates his human friends to supply him with details about spaceflight. In the sequel, the human handlers have become a little more interesting and various. The human life span is much shorter than that of Mesklinites, so Lackland has been replaced by a team in orbit that includes some eager juveniles.

By the end of the two adventure stories, the characters have learned a lot about Mesklin and Dhrawn, as well as about the competition for knowledge among species and about what can be learned cooperatively. In *Star Light*, they discover that Dhrawn, like Jupiter in the Milky Way, may be closer in nature to a star than to a planet. Furthermore, the explorers find out by necessity how to survive in alien conditions; Dhrawn is home for neither Mesklinites nor humans. A final fascination in the plot and in the environmental details, which in Clement's work are closely tied, is that by the end of the sequel, humans have learned to communicate in the Mesklinite language, called Stennish. The wonder in that comes from the fact that Mesklinites have no lungs, so that sound is generated from a sort of siphon in their small bodies.

Analysis

Clement's narratives create the impression that the reader is a scientist. In fact, many of Clement's readers are scientists who delight in the accurate references to astronomy, planetary dynamics, strange variations in weather, and alien evolution. The elements of learning in Clement's work make it science fiction, whereas in its strong story lines about survival, it reads like adventure fiction.

The other element that strongly dominates these novels, as well as much of the rest of Clement's hard science fiction, is the sense of hope and exuberance associated with travel and adventure books written for young people. The history of such books begins with the eighteenth century writings of Jonathan Swift and Daniel Defoe. In the size differentials between the humans and Mesklinites and in the sheer inventiveness of details, the reader is reminded of Swift's *Gulliver's Travels* (1726) and of Defoe's *Robinson Crusoe* (1719). The awareness of and attempt to map variability and possibility in nature fuses nicely with youthful hope in Clement's work, as in that of these predecessors.

In this set of Mesklinite novels in particular, as well as in *Cycle of Fire* (1957) and *Close to Critical* (1964), Clement postulates an ominous cycle for civilization in which creatures must learn to use the knowledge they acquire about nature and not to destroy themselves with that knowledge. This classic dilemma is discussed as the "energy crisis" in *Star Light*, and it adds a sense of urgency to these essentially problem-solving adventure tales. Clement is a technically accurate and fascinating writer of science and should be read as an important thinker on the problems and challenges related to science.

—*Donald M. Hassler*

The Mists of Avalon

King Arthur's half-sister, Morgaine, fights to keep Avalon, the Goddess's sacred island, from forever disappearing into the mists

Author: Marion Zimmer Bradley (1930-1999)
Genre: Fantasy—mythological
Type of work: Novel
Time of plot: The Middle Ages
Location: Great Britain
First published: 1982

The Story

Marion Zimmer Bradley's *The Mists of Avalon* retells the legend of King Arthur. Like most versions of what has come to be known as the "matter of Britain," the story chronicles the monarch's rise to power, his glorious but troubled reign, and his downfall and eventual death. Bradley's tale also offers a revised view of Arthur, of his changing world, and, more specifically, of the transition from pre-Christian Goddess worship to Christianity. Narrated by Arthur's half-sister, Morgaine, *The Mists of Avalon* brings to life the Cult of the Goddess, paying homage to the women in Arthur's life.

Arthur's rise to power begins with his and Morgaine's mother, Igraine. As Igraine's fate unfolds, so do the futures of both Great Britain and Avalon, the sacred island of the Goddess. In her role as High Queen to Uther Pendragon, Igraine serves the Goddess by keeping Avalon, her homeland, alive in the minds and hearts of her subjects. As giver of life to Morgaine and Arthur, she is also mother to both Avalon and Great Britain, for through her, Avalon finds a successor to Viviane—the reigning high priestess—and Great Britain acquires its next High King.

Aided by the women of Avalon, Arthur ascends to the throne and marries Gwynhwyfar, the antithesis of his female relatives. She becomes a defender of the Christian faith and an enemy of Avalon, and thus a source of conflict and a catalyst for change. To appease Gwynhwyfar, Arthur forsakes his oath to Avalon—a promise not to favor one religion over another—and musters his armies under a Christian banner. Ultimately, Gwynhwyfar's piety prompts Morgaine to assume a new role as protector of Avalon, a role requiring her to plot her own brother's overthrow.

Arthur's downfall does occur, but not as Morgaine originally plans, because the Goddess has devised another destiny for Arthur and his sister. Possessed by the spirit of an outraged Goddess, Morgaine delivers an enchantment that leaves the High King with neither military power nor trustworthy counsel. A vulnerable Arthur falls prey to the wiles of his son Gwydion. Conceived by Morgaine during a fertility rite in Avalon, Gwydion is the son that no Christian king can claim.

Prodded by his Aunt Morgause, who represents the dark aspect of the Goddess, Gwydion leads an attack against Arthur. Father and son battle and kill each other. Morgaine, in the role of the Death Crone, takes her brother's body to Avalon, then visits Viviane's shrine at Glastonbury's convent. In this most Christian of places, Morgaine plants a twig from Avalon, and she realizes that the sacred isle will endure because the Goddess is reborn not only through Avalon's women but also through women who live outside the mists of Avalon.

Analysis

Bradley's story blends the supernatural and the ordinary to create fantasy. The Goddess of Avalon is not simply an unseen force but also an aspect of living women. At times, reincarnation and karmic destiny drive the plot, and throughout the story, psychic visions, called Sight, give glimpses of the future and of several pasts, including one in Atlantis. Faeries kidnap lost travelers, Druids forge the legendary Excalibur, and ceremonial magic is a part of daily life. In short, Bradley's tale depicts a fantasy world fraught with mysticism and mythic figures.

A complex novel about the mythical King Arthur, *The Mists of Avalon* joins a distinguished body of late twentieth century Arthurian fiction. Like T. H. White's two-part story—*The Once and Future King* (1968) and *The Book of Merlyn* (1977)—Bradley's novel translates medieval concepts into images that twentieth century readers can understand. Unlike White's account, Bradley's rendering of the myth tells little about the specifics of war and battle, focusing instead on characters and their intricate relationships. In doing so, *The Mists of Avalon* resembles Mary Stewart's Merlin trilogy—*The Crystal Cave* (1970), *The Hollow Hills* (1973), and *The Last Enchantment* (1979). By salvaging the character Morgaine from her traditional role as an evil sorceress, Bradley's novel adds a decidedly feminist voice to a body of literature that includes White's and Stewart's more male-oriented narratives.

Female characters in *The Mists of Avalon* have much in common with their late 1970's and early 1980's counterparts in popular feminist fantasy and science fiction. Similar to the women in Joanna Russ's *The Fe-*

male Man (1975), the priestesses of Avalon live in their own world, trace their family histories through their mothers, and contend with male outsiders. Like the Tribeswomen in Suzy McKee Charnas's Motherlines series, Bradley's women collectively challenge conventional gender roles and redefine the meanings of "mother" and "mothering." Although they struggle against men, the women of Avalon seek what neither Russ's nor Charnas's female utopian societies value: egalitarian alliances with males. Nevertheless, when necessary, Bradley's women defend Avalon as fiercely as might the female knights in Jessica Amanda Salmonson's "The Prodigal Daughter" (1981). Like much of the female-authored fantasy literature of its time, *The Mists of Avalon* reclaims political power for women. It goes a step further, however, by making Goddess worship the core of women's power as well as the commanding force behind the legend of King Arthur.

The Mists of Avalon was published twenty-five years into Bradley's career, and it builds on feminist themes in her earlier works, especially the well-known Darkover series. Bradley, in fact, may have modeled the women of Avalon after such characters as her Free Amazons in *The Shattered Chain* (1976). Lengthier and more historically sophisticated than her previous fantasy novels, *The Mists of Avalon* also marks Bradley's conscious attempt to write more scholarly fiction. That shift produced another feminist mythological fantasy, *The Firebrand* (1987), and demonstrated that she can outgrow categories in writing.

—*Debra G. Miller*

Mockingbird

Toni Beauchamp wrestles with the unwanted inheritance of her mother's magical powers and the possibility that she will hand them on to her own unborn daughter

Author: Sean Stewart (1965-   )
Genre: Fantasy—Magic Realism
Type of work: Novel
Time of plot: Contemporary
Location: Houston, Texas
First published: 1998

The Story

On Elena Beauchamp's tombstone is carved the legend, "There are some gifts which cannot be refused." Elena had the gift of magic and passed on part of it to her daughter Candy, who can see certain aspects of the future. However, her other daughter, Antoinette, who is determined to be as unlike her mother as possible, receives the darker part of her mother's magic. In a cabinet in the family living room are dolls representing spirits called Riders: the Mockingbird, the Widow, Pierrot, Mr. Copper, Sugar, and the Preacher. Another spirit, the Little Lost Girl, inhabits the house but has no doll of her own; she figures prominently in all of the stories told about the other Riders.

Each Rider has particular qualities. Sugar is flirty and loving, the Mockingbird assimilates different personalities, the Preacher is grim and bitter, Pierrot is a funny but cruel clown, Mr. Copper never loses at games, and the Widow rules the family with an iron fist. Any of them can take over Toni's body without warning, completely suppressing her personality and absolutely controlling what she does. She hates this legacy from her mother, but can do nothing about it. When she loses her job soon after becoming pregnant, Toni is in deep trouble both financially and emotionally. In addition, her sister is getting married, and she has put a curse on her former boss without actually meaning to do so. Meanwhile, an old family friend has recently died, and her mother's other daughter—about whom Toni never knew—is coming to Houston for a visit. The cold spirit of the Widow is taking her over.

Candy's boyfriend Carlos knows something about magic too, and he takes Toni out one night to intercede with the Riders on her behalf. On a Houston street, they nearly hit a young girl, who, it becomes clear, is the Little Lost Girl.

The Riders make things worse at times, as when the Widow terrifies Candy by demanding that she marry Carlos or when Sugar spends hundreds of dollars on clothes—but then occasionally the Riders help, too. Toni is an insurance company actuary, with a sharp eye for figures and a basic understanding of markets, but when she is contemplating day-trading for a living, she is too frightened to risk her savings on the kinds of trades she will need to make it work. However, Mr. Copper takes over her body one morning; in his calculating way, he makes her several thousand dollars, getting her started. Soon afterward, Candy and Carlos agree to marry, and even the approach of a hurricane and Toni's labor cannot prevent things from coming out right.

Analysis

Mockingbird is a kind of novel not often written by North American writers. Magic in the book is not condensed into spells or held apart as the province of wizards. Nor is it particularly marveled at by any of the characters. Magic exists. It is something certain people can do. It has its benefits and costs. Treating magic in this way allows Stewart to spend more time examining the subtle changes this kind of magic creates in the Beauchamp family, the way that unpredictable power subtly deforms the interactions between people. Magic permeates every moment of *Mockingbird*, even when it is not actually happening. The Beauchamp magic is just there, in the same way that the troubled relationships between the Beauchamp women are just there, intractable and frustrating and occasionally wonderful.

The motif of the Little Lost Girl echoes throughout *Mockingbird*. Candy, who is struggling to leave behind an adolescence of promiscuity, is lost because of her feeling that Toni was the favored sister; Toni herself is lost because of her denial of the family gifts; their other sister Angela was literally lost in Canada. Elena Beauchamp, too, was lost, a woman with a terrible gift who tried and failed to go against her nature in the interest of her family. Each of them is found during the course of the story, but they must find each other, and the figure of the Mockingbird stays in the background looking over it all: one person who adopts many voices. The three sisters, for all their differences, ultimately speak with the Beauchamp voice; or, as the novel's final line has it, "We are singers, in this family, and we are also songs."

—*Alex Irvine*

The Moon Is a Harsh Mistress

An unlikely combination of an eccentric professor, a political agitator, a computer technician, and a self-aware computer plot a revolution that gives the Lunar colonies independence

Author: Robert A. Heinlein (1907-1988)
Genre: Science fiction—future war
Type of work: Novel
Time of plot: May 13, 2075-October 14, 2076
Location: The Moon (primarily Luna City) and Earth
First published: 1966 (serial form, *If*, December, 1965-April, 1966)

The Story

The Moon Is a Harsh Mistress is the story of the successful revolution of the Lunar colonies against the Lunar Authority on Earth. It is presented as the memoirs of one of the architects of the revolution, Manuel Garcia O'Kelly Davis, known throughout the novel as Mannie.

A computer repairman with virtually no interest in politics, Mannie appears to be the least likely of Luna City's citizens to become involved in a revolution against the oppressive Authority. He hates it as much as any other Lunar Citizen, or "Loonie," but sees its interference as inevitable. One day, however, he stumbles into a secret meeting of a revolutionary group, following a tip given to him by the main computer at Lunar Authority Complex. This computer, which Mannie has named Mycroft (or Mike), after Sherlock Holmes's elder and smarter brother, recently became self-aware, developing a humanlike personality. Mannie keeps that unprecedented development to himself.

When the secret meeting is interrupted by the Lunar Authority's armed guards, Mannie helps one of the agitators escape. She is Wyoming "Wyoh" Knott, a tall, blond woman from Hong Kong Luna whose beauty charms him. Ducking into a hotel room to escape detection, Wyoh and Mannie continue the political discussion, his cynicism clashing with her idealism. Nevertheless, they have enough of a common cause for him to trust her with his secret that the main computer has "come alive." Professor Bernardo de la Paz, Mannie's former mentor, joins them in the secret, and with his knowledge of revolution theory, combined with Mike's knowledge of literally everything else, they plan the Lunar revolution.

Taking over the Authority offices on the moon is relatively easy, though the date of the coup has been rushed, precipitated by the rape and murder of a Lunar woman by Authority Peace Dragoons. The guards are killed, and the Lunar Authority's representative, Warden Mortimer Hobart, suffers an irreversible coma. For the first time in history, Loonies control Luna.

Authority on Earth is still to be reckoned with, however. Mannie and the professor come down to Earth to negotiate peace, but the negotiations fail. Having no weapons, the Loonies catapult moon rocks toward selected targets on Earth. The rocks hit with the force of bombs, and Earth governments capitulate. The Loonies thus win the Lunar revolution.

Analysis

Undoubtedly one of Robert Heinlein's greatest achievements in this Hugo Award-winning novel is the creation of Mike, the supercomputer that comes alive. Heinlein realizes the character effectively through Mannie, who admits in chapter 15 that he understands machinery better than he understands people. By giving Mannie the sort of symbiotic relationship with computers that a good technician needs, Heinlein prepares the reader for the humanization of the computer. Furthermore, Mannie himself has a cybernetic element: Having lost his left arm in a mining accident, he is outfitted with mechanical prosthetics, making him part machine. While presenting Mannie's rapport with machinery as extraordinary, Heinlein nevertheless universalizes Mannie by making him the narrator and by naming him Manuel. Mike shortens that to Man. To Mike, Mannie represents the human race as it could be in the technologically complex twenty-first century.

A second great achievement in the novel is Heinlein's creation of a Lunar "dialect" of English, which is an amalgam of Russian with American and Australian slang. Although fellow science-fiction writer Alexei Panshin ridiculed it as "babu Russian," it is a rare accomplishment: a language that is self-consistent and a logical extrapolation of the language Lunar colonists might speak, as well as being unobtrusive and intelligible to the reader. Its form is simple, with American speech patterns and Russian syntax—articles, pronouns, and expletives pruned where unnecessary for meaning. The second sentence of the novel is a good example: "I see also is to be mass meeting tonight."

One element of Heinlein's consistent success in science fiction is his ability to make a future culture seem real. Early science fiction did so mostly by making the technology scientifically accurate. There is some element of this engineer's perspective in *The Moon Is a Harsh Mistress*, particularly in the accurate and plausible portrayal of a Lunar catapult throwing moon rocks, with tremendous destructive force, at Earth. Equally effective is Heinlein's use of a technique that Russian formalist critics called defamiliarization. Nothing emphasizes the reality of Lunar life more than presenting what is unusual as common and vice versa. When Mannie finds a hidden computer file he needs, he speaks of striking not gold but ice. If there is water on the moon, it is beneath the surface, frozen, and a valuable find. Similarly, the boundaries of Luna City are not spoken of as "city limits" but "municipal pressure," for where the air stops is the end of habitable space. Furthermore, "pressure" is turned into a verb without the cumbersome "-ize" suffix, a logical extrapolation of how a Loonie might talk.

The novel took many of Heinlein's detractors by surprise. He had built a reputation after *Starship Troopers* (1959) for mixing conservative polemics with his science fiction. In this novel, one of the major characters, Professor la Paz, spouts very liberal (or perhaps anarchical, the term la Paz prefers) political theory that the narrator presents sympathetically. The novel also popularized a political slogan. The third section of the novel is titled "TANSTAAFL," standing for "There Ain't No Such Thing As a Free Lunch." This became the unofficial slogan of the Libertarian party within a decade after the novel appeared.

—*John R. Holmes*

More than Human

Six people with psionic powers join to form a superhuman entity classified as *Homo gestalt*

Author: Theodore Sturgeon (Edward Hamilton Waldo, 1918-1985)
Genre: Science fiction—superbeing
Type of work: Novel
Time of plot: The 1950's
Location: The midwestern United States
First published: 1953

The Story

More than Human is an expanded version of "Baby Is Three," a novella published in *Galaxy* in 1952. The novella forms the central part of the novel, which deals with the joining of six people to form a new form of humanity, *Homo gestalt*.

The first section of the novel, "The Fabulous Idiot," focuses on Lone, a mentally impaired man described as purely animal, who has parapsychic powers. Alicia and Evelyn Kew are sisters whose unconventional upbringing has kept Evelyn in a state of innocence. Evelyn's psychic plea, "touch me," is answered by Lone, but their merging is interrupted by her father, who kills Evelyn and beats Lone. Emotionally awakened and physically wounded, Lone is taken in by the Prodds, a farm family whose care makes him human for the first time.

When Mrs. Prodd becomes pregnant, Lone leaves the farm to live in a cave he constructs in the woods. There he is joined by Janie, a precocious five-year-old with telekinetic abilities, and Bonnie and Beanie, African American twin toddlers who are able to teleport. Mrs. Prodd dies in childbirth, and her baby is born with Down syndrome. Lone brings the Prodd child, whom he christens "Baby," back to the cave, to become the computerlike repository of information for the new organism. Together, the four children and Lone function as a single being, *Homo gestalt*. To help the grieving Mr. Prodd, Lone and the children construct an antigravity device to attach to his mired pickup truck, thus demonstrating the superhuman capacity of the new organism.

The middle section, "Baby Is Three," is the account of a psychiatrist's uncovering of the repressed memories of fifteen-year-old Gerry, who is

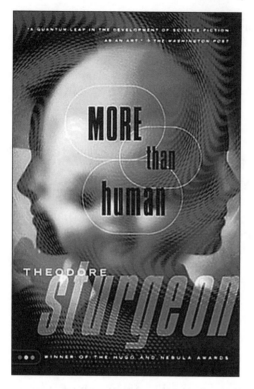

now the central ganglion of the *Homo gestalt*. By focusing on the triggering phrase "baby is three," Gerry remembers his flight from an orphanage and his rescue by Lone from death by exposure. When Lone is killed by a falling tree, Gerry assumes the leadership role within the gestalt organism. Gerry and the other children are taken in by Alicia Kew, who provides them with security and raises them as "normal" children. Once they are no longer outcasts dependent on one another, their bond begins to disintegrate, and they cease to be *Homo gestalt*. Gerry kills Miss Kew to recover the organism's autonomy.

The final section, "Morality," takes place nine years later. Under the leadership of Gerry, *Homo gestalt* has achieved superhuman powers but shares all of Gerry's personality traits—immaturity, manic depression, viciousness, and vengefulness. As this section opens, Janie is trying to rehabilitate the mentally and physically ruined Hip Barrows, whose investigation of *Homo gestalt*'s antigravity device had threatened to expose them. Gerry had intervened to destroy all evidence that the device existed, causing Hip to spend seven years trying to trace its origins. As Hip draws closer, Gerry commands him to "curl up and die." Only Janie's care prevents Hip's death. After Hip recovers his memory, Hip and Janie confront Gerry, convincing him that *Homo gestalt* must have an ethos to survive. Hip is integrated as the final component in *Homo gestalt*, its conscience. With this addition, *Homo gestalt* achieves maturity and is welcomed into the company of other immortal gestalt organisms who have existed for aeons to protect and guide humanity.

Analysis

Theodore Sturgeon is recognized as part of the Golden Age of science fiction. Unlike other famous members of this select group, including

Robert A. Heinlein and Isaac Asimov, he was conspicuous for rejecting the scientific and technological trappings that marked much of the fiction from that era.

More than Human is Sturgeon's most enduring novel. It was lauded upon its publication for the literary quality of its writing and awarded the 1954 International Fantasy Award. It is the second in a trio of parapsychological novels that Sturgeon wrote in the 1950's; the others are *The Dreaming Jewels* (1950; also published as *The Synthetic Man*, 1957) and *The Cosmic Rape* (1958).

Despite its modern setting and psychoanalytic jargon, *More than Human* is part of one of the oldest literary genres, the creation myth. Sturgeon emphasizes this aspect by employing echoes of Genesis. Evelyn is the new Eve, Lone ("All Alone") is Adam, and their meeting in the garden is a retelling of the biblical story in which the forces of evil try to prevent human union. The metaphor is extended into the New Testament in the book's final section. Hip Barrows—whose full name is Hippocrates, the healer—must suffer spiritual death and be resurrected through joining with the gestalt (a reference to an expanded Trinity) before the entity can achieve eternal life and enter the realm of the immortals.

By linking the emergence of his superbeing to human creation myths, Sturgeon rejects the science-fiction tradition of seeing emergent and created life-forms as unnatural or deviant. Unlike the monster in Mary Shelley's *Frankenstein* (1818), *Homo gestalt* creates itself out of the human desire to establish connections of love and compassion. Although Gerry utilizes the entity in negative ways, readers understand that this is a result of the alienating effects of his own horrible childhood, not the alien nature of *Homo gestalt* itself. Antisocial, superhuman children are a staple of horror literature, as exemplified by Stephen King's *Carrie* (1974), but Sturgeon ignores the seductions of horror and looks into the heart of the problem—their mirroring of what is evil within society itself. He reasons that all children must grow up, and any created being or race also goes through progressive stages of growth in order to realize its potential. Sturgeon's novel is unusual in emphasizing what is best in humanity through its depiction of what is more than human.

—*Katharine Kittredge*

The Mote in God's Eye and
The Gripping Hand

The human race overcomes a threat from an alien species through biological manipulation

---

Authors: Larry Niven (1938-   ) and Jerry Pournelle (1933-   )
Genre: Science fiction—alien civilization
Type of work: Novels
Time of plot: The thirty-first century
Location: The Trans-Coal Sack Sector of the Empire of Man
First published: *The Mote in God's Eye* (1974) and *The Gripping Hand*
   (1993)

The Story

The Mote in God's Eye and *The Gripping Hand* concern the conflicts attending humanity as it expands its reach into the galaxy. Primary among these conflicts is the encounter with an alien species from a star system called the Mote. This species differs from humans, particularly in its highly stratified social organization, which has evolved out of biological stratification, creating what are effectively subspecies. Each subspecies has its own peculiar social task: Warriors, Engineers, Mediators, Masters, and many others adapted for various specific tasks. This makes the Moties, as they are called, more similar to the social insects than to humans, who can perform a wide variety of tasks. The Moties' efficiency is increased by specialization, making them formidable opponents both in war and in peaceable endeavors.

The Moties' alarming rate of population increase causes a cycle of boom and bust on the Motie planet—civilization is followed by chaos in cycles of a few hundred years. The hope of certain Moties is to expand beyond their home planet into the galaxy and thereby find "living room" where the species can expand boundlessly. This, however, is what other Moties term a "Crazy Eddie" solution. They point out that the galaxy is not boundless and that eventually, once filled with Moties, it will be subject to the same cycle.

This fact establishes the basis for conflict between humans and Moties. The first human contact with Moties generates considerable enthusiasm, at least among scientists and merchants, groups that stand to gain new knowledge and new markets. The scientists are represented by Dr. Anthony Horvath, who heads the scientific expedition sent to the Motie star system and whose naïve trust of the Moties gives them access to the space drive technology they need in order to break free of their planet. The principal merchant is Horace Bury, whose greed parallels Horvath's naïveté. At one point, hoping to cash in on the Moties' engineering efficiency, he decides to smuggle a Motie engineer back into human space, a plan that is disrupted in such a way as to make him permanently and venomously opposed to the Moties.

The military is much warier of the Moties. Rod Blaine, who commands the warship carrying the human expedition to the Moties, has his hands full trying to maintain tight security on his ship. Ultimately, he fails, losing the ship to a burgeoning population of the Motie class called Brownies, small idiot savant engineers who redesign the ship into warring Brownie fiefdoms. Kevin Renner, the flight commander, is crucial in exposing the Moties' true intentions. Admiral Kutuzov, who commands the fleet that accompanies the expedition, waits silently, ready to blast the expedition and the Moties' planet into oblivion at the slightest sign of danger.

The danger, however, is not perceived until the expedition has returned to the Empire with three Motie ambassadors. When the Moties' intentions are discovered, the humans decide to blockade the Moties within their own star system, at least until the collapse of the present civilization, at which time it would be safe to exterminate the species if necessary. With the blockade in place, *The Mote in God's Eye* ends.

The Gripping Hand picks up the story twenty-five years later, when Motie ships begin to penetrate the blockade. After considerable confusion, it is determined that this is a different civilization of Moties, a space-based colony that survives by scavenging the remnants of past Motie space colonies. Fortunately, a way to neuter Moties through the use of a bacterial agent has been discovered. The Moties are engaged in battle, the agent is introduced into the population, and the book ends with humanity saved from the encroachments of an alien species.

Analysis

The Mote in God's Eye and *The Gripping Hand* draw together a number of common science-fiction tropes, primarily that of the encounter with an alien civilization. This is a venerable tradition; precursors could be said to include Cyrano de Bergerac's seventeenth century descriptions of the peoples of the Moon and Sun in *Other Worlds* (1965; original publications in 1657 and 1659) as well as Jonathan Swift's *Gulliver's Travels* (1726), with its Lilliputians, Brobdingnagians, and talking horses. The early modern precursors include Sydney Wright's *The Amphibians: A Romance of 500,000 Years Hence* (1924) and *The World Below* (1929), Edgar Rice Burroughs's Venusian and Martian series, and Stanley Weinbaum's *A Martian Odyssey, and Others* (1949; *A Martian Odyssey and Other Science Fiction Tales*, published in 1975, contains the stories from that work and the 1952 *The Red Peri*), in which are found some of the most imaginative renditions of alien creatures for its time. More recent, and highly acclaimed, additions to this genre are Frank Herbert's Dune series (1965-1985) and Roger Zelazny's *This Immortal* (1966).

The Mote in God's Eye constitutes the largest commercial and critical success resulting from the collaboration between Larry Niven and Jerry Pournelle. It was nominated for several major awards. Other successes have been *Inferno* (1976), which also was recognized with award nominations; the mainstream best-seller *Lucifer's Hammer* (1977); and *Footfall* (1985) and *The Legacy of Heorot* (1987), which added Steven Barnes to the writing team. Niven has also collaborated with Barnes to produce the Dream Park sequence, consisting of *Dream Park* (1981), *The Barsoom Project* (1989), and *Dream Park: The Voodoo Game* (1991; U.S. publication in 1992 as *The California Voodoo Game*). Niven generally is recognized as having produced better solo work than Pournelle. His *Ringworld* (1970) won both the Hugo and Nebula Awards. Another popular novel is *A World out of Time* (1976).

Although *The Mote in God's Eye* was identified immediately as a classic of science fiction, *The Gripping Hand* met with much less acclaim. Seen as a generally inadequate successor, it has been criticized for being too involved with plot and space maneuvers, to the detriment of the subject development that characterized the earlier novel and made it especially interesting. Readers lose the Motie-eye view, employed in the first novel, that gave such engrossing insights into the workings of an alien mind. In the sequel, the Moties are cardboard characters, as are the humans with whom they do battle.

The basic elements of both stories offer a number of interesting themes: adaptability versus efficiency, types of social organization, parallels with human society and history, xenophobia, and ethnocentrism. In the earlier book, these themes were at least acknowledged, if not satisfactorily developed. Reading *The Gripping Hand*, one suspects that its writing was propelled by a desire to cash in on its predecessor's status rather than to enlarge the authors' claim on their readers' imaginations.

—*Peter Crawford*

The Mythago Cycle

Three novels describe adventures in the magical Ryhope Wood, where figures from history and myth are reborn as mythagos

Author: Robert Holdstock (1948-   )
Genre: Fantasy—magical world
Type of work: Novels
Time of plot: The mid-twentieth century
Location: Ryhope Wood, an old English forest
First published: *Mythago Wood* (1984), *Lavondyss: Journey to an Unknown Region* (1988), and *The Hollowing* (1993)

The Story

Ryhope Wood stands in southeastern England, in the county of Herefordshire, near the village of Shadoxhurst. One of the few remaining ancient forests of England, it is a place where times long gone elsewhere still live. Ryhope is a small woods, measuring only three square miles, but within the forest time and distance bear little relationship to the outside. Narrow creeks become great rivers, several days become decades, and a few hundred yards of trail become a track of many miles. Ryhope Wood serves as the focus of the three fantasy novels composing the Mythago Cycle.

Within these primal woods are mythagos, or myth images, created from the minds of individuals who live nearby and who are somehow drawn to Ryhope. A mythago might reflect something out of an individual's past—from stories and tales heard as a child or learned in school—but can also represent or replicate the histories and myths of all who lived and died since the last ice age. The mythagos are not imaginary fictions: They are real, at least within the confines of Ryhope Wood, but not precisely as the outside world understands reality.

Mythago Wood is the story of George Huxley, his two sons, Christian and Steven, and George's colleague from Oxford, Edward Wynne-Jones. In the years before World War II, Huxley becomes obsessed with Ryhope and the mythagos to the extent of ignoring his family. He is entranced with one of his own mythago creations drawn from ancient myth, a young woman named Guiwenneth.

Steven, returning from military service, discovers that his father has died. Christian, Steven's brother, has become ensnared by Ryhope and by the now-dead Guiwenneth. In his woodland search for a resurrected Guiwenneth, Christian is pursued by his mythago of his dead father, a part-boar, part-man, the Uscrumug. Guiwenneth returns, but to Steven. In his jealousy, Christian, whose time in the woods has transformed him into a brutal warrior, kidnaps Guiwenneth. Steven, joined by Harry Keaton, a badly burned former air force pilot, pursues his brother. His quest takes years as measured in Ryhope time, and many mythago challenges are faced and overcome. Eventually Steven finds Christian. Fulfilling an oft-told myth, Steven, the Kinsman, kills the Outsider, his brother, who has been wreaking havoc in the land. A badly injured Guiwenneth appears, followed by George Huxley as the mythago Uscrumug who gently takes Guiwenneth from Steven's arms and carries her across the fire into the land of ice, Lavondyss, the place of redemption. *Mythago Wood* ends with Steven waiting for Guiwenneth's return.

The central character of Robert Holdstock's subsequent novel, *Lavondyss*, is Tallis Keaton, the young sister of Harry Keaton. In *Mythago Wood*, Harry had left Steven to pursue his own quest for release from his traumatic wounds. He had gone to Lavondyss, the place of peace beyond fire and ice. As Tallis grows to adolescence she, too, is caught up in mysterious Ryhope Wood and its mythagos. She feels called to save her brother Harry, who is somehow trapped within the wood. At the urging of Scathach, a warrior whom she had previously observed dying, she penetrates Ryhope's vastness. She and Scathach discover the latter's non-mythago father, Edward Wynne-Jones, George Huxley's colleague, now the shaman to a neolithic mythago tribe. Tallis and Scathach part, he to follow his destiny to die on that battlefield earlier observed by Tallis and she to search for Harry.

Tallis is transformed into a tree. The tree eventually falls, and she is carved into a mask of power for a starving ice age family. Again transformed, now as a holly tree, a mythago holly that can move, have intercourse, and give birth to birds, she observes the original Tallis prior to her arboreal transformation. The holly-Tallis sleeps and then awakes as the human Tallis, but as an old woman. As she approaches death, Harry appears and perhaps takes her back through time to her childhood and out of Ryhope. The novel ends with Tallis's aged corpse being burned on a funeral pyre. Her voice, coming from a mask, asks Harry to wait for her.

Holdstock's third Ryhope novel is *The Hollowing*. When Tallis entered Ryhope with Scathach, her father, James Keaton, attempted to follow her but disappeared. After a year of outside time he reappears, apparently deranged, telling stories of Ryhope. The only person with whom he can communicate is Alex Bradley, a friend of Tallis. James soon dies, shortly followed by Alex. Alex's father, Richard Bradley, is devastated.

After six years have passed, Richard is contacted by several scientists who have been exploring Ryhope. They reveal that Alex is not dead and is still only about twelve years old, although in the world outside Ryhope he would be almost twenty. Because of his imaginative powers, Alex is a mortal danger to the woods through the mythagos he creates. In spite of his doubts, Richard joins the explorers, searching for "hollowings" that allow the passage from one part of the woods to another. They hope that one of the hollowings will lead to Alex and his mythago world. The quest is filled with dangers.

Richard falls in love with Helen Silverlock, a Native American and one of the explorers. Through a mask tree created by Alex, James Keaton appears, calling for Tallis. Finally Richard finds Alex, pursued by Gawain and the Green Knight of literature and myth. The novel ends with Richard and Alex waiting in the woods for Helen, who has been pursuing her own mythago nemesis.

Analysis

Holdstock's three novels about the primeval forest of Ryhope Wood are very much in the genre of fantasy and have been recognized as such. *Mythago Wood* won both the World Fantasy Award and the British Fantasy Award for best novel. Holdstock also published a long novella about Ryhope Wood, "The Bone Forest," contained in a 1991 collection with the same title. This latter work, which discusses at length the relationship between George Huxley and his two sons, is the first narrative segment of Holdstock's multivolume saga and is preliminary to the events narrated in *Mythago Wood*.

Much of the fascination for Holdstock's readers comes from his myth-making and myth-using abilities. His mythagos, the myth images that are the products of the imaginations of the characters, are drawn from various historic and mythic traditions, including the Celtic, Greek, and Anglo-Saxon. Figures from many different pasts, from a World War I soldier to a middle-aged Jason and his fellow Argonauts to ice age hunters, cross paths in Ryhope Wood. Although George Huxley, Edward Wynne-Jones, and the explorers in *The Hollowing* are convinced that there is a scientific explanation for the events and transformations associated with Ryhope Wood, the element of science is submerged by the unexplainable: Scientific rationality seemingly cannot explain the long-held secrets of Ryhope.

The forest follows its own laws, if any. At times the events within Ryhope nearly replicate the historic past, but equally often they have evolved far beyond historical recognition. The mere passage of time could easily distort that actual past, but one could argue that Ryhope's mythagos reflect archetypes found in the deepest recesses of the individual or collective unconscious rather than showing objective history.

The novels need not be read sequentially. *Mythago Wood* is the story of Steven Huxley, his rivalry with his brother, and his search for Guiwenneth. *Lavondyss* relates the tale of Tallis Keaton and her quest for her brother, Harry. *The Hollowing* revolves around Richard Bradley's seemingly hopeless search for his presumedly dead son, Alex. The close and compulsive relationships of the characters, their passions and complexities, dominate Holdstock's writings. The dragons to be slain are personal. Ryhope Wood is a magical and even surreal place, and although Holdstock's descriptive passages of the woods compellingly enrich the stories, the background does not overwhelm the consuming interrelationships of the major characters. Ryhope Wood is the necessary stage on which the events take place.

Holdstock has successfully re-created the traditional English landscape. His novels are grounded in a very real English countryside with its small rural village, local manor house, and nearby woods. There is, however, another feeling to Ryhope. One critic described what Holdstock accomplished as creating a "landscape between history and dream." There are, in his writings, the elements of dream, sometimes nightmarish, sometimes not. The quality of his artistic vision and his literary talents make his novels and stories impossible to simply read and cast aside. They, like his mythagos, linger on for the reader, at the edge of consciousness, a captivating landscape of memory.

—*Eugene Larson*

The Neuromancer Trilogy

Cyberspace jockeys struggle against powerful entities for access to information and knowledge on Earth's computer matrix

Author: William Gibson (1948-   )
Genre: Science fiction—cyberpunk
Type of work: Novels
Time of plot: The near future
Location: Earth, several orbiting space stations, and the cyberspace matrix, a computer-generated alternative reality
First published: *Neuromancer* (1984), *Count Zero* (1986), and *Mona Lisa Overdrive* (1988)

The Story

These three novels constitute a loose trilogy. Several characters recur, and the stories are set at roughly the same time, involving many of the same locations, particularly the Sprawl, the megalopolis stretching from Boston to Atlanta. All three novels deal with computer "cowboys" surfing for information on the world's cyberspace matrix.

Neuromancer begins in Japan with the recruitment of Case, a burned-out matrix-cowboy-turned-hustler, by Armitage, an agent for persons unknown. Armitage uses Molly, a street warrior, to collect Case. They build a team that includes Dixie Flatline, a cyberspace replica of a deceased hacker's consciousness, and Rivera, who can create holographic illusions telepathically. They travel to Freeside, an orbiting space station, and learn that their employer is actually an artificial intelligence, code-named Wintermute, that is seeking illegally to augment itself. It hired the group to hack into its own core and remove the limits placed on its capacity to grow.

At the tip of Freeside, the team penetrates the Villa Straylight, home of the Tessier-Ashpool dynasty that created Wintermute. The team meets 3Jane Marie-France Tessier-Ashpool, one of the dynasty's cloned "daughters." Armitage and Rivera are killed. 3Jane gives up the password that allows for the transformation of Wintermute, which then joins with another artificial intelligence called Neuromancer. The two attain full sentience, becoming Earth's computer matrix itself.

Count Zero braids together three main narrative threads. Seven years after the events in *Neuromancer*, strange "ghosts" appear in the computer network. Bobby Newmark, known as Count Zero, is a novice hacker on his first "run" in the matrix using some hijacked software. He is nearly killed but is saved by a mysterious female presence, whom his voodoo-practicing mentors call the Holy Virgin. Newmark is pursued by un-known agents but hides in a nightclub in the Sprawl.

Meanwhile, art dealer Marly Krushkova is hired by Josef Virek, the richest man in the world, to trace the origins of a strange art object. Virek's body has been eaten away by cancer; what remains of him "lives" in vats in Sweden, and he projects himself through the matrix us-ing virtual reality. Marly discovers that the artist is a sentient machine orbiting in the wreckage of the Tessier-Ashpool computer cores, whose knowledge Virek seeks in order to liberate himself from his confine-ment. He secretly has ordered the extraction of a scientist named Chris-topher Mitchell, who pioneered "biosoft," an elaborate interface of ma-chine and organism. Turner, a mercenary, bungles the extraction and ends up with Mitchell's daughter Angela, who has a strange graft in her brain that she uses to "dream" her way into the matrix. Christopher Mitchell turns out to be a fraud, having been sent details on the construc-tion of biosoft from the orbiting artist-machine. Virek purchases the orbiting ruin but is killed by one of the voodoo "lords" haunting the ma-trix. They are apparently fragments of the artificial intelligences con-joined in *Neuromancer*. Angela is revealed as the Holy Virgin, and she and Bobby go off with the voodoo practitioners. Marly becomes an afflu-ent gallery owner, and Turner settles down to rear a family.

Mona Lisa Overdrive has four interconnecting plot lines. It picks up the story of Angela Mitchell seven years after *Count Zero*. She has become a star on Sense-Net, a form of virtual reality through which viewers expe-rience the sensations of another's body. She has lost most of her ability to interface with the matrix because her brain implants have been dam-aged by drug abuse. A mentally unbalanced computer construct of the consciousness of 3Jane Tessier-Ashpool plots to kidnap her and has the features of a prostitute named Mona altered to resemble Angela. Sally Shears, who is actually Molly from *Neuromancer*, is blackmailed into car-rying out the kidnapping but realizes that she is also a target of 3Jane's conspiracy.

Molly/Sally cuts a deal with the matrix voodoo-gods and kidnaps both Mona and Angela a week ahead of schedule. She transports them to the nearly deserted Factory, where Bobby Newmark/Count Zero is hid-den. His body is plugged into an aleph, or soul-catcher, a huge mass of "biosoft" material. The Factory is attacked by mercenaries employed by

William Gibson.
(Courtesy of the D.C. Public Library)

3Jane, who owns the aleph. The aleph is jacked into the matrix. Angela dies along with Bobby, but her interface has been restored, and her consciousness, along with Bobby's, is preserved in cyberspace.

Kumiko Yanaka, daughter of a Yakuza warlord hiding in London because of a clan war, runs away from Swain, an agent of 3Jane. Along with her "ghost" protector Colin, a biosoft program, Kumiko jacks into the matrix to observe a new data construct that has emerged with the intrusion of the aleph into cyberspace. She is captured, but the security program in Colin defeats 3Jane. In the Factory, Molly completes her mission and hides the aleph. The cyber-psyches of Angela and Bobby learn the shape of the matrix and part of the reason why it divided into various "gods" after the events in *Neuromancer*. There is another sentient matrix on Alpha Centauri, which they set out to discover. Mona takes Angela's place as a Sense-Net star.

Analysis

Stylistically, William Gibson draws heavily on the hard-boiled detective fiction of Raymond Chandler, James M. Cain, and Dashiell Hammett. The term "cyberpunk" came into being with Bruce Bethke's 1983 story of the same name, but Gibson and occasional collaborator Bruce Sterling quickly became the most famous writers in the cyberpunk subgenre. As a cyberpunk novelist, Gibson combines gritty realism and violent action with a sophisticated sense of what a computer-saturated world might be like. His language melds streetwise dialogue and hard-hitting narration with technological and consumer jargon.

The Neuromancer novels are mysteries that become increasingly complex, as the multidirectional plots of the later two texts indicate, and difficult to solve. Where a Hammett or Cain novel might involve a missing person or a strange crime, Gibson centers on the pursuit of knowledge, particularly the hidden keys to structures of information and to the nature of consciousness itself. The questions posed by Gibson's protagonists about themselves or their world remain largely unanswered. Even if some solution is found, it is often abortive, incomplete, or unsatisfying. Often, as in *Neuromancer,* those involved in a "run" on the matrix or a quest in the physical world are unaware of who employs them, of what they are looking for, or of the exact nature of their task. They simply act according to orders or instinct, sometimes groping blindly with no sense of direction or position. A pervasive sense of confusion and failure informs the worldview expressed in all three of these novels.

Coupled with the often disinformational nature of Gibson's narratives is a recurrent preoccupation with conspiracies. Gibson's characters are either ultra-rich power brokers or powerless outcasts such as addicts, prostitutes, mercenaries, and hackers. Even those who believe they are in control of their world soon discover that the information they barter for money and position seems to have a life of its own and, in subtle and unforeseeable ways, exerts an influence that lies beyond human agency. The fates of any number of people and institutions are affected by indifferent, chaotic forces that work according to their own inscrutable agendas. This fundamental disorder gives rise to what one of Gibson's characters calls "a certain tame paranoia" that colors everything a person thinks and does.

Gibson's novels also interrogate the nature of subjectivity, of stable selfhood. He explores the radical separation of mind and body (or what Case, in *Neuromancer,* disparagingly calls "meat") in the artificial frameworks of the computer matrix, forcing his characters and readers to confront what "consciousness" possibly could be. Some of his characters are physically dead but have their selves or "souls" preserved in a configuration within cyberspace; they exist there as sentient beings. Computers attain their own equivalent of selfhood and act as autonomous individuals. Gibson, without necessarily providing any clear answers, examines the gray zones between life and death, sentience and automation, and reality and illusion. He suggests that, in the "consensual hallucination" of an artificial world (an analogue perhaps for the art of fiction as Gibson himself practices it), thought itself can find a true form of liberation.

Gibson's texts present warnings. As liberating as it may be, technology is also threatening, addictive, and perniciously delusive. A number of his protagonists—Case and Turner in particular—want to escape from the vicious circle of paranoia and inhumanity that cyberspace presents, and they withdraw from the vast systems of information and money to a simpler domestic life, each rearing a family. For all those who find a release from their bodily limitations in the imaginative potential of Gibson's "matrix," there are an equal number who are thoughtlessly killed or have their lives destroyed by technocratic advancement. People might do well, Gibson's novels suggest, to reconsider the human consequences of technological ambitions.

—*Kevin McNeilly*

Nineteen Eighty-Four

Winston Smith struggles unsuccessfully to preserve his individuality against the brainwashing efforts of O'Brien, Big Brother's representative

Author: George Orwell (Eric Arthur Blair, 1903-1950)
Genre: Science fiction—dystopia
Type of work: Novel
Time of plot: 1984
Location: London, England (Airstrip One, Oceania)
First published: 1949

The Story

Winston Smith begins a diary, an act tantamount to signing his own death sentence in a ruthlessly totalitarian state bent on eradicating individuality. He is determined to stay alive—and "human"—as long as he can. To do so, he must escape the all-seeing eye and all-hearing ear of the Thought Police behind the omnipresent telescreen.

Winston and Julia, who work in the Ministry of Truth, become lovers and find an illusory haven above Charrington's shop in the district of the "proles," or masses outside the Party. Earlier, the lovers revealed themselves to O'Brien, allegedly a member of the "Brotherhood" intent on toppling Big Brother. O'Brien sends them "the book," supposedly written by Goldstein, Big Brother's enemy. The Thought Police smash into the lovers' refuge and drag them away to the Ministry of Love.

As he expected, Winston is tortured, but to his surprise his torturer is O'Brien, a self-styled therapist, determined to return Winston to "sanity." Winston masters "doublethink," or the capacity to believe that two plus two equals five, or any other number suggested. Confident that he has satisfied O'Brien's insane demands without betraying the self that loves Julia, Winston is totally unprepared for the horror of what awaits him in Room 101. Knowing that Winston has a phobia of rats, O'Brien has devised a wire mask to fit over his head with a door his tormentors can open into a cage of starving rats. Winston in mindless terror screams, "Do it to Julia! Not me!" Internally devastated by the horrible recognition of his betrayal, Winston accepts self-annihilation as a "victory over himself." The last sentence confirms his conversion: "He loved Big Brother."

Analysis

Few novels have had the impact of *Nineteen Eighty-Four*. Even those who have not read the novel are familiar with terms such as "Big Brother" and "doublethink." Although the novel may be read as a grim political satire on George Orwell's time—the horrors of the modern totalitarian state, whether Joseph Stalin's Soviet Union in the 1930's or Adolf Hitler's Third Reich in the 1940's—it easily qualifies as a dystopic vision of a nightmarish future awaiting the world if it ignores modern assaults on human freedom. Its warning of a negative utopia has not diminished with the passage of the year 1984, for its menace is just as possible for 2084 or 2184.

Clearly, Oceania, like the other superstates of Eurasia and Eastasia, is an extension of twentieth century totalitarianism's efforts to eradicate individuality. Orwell's analysis of the planned exhaustion of excess economic productivity on military expenditures to preserve the inequities of a traditional class system is brilliant. In fact, "the book" that O'Brien claims he coauthored with the Inner Party reads like the secret history of twentieth century political economics.

Unlike other classics of speculative or science fiction such as Aldous Huxley's *Brave New World* (1932), Orwell's science fiction lacks much of the advanced technological hardware readers associate with the genre. That lack, however, is justified within *Nineteen Eighty-Four* by Oceania's spokesman, O'Brien, who tells Winston that science and technology persist only as weapons of oppression. These weapons include use of psychology to engineer pain or technology like the telescreen for surveillance. Weaponry itself has retreated to pre-Hiroshima levels, nuclear weapons having been eliminated as threats to the status quo of the three superstates. Science and technology, Orwell suggests, had to be curtailed because in their purest forms they are grounded in the spirit of innovation and free inquiry. As O'Brien brags, Big Brother could rewrite astronomy to make the stars mere miles away from Earth if such a "truth" accorded with unrestrained exercise of power by the Party.

It is no coincidence that Winston works in the Ministry of Truth. Like other totalitarian leaders in the twentieth century, "Big Brother," or the Inner Party collectively, knows that truth is textual. The most successful dictators control their subjects through propaganda and the manipulation of history. Winston wanders through the proles' district hoping to find some corroboration of his own recollection of life before Big Brother but discovers the unreliability of the proles' memory and returns to his own job of rewriting history, a job he finds so stimulating that he passes up the opportunity to fade into the proles' world with Julia. Besides, in

*Film still from Michael Anderson's 1956 film adaptation
of George Orwell's 1984. (Library of Congress)*

this hierarchical system, Winston prides himself on his superiority to these "masses."

Winston envisions his experience in the novel as a tragic contest with the state to demonstrate his own superiority as an individual. Time and again, he boasts to Julia that although they will inevitably be tortured and killed, they, or at least *he*, will never surrender his humanity. Love, loyalty, decency, and nobility represent "humanness" to Winston and also to Orwell. Tragedy, the narrator indicates, may no longer be possible because the privacy and family loyalty on which it depends are under threat. Winston casts himself in the role of a traditional tragic hero, flaunting his pride in the individual's capacity to suffer all yet maintain dignity. When Winston proclaims the "spirit of Man" and O'Brien tells him to look in a mirror, Winston sees an image chillingly like those that confronted the liberators of the Nazi concentration camps. Winston embodies the tragedy of liberal humanism, naïvely confident that it could withstand any suffering without the surrender of a quintessential "humanity."

As a vision of a dystopic future, *Nineteen Eighty-Four* is grounded in a psychology Orwell both fears is valid but hopes is not. First, the novel asks whether a state constructed on terror and unrestrained power can survive without a collective "mental breakdown." O'Brien's insane lust for the sadistic exercise of power has seemed to some more terrifying than his menacing rats. Another question on which the novel's psychology rests is whether the "spirit of man," or faith in the individual, can be destroyed by torture and brainwashing such as Winston's in Room 101. How responsible are individuals for what is beyond their control? Finally, the novel poses the question of the individual's ability to stay sane in an insane world, where all the texts that might confirm reality are manipulated by a state intent on serving its mad religion of power. Readers must answer these profound questions for themselves.

—*Earl G. Ingersoll*

No Enemy but Time

A contemporary American who has dreamed of ancient Africa his entire life is sent back in time two million years

Author: Michael Bishop (1945-   )
Genre: Science fiction—time travel
Type of work: Novel
Time of plot: 1963-2002 and two million years in the past
Location: East Africa
First published: 1982

The Story

The novel is composed of chapters that alternate between two narratives. The first begins in 1986 as protagonist John Monegal, a twenty-three-year-old black American, is undergoing survival training in a fictional East African country in preparation for a trip back in time to study proto-humans. The narrative, told in first person, centers primarily on his two years spent two million years in the past.

The other, third-person narrative begins in 1963 with John as a small child in Spain. John's mother was a mute prostitute in Seville. Fearing that she would be unable to provide for her son, fathered by a black member of the U.S. Air Force, she gives the baby to a randomly selected Air Force family. John grows up as the adopted son of an enlisted man. Initially slow to develop, he adapts to his new life but is haunted by vividly realistic dreams of a primitive world that he slowly realizes is East Africa two million years ago.

After John's adoptive father dies in a car accident, John moves to the Bronx with his mother and sister. When he discovers that his mother is writing a book about his dream experiences, he runs away to Florida. He works odd jobs, under the name Joshua Kampa, for eight years. His vivid dreams of Pleistocene Africa recur, and he avidly reads about anthropology and paleontology, becoming an amateur expert. He gets the attention of a famous hominid paleontologist from the African country of Zarakal, who offers him a chance to travel back in time.

After months of survival training with a local tribesman in Zarakal, Joshua is sent into the past. He tries to send back his observations, but his communicator fails. He meets a band of proto-humans, one female

member of which seems closer to modern humans. He becomes tolerated and then accepted by the hominids, especially the female he calls
Helen, with whom he falls in love. The hominids are fascinated by his
technological artifacts, which include a handgun that he uses only when
absolutely necessary. The death of a male member of the group who kills
himself playing with the gun brings Joshua closer to the tribe. Helen becomes his mate.

A drought forces the hominid group to migrate. Helen adopts an
Australopithecus baby who is later killed. Joshua then realizes that Helen,
formerly barren, is pregnant. Joshua and Helen spend happy months together before the baby is born. Helen dies in childbirth. Stricken with
grief, Joshua takes his baby and flees as an erupting volcano disperses
the tribe. He barely makes it back alive to his time machine, then returns
to the present with his daughter.

The final chapters of the book cover the next fifteen years, as Joshua
and his daughter Monicah first live in the United States, then move to
Zarakal. Under the patronage of Zarakal's leader, Joshua becomes an
important government official. Monicah also has vivid dreams, but of
the far future, not the far past. The novel ends with her decision, against
her father's wishes, to use the time machine to visit the future world of
her dreams.

Analysis

Michael Bishop's *No Enemy but Time* is a vivid and convincing vision of
what modern humanity's ancestors might have been like, and it is one of
the most profound dissertations within the science-fiction genre on the
nature of humanity. The story of Joshua Kampa (John Monegal) and his
association with the Pleistocene hominids and their way of life is both
compelling and convincing, and several scenes in the book, including
the death of Helen, are among the most moving to appear in any science-
fiction novel. The book also has a protolerance subtext that true human
love can exist between people with noticeable differences.

Bishop obviously spent considerable time researching anthropology
and theories about various proto-human species. The verisimilitude of
his Pleistocene East Africa far exceeds that of Jean Auel's Earth Children
series (1982-1990). As it relates to anthropology and paleontology, *No
Enemy but Time* is clearly scientific, but Bishop is unable to attain the
same verisimilitude in relation to the operation of the time machine, the
explanation of which teeters uncomfortably between physics and sheer
mysticism. The text does not explain why John (and a handful of others)
can receive accurate information through time in their dreams, and it

provides conflicting explanations and evidence regarding whether the past into which they travel is the actual past, a re-created alternative past, or a mental construct without tangible reality.

Another minor problem is that the narrative track in the Pleistocene section is so compelling that the merely very good narrative track that tells of the protagonist's life prior to his time travels pales in comparison. The story of John's early life at times seems to be an annoying sidetrack that gets in the way of the primary narrative.

Both of these problems are attenuated, however, by Bishop's parallel narrative structure. Bishop saved the weak explanations of the scientific operation of the time machine, for example, until three-fourths of the way through the novel, after the verisimilitude of time travel was firmly established. He also used the dual narrative structure to keep a more even pacing throughout the novel than would have occurred if the entire narrative had been conveyed chronologically. This also allowed the time-traveling chapters to be placed in the first person, bringing the reader much closer to the distinctive personality and views of the protagonist.

The stylistic excellence of *No Enemy but Time* earned it a well-deserved Nebula Award for best novel. Its uneven underpinnings in the hard sciences, however, may have been a factor in its failure to be nominated for the Hugo Award. Despite its minor flaws, *No Enemy but Time* is one of the most important statements yet published within the science-fiction genre on one of the most important themes in literature—what it means to be human.

—*D. Douglas Fratz*

Non-Stop

Members of a savage tribe leave their home to explore their world, which turns out to be a vast starship, on a voyage that lasts several generations

Author: Brian W. Aldiss (1925-   )
Genre: Science fiction—closed universe
Type of work: Novel
Time of plot: Around the year 3000
Location: A vast starship
First published: 1958

The Story

Brian Aldiss's first science-fiction novel tells about a primitive tribe that unknowingly inhabits the corridors of a vast spaceship traveling among the stars. Members of the tribe venture into unknown sections of the ship and discover that it has already reached its destination and that they have been watched secretly by the Outsiders, a maintenance crew from Earth. The book was first published in Great Britain and underwent some textual changes before being published in the United States under the title *Starship* in 1959.

Roy Complain is a hunter for the seminomadic Greene tribe that lives in a place called the Quarters. The tribe constantly moves through corridors by pushing barricades in order to gain new land. Its members find artifacts, presumably left behind by the mysterious race of Giants that built their world. There are legends about the Forwards, a distant region of their world, where a more civilized tribe lives. One day, Complain, the priest Marapper, and three other tribe members set out on an expedition to the mythical Forwards section. Marapper, who believes that the world is in fact a ship traveling through space, owns a book containing a map of the ship. He plans to reach the Control Room and take over the ship.

After various adventures, Complain is captured by the Giants and taken to their secret headquarters. They release him, and he is reunited with his comrades. Soon afterward, the group is captured by the Forwards tribe. Marapper tries in vain to convince the Forwards that the Control Room exists. During the following interrogation, it becomes clear that Fermour, one of the members of the expedition, is in reality an Outsider. Complain and Marapper learn more about the their world from Master Scoyt. They find out that the spaceship had been taking colonists to Procyon, eleven light-years from Earth. After dropping off the colonists, the ship started on its return journey. Something appears to have gone wrong, and twenty-three generations have lived on the ship since.

The diaries of Gregory Complain, first captain of the homeward voyage, reveal that the water taken on board the spaceship *Procyon V* had contained a new amino acid that disrupted the crew's genetic sequence. Most of the crew died, and many of the plants and animals on board mutated. Eventually, the Giants reveal to Complain and the Forwards that this disease sped up the surviving crew's metabolic rate, so that they lived only for about twenty years. The lack of proper nutrients also turned them into dwarves. The ship itself already had reached Earth and was orbiting it, but the World Government was afraid that the crew would not be able to survive beyond the ship. In an apocalyptic ending, Fermour separates the individual levels from one another, so that the ship breaks apart into disk-shaped sections that begin to circle Earth.

Analysis

The so-called generation ship novels are a subgenre of the space opera. Whereas the scope of the space opera is concerned with the vastness of the universe, galactic empires, and interstellar wars, the generation ship novels have their main focus on the social structures and human interaction in the limited confines of the ship. The vastness of space is contradicted by the relatively limited space on board the ship, which, for its inhabitants, represents the universe because they usually have forgotten earlier technical knowledge and are on a voyage between planets. They are unaware of any reality outside the ship.

This type of book offers an interesting perspective on the human condition and possible circumstances for devolution. The spaceship can be viewed as an allegory of the spaceship Earth, which could have a similar fate. Aldiss uses all the typical characteristics of a generation ship novel: The inhabitants of his ship have only partial knowledge about where they are and have been subject to significant devolution. The interesting twists in this book are the fact that the so-called Outsiders seem to control everything and that these people are actually humans from Earth. Another imaginative plot twist is revealed at the very end, when the savages find out that their expedition actually reached its destination of Earth three generations ago.

The first archetypical generation ship story was Don Wilcox's "The Voyage That Lasted 600 Years" (1940). The subgenre became popular with Robert A. Heinlein's two short stories "Universe" (1941) and "Common Sense" (1941), in which a mutiny on board a generation ship causes the death of all navigators and sets the descendants of the passengers adrift in space. Another important work in the subgenre is E. C. Tubb's *The Space-Born* (1956). Aldiss's book is part of this movement in the field, which lasted from about 1940 to 1960. The decline in popularity of the generation ship book followed the decline of the space opera in general in the early 1960's.

Non-Stop was Aldiss's first science-fiction novel. His first book was *The Brightfount Diaries* (1955), but the generation ship story brought him his first critical acclaim. The book is a serious discussion of the character of humanity, showing ultimate destruction of the world of the spaceship. Aldiss often points out in interviews that he regards the human race as essentially flawed. The senseless destruction of the spaceship at the end of *Non-Stop* is nothing less than a warning not to do the same with spaceship Earth. Aldiss continued his vision of a dark future for humanity in many of his later works. *Greybeard* (1964) and *Earthworks* (1965) are two other grim visions of the sterility of humanity and Earth itself.

—*Jörg C. Neumann*

The Once and Future King

The orphan Arthur grows from a sensitive boy to a just and philosophical king in this retelling of Thomas Malory's *Le Morte d'Arthur*

Author: T(erence) H(anbury) White (1906-1964)
Genre: Fantasy—alternative history
Type of work: Novels
Time of plot: About the twelfth century
Location: England
First published: *The Once and Future King* (1958), which includes *The Sword in the Stone* (1938), *The Witch in the Wood* (1939; titled *The Queen of Air and Darkness* in the collection), *The Ill-Made Knight* (1940), and *The Candle in the Wind* (1958); and *The Book of Merlyn* (1977)

The Story

The Once and Future King and *The Book of Merlyn* together constitute T. H. White's retelling of Thomas Malory's *Le Morte d'Arthur* (1485). White began writing *The Sword in the Stone* in 1936; *The Witch in the Wood* and *The Ill-Made Knight* soon followed. *The Book of Merlyn* was completed in 1941 and was intended, along with *The Candle in the Wind* (which was later adapted for the 1961 musical *Camelot*, which was filmed in 1967), for simultaneous publication with the three previously published novels. When *The Once and Future King* finally appeared, it incorporated a number of the author's revisions but not the concluding volume. *The Book of Merlyn* was not published until 1977. Although it rounds out the series, briefly describing the death of Arthur and the religious retirement of Lancelot and Guenever, it is chiefly a philosophical forum in which Arthur, Merlyn, and a number of animals debate the nature of humankind.

Merlyn guides the events of *The Sword in the Stone*. The magician tutors the young orphan Arthur (derisively nicknamed "the Wart" by his foster brother, Kay), at times magically turning him into a goose, an ant, a fish, and a hedgehog. Merlyn uses the natural world to demonstrate the various forms of government and impresses upon the future king the cruelty of aimless military strength. Under Merlyn's influence, Arthur's maturing philosophy reverses the common notion of the day and concludes that "right makes might."

Upon the death of Uther Pendragon, a tournament is called to discover who might release the prophetic sword from the stone in which it is embedded, thereby indicating his right to become king. Serving as squire to Kay, Arthur is dispatched to retrieve Kay's forgotten sword. He returns with the magic sword, ignorant of its significance. He is reluctantly proclaimed king. Merlyn reveals him to be the son of Pendragon. Living backward through time, Merlyn bears the wisdom of hindsight. He is, however, without foresight and therefore becomes easily muddled, fatefully forgetting to brief Arthur on the maternal side of his family tree.

When *The Witch in the Wood* was rejected on initial submission, the publisher expressed his discomfort with White's handling of the subject matter. His discomfort was not, however, with the incestuous conception of Arthur's son, Mordred; rather, a readership primed by the earlier book's lighthearted tone might be appalled by the second book's horrifying combination of twisted filial duty and seething hatred toward a dazzlingly erotic mother who demands affection but returns none. Retitled *The Queen of Air and Darkness* when it was included in *The Once and Future King*, this book introduces the young Orkney brothers, Gawaine, Garheris, Gareth, and Agravaine. The morality of the future knights ranges from confused to deranged. The problematic nature of Arthur's struggle to establish his claim to the throne and to unify Britain, the story of which White threads into the Orkney narrative, becomes clear.

The ill-made knight of the third book is Lancelot. White's "best knight of the world" is as hideously ugly as he is graceful and as deeply religious as he is sinful. He is driven to overcompensate for every deficiency, and he is torn by his love for both Arthur and Guenever. His greatest wish is to be allowed to make a miracle, which requires moral purity. In the end, although he is unfaithful to his king and to his lovers and although he twice loses his mind, is at last unhorsed, and fails the Grail Quest, he is allowed his miracle.

The disintegration of the Round Table is described in *The Candle in the Wind*. The Orkneys, who have long been in Arthur's service despite the ancient enmity, have been joined by Mordred. The youngest brother poisons the hard-won tranquillity of Arthur's reign and expertly prods his brothers into exposing Guenever's adultery, thereby initiating the events that force Arthur to make disastrous war on his best knight and best friend. As Arthur lays siege to Lancelot's castle, Mordred treacherously assumes his father's throne and Arthur returns to England for his fateful confrontation with his son.

Analysis

Arthurian legend has its roots in pre-Christian Welsh mythology. By the Middle Ages, Arthur and his knights of the Round Table were well known across Europe. Arthur was ranked prominently in Geoffrey of Monmouth's *The History of the Kings of Britain* (1137), and his court was celebrated in the French and German epic poetry of the eleventh and twelfth centuries. The definitive British narrative did not appear until the fifteenth century, when Thomas Caxton printed Thomas Malory's *Le Morte d'Arthur*.

In Arthur, Lancelot, and Guenever, White discerned a timeless nobility. He imbued his heroes with his own doubts, his self-perceived sadism, and his concern for a just and peaceful social order. A conscientious objector, White avoided conscription but brooded over the spread of Nazism. Impending war made Arthur an attractive subject; the "future king" was, after all, prophesied to return in England's time of need. C. S. Lewis, in *That Hideous Strength* (1945), chose a variation in which Merlin returns to save England. The long shadow of World War II, which only began to fade near the end of the twentieth century, inspired many apocalyptic visions in literature, and such works frequently ring with Arthurian overtones. J. R. R. Tolkien's *The Lord of the Rings* trilogy (1954-1955) owes much to Arthurian legend, including a king of obscure though royal birth, a prophetic sword, and a wizard. These motifs, as well as the quasi-medieval settings of many fantasy novels, almost define a subgenre of fantasy literature.

The Sword in the Stone was for White a wishful reenactment of childhood, full of haymaking and hawking; long, brave nights in the forest; and magic. Far from the somber, druidical Merlins of other versions of the Arthurian legend such as Mary Stewart's Merlin trilogy (1970-1979), White's wizard is a dithering bundle of anachronisms; he is comic and ridiculous but wise. The ghastly opening of *The Witch in the Wood*, in which Queen Morgause idly boils a cat while her young sons recount the rape of "Granny" by Uther, was a sharp departure from the lightheartedness of the earlier work. In Morgause and her sons, White contrasts the loveless and arbitrary rearing of the Orkneys with the relatively idyllic orphanhood of Arthur. Isolation and ethnic pride, neglect, and ignorance are at the root of Britain's fragmented and violent social order.

Although the project began with White's psychological analysis of *Le Morte d'Arthur*, it is only in *The Ill-Made Knight* that White began to borrow heavily from Malory. Far from the image of perfect masculine beauty that has usually defined Lancelot, White's best knight is a human gargoyle, a misogynist with a weak mind and a streak of cruelty. As a misogynist himself, White was at first stumped by Lancelot's foil, Guenever. The contrast between Arthur's sorceress sister and his Christian wife has been played upon since the Middle Ages. Marion Zimmer Bradley in fact refocused the entire Arthurian legend on the epic's women in *The Mists of Avalon* (1982). For White, too, it seemed necessary that Guenever should be a more substantial character than Malory's shrewish, adulterous queen but of an entirely different mold from Morgause, particularly because Lancelot loved her. The Guenever that emerged is unencumbered by Pre-Raphaelite charms or feminist platforms, an ordinary woman in an oversized role. Pity is the root of Lancelot's love. White's queen is tenacious and loyal despite her petulance and jealousy; she is also intelligent and thoroughly pragmatic.

White, who nearly converted to Roman Catholicism while writing his Arthur books, treats religion warily but respectfully. Unlike Tolkien or Lewis, for whom good and evil were clearly defined, White sensed that the "moral" thing was not necessarily the "right" thing. Lancelot's son Galahad achieves the sinless perfection his father strives for, and though he seems scarcely human and is thoroughly unlovable, he finds the Grail. In contrast, Lancelot blunders through his moral dilemmas. When Lancelot heals Sir Urre's hexed wounds, he knows that the "miracle was that he had been allowed to do a miracle." White sees the Grail Quest as a horrible failure, destroying or demoralizing Arthur's knights. When Mordred appears at court, the Round Table is already set to crumble.

With the hasty conclusion of *The Book of Merlyn*, White returned to England to involve himself in its defense, though England ultimately found him more useful as a writer. His only other notable work of fantasy, *Mistress Masham's Repose* (1946), a satire about a community of Lilliputians and their struggle to remain unexploited in the modern world, was written while he was still composing his Arthur books. White continued to publish to popular and critical acclaim, but none of his other works met with the enduring popularity of *The Once and Future King*.

—*Janet Alice Long*

Only Begotten Daughter

Julie Katz, "immaculately" conceived through the sperm donation, seeks her destiny as the divine daughter of God

Author: James Morrow (1947-   )
Genre: Fantasy—Magical Realism
Type of work: Novel
Time of plot: 1974-2012
Location: New Jersey
First published: 1990

The Story

Murray Katz, a celibate Jewish recluse living in southeastern New Jersey, discovers that his most recent sperm donation has fertilized an egg.
He then steals an ectogenesis machine and cares for the developing fetus
in his abandoned lighthouse on Brigantine Point. Nine months later the
daughter of God is born—Julie Katz, immaculately conceived half sister
to Jesus and modern-day deity. Raised by Murray and his lesbian partner Georgina Sparks, Julie discovers her divinity early. By the age of two
she is walking on water. Shortly afterward, she restores a dead crab to
life. Murray, haunted by visions, makes Julie promise to stop performing miracles to remain hidden from her enemies. However, he does allow her to breathe in water and to continue visiting Absecon Inlet,
where she maintains her friendship with a sponge named Amanda.

Tormented by the lack of communication with her divine mother,
Julie struggles to determine her purpose on earth. She meets Andrew
Wyvern, a self-described "man of wealth and taste" who is actually the
Devil. He tricks her into displaying her powers by healing Timothy, the
blind son of fanatical Revelationist Billy Milk. Questioning the wisdom
of direct intervention, Julie opts for miracles by writing an advice column called "Heaven Help Us" for a tabloid.

When this plan backfires, Julie joins Wyvern for a sojourn to Hell,
where she meets her half brother, Jesus, and learns the truth about
divinity. She returns to earth fifteen years later—without her divine
powers—and finds herself in New Jerusalem, a fanatical society run by
the Revelationists. Threatened by the underground Uncertainty movement—a religion based on her own advice columns—Julie is captured

and crucified by the Revelationists, who want to trigger the redemption of New Jerusalem and the return of Christ. She is saved, however, by the divine intervention of Amanda the sponge.

Analysis

Morrow regards satire as "a deadly serious business," used "to get the reader's attention." His humor provides a thin layer between the reader and troubling questions. For example, his character Julie wonders what sort of deity she is: "A deity of love, or of wrath? Love was wonderful, but with wrath you could do special effects." Morrow uses *Only Begotten Daughter* to suggest that what many believers seek in religion is the "special effects." He dramatizes the dichotomy between the rational and the irrational. Divine or not, Julie believes in the uncertainty of life and the wonder of science. However, when she performs a miracle, her followers create a religion based upon her advice columns. Her foe, Billy Milk, believes in the Second Coming, resurrections, and burning bushes. He sacrifices an eye to persuade God to heal his blind son. Morrow regards this fascination with miracles and the need for "special effects" as irrational. The challenge is to view the world rationally, appreciating the world for the wonders that it holds, without relying on mysticism.

Existential pain pervades the novel, and each character struggles with the pain of existing as a thinking being in an unpredictable world. Julie creates a temple of pain, and fills it with photos of human suffering. She cannot understand why her Mother does not intervene. She asks Jesus, "Put me in charge of the universe, and my first act will be to arrest my mother for criminal neglect." Jesus responds that maybe God cannot intervene, that perhaps he created humans to solve these injustices.

Morrow offers hope through another theme: the power of love to soothe this pain. Julie craves attention from her mother, yet acknowledges that Murray's love always did the work of two parents. In the end, when Amanda saves Julie from death, she implies that she is Julie's mother. When she asks the sponge if she is God, the sponge replies, "Just a theory, but the data are provocative. I mean, look at me. Faceless, shapeless, holey, undifferentiated, Jewish, inscrutable . . . and a hermaphrodite to boot." Amanda points out that sponges, when pulled apart, form new sponges. She is both immortal and infinite, offering an alternative to belief in an anthropomorphic God incapable of a sponge's power to absorb and assimilate. A complex novel, *Only Begotten Daughter* raises questions about religion, intellect, beliefs, and relationships in a stunningly original and entertaining way.

—Michael-Anne Rubenstien

The Orange County Trilogy

Three thematically connected novels set in Southern California of the twenty-first century provide very different visions of the future of the region and its society

Author: Kim Stanley Robinson (1952-   )
Genre: Science fiction—extrapolatory
Type of work: Novels
Time of plot: 2027, 2047, and 2065
Location: Orange County, California
First published: *The Wild Shore* (1984), *The Gold Coast* (1988), and *Pacific Edge* (1990)

The Story

The Orange County trilogy is set in three different extrapolated futures. In each novel, a small group of people become involved in events that change their lives. Each novel takes place over a single summer, almost solely in Orange County, California.

The Wild Shore takes place in 2047 in San Onofre, six decades after a nuclear war devastated the United States but left the rest of the world intact. The remaining world powers have quarantined the United States and use satellite-based defenses to prevent the country's redevelopment. Teenager Hank Fletcher lives in a valley populated by a handful of families struggling for survival.

Hank's life involves farming, fishing, going to swap meets, and learning from his eighty-year-old uncle, Tom Barnard, about pre-disaster America.

Strangers arrive from San Diego by rail handcar, seeking to form an alliance to fight against the Japanese patrolling the coast. Hank and Tom travel with them to San Diego and learn how Russian terrorists exploded two thousand neutron bombs, one in each major U.S. city and town. On their return trip, they find rail bridges destroyed, so they must travel by sea. Japanese forces sink their boat, and Hank is captured. He escapes, swims to shore, and barely survives to walk home.

The San Onofreans decide not to help the San Diegans, but Hank and his friends choose to do so secretly. While Tom is ill, Hank learns about some Japanese "tourists" illegally visiting. He leads a small army of San

Diegans to ambush them. They themselves are ambushed, however, and barely escape to return home. One of Hank's friends is wounded and later dies. Tom recovers and convinces Hank to write a book about his life in San Onofre and the events of that summer.

The Gold Coast portrays a very different future. It is 2027, and Orange County has been developed into an endless tangle of condominiums, malls, freeways, and defense construction plants. Twenty-seven-year-old Jim McPherson, son of a weapons engineer, works part-time and writes bad poetry. His vague desire to rebel against the status quo has no focus; he spends his time cruising the freeways and going to wild parties centered on sex and consumption of designer drugs. His only serious intellectual pursuit is the history of Orange County, learned from his grandfather, Tom Barnard.

While Jim's father is involved in struggles to gain new contracts and salvage one gained on fraudulent data, Jim is recruited by a friend to help sabotage military contractors. As he gets further involved, his turbulent love life, estrangement from his father, and friends' problems strain his mental stability. After a madcap tour of Europe with his friends, Jim's problems become unbearable. While Jim is picking up a shipment of small missile launchers to be used to attack his father's company, his mental state becomes further disturbed. He spends the night driving around and randomly bombing buildings, then escapes into the mountains with a friend. When he returns, he finds that his terrorist friends were not idealists: Their sabotage was assisted by both defense contractors and drug smugglers. The events of the summer inspire Jim to write about the time when the orange groves of Orange County were destroyed, changing the area forever.

Pacific Edge is set in the year 2065, in the small village of El Modena. Its citizens are seeking to maintain an ecological utopia in a world that is itself peaceful and prosperous. Kevin Claiborne is a thirty-four-year-old building renovator with a love for softball, bicycling, and the land, especially Rattlesnake Hill, the only undeveloped area in El Modena.

Kevin joins the city council and is soon leading the opposition to a secret plan to develop Rattlesnake Hill. With the help of both the town legal counsel and his grandfather, Tom Barnard, Kevin slowly learns that the plan involves use of capital earned by illegal means. Tom was one of those instrumental in changing to the new world order, primarily through dismantling large businesses. Kevin falls in love with the estranged mate of the mayor, and Tom is drawn out of his hermitlike existence by a visiting female professor from India. Tom and his friends watch the first Mars landing while sitting naked, wearing animal masks, and drinking tequila in a natural hot springs pool. During a trip to visit an expert in California water law, they spend a beatific few days camping in the Sierras.

The battle for development of Rattlesnake Hill continues, and Kevin's new love returns to the mayor. Tom leaves, by sailing ship, with his new Indian friend. He continues to work to get the proof needed to sway the final town vote on development of Rattlesnake Hill. He eventually obtains the proof but is killed in a hurricane before he can get it to Kevin. The town votes to develop, but Kevin finds a solution, arranging a ceremony to dedicate a plaque atop Rattlesnake Hill to commemorate Tom's death, making the hill an untouchable shrine.

Analysis

Kim Stanley Robinson's Orange County trilogy (also called the Three Californias novels) is a unique creation and one of the most interesting extrapolative works in science fiction. Each novel presents a consistent vision of the future of both Southern California and the world of which it is an integral part. *The Wild Shore* features pastoral innocence in a world determined to keep America from ever again exerting influence, *The Gold Coast* shows technological extremes in a world dominated by American military might, and *Pacific Edge* posits an ecological utopia in a peaceful and prosperous global village. The thematic interplay among the novels makes the trilogy a profound treatise on the future of humanity, a coherent whole that is more than the sum of its parts.

As with all of Robinson's novels, place and character dominate plot. Each novel consists of numerous intertwined subplots whose importance is in showing character development, illustrating the innate beauty of landscapes both natural and artificial, and developing themes. It is clear that Robinson loves the landscapes of California but also that he loves all his diverse characters. Even minor characters come alive as well rounded and sympathetic, never reduced to mere caricatures. All the protagonists have flaws, and even the antagonists are sympathetic, motivated by what they believe is right.

Robinson's stated intention was to write a dystopia (*The Wild Shore*), an extrapolation of current trends (*The Gold Coast*), and a utopia (*Pacific Edge*). It is a testament to the verisimilitude of his treatments that with only a minor shift in sensibilities, one can imagine *The Wild Shore* as a pastoral utopia, *The Gold Coast* as a war-filled dystopia, and *Pacific Edge* as the most likely future. Shifting paradigms, the three books can be viewed as reflecting different periods and sensibilities in the author's own life. In this view, *The Wild Shore* reflects Robinson's innocent teenage years in Orange County, *The Gold Coast* the hedonistic life of his twenties, and *Pacific Edge* his more idealistic thirties.

Despite the diverse scenarios presented, the three novels have much in common. Each has moments of extreme joy and beauty interspersed with moments of intense anguish. Tom Barnard plays a similar role in each as the primary source of historical knowledge. Each protagonist belongs to a small group of close friends and has a turbulent love life. All three books exude a strong love for the land and the sea, with camping in the mountains and sailing the ocean being common experiences. Robinson flawlessly weaves his encyclopedic knowledge of numerous subjects, from ecology to defense contracting to the history of Orange County, into the narrative.

The few logical inconsistencies are necessary for the goals of each book and are well hidden. Robinson is a master of showing first and explaining later, after the verisimilitude of the scenario is unquestionably established. In *The Wild Shore,* no one manages to establish mass communication even though the technology should be readily salvageable; the San Diegans are working on a shortwave radio receiver that sounds like it is from the 1930's. Mass communication would have ruined the mystery and pastoral ambience of the novel. Jim's drug-dealing friend in *The Gold Coast* apparently is a one-man corporation, performing manufacturing, research and development, safety testing, purchasing, marketing, and sales tasks on his own, even though his life is depicted as a constant party.

The utopian life in El Modena seems in retrospect to be primarily based on the disappearance of 90 percent of the population; everyone who remains is an intellectual, no matter what his or her occupation. None of these inconsistencies adversely affects the believability of the scenarios or the flow of the narrative.

Robinson's Orange County trilogy is a unique accomplishment, an intricate interplay of character and philosophy, didactic but entertaining. It utilizes the potential of science fiction to overcome the despair of what the world is like and glory in the potential of the future.

—*D. Douglas Fratz*

Orlando

While seeking perfection in poetry and love between the late sixteenth and the early twentieth centuries, English aristocrat Orlando meets famous people, becomes a woman, and meditates on change

Author: Virginia Woolf (1882-1941)
Genre: Fantasy—cultural exploration
Type of work: Novel
Time of plot: The late 1500's to 1928
Location: Mostly England, with some scenes in Constantinople and Thessaly
First published: 1928

The Story

In the late 1500's, Orlando, a young nobleman from an ancient British family, dedicates himself to literature. He encounters William Shakespeare and is appointed by Queen Elizabeth to be her companion. In London, he falls in love with a mysterious Russian beauty who soon abandons him. Devastated, he turns to poetry, but when one of his tragedies is ridiculed publicly by a London poet, Orlando retreats to his family's magnificent estate and burns all his poems except one, titled "The Oak Tree."

When a strange guest arrives, introducing herself as the Archduchess Harriet Griselda of Roumania, Orlando becomes increasingly uncomfortable and decides to leave England. At his request, he is appointed as ambassador extraordinary to Constantinople and is next seen performing his official duties in that post. Life is generally tedious until he suddenly falls into a coma. After several days of suspended animation, Orlando awakes, having somehow been transformed into a woman.

Orlando joins a band of Thessalian gypsies, with whom she lives contentedly for some time. Finally, however, she is inspired by a vision of her ancestral home to return to England, where she finds herself in the eighteenth century and soon befriends such famous writers as Jonathan Swift and Alexander Pope. Much of Orlando's time is engaged in meditation about fame, time, and the nature of literature. Soon, with the remarkably elusive lapsing of time that characterizes this novel, the nineteenth century arrives, and Orlando finds herself unable to write meaningful poetry. Out one day for a long walk in the country, she experiences a sudden overwhelming vision of her innate kinship with nature, and, as she lies on the ground afterward, she is discovered by Marmaduke Bonthrop Shelmerdine, with whom she immediately forms a passionate intimacy.

Virginia Woolf.
(Courtesy of the D.C. Public Library)

Shortly after meeting, Orlando and Shelmerdine marry, and Orlando finds that she is able to write again. She completes her poem "The Oak Tree," on which she has been working for some three hundred years, and takes it to London, where an old friend promises to see that it is published. She makes an effort to acquaint herself with Victorian literature, to which she generally objects, and, without warning to the reader, gives birth to a son.

At the end of the novel, Orlando finds herself in the year 1928, driving an automobile and trying to cope with shopping. Her poem has been a success, and she returns to her estate and visits the great oak that has been her refuge and inspiration over the centuries. At the oak, at exactly midnight, Orlando's husband arrives in an airplane.

Analysis

Virginia Woolf achieved literary fame as an innovator in literary form, and her novels reflect various experiments and unique effects of the type associated with the early twentieth century aesthetic movement called modernism. *Orlando* (subtitled *A Biography*) is of particular interest because of its fusion of autobiographical elements, technical innovation, fantasy, satire, and preoccupation with the Western literary tradition. All these ingredients are interwoven to create an apparently central theme of mutability or change, a traditional theme developed extensively in Renaissance England by Edmund Spenser (c. 1552-1599) and in the ancient world by Lucretius (c. 98-55 B.C.E.).

The two most conspicuous manifestations of such change appear in the dizzying time shifts that occur in Orlando's long life and in the protagonist's unexpected and unexplained change from male to female. These shifts and shuffles serve principally to maintain a focus on an underlying theme informing the entire novel: the anxiety of the literary artist.

When Orlando, as a boy, hikes to the great oak on his family's estate, he already has defined himself as a poet. From the oak, he is able to see incredible distances across England, and it is this tree that symbolizes nature, inspiration, and durability in time, for the oak both changes and remains the same, just as Orlando's poem "The Oak Tree," on which he/she works for three centuries, develops and remains. Throughout the bewildering chronological developments of the novel, the constant, abiding tree awaits Orlando's maturation and return—and the perfection of her art. At the end of the novel, Orlando brings her poem, now published and famous, back to the ancient oak. She is rejoined there by her husband, thus completing two different thematic circles of separation and reunion.

Woolf's novel deliberately incorporates many literary influences. Because it is a novel about writing, Woolf often echoes authors—especially great innovators—from earlier periods of English literature, notably Laurence Sterne, Alexander Pope, and Jonathan Swift. Although Woolf's works often focus on the artist's creative anxieties and imagination, as in her novel *To the Lighthouse* (1927), *Orlando* is a fantastic tour de force exploring the artist's power to manipulate multiple dimensions of a work.

Another aspect of *Orlando* is that it naturally reflects Woolf's own experience. As the daughter of distinguished writer Sir Leslie Stephen and as a member of the Bloomsbury Group of writers and other artists, Woolf was deeply involved in writing and criticism throughout her life. Her relationship with Vita Sackville-West, to whom *Orlando* is dedicated, is also reflected in the sexual ambivalence of Orlando, of Shelmerdine, and of the Archduchess Harriet. Many passages also reveal the hypersensitivity of the novel's protagonist, thus suggesting Woolf's own unfortunate psychological instability that ultimately led to her suicide in 1941. Perhaps it is the fantastic artistry of this novel that provides enough distance between author and protagonist to make it possible for Woolf to come to terms with her own genius in her own time.

—*Robert W. Haynes*

Our Lady of Darkness

A San Francisco writer of weird tales is haunted by a "para-mental," a ghostly presence born of the unnatural urban environment

Author: Fritz Leiber (1910-1992)
Genre: Fantasy—occult
Type of work: Novel
Time of plot: 1976
Location: San Francisco, California
First published: 1977 (revised and expanded from "The Pale Brown Thing," *The Magazine of Fantasy and Science Fiction*, January-February, 1977)

The Story

Franz Westen, a writer of weird tales, has moved to a San Francisco apartment house following the death of his wife, Daisy, and a period of alcoholism. He has begun a tentative affair with Cal, a harpsichordist living in the apartment below whose music has a supernaturally healing influence. Still grieving, Franz avoids commitment with Cal, finding solace in his "Scholar's Mistress," a heap of occult books and weird pulp magazines, which he lines up every night on Daisy's side of the bed.

While in an alcoholic haze, Franz had purchased two books: *Megapolisomacy: A New Science of Cities*, by Thibaut de Castries, and a diary written by one of de Castries' disciples, whom Franz believes to be Clark Ashton Smith. De Castries and his book are imaginary, but Smith was an actual fantasy writer, a friend of H. P. Lovecraft, a writer of tales of cosmic terror. In his book, de Castries maintains that conglomerations of large buildings produce noxious residues and become breeding grounds for "paramental entities." Franz gradually becomes certain that a pale brown dancing figure he sees from his window is such a being. When he walks to the Corona Heights area in pursuit, he is horrified to see the figure waving to him from the window of his own room.

Franz visits the sybaritic Jaime Donaldus Byers, a poet and authority on Clark Ashton Smith, who confirms that the diary is indeed by Smith. Byers, who also owns a copy of the rare *Megapolisomacy*, tells Franz about an anti-urban cult established by de Castries and describes de Castries' mistress, a mysterious woman in a black veil. Examining Smith's journal, Byers finds a cryptically written curse hidden between two pages.

Franz spends the day researching the history of the apartment building in which he lives, ultimately learning that Smith had inhabited the room in which Franz now lives. That evening, Franz attends Cal's harpsichord concert but leaves in the middle, preoccupied with the curse. At home he decodes the cryptogram and realizes that de Castries had set a trap for Clark Ashton Smith; Smith had died before the tall buildings needed to spring the trap were constructed. After placing on the bed the works of occult and weird fiction that make up his "Scholar's Mistress," Franz lies down. He dreams that Daisy is alive and caressing him, then that she is dead and that what he had taken for fingers are black vines growing out of her skull. He awakes to find that his "Scholar's Mistress" has come to life and is attacking him. Cal arrives barely in time to exorcise the evil being by invoking the names of musicians and scientists, representing the principles of order and harmony. Cal and Franz move together to another apartment but do not marry.

Analysis

Our Lady of Darkness is Fritz Leiber's most sophisticated, extended treatment of the urban supernatural. Ghosts born of urban pollution and the impersonality of city life are found in such early Leiber stories as "Smoke Ghost," "The Hound," and "The Inheritance." Like its predecessors, the ghost in *Our Lady of Darkness* is obliquely perceived against a cityscape that distorts perspective. Leiber further suggests the unnaturalness of urban life by repeated images and metaphors involving paper. A skyscraper, for example, is several times compared to a vertical punch card. Tracing his building's history, Franz is sent on a paper chase, from one document repository to another. The paper imagery suggests that in a city, unlike in a small town, human interactions are carried on indirectly.

One of the pleasures of *Our Lady of Darkness* is Leiber's wide-ranging allusiveness and skill at parodying the styles of other writers, particularly H. P. Lovecraft. Like Lovecraft, Leiber mixes references to imaginary and actual writers and books. Along with Clark Ashton Smith, the writers Jack London and Ambrose Bierce were members of the cult of the fictional de Castries. Leiber has borrowed from Lovecraft the creation of an imaginary book with evil powers: *Megapolisomacy* is based on Lovecraft's fictional *Necronomicon*.

Although *Our Lady of Darkness* is not as overtly misogynistic as some of Leiber's writings, such as "The Girl with Hungry Eyes," much of its imaginative energy comes from fear of female sexuality. Franz must make a stock choice between Cal, who is a practitioner of white magic, and the sinister dark lady of the title. At the outset, Franz resists involvement with Cal, playfully telling his "Scholar's Mistress" that she will always be his "best girl." Grieving for his dead wife, Franz prefers vicarious thrills of works of supernatural horror to the give-and-take of a relationship with a real woman. Shortly before his "Mistress" comes to life, Franz speculates that the entire purpose of supernatural horror is to make death exciting. The "Scholar's Mistress" seems to be a combination of Franz's dead wife (or the horror her slow death inspired) and de Castries' reanimated dark mistress. Her attack on him is described as a rape. Ultimately, Franz rejects his necrophilic attraction to death by loving Cal, but he cannot fully commit himself to her because he fears her supernatural power, however benign.

Winner of the World Fantasy Award in 1978, *Our Lady of Darkness* is perhaps Leiber's best novel. In the eighteenth century sense, it inspires terror rather than horror; that is, sinister, dreamlike threats impend but never culminate in physical violence. *Our Lady of Darkness* is a stylistic tour de force, with its wide-ranging allusiveness and striking metaphors. This is not, however, a novel for feminists. Fear of women is at the heart of its most powerful imagery and effects.

—*Wendy Bousfield*

The Owl Service

Three teenagers find themselves acting out the latest cycle of a
timeless tragic legend

Author: Alan Garner (1934-   )
Genre: Fantasy—inner space
Type of work: Novel
Time of plot: The 1960's
Location: North Wales
First published: 1967

The Story

At the heart of this story is an old Welsh legend from the fourth branch of
Mabinogion. The legend is that of Blodeuwedd, the woman of flowers
whom Gwydion the magician created for Lleu Llaw Gyffes, after his
mother, Arianrhod, decreed that he would not wed a mortal woman.
Blodeuwedd fell in love with Gronw Pebyr and plotted with him to kill
Lleu. Lleu was turned into an eagle and later rescued by Gwydion, but
Blodeuwedd, as a punishment, became an owl. Alan Garner takes up the
idea of this eternal triangle and translates it to modern Wales.

The story opens by introducing a family newly created by the marriage of the mother and father, who bring with them daughter Alison
and son Roger, respectively. There are tensions within the family as the
members get to know one another, and also between Nancy, the house-
keeper, and her son Gwyn, whom she has brought up outside the valley,
which she hates, although she cannot get it out of her mind. Gwyn, as he
admits, knows as much about the place as does his mother, although he
has never lived there. In particular, Nancy is concerned that he should
not consort with Huw Halfbacon, known as Huw the Flitch, the handyman and gardener, who seems to be half-witted.

In the midst of these tensions, Alison hears strange scratching noises
in the attic above her room. When Gwyn investigates, he discovers a pile
of plates decorated with patterns, in which Alison can see owls. Meanwhile, Roger, her stepbrother, sunbathing by a mysterious standing
stone, experiences an impression of something being thrown past him.

These are only the first in a long series of supernatural events. Several sets of paper owls that Alison makes from tracings of the patterns on the plates go missing, and the plates themselves are destroyed. Hurled against a section of wall, they dislodge a coating of plaster, revealing a wall painting of a beautiful woman, surrounded by flowers that have claws for petals. Later, the painting mysteriously vanishes. When Roger photographs the scene through the hole in the standing stone, a strange figure is revealed, either mounted on horseback or on a motorbike. Throughout the valley, it is clear that people are expecting an event. They talk of the lady coming, and that it is to be owls "this time."

Eventually, it becomes clear that the reader is witnessing a cyclical tragedy, in which the story of Lleu, Blodeuwedd, and Gronw is reenacted, generation after generation, and that Blodeuwedd returns again and again, despite the efforts of generations of magicians to stop her. The painting and the plates were two such efforts to pin down her power. Only if the woman can be persuaded to see her as flowers rather than as an owl will the reenactments cease. It is up to Gwyn, the new magician in the valley, to attempt this; he is, as readers perhaps have suspected, Huw Halfbacon's son. In a terrifying conclusion to the story, Alison is persuaded by her stepbrother rather than Gwyn that she should see flowers.

Analysis

The Owl Service is the only one of Garner's novels to be set away from his native Cheshire, in North Wales, but it nevertheless still incorporates his major themes and preoccupations, not least the vivid sense of place and the need to be rooted, as well as the continuing importance of myth in modern society. Gwyn's mother, Nancy, has rejected her destiny but nevertheless, as becomes clear, she cannot break free from the valley and its history. She has told her son much about the valley, thus unwittingly fulfilling a part of his destiny. It is surely not chance that they have been called back to the valley to be present at Blodeuwedd's appearance.

Garner emphasizes the sense of being tied to the land by juxtaposing Gwyn's intimate secondhand knowledge of the place with Alison's firsthand ignorance. She has spent holidays at the house since childhood yet knows nothing of its history and is unable to fathom what is happening, although she is clearly the catalyst for the events through her discovery of the owl plates.

Garner also is concerned with the effects of severing a relationship with the land. Nancy already has rejected the valley, and Gwyn, like his father and grandfather, is destined to fail in stopping Blodeuwedd. Hints are given that although she is once again calm, she will return yet again, leaving open the question of what will happen to the valley if Gwyn, as his mother wishes, moves away. He already is uncomfortable with his heritage, although the local people take it as a part of their daily lives.

Although the supernatural events of *The Owl Service* are perhaps less overt than those of Garner's *The Weirdstone of Brisingamen* (1960) or *The Moon of Gomrath* (1963), both for younger children, this book's atmosphere is nevertheless far more menacing. Garner has stepped beyond a neat, simplistic world in which magicians always triumph and good overcomes evil. He presents a world of ambiguity in which magicians are as frail as mortals, subject to human weakness and failure. Readers are never clear whether the situation is genuinely magical or simply brought about by the tensions of a "made" family whose members do not yet know how to live together, class pretensions between generations and social classes, or the genuine visitation of Blodeuwedd. Garner's portrayal of this confused scene is powerful, almost brutal at times in its simplicity but also subtle, a few words speaking volumes for all that is left unsaid.

—*Maureen Speller*

The Paper Grail

Howard Barton journeys to Northern California in search of a sketch by the legendary Japanese artist Hoku-sai that is said to possess magical powers

Author: James P. Blaylock (1950-   )
Genre: Fantasy—Magical Realism
Type of work: Novel
Time of plot: The 1990's
Location: The Mendocino County area of Northern California
First published: 1991

The Story

On receiving the news that he has been willed a rare sketch by the Japanese artist Hoku-sai, Howard Barton returns to his old stomping grounds in Northern California. Once there, he quickly, if unexpectedly, falls in with a group more or less led by his eccentric Uncle Roy, the perennially improvident proprietor of a haunted museum. Roy's group includes his wife, Edith; his attractive daughter, Sylvia; Artemis Jimmers, an aged, oddball inventor; Mr. Bennett, a handyman with a predilection for making and displaying huge plywood cutouts on his property; and, in the background, the "gluers," called so because of their habit of gluing bizarre decorations and objects on their vehicles.

Feuding with Roy's group is an equally offbeat gang led by Roy's landlady, Heloise Lamey, a witchlike old woman who tends a bizarre garden and owns most of the town. Mrs. Lamey's unlikely gathering of villains includes Stoat, a slick, wheeler-dealer type; Glenwood Touchey, a disgruntled literary critic; Gwendolyn Bundy, a feminist poet who writes of the "existential woman" in "flat verse"; the Reverend White, a hard-drinking preacher; and Jason, a would-be painter. The feud has been accelerated by news of the death of Michael Graham, the old man who owned the sketch and presumably willed it to Howard. As tensions rise and conflicts intensify, the confusion increases and the questions become more and more bizarre. Are the ghosts in Uncle Roy's "museum" real or fake? Is Graham really dead? What strange inventions is Jimmers secreting in his mysterious tin shed? Does he have the sketch, along with several forgeries? What are its powers, if any?

Rhetorical agitation escalates quickly into acts of strange, often ridiculous, violence. The contesting groups chase each other around like Keystone Kops. Mrs. Lamey's gang destroys Bennett's plywood Humpty Dumpty, Howard destroys her clothes drier, Uncle Roy's museum goes up in flames, and Jimmers's tin shed is stolen. Finally, Uncle Roy and his wife are kidnapped and their lives threatened by Mrs. Lamey, who demands the sketch along with proof of its powers. Having received the drawing from Jimmers following Graham's demise, Howard agrees to a meeting. At last, he confronts his hysterical female nemesis in the middle of a raging storm that may or may not have been caused by the sketch.

Analysis

James Blaylock has stated that his favorite novel is Laurence Sterne's *Tristram Shandy* (1759-1767), and this explains much about not only *The Paper Grail* but also, in varying degrees, the rest of his fiction. Nothing much happens in Sterne's novel, but a grand time is had by all, especially the reader. Much of the point of Sterne's book is that life is such a complicated and ambiguous activity that very little purposeful action is possible. One distraction leads to another, which leads to another, and so on, a process that rarely ends where initially intended. Blaylock's novels are not that diffuse, but it is obvious that his characters are more interested in the side trips than in the destination.

The Paper Grail follows the personal formula that structures most of Blaylock's fiction, whether set in the contemporary world, Victorian England, or an alternative universe. A group of likable, comical, obsessive eccentrics does battle with a group of hateful, comical, obsessive eccentrics. Into this mix comes a single "normal" individual, the "hero," on a mission of some sort. He gets ambiguous assistance from the good grotesques and faces obstacles—some ludicrous, some dangerous, some both—from the bad ones. After many episodic, bizarre, funny encounters, the hero finally clears up the mysteries, fulfills his mission, and "gets the girl," if there is one to get.

For better or worse, Blaylock's novels lack the plot-driven pacing of most popular fiction. His characters, even his most grotesque villains, seem in no hurry; they enjoy indulging their eccentricities. In the midst of a violent showdown, they are all ready to stop for the dinner bell. If this takes the edge off the story's urgency, it underscores another important aspect of this author's fiction: its basic amiability. Although *The Paper Grail* has an abundance of villains, it lacks any real sense of evil. The bad characters are more goofy than malevolent. Despite the property destruction, threats, and violent activity in the book, there is only one fatality, that of a very old man from natural causes. In the end, the secondary villain, Stoat, reforms, and the other lesser conspirators simply stumble off. Even Heloise Lamey is forgivable. Her hysteria and blundering badness backfire; she is, finally, more to be pitied than censored.

Blaylock writes what might be termed literate slapstick. In *The Paper Grail*, he juxtaposes his comedic quest with the original legend of the Holy Grail, with frequent ironic references—Graham dies while fishing (hence, the Fisher King), his cane becomes Howard's Excalibur, Jimmers's shed is referred to as The Castle Perilous, and the sketch often is called the "Grail."

Blaylock's fiction probably can be shoehorned into the Magical Realism category, but of the Ray Bradbury, not the Gabriel García Márquez, type. His grotesque characters and their bizarre activities certainly belong in a distorted, heightened world, but one that, for the most part, is not totally impossible. It is not until the final chapters that *The Paper Grail* crosses the line into the overtly fantastic as the real powers of the Hoku-sai sketch and the truth of Jimmers's ghost machine are revealed. Conversely, these fantastic intrusions do not surprise the reader. Blaylock's is a fast, funny, bizarre world in which the fantastic occurs whenever the characters get around to it, except when they are distracted by the wonders of their own peculiarities.

—*Keith Neilson*

The Patternist Series

Over a period of four thousand years, a race of paranormal humans gradually comes into existence to displace or coexist with Clayarks (humans mutated by an extraterrestrial organism) and original humans

Author: Octavia E. Butler (1947-   )
Genre: Science fiction—alternative history
Type of work: Novels
Time of plot: About 1700 B.C.E. to 2300 C.E.
Location: Earth and the planet Kohn
First published: *Patternmaster* (1976), *Mind of My Mind* (1977), *Survivor* (1978), *Wild Seed* (1980), and *Clay's Ark* (1984)

The Story

The five novels of the Patternist series were not written and published in the order of their fictional chronology. Chronologically, the tale begins with *Wild Seed*, which covers the period from 1700 B.C.E. to 1830 C.E. It presents Doro, the oldest known of all the patternist paranormal humans. Born a Nubian in the upper Nile region of Africa around 1700 B.C.E., he died at the age of thirteen in a transition, the equivalent of a vastly accelerated adolescence. He can live only by taking the body of another nearby living human, which, used up, is left dead, to be replaced by yet another living human. Doro's mind and spirit displace those of the body's owner. He must kill to survive and has done so thousands of times. Doro's taste for the bodies of other humans with paranormal abilities (limited to forms of telepathy and psychokinesis; Butler eschews precognitive powers) drives him to hunt them, relocate them in isolated villages, and breed them through many centuries.

Around 1690, his homing sense for paranormal humans takes him to the extraordinary Anyanwu in the Ibo/Nigerian region of West Africa. At this time, Anyanwu is already three hundred years old because she is a shape-shifter and a healer. She can take many forms, including that of an eagle, a panther, a dolphin, and a wolflike dog. She has enormous physical strength and does not age.

From 1690 in West Africa, through the "middle passage" period of the slave trade, to the early nineteenth century in America, Doro and Anyanwu engage in a struggle of love, hate, and, finally, truce. During these years, Anyanwu has children by members of Doro's breed population of paranormal humans, often with Doro inhabiting the breed father's body. She eventually establishes herself as a white male Maryland plantation owner to give a home to what has become her own extended family of paranormal people. Prior to the Civil War, Anyanwu moves her people out of the war's path to California, where she soon takes the name Emma. It is by this persona that she will be known in her role as a secondary character in *Mind of My Mind*, set in the late twentieth century.

In *Mind of My Mind*, Doro searches for stabler paranormal individuals. Most young paranormals manifest psychologically unbalanced behaviors that are destructive to themselves or others before transition. Especially with Emma's help, Doro breeds increasingly powerful people, culminating in Mary, whose powers are as Doro's would be had he not "died" in transition. Mary eventually unites a large population of paranormals, with herself at the center of a telepathic web, or pattern. Thereafter, the paranormals are never again alone. Because Doro cannot tolerate his displacement as the virtual owner of these patternist people, Mary regretfully kills him.

In *Clay's Ark*, set in about 2020 but retrospective to the 1970's, the account of patternist history is recessed to tell the origin of the Clayark disease that transforms infected humans into catlike humanoids with super strength, health, and sensitivity. The disease actually is an organism imported from Proxima Centauri Two by an African American geologist crew member, Eli Doyle, who survived the crash and destruction of a spaceship named *Clay's Ark* on its return to Earth. In spite of Eli's efforts, the organism infects Earth's major population centers. Eventually, three women give birth to mutated children fathered by Eli, the first of the Clayark humans. The drive of the *Clay's Ark* starship utilizes the psionic or paranormal powers of average humans.

In *Survivor*, also set in the early twenty-first century, such a starship takes a group of ordinary (nonparanormal) people of an apparently Judeo-Christian religious cult to the planet of the kohn—analogous to Earth's mammal—to escape Earth's gradual descent into savagery. The paranormal patternists and Clayark-mutated people are part of the populations deliberately left behind. The heroine is Alanna, a wild African-Asian human who had been saved at eight years of age from abandonment and death by the cult leader, Jules, and his wife. Alanna lives with them on the new world with the Garkohn, a tribe of kohns addicted to meklah, withdrawal from which is usually fatal. The Garkohn cause the humans to be addicted as well. Alanna is captured by and bears a child of the Tehkohn people, enemies of the Garkohn, proving that the kohn and human species can breed. The Tehkohn are not addicted to meklah. Alanna survives withdrawal from her addiction and remains with the Tehkohn, who defeat the Garkohn in war.

Patternmaster is set in a quasi-medieval, twenty-third century California. There is a large population of Clayarks, some "mutes" (humans without paranormal powers), and patternists. The first pattern-master, Mary (of *Mind of My Mind*), is long since dead. One of her successors, Rayal, is about to die, and his rule is contested by his two powerful paranormal sons, Coransee and Teray. Teray, who has been reluctant to pursue the role of pattern-master, wins it. The Clayarks appear to remain in a savage or primitive state, though in a brief episode, Teray and a Clayark have a respectful conversion. The narrative is arrested with the patternists in power in North America and presumably on all of Earth. The prospects for patternist humans are bright.

Analysis

The patternist novels feature many established science-fiction topics: psionic powers, genetics and mutations, extraterrestrial travel, extraterrestrial species, actual history refurnished with science-fictional characters and effects, and postcatastrophe future history wherein the future is made to be significantly like the past by being more elementary and even medieval in surviving technology—perhaps a better setting for Octavia Butler's exploration of her characters. Each novel is different in mood. *Survivor*, with its subtext of reverence for harmonious existence with nature, is reminiscent of Ursula K. Le Guin's *The Word for World Is Forest* (1972). *Clay's Ark*'s action and setting of violence along southwestern U.S. country roads and highways recalls the film *Road Warrior* (1981). *Patternmaster* and *Mind of My Mind* are in the tradition of works Butler admires: Theodore Sturgeon's *More than Human* (1953) and John Brunner's *The Whole Man* (1964). *Patternmaster* and *Mind of My Mind*, however, are anchored in the luminous originality of *Wild Seed*, the style and setting of which echo the oral narrative discourse of Nigerian West African storytelling and the horrific historicity of the centuries of the African slave trade, the middle passage, and the captivity of the African slave populations in the Americas.

Part of the genius of *Wild Seed* is that there are no antecedents for it in the science-fiction genre. Moreover, it grandly merges meanings traditionally represented in the Faust myth, vampire lore, and the Greek and Hebraic genesis stories. Doro is Faust and vampire, voracious in his appetite for existence. His life is a progression of murders of the humans whose bodies become the hosts for his spirit. Anyanwu is an Earth Mother, strong enough to bear a species and even sometimes to protect her children from infanticide by Doro. *Wild Seed*, furthermore, is the touchstone work for Butler's nonpatternist novels. It connects the optimism of the extraterrestrial gene trading of her *Xenogenesis* trilogy (1989), the "seed" implied in the title of her *Parable of the Sower* (1993), and the fictional slave narrative of her brilliant *Kindred* (1979).

Butler makes the calendar of the patternist novels clear, but they are not fully linked. *Wild Seed*, *Mind of My Mind*, and *Patternmaster* deal with the patternist paranormal humans. *Patternmaster* and *Clay's Ark* deal with the Clayark-mutated humans, and *Survivor* deals with original humans and an alien humanoid species, the kohn. They are, moreover, like all of Butler's stories and novels, tapestries of often bizarre violence, both physical and psychological, and read as excellent adventure tales. Butler has a more pressing agenda for the meaning of the patternist works, however. The novels are primarily stories of the love affairs of individuals who combine radically unique identities with powerful desires for relationships that will validate and nourish them. The relationships transcend ethnicity, race, species, and, ultimately, extraterrestrial DNA. Moreover, from them issue biologically beautiful children.

Although Butler is the author of few works of shorter fiction, her "Speech Sounds" (1983) won the Hugo Award for best short story; "Bloodchild" (1984) won the Hugo, Nebula, and Locus awards for best short novelette; and "The Evening and the Morning and the Night" (1987) earned a Hugo nomination. *Parable of the Sower* was nominated for a Nebula. *Kindred* and *Wild Seed* remain among the very best novels of modern science fiction.

—*John R. Pfeiffer*

The Phoenix and the Mirror

Vergil Magus creates a virgin mirror to locate the missing daughter of Queen Cornelia of Carsus

Author: Avram Davidson (1923-1993)
Genre: Fantasy—alternative history
Type of work: Novel
Time of plot: The first century C.E.
Location: Italy, the Mediterranean Sea, and North Africa
First published: 1969

The Story

An Ace Science Fiction Special, with appropriately enigmatic cover art by the husband-and-wife team of Leo and Diane Dillon, *The Phoenix and the Mirror: Or, the Enigmatic Speculum* was the first book in a projected series titled *Vergil Magus*. The second and only other book, *Vergil in Averno*, was published in 1987. Its events precede those of *The Phoenix and the Mirror*. In both novels, Avram Davidson expands on the medieval conceit that the Roman poet Vergil was a magician.

Lost in a labyrinth of tunnels and pursued by manticores, Vergil escapes with the assistance of Queen Cornelia of Carsus and her servants. When Cornelia discovers who the magus is, she uses magic to take his masculinity hostage, then orders him to make her a virgin mirror, with which she can locate her daughter, Laura, who has been lost on the way from Carsus to Naples. Once the device is made and used, Cornelia will allow Vergil to become a whole man again.

A virgin mirror is made of tin and copper ores smelted and blended with care. Never exposed to light as it is polished, lidded, and closed with a clasp, it will show whoever first uncovers it whatever he or she desires to see. Such a device could take a year to make, and Vergil knows the queen will not be patient. She plans to use the princess's marriage to advance political aims.

Tin is a monopoly of Tartismen, who import it from a fabulous distance, already cast into ingots. Vergil must obtain raw ore quickly. He goes to the traders' Cyclopean castle in Naples to ask their help. While there, he meets a Phoenician captain, Ebbed-Saphir, and thwarts an assassination attempt. In gratitude, the Tartismen's Captain-Lord sends a messenger-bird and two falcons to attempt to obtain a small quantity of tin ore.

Copper, too, is customarily imported in ingots, although the source is much nearer at hand. Because of the Sea-Huns, the ships that bring it from Cyprus travel in yearly convoys. Vergil cannot wait, so Ebbed-Saphir agrees to lend his ship. The magus decides to seek permission to pass from the barbarian Sea-Huns themselves.

The Sea-Huns have three nominal kings because the shaman who "put on the bear-skin" to find out which of the old king's three sons should inherit the throne has remained a bear. Two of the kings are out of reach, but the third, Bayla, wishes to worship the goddess Aphrodite as embodied in her priestesses. He is willing to make the voyage with Vergil so that he can visit the Temple of Aphrodite on Cyprus.

They find the blockaded island of Cyprus overrun by religious cults of all kinds, including that of Daniel Christ, whose leader gives Vergil the information required to compel the evasive Cypriots to provide the magus with copper ore. Vergil then sails back to the Sea-Huns' camp to find that the shaman has at long last changed back into a man and announced that Bayla is the one true king.

Returned home, Vergil finds that the tin ore has arrived. Work on the mirror, though tedious, goes well. When the major speculum is completed, Cornelia comes to discover where the princess may be. At the stroke of noon, she touches the newly revealed polished bronze with a golden pin and sees her daughter on Cyclopean steps.

Virgin no longer, the mirror reflects only the faces of those who look into it. Vergil sees himself and knows that he is a whole man again. He also knows that he has fallen in love with the first woman he has really looked at since Cornelia took his masculinity hostage: the girl in the mirror. He must, and will, find her.

Beginning with the Tartismen's castle in Naples, Vergil searches all known castles of Cyclopean work without success, until it becomes plain that Laura must be in Thither Lybia. Taking Ebbed-Saphir as his guide once more, the magus sets out. Once within sight of the ruin, Vergil goes on alone and finds the last of the Cyclops unwilling to give up his companion. The magus temporarily blinds it with dust and escapes with the girl.

The Phoenician captain rejoins them and leads them to a pyre. No true man, but a phoenix, Ebbed-Saphir intends to renew himself by burning himself and the daughter of his promised bride, Cornelia. By becoming his mate, Cornelia has lived hundreds of years, but she has evaded the final part of the bargain. Vergil overcomes the phoenix, and Laura is saved.

In Naples, Vergil reveals that the girl he has rescued is not Laura but her half sister, Phyllis. Cornelia had concealed the girls' true identities even from them, hoping to use her husband's bastard child to cheat Ebbed-Saphir, who she thought would be killed in the regeneration process if he underwent it with Phyllis rather than Laura. Vergil claims Phyllis as his wife.

Analysis

The Phoenix and the Mirror is set in a world in which classical mythology and medieval alchemy are true. Though not based on the historical Vergil or on any of the later legends—most of which involve a misperception of Vergil as a Christian before his time—this book draws freely on classical, medieval, and renaissance sources for background and detail.

The Phoenix and the Mirror is built on a series of dual images: sun and moon, tin and copper, and male and female. Throughout the story, from the simple lust of Bayla King for Aphrodite's priestesses to the momentary terror of the final union of Ebbed-Saphir and Cornelia, sexuality affirmed is positive, and sexuality denied or cast aside is negative. In the end, Vergil not only regains his masculinity but also finds his feminine complement.

—*Catherine Mintz*

The Picture of Dorian Gray

> Dorian's soul goes into his portrait, which shows the effects of sin and age as his body stays young

Author: Oscar Wilde (1854-1900)
Genre: Fantasy—cautionary
Type of work: Novel
Time of plot: The 1870's and 1880's
Location: London and the British countryside
First published: 1891 (serial form, *Lippincott's Monthly Magazine*, July, 1890, without chapters 3, 5, 15, 16, 17, and 18; "The Preface" in *The Fortnightly Review*, March, 1891)

The Story

Basil Hallward, a painter, reluctantly introduces his jaded friend, Lord Henry Wotton, to the young man Basil is painting. Dorian Gray, at the age of twenty, is outstandingly beautiful, wealthy, and inexperienced. Lord Henry tells him that "beauty is a form of genius" and that he must live the wonderful life inside him, giving form to every feeling, expression to every thought, and reality to every dream. Lord Henry believes that this form of fulfillment results in an ideal life.

Dorian realizes with horror that he will grow old as the portrait stays young and beautiful. He states that he would give his soul to stay young while the portrait ages. Immediately, Dorian's character changes; he cruelly taunts Basil as Basil gives him the painting.

Dorian flings himself into life. He falls in love with a young actress, Sibyl Vane, who plays Shakespearean roles in a seedy theater. They declare their love the afternoon before Basil and Harry first see her. That night, her performance is terrible; having felt real love, she can no longer pretend it as Juliet. Dorian, however, loves only the images; he coldly rejects the woman. On returning home, he sees that the portrait reflects his cruelty. Horrified, he resolves to marry Sibyl, but he cannot; she has committed suicide. At first, Dorian is shocked, but he soon rationalizes that Sibyl deserved her fate because she failed to live up to his expectations.

The day after Sibyl's death, Lord Henry sends Dorian a "poisonous book." Symbolist in style, the book is said to tell of a young Frenchman

Oscar Wilde. (Library of Congress)

who tries to recapitulate the emotional, spiritual, and intellectual history of the world in his own life, "loving for their mere artificiality those renunciations what men have unwisely called virtue, as much as those natural rebellions that wise men still call sin." Dorian comes to feel that the hero of the book is "a kind of prefiguring type of himself." He patronizes the arts, flirts with Roman Catholicism, and studies perfumes, exotic musical instruments, jewels, and embroideries.

For seventeen years, Dorian enjoys the life of a wealthy man, remaining young and beautiful. Rumors circulate about him: He ruins women's reputations, he frequents strange places, and his friends come to bad ends. Seeing him, however, few can believe him to be evil. Late one night, Basil visits, insisting he must know if the rumors about Dorian's evil lifestyle are true. Dorian offers to show Basil his soul, as contained in the portrait. Basil is horrified at the cruel, sensual face. Dorian stabs him to death and blackmails a friend into disposing of the body.

Plagued by fear and guilt, Dorian escapes Sibyl Vane's brother, who has sought vengeance all these years, but that does not help, and even opium yields only temporary forgetfulness. He resolves to change and refrains from seducing a village girl. The portrait reveals hypocrisy in addition to evidence of various sins and flaws. Dorian grows angry, determining to destroy the painting and, with it, his past. He stabs it. Passersby hear a horrible cry. When the servants enter the room, they find "a splendid portrait of their master" and a body they recognize only by the rings it wears.

Analysis

Oscar Wilde's only novel, *The Picture of Dorian Gray*, was written during the years that Wilde was writing fairy tales and short stories such as "Lord Arthur Savile's Crime" (1887), which the novel resembles in milieu. Aside from the fairy tales and "The Canterbury Ghost" (1887), the novel is his only prose fantasy. His dramas appeared from 1892 onward, and *The Picture of Dorian Gray* prefigures them in its witty dialogue and portrait of London social life.

The first critical question raised about *The Picture of Dorian Gray* concerned its morality, although, except for the murder of Basil, no immoral acts are described. Wilde stated that the story's moral was that all excess, as well as all renunciation, brings its own punishment. The nature of Dorian's sins is never clear, though a few hints were added after newspaper reviews attacked the original version. In the context of the book, Dorian's chief sin seems to be a desire for experience and knowledge of all kinds.

What connection exists between Dorian's crimes and his interest in art? Adjectives such as "monstrous," "terrible," "maddening," and "corrupt" are applied with little apparent regard to their subject in the descriptions of the "poisonous book" and of Dorian's interests and activities. Scholars have speculated that Wilde's own underground homosexual life was hinted at by Lord Henry's cynical statements and the vagueness of Dorian's sins. This may have been what made newspaper critics uncomfortable. For Wilde, sin and art seem one in life and in literature; the Platonic ideal of beauty can be worshiped as easily in a young man as in a beautiful object.

Other criticism has focused on influences, especially the identity of the poisonous book. Wilde himself said his novel bore a resemblance to *A rebours* (1884) by Joris-Karl Huysmans, but that resemblance cannot be pushed too far. Other strong influences are *Vivian Grey* (1826-1827) by British novelist and prime minister Benjamin Disraeli and *Melmoth the Wanderer* (1820) by Wilde's great-uncle, Charles R. Maturin. Finally, *Studies in the History of the Renaissance* by Walter Pater, with its philosophy of living life to the fullest, was a prime source of the decadent philosophy, which Wilde exemplifies so thoroughly in Dorian himself.

—*Edra C. Bogle*

Planet of the Apes

Three men land on a planet where civilized apes are the dominant
species and human beings exist in a wild state as dumb animals

Author: Pierre Boulle (1912-1994)
Genre: Science fiction—evolutionary fantasy
Type of work: Novel
Time of plot: After 2500
Location: Soror, a planet in orbit around Betelgeuse
First published: *La Planète des singes* (1963; English translation, 1963)

The Story

Xan Fielding's translation of *La Planète des singes* was known in some
quarters by another title, *Monkey Planet* (1964), a phrase lacking the dignity Pierre Boulle had conferred on his simian civilization. The dignity
of a simian society that, whatever its many ineradicable imperfections,
has eliminated war and the serious consequences of racial and class conflicts is somehow associated less with the prank-suggestive adjective
"monkey" than with the more substantial noun "apes." It is dignity, or
the quality of worth, with which the story is largely concerned.

The story's frame is the discovery of a manuscript inside a bottle that
is floating in space. Its retrievers are Jinn and Phyllis, a wealthy couple
enjoying a holiday as they cruise in their private spaceship. Jinn, who
knows the Earth language in which the manuscript is written, reads it to
Phyllis, after which both react to it incredulously.

The manuscript contains the account by a French journalist, Ulysse
Mérou, of his two-year stay on an Earth-like planet on which the Earth's
situation of civilized humans and wild apes has been reversed. Humans
lack intelligence and speech, live naked in the wild, and are preyed on
by apes, who use them as objects of study in physiological research.
Ulysse and his companions, scientist Professor Antelle and physician
Arthur Levain, are captured by gorillas after landing on the planet,
which they christen Soror because it is like a sister to Earth. Levain is
killed by the hunters, and Professor Antelle reverts, in extended captivity, to the brute animal state of Soror's humans. Ulysse manages to survive by ingratiating himself with two chimpanzee scientists, Cornelius
and his fiancé, Zira. He learns the simian language, wins the respect of

the scientific community, and is allowed finally to wear clothing, as do the planet's apes, but not its humans.

The villain is an orangutan named Zaius, who contests the research of Cornelius and Zira and plots the liquidation of Ulysse. The cohabitation of Ulysse with a beautiful but primitive human female, whom he names Nova, results in the birth of their son, Sirius. The family escapes from Zaius and the planet with the help of Cornelius and Zira. Ulysse takes Nova and their child to Earth, which, owing to the relativistic variations of space-time, is now seven hundred years older than when he left it less than a decade before. Landing in Paris, Ulysse discovers that Earth's evolutionary processes have turned it, like Soror, into a planet of apes. He escapes with his family, writes his account, and casts it adrift in the bottle picked up by Jinn and Phyllis, who, the reader learns, are chimpanzees.

Analysis

The values intimated by the plot are those of individual worth, including personal responsibility, objective inquiry, disregard of physical differences, and familial cohesion. The society on Soror from which Ulysse escapes is the same as that of twentieth century Europe and America, with some utopian exceptions. Its members have resolved the problems that culminate in war and racial violence. There are no national divisions. The entire planet is governed by an egalitarian parliament representing the unilingual races of Gorillas, who are the executives and hunters, Orangutans, who are the traditionalist academicians, and Chimpanzees, who are the true intellectuals and enlightened scientists. Criminal activity is contained by effective police forces, and political ambitions are checked by administrative balances and interdependence.

The tripartite society recalls that of Plato's Politeia. The Gorillas are closely akin to Plato's powerful *epikouroi* (auxiliaries); the Orangutans are *phylakes* (guardians) but less noble, because of their reactionary pettiness, than Plato's guardians; and the Chimpanzees are, as *demiourgoi*, superior to Plato's craftsmen because of their heightened intellectualism.

The reluctance of Soror's guardians to accept the findings of objective research—especially the discovery that their civilization derived from a preexistent human civilization—is a satirical comment on the obtuseness of twentieth century conservatives in their resistance to what have become ecological certainties and technological truths. At the same time, the ability of the apes to achieve social equality and global tranquillity is a satiric reminder of the human disinclination to do so.

Planet of the Apes forms part of Boulle's extended commentary on the stubborn incapacity of human beings, collectively, to adjust themselves to their own technological achievements and, in consequence, to one another. Other parts of this commentary include, for example, *Le Pont de la Rivière Kwai* (1952; *The Bridge on the River Kwai*, 1954) and *Le Jardin de Kanashima* (1964; *Garden on the Moon*, 1965), the first exemplifying Boulle's use of World War II as a reflection of human fallibility, the second rehearsing the missile race madness that followed World War II.

Within its effective framing device, Boulle's narrative provides a quickening of pace that contributes to the sense of anxiety that his evidences of civilizational folly induce in his reader. The three parts of the novel comprise thirty-eight chapters. In chapter 29 (chapter 3 of part 3), the past tense yields to the present perfect; and from chapter 32 (chapter 6 of part 3) to the end, the present tense is used as Ulysse describes his hectic escape from Soror and his shocking return to Earth.

—*Roy Arthur Swanson*

The Prydain Chronicles

Taran, an Assistant Pig-Keeper, comes of age to become a hero and a king in the land of Prydain, a magical kingdom struggling against the forces of evil

Author: Lloyd Alexander (1924-   )
Genre: Fantasy—heroic fantasy
Types of work: Novels and stories
Time of plot: Various periods in the history of Prydain
Location: The land of Prydain
First published: *The Book of Three* (1964), *The Black Cauldron* (1965), *The Castle of Llyr* (1966), *Taran Wanderer* (1967), *The High King* (1968), and *The Foundling, and Other Tales of Prydain* (1973)

The Story

The Prydain Chronicles primarily are a history of the adventures of Taran, a young orphan in the care of the wizard Dallben and the old warrior Coll. In a series of heroic quests, Taran, given the title of Assistant Pig-Keeper, finds the excitement he craves along with his share of despair and heartache as he grows up to become the High King of Prydain.

Taran's adventures begin in *The Book of Three*, when Hen Wen, the oracular pig who is Taran's charge, runs away to escape capture by the Horned King, champion of the evil King Arawn, Death-Lord. Taran, while following the pig, is introduced to the cast of characters who become his companions on this quest and will also appear in subsequent adventures. These include Prince Gwydion, war leader for High King Math and the forces of good; Gurgi, a strange creature who becomes half pet, half servant; the beautiful Princess Eilonwy, orphaned daughter of a line of enchantresses who helps Taran escape from the castle of the wicked Queen Achren; wandering bard and king Fflewddur Fflam; and Doli the dwarf. Taran, aided by a magical sword, helps to defeat the Horned King and restores at least a temporary peace to the kingdom.

Taran's adventures continue in *The Black Cauldron*. He is reunited with his companions to begin a new quest, that of destroying the cauldron in which King Arawn creates his deathless warriors, the Cauldron-Born. Taran must suffer wounded pride at the hands of the arrogant Prince Ellidyr, deal with his grief over the loss of his friend, Adaon the warrior and bard, and bargain with Orddu, Orgoch, and Orwen, the three mysterious enchantresses who hold the cauldron. Taran learns the meaning of sacrifice when he must give up his most precious possession, Adaon's brooch, to obtain the cauldron; and he learns humility when Ellidyr betrays him and threatens to claim the credit for all of Taran's triumphs. It is Ellidyr, however, who sacrifices his life to destroy the cauldron.

In *The Castle of Llyr*, Taran begins to acknowledge his feelings for Princess Eilonwy when he and Prince Rhun of the Isle of Mona escort her to the prince's home, where she will begin her training in the ways of the court. Taran reaches Mona and finds Prince Gwydion, who warns him that Queen Achren is plotting revenge on Eilonwy. Chief Steward Magg, conspiring with Achren, kidnaps Eilonwy, and Taran and his companions seek to rescue her. Achren knows that Eilonwy, as a daughter of an enchantress, has access to great powers. Eilonwy chooses to forsake her potential power and uses her magic only to defeat Achren.

Taran Wanderer tells of Taran's quest to discover the mystery of his parentage. He journeys around the kingdom, hoping that the truth of his past will make him worthy of asking Eilonwy to marry him. In the course of his travels, Taran acquires wisdom. He learns skills of judgment and negotiation when he settles a dispute between two nobles. When Craddoc the shepherd falsely claims to be Taran's long-lost father, Taran must face his own guilt over being ashamed of his modest parentage. After Craddoc dies, Taran travels among the Free Commots, a group of self-governing villages. There he learns the importance of skilled craftsmanship as well as the value of working hard to make a living. Taran finally learns to accept himself despite his unknown parentage.

The High King is the last adventure for Taran and his friends. Arawn makes his last stand by stealing Gwydion's magical sword. Gwydion rallies Taran and his companions to begin a quest to retrieve the sword. Taran, benefiting from the time he spent making friends among the Free Commots, raises an army that he leads to Caer Dathyl, home of High King Math.

The forces of evil, which include the deathless Cauldron-Born warriors, initially prove too strong for the combined armies of Gwydion and Taran. Caer Dathyl falls, and King Math is slain. Gwydion risks everything on a desperate raid on the now-unguarded Annuvin, stronghold of King Arawn, hoping to find the sword. He charges Taran with the task of delaying Arawn's forces on their return march back to Annuvin. Taran fulfills his task and finds the magical sword, learning its secret: It alone can kill the Cauldron-Born warriors. Taran also destroys King

Arawn, ending an era in which magic was a major force in Prydain.

Taran must face the high cost of his victory: Prince Rhun, his old teacher Coll, and many of the friends he made among the Free Commots are killed in battle. Taran must say goodbye to Gwydion, Dallben, Fflewddur, and Gurgi, who must now leave Prydain to return to the kingdom of magic. The land of Prydain will belong to mortals, ruled by the hard-earned wisdom of King Taran and Queen Eilonwy.

The Foundling, and Other Tales of Prydain is a collection of six short stories set in Prydain before Taran's time. "The Foundling" tells of Dallben's childhood and how he became an enchanter by accidentally tasting a magic brew. In "The Stone," Doli the dwarf teaches a farmer a lesson on why mortals should not meddle with magic. "The True Enchanter" is the story of how Princess Angharad, Eilonwy's mother, chooses a mortal for her husband rather than an enchanter. "The Rascal Crow" is an adventure of the animals of Prydain, who also struggle against Arawn Death-Lord. "The Sword" is a history of Gwydion's sword Drynwyn and how it came to be lost. "The Smith, the Weaver, and the Harper" reveals how Arawn Death-Lord stole many secrets of craftsmanship from the people of Prydain.

Analysis

Originally inspired by the Mabinogion, a collection of Welsh legends, Lloyd Alexander evoked his memories of the time he spent in Wales during World War II to build the fantasy land of Prydain. The critically acclaimed series of novels and short stories is populated by numerous unforgettable characters and is full of daring adventures in which these characters are forced to confront the consequences of their actions. Although the setting undeniably is a fantasy realm, Taran struggles with the same kinds of problems that might trouble a contemporary young man.

Alexander has been compared with both T. H. White and J. R. R. Tolkien for his use of well-known legends as a basis for his writing. Alexander is able to strike a balance between heroic epic and modern realism that makes the books accessible to young people of various generations. The books are considered classics by many in the field of children's literature.

The Book of Three, the first of the series, was published after Alexander already had published several adult novels. His first children's book, *Time Cat: The Remarkable Journeys of Jason and Gareth* (1963), led him to explore further his research into Welsh folklore. Rather than merely retelling the old legends, Alexander added his own created characters along with contemporary conflicts of values and ethics. In each of the novels, the themes of heroic quests are enriched by Taran's personal quest: the search for his identity. Taran and the other characters also are tested by dilemmas brought on by the universal battle between good and evil.

The Foundling, and Other Tales of Prydain was published several years after the last Prydain novel. This collection of short stories was intended, along with Alexander's books *Coll and His White Pig* (1965) and *The Truthful Harp* (1967), to introduce younger children to the land of Prydain. Each story picks up and explains in more detail a tale that was hinted at in the novels. The mood of each story is different, covering a range including romantic, humorous, grim, and triumphant.

The Prydain Chronicles firmly established Alexander's reputation as a major children's author. The books garnered Alexander numerous prestigious awards, including the Child Study Association of America's Children's Book of the Year citation, *The New York Times*'s Outstanding Books of the Year citation, *School Library Journal*'s Best Books citation, the American Book Award, the American Library Association's notable book citation, and the Newbery Medal. The well-received series was praised for its sophisticated storytelling and richly developed mythological background. Critics also appreciated Alexander's realistic characters, who strive to overcome both internal weaknesses and external enemies. The books' tones vary from lightheartedness to somberness, but a level of humor is maintained throughout.

—Quinn Weller

The Psammead Trilogy

Five siblings go on a series of magical adventures when their wishes are granted by a sand-fairy, a magic carpet, and a magic amulet

Author: E(dith) Nesbit (1858-1924)
Genre: Fantasy—Magical Realism
Type of work: Novels
Time of plot: About 1902-1903, with excursions to antiquity and the future
Location: London and Kent, England, and various other locations on Earth
First published: *Five Children and It* (1905; serial form as *The Psammead, The Strand Magazine,* 1902), *The Phoenix and the Carpet* (1904; serial form, *The Strand Magazine,* 1903-1904), and *The Story of the Amulet* (1906; serial form, *The Strand Magazine,* 1905-1906)

The Story

The Psammead Trilogy was written as three separate commissioned serials for *The Strand Magazine.* Although *The Story of the Amulet* was finished and published last, E. Nesbit began work on it before *The Phoenix and the Carpet. Five Children and It* contains eleven adventures that begin when five children (in order by age), Cyril, Anthea, Robert, Jane, and their baby brother, called The Lamb, go to the Kentish countryside for a summer vacation. While exploring an abandoned gravel quarry, the children find a psammead (pronounced Sammy-add) or sand-fairy. The Psammead, a tubby, furry creature with bat's ears and telescoping eyes, proves capable of granting wishes that last until sundown. A grudging and cantankerous ally at best, soon the Psammead bargains that wishes be restricted to one a day. Among other wishes, the children wish to be as beautiful as the day, to be rich beyond the dreams of avarice, to have wings, to be in a besieged castle, and for The Lamb to be grown up. Each wish, wild and wonderful as its consequences are, proves troublesome and disconcerting. When the most ill-considered wish of all plants burgled jewels in their mother's bedroom, the children get the Psammead to grant immediately all the wishes needed to set things right in return for their promise to leave him alone and never to ask him for another wish.

The Psammead includes in the last wishes Anthea's polite hope to see him again one day.

The Phoenix and the Carpet takes place the following fall, with the five children back in London. Their new adventures begin when their ruined nursery carpet is replaced with a secondhand Persian carpet in which a phoenix egg is wrapped. When the children accidentally knock the egg into the fireplace, the flames cause it to hatch. The Phoenix informs them that the carpet is, in fact, a magical wishing carpet that can take them anywhere. Accompanied by the vain but agreeable Phoenix, the children wish themselves to a tower in France that contains a hidden treasure, to a southern shore where one cannot possibly have whooping cough, and to a bazaar in India. These adventures also are fraught with difficulties. Worse embarrassments occur when the Phoenix accompanies them around London, especially because, when excited, it is apt to start fires. Furthermore, the children's hard use of the carpet is causing it to wear out. Precisely when the children decide they must ask the Phoenix to leave, it informs them that a few months with them have been as wearying as its usual five-hundred-year life span. With relief, they grant its request to immolate itself and have the carpet transport itself and the Phoenix's egg to a place where they will not be found for two thousand years.

The Story of the Amulet is set during the following summer. The children's father is away working as a war correspondent, and their mother, taking The Lamb with her, has gone to Madeira to recuperate from an illness. The children are staying in London at the home of their old nurse. They find the Psammead caged and up for sale in a pet store. The children rescue him by buying him. He still cannot grant them wishes, but in gratitude, he offers to help them to their hearts' desire, which is the safe return home of their parents and brother. He directs them to buy a magic amulet in a secondhand shop. The amulet, when whole, grants one's heart's desire, but half of it was long ago crushed to dust. The remaining half, however, has the power to take the children through time so that they can look for it in its whole state. The children learn how to pronounce its inscription from Jimmy, a learned gentleman living in rented rooms upstairs. They search for the whole amulet in ancient Egypt, Babylon, Tyre, and England of the future. On a separate quest, they also travel in time to England at the time of Julius Caesar's invasion. The queen of Babylon, through a wish granted her by the Psammead, visits them in their own time. With the unwitting help of Jimmy and the self-interested help of Rekh-marā, a priest of Amen-Rā, they eventually succeed in finding the amulet. Their hearts' desire granted, they give the amulet to Jimmy. Jimmy and Rekh-marā also find their hearts' desire in great learning.

Analysis

From her teens on, Nesbit was a published author of poems, short stories, novels, articles, and children's stories, but not until she was nearly forty did she begin to write the humorous and sparkling children's novels for which she is best remembered. Some of those, such as the Psammead Trilogy *House of Arden* (1908), and *The Enchanted Castle* (1907), incorporate fantasy; others, for example, *The Treasure Seekers* (1899), *The Wouldbegoods* (1901), and *The Railway Children* (1905), do not. In both types of story, Nesbit was among the first to depict children realistically.

Similar to the boys in Rudyard Kipling's *Stalky & Co.* (1899; collects eight stories published 1897-1899), the children in her books are neither unbelievably good nor unbelievably bad, as so many fictional children were in her day. They bicker and make up, and they are frightened and brave by turns. Unlike Kipling, Nesbit depicts both boys and girls and has neither group completely conform to the stereotypes then current. The boys, though brave, on occasion cry. The girls, though usually gentler, hurl stones at a castle-besieging army and take charge of dangerous situations.

The Psammead Trilogy, standing with *The Treasure Seekers* at the beginning of a burst of creative activity, uses many themes to which Nesbit returned in later books. First and foremost, the trilogy deals with the subject of wish fulfillment, continually stressing the adage, "Watch out what you wish for; you might get it." The children's wishes, except for those few in which they wish good for others, do not turn out as expected. They wish for gold, for example, and get ancient money they cannot spend. Furthermore, they are suspected of stealing it. Annoyed with taking care of their baby brother, they wish others would want to take him off their hands, then discover how much they love him and want him when every passing stranger tries to take him away.

Magical time travel is another theme to which Nesbit returned often. As her text acknowledges, it was suggested to her by H. G. Wells's *The Time Machine* (1895), but she was probably the first to incorporate time travel into a children's story. Wells's *A Modern Utopia* (1905) also influenced the trilogy. In *The Story of the Amulet*, the children travel to the future and see a Wellsian utopia from a child's point of view; they notice child-safe playrooms and desirable schools.

A committed socialist, Nesbit occasionally indulges in social criticism. The queen of Babylon comments that London's slaves, as she calls the working people, do not look well treated, and the children find that they cannot explain why having the vote should make them contented. In another adventure, the children can rescue an orphaned girl from the workhouse only by finding her a home in the past; children in their present are not properly valued by society.

Nesbit's influence was felt by many subsequent writers for children. C. S. Lewis admired the Psammead Trilogy and drew on his memories of it in creating *The Chronicles of Narnia* (1950-1956). Edward Eager acknowledged her influence on his work in *Half Magic* (1954). Her keen eye for what children feel, say, and do, and her serious exploration of the gifts and the dangers of imaginative play as a tool for both exploring and escaping reality, make her one of the shapers of early twentieth century children's fiction.

—Ronnie Apter

Rashomon and Other Stories

A collection of six stories, the most famous of which accents the distortions of memory by describing a single incident through three widely divergent testimonials

Author: Ryūnosuke Akutagawa (Ryūnosuke Niihara, 1892-1927)
Genre: Fantasy—medieval future
Type of work: Stories
Time of plot: Medieval times through the sixteenth century
Location: Japan
First published: 1952

The Story

The title *Rashomon and Other Stories* has been used for several collections of Ryūnosuke Akutagawa's work. "In a Grove" (published in Japanese as "Yabu no naka," 1922), the opening story and centerpiece of this 1952 anthology, consists of the testimony of several different speakers responding to a government official's investigation of a woman's rape and her husband's subsequent death in a secluded forest. The most intriguing testimony springs from the bandit who raped the wife, the wife herself, and the dead husband, who speaks through a spirit medium. Each of the three recounts with dogged assuredness a version of the events that is radically different from those of the others; each version elevates the motives of the speaker at the expense of the perceived motives of the other two persons present. The mixture of cogency and implausibility in all three accounts suggests that nobody can be certain about all the details of that day in the grove—or throughout much of recorded history.

The story "Rashomon" is named for the largest city gate in medieval Kyōto, Japan's former capital. This gate and the corpse-laden room in it serve as the story's setting, and its state of disrepair is emblematic of the grim period of famine and concomitant moral decay gripping Japan at that time. Desperate to earn money for food, a shriveled old woman is pulling the hair from corpses in the gate in order to make wigs from it. The male protagonist, who happens by, threatens to kill her in disgust for defiling the dead, but she argues that many of these dead people had benefited from shady business practices when still alive. He spares her and leaves, but not before stealing her kimono.

The remaining four stories are interesting, even if they do not rivet one's attention like the first two. "Yam Gruel" recounts the story of a low-ranking samurai often mocked as a provincial pauper. His intense yearning for a rare dessert delicacy, yam gruel, leads him into encounters with a supernatural fox, at which point he begins to realize the hollowness of his craving. In "The Martyr," a young priest accused of impregnating an unmarried young woman is driven from his church in Nagasaki and must resort to begging for a living. When the young woman's baby daughter is caught in a burning house, nobody but the excommunicated priest dares to rush in to save the infant. Although the infant escapes harm, the priest soon dies from severe burns. It turns out that the priest was in fact a woman and thus blameless from the start. "The Dragon" portrays the excitement surrounding a dragon sighting, and "Kesa and Morito" renders the monologues of two guilt-ridden adulterous lovers who feel compelled either to murder or to be murdered.

Analysis

Akutagawa is one of Japan's most famous writers, and "Rashomon" has been cited as establishing his style and becoming the prototype for historical fiction in Japan. Most of Akutagawa's fiction contains a core of realism embellished with the casual incorporation of fantasy. Akutagawa's work thus resembles that of the late twentieth century Latin American Magical Realists, whom he anticipated by roughly half a century.

"In a Grove" was the primary inspiration for Akira Kurosawa's award-winning film *Rashomon* (1951) and is Akutagawa's most famous story internationally. It also is his most experimental short story, for it involves seven different narrators, none of whom can be said to be central in terms of reliability or thoroughness of presentation.

"In a Grove" contains neither a prologue nor a conclusion or denouement, leaving readers with no overarching authorial interpretation to help resolve the numerous conflicting points of testimony. In this way, Akutagawa's scenario differs substantially from that of Kurosawa, who inserted a woodcutter's eyewitness account of the rape and suicide near the film's conclusion in order to tie together the loose ends intentionally left dangling by Akutagawa. The self-deluded aspects of the testimony of Tajōmaru (the bandit), Masago (the wife), and Takehiro (the husband) remain implicit with Akutagawa, whereas Kurosawa makes them explicit in his film.

The major difference among the three conflicting testimonies is the nature of Takehiro's death. Tajōmaru claims to have stabbed Takehiro to death after a lengthy and valiant sword fight. In contrast, Masago testifies that after witnessing the rape, a dumbstruck Takehiro shamefacedly agreed to her plan for a double suicide; she stabbed him to death shortly before failing in an attempt to cut her own throat. Finally, Takehiro's ghost claims that he committed suicide in despair over his wife's urging of Tajōmaru to kill him where he sat, tied to a tree, shortly after he witnessed Tajōmaru rape her.

Tajōmaru's account of the final spirited sword fight with Takehiro is implausible, in that risking one's life to duel with a captive seems out of character for a bandit who had used underhanded schemes to tie Takehiro to a tree and rape Masago. The crux of the controversy over Takehiro's death thus lies in the conflicts between the accounts of Takehiro and Masago. Takehiro's cold and despondent gaze in Masago's direction after the rape suggests that he believed that she had not struggled tenaciously enough with Tajōmaru before succumbing to his erotic aggression and perhaps had found it even more to her taste than her husband's weak and tepid embrace. Blaming his sorely deflated manhood on Masago instead of the rapist, Takehiro goes so far as to imagine that his raped wife had implored Tajōmaru to kill him so that she could belong to the bandit body and soul thenceforth. Masago's account also refers to Takehiro's cold and silent stare, but she excises the painful element of Takehiro's resentment toward her, explaining away his subsequent death in sketchy terms and lamenting the worthlessness of her present reclusive existence.

What really happened during a particular incident such as this may be impossible to ascertain, but it does not follow that truth itself is an impossibility, as some pessimistic commentators have concluded with alarm. Despite uncertainties hanging over the specifics of these events, readers can confidently conclude that Tajōmaru's rude intrusion sparked a severe breakdown in communication and trust between Takehiro and Masago that would doom the couple's prospects for eventually resuming a normal existence.

—*Philip F. Williams*

Riddle of Stars

Morgon of Hed and Raederle of An must answer the riddle of their own powers in order to fulfill their destinies and save the High One's Realm from destruction

Author: Patricia A. McKillip (1948-   )
Genre: Fantasy—high fantasy
Type of work: Novels
Time of plot: Undefined but resembling medieval Europe
Location: The High One's Realm
First published: 1979 (contains *The Riddle-Master of Hed*, 1976; *Heir of Sea and Fire*, 1977; and *Harpist in the Wind*, 1979)

The Story

Riddle of Stars was first published in three separate volumes. *The Riddle-Master of Hed* concerns itself primarily with Morgon, the Land Ruler of Hed, a young man with three mysterious stars on his forehead. Morgon has won a riddle game with a dead king, entitling him to the hand of Raederle, the second most beautiful woman in An. When he leaves Hed to ask Raederle to marry him, he is attacked repeatedly by Shape Changers. Morgan discovers that the Shape Changers were responsible for the deaths of his parents, who were trying to bring him a harp with three stars. The Shape Changers are wild and lawless killers. They do not care whom they hurt as they pursue and harass Morgan.

Under a mountain in Isig, Morgan discovers a cave containing the children of the Earth Masters. These children have been turned to stone, but Morgan's presence revives them long enough for them to give him a sword with three stars embedded in it and to name him the Star Bearer. After he receives the sword, Morgan, who has been trying to avoid his destiny and return to Hed, bows to the inevitable. He follows Deth, the High One's harpist, to Erlenstar Mountain. There, instead of receiving answers from the High One, his mind is painfully stripped of the awareness of the Land Rule of Hed by the wizard Ghisteslwchlohm. As Morgan lies in torment in the darkness, he is haunted by the sound of Deth's harping.

Heir of Sea and Fire begins with Raederle of An, Morgan's sister Tristan, and the Land Heir of Herun, Lyra, commandeering a ship and sailing toward Erlenstar Mountain, where they hope to get answers from the High One about whether Morgan is alive and why the High One allowed him to be tortured. While they are traveling, Raederle is set upon by Shape Changers. One of the Shape Changers informs Raederle that she has inherited their magical abilities. Raederle realizes she desires that incredible power, and the desire scares her.

When the women learn that Morgan is still alive, Lyra and Tristan return to their own lands, but Raederle goes to the College of Wizards seeking answers to the riddle of her own powers. Morgan finds her there and warns her that even though Ghisteslwchlohm is tracking him, he is still seeking Deth in order to kill him. When Morgan leaves, Raederle uses her powers to bargain with the ghosts of An, forcing them to protect the stranger abroad in their land so that he can arrive safely in her family's hall. She intends that the ghosts should protect Morgan, but they mistakenly escort Deth to the hall, where Morgan finds him. When Morgan raises his sword to kill Deth, the harpist sets him a riddle, and Morgan allows Deth to depart. Raederle is afraid that she has become something so powerful that it is nameless, but Morgan sees her for herself and names her. Raederle vows that she shall remain with Morgan, no matter how perilous his future path, as he seeks the answers to the riddles of his destiny.

Harpist in the Wind follows the adventures of Morgan and Raederle as they travel the High One's Realm. Raederle still fears her legacy and refuses to change shape. It is dangerous for her and Morgan to travel in their own forms because the Shape Changers and Ghisteslwchlohm are following them.

Morgan and Raederle meet Deth, who has been scarred by Ghisteslwchlohm. When, with Deth's help, Ghisteslwchlohm captures them, for love of Raederle and the Morgan of Herun, Deth refuses to help the wizard bind Morgan. The Shape Changers attack, and Deth apparently is killed. Morgan and Raederle manage to escape, and Raederle finally agrees to learn how to change shape.

Morgan eventually realizes that the Shape Changers are really Earth Masters, a race so powerful that they created, then nearly destroyed, the High One's Realm. He begins gathering the power of Land Law to him. This involves interfering with the bindings between the Land Rulers and their realms, but the rulers trust Morgan and give him access to their minds and their secret stores of knowledge.

When it becomes apparent that the final battle for the Passing of the Age will be fought on Wind Plain, all the rulers gather their armies and go there. On Wind Plain, at the top of a tower hidden by illusion, Morgan finds Deth, who turns out to be the High One. Deth explains that he needed to hone Morgan into a wild and powerful weapon so that he could both understand the lawless power of the Shape Changers and be strong enough to overcome them. Deth then looses the winds. A great battle is fought during which Deth dies. Morgan's heritage passes into his mind, and he uses the winds to bind the Earth Masters, alive but harmless, inside Erlenstar Mountain. As the trilogy closes, Morgan joins Raederle in Hed and finally begins to feel his beloved realm settling down to its well-earned peace.

Analysis

Riddle of Stars is considered one of the classic works of high fantasy. Its plot unfolds like a riddle, and the reader is forced to solve the puzzles of the world in the same manner the characters must solve the riddles that are put to them. The trilogy follows in the traditions of J. R. R. Tolkien's *The Lord of the Rings* (1968) and Ursula K. Le Guin's *Earthsea* trilogy (1977) but creates its own highly complicated, impressively detailed, beautifully described world in which language and power are linked inextricably.

Like the Tolkien and Le Guin trilogies, *Riddle of Stars* uses the idea that by naming a thing a person gains power over it. Although in Tolkien's trilogy the underlying assumption is that absolute magical power is destructive and eventually will corrupt even a benevolent ruler, Patricia McKillip's wizards believe that arcane knowledge is meant to be explored and utilized. Magic does not necessarily corrupt, as long as it is tempered with love. The bonds that keep McKillip's characters from becoming wild and lawless are their desires to protect humble things such as family, hearth, and home.

Riddle of Stars, like most of McKillip's novels, has a strong streak of feminism running through it. Her women must pit their wills and intellects against a frequently male-dominated world, earning the privilege of wielding the power that is their birthright. One of the things that makes her books so popular is that, unlike many fantasy novels with strong female protagonists, her characters generally manage to make peace with the men they love without having to deny their own urges or bend their principles.

McKillip is considered one of the great prose stylists in the fantasy genre. Her short fiction can be found in many of the more prestigious fantasy anthologies. Her earlier novels were heralded with critical acclaim, and in 1975 she won the first World Fantasy Award ever given for her novel *The Forgotten Beasts of Eld* (1974). That novel contains the themes McKillip uses in most of her adult works, having as its protagonist a strong-willed woman who uses her wizardry to name the beast she most fears and desires.

After writing *Riddle of Stars*, McKillip primarily wrote young adult fiction and short stories until she created the world of *The Sorceress and the Cygnet* (1991) and its sequel, *The Cygnet and the Firebird* (1993). These two books continue her themes of strong, magic-wielding men and women who must fight to attain their power and learn to take control of their own destinies. The world created in these two books is rich and complex, a place where the constellations of myth and legend can come to life to warn humans to remember their attachments to home and humanity.

McKillip's next novel, *Something Rich and Strange* (1994), won the Mythopeic Society Award. *The Book of Atrix Wolfe* (1995) continues the theme of names and naming, playing especially on the pun of an inhuman creature learning about sorrow and then being trapped within the concept and being called "Saro." Although *The Book of Atrix Wolfe* is a beautifully written novel, it is less strongly plotted than some of McKillip's earlier pieces and rehashes themes she previously used to greater effect. *Riddle of Stars*, for its imaginative landscape, strong characters, intriguing riddles, and glorious prose, is aptly considered the benchmark against which all of McKillip's work, and indeed most high fantasy, tends to be judged.

—*Shira Daemon*

Ringworld and The Ringworld Engineers

A team of explorers from various races investigates the Ringworld, a vast artificial planet; members of the team later return to save it from destruction

Author: Larry Niven (1938-   )
Genre: Science fiction—future history
Type of work: Novels
Time of plot: 2850 and 2873
Location: Earth and the Ringworld
First published: *Ringworld* (1970) and *The Ringworld Engineers* (1979)

The Story

The Ringworld novels take place in Larry Niven's own particular future history, Known Space. Like Isaac Asimov's and Robert A. Heinlein's Future History stories, it has been charted and time-lined, but unlike theirs, it includes a variety of sentient alien species and several million years of prehistory. According to this schema, humanity arose not simply because of evolution on Earth but also because the attempt of a race known as the Pak to establish a colony on Earth went awry. Human beings are the mutated remnants of the Pak breeder stage, which could not metamorphose into the protector stage because the necessary catalytic plant could not be grown on Earth.

At the time of the novels, the two most important alien races are the kzinti, a fierce race of large felinelike carnivores whom humans have beaten in a series of savage wars, and the puppeteers, so called because of their two heads, which resemble human hand puppets. The character of the puppeteers is the exact opposite of that of the kzinti: They are diffident herbivores who would rather flee than fight. The puppeteers, however, disappeared from Known Space some two hundred years before the novels open, because they discovered that the core of the Milky Way is exploding. Even though a deadly wave of radiation from it will reach Known Space in the distant future, the puppeteers are moving their entire race now.

In their migrations, they have discovered the Ringworld, an artificial ring of matter forming a band around its sun, at roughly Earth's distance from Sol. Its land area is that of three million Earths. Because the civilization that built such an artifact must be immeasurably powerful, the puppeteers organize an expedition to examine the Ringworld more closely. The team consists of the puppeteer Nessus, who is considered insane by puppeteer standards because he is willing to take risks; Louis Wu, a two-hundred-year-old human who is known for his habit of taking solitary journeys to escape from any kind of company; Speaker-to-Animals, a kzinti junior diplomat trained to deal with other species without reflexively killing them; and Teela Brown, a human whose ancestry involves several generations of winning the Birthright lotteries and who is thus considered by the puppeteers to be lucky by reason of genetics.

Forced to crash land when their ship's slower-than-light engines are destroyed by the Ringworld's meteor defenses, the team must figure out a way to leave the Ringworld without the use of conventional means of propulsion. During their journey across an infinitely small portion of the Ringworld's surface, which nevertheless seems impressively large to them, they discover that the Ringworld's main sentient inhabitants are all descended from human beings. More important, they learn that the puppeteers have manipulated both human and kzinti history for their own ends. Most of the once-advanced civilization of the Ringworld has reverted to savagery because of a biological plague that destroyed its superconducting material. With the help of a native spacewoman, the team is able to escape from the Ringworld, but Teela Brown remains, because apparently she is destined to live there.

In *The Ringworld Engineers*, two members of the former team, Louis Wu and Speaker (now named Chmee), return to the Ringworld after being kidnapped by the deposed leader of the puppeteers, the Hindmost, who hopes to discover on the Ringworld a transmutation device, the secret of which will restore him to his former rank. During this journey, the team meets a much greater variety of Ringworld inhabitants, ranging from giant grass eaters to nocturnal vampires. Each hominid group has evolved to occupy an ecological niche occupied by animals on Earth. The team also learns that the Ringworld will soon be destroyed because its orbit has been shifted by solar flares.

Wu is determined to save the Ringworld. He learns that the Ringworld was constructed by Pak protectors, all of whom died a quarter of a million years ago. One human, however, has been transformed into the protector stage since then—the former Teela Brown. She cannot save the Ringworld because doing so would mean the death of 5 percent of the Ringworld's population, one and one-half trillion lives that, as a protector, she instinctively must protect. Wu and the others manage to save the planet but at a terrible cost.

Analysis

A typical story by Larry Niven involves the solving of some technological or scientific dilemma within the framework of his Known Space. Niven came up with the idea for the Ringworld itself as a variation of the Dyson sphere, a planetary construct by the physicist Freeman Dyson in which an advanced civilization could take advantage of all of its sun's energy. Niven had to fit this concept within the future history he already had imagined. In many respects, the Ringworld novels (particularly *Ringworld*) represent his finest novel-length achievement using this strategy. *Ringworld* won the Hugo and Nebula Awards for best novel of the year.

One reason for the novel's immense appeal is the strength of its characters. Louis Wu is both a typical and atypical science-fiction hero. He is typical in that he is driven by an immense curiosity about the universe he inhabits and is able to exist on his own as a solitary agent; he is atypical in that he is not extraordinarily competent in solving his problems, either physically or intellectually. He realizes that he needs the ideas and perspectives of others, and indeed he craves them. He is a xenophile, not a xenophobe, and relishes the prospect of working with aliens. Similarly, Speaker and Nessus are typical and atypical: They are representative of their species, in one case ferocious and honor-driven, and in the other cowardly and manipulative. They become unique characters because of their differences from their norms. Speaker is able to control his temper and instincts, and Nessus is able to exhibit courage and martial capabilities.

Teela Brown is an entirely different matter. She is unique in that because of her inherent luck, she never has been hurt. She must travel to the Ringworld because it is the only place in the universe that can educate her. Her case introduces one of the primary themes of the novel, that of control: *Dei ex machina* keep popping up in the narrative to confound reader expectations. The puppeteers turns out to be exactly that: They have pulled the strings in the outcomes of the human-kzinti wars in order to produce more docile kzinti and have manipulated the human Birthright lotteries in order to produce a character like Teela Brown. Evolution is not the result of blind chance or random occurrence; all the main species in the novel have been tailored in their development toward some specific end. Teleology has been replaced by tinkering.

One of the most famous analyses of *Ringworld*, one that Niven himself discusses, is that its plot is based on that of L. Frank Baum's *The Wonder-*

ful Wizard of Oz (1900). Certainly, in *Ringworld*, a series of curtains is pulled aside to reveal the mortal hand behind seemingly arbitrary events. This strand culminates in Teela Brown's eventual fate. She teams up with a gigantic "sword-and-sorcery" hero on his quest to find the base of the Ringworld, and she seems to pass from the genre of science fiction directly into fantasy.

Niven declared that *Ringworld* needed no sequel, but fan pressure and suggestions resulted in *The Ringworld Engineers*, in which Niven cleared up some of the scientific inaccuracies of the first novel. Some critics have declared that the second novel is by far the weaker; however, in many ways it is a satisfying conclusion to the main narrative and previously introduced themes. The purpose of the Ringworld itself is made somewhat clearer; initially, it seemed no more than narrative convenience that all of its inhabitants were hominids. Louis Wu's story involves a continuation of the theme of control. At the beginning of the novel, he is a current addict, enslaved to a trickle of electricity into the pleasure center of his brain. The Hindmost thinks that he will be able to control Wu through this addiction, but Wu is able to overcome it by his own will, and by the end of the novel he is able to withstand the irresistible lure of the scent of the plant that turns humans into protectors. By controlling himself and continuing to enlist the aid and perspectives of others, Wu is able to save the Ringworld as well as himself. Human beings, Niven implies, no matter how they are manipulated, will be able to control their own destinies.

—William Laskowski

Roderick and Roderick at Random

The life history and adventures of a robotic learning machine as it wanders through America trying to understand and become part of human culture

Author: John Sladek (1937-2000)
Genre: Science fiction—artificial intelligence
Type of work: Novels
Time of plot: The late twentieth century
Location: The United States
First published: *Roderick: Or, The Education of a Young Machine* (1980) and *Roderick at Random: Or, Further Education of a Young Machine* (1983)

The Story

Roderick is a robot manufactured at the University of Minnetonka at a time when research into artificial intelligence has been outlawed. The opening chapters depict the efforts of Dr. Lee Fong, the director of the project, to gain funding for his work from the university following withdrawal of his federal funding, which turns out to have been secret and illegal. Meanwhile, two forces threaten Roderick. The government-run Orinoco Institute and a loathsome industrialist named Kratt are both intent on destroying the robot and its creators.

To prevent destruction of the robot, the inventors first send Roderick to Hank and Inca Dinks, who ignore him and allow him to begin a lifelong fascination with television. He is then sent to an older couple, Ma and Pa Woods of Newer, Nebraska, who try to raise him more or less as a human child. Unfortunately, a wandering band of gypsies kidnaps Roderick from his front yard. They sell the robot to Kratt, who puts Roderick to work telling fortunes in a carnival. He is rescued from this situation, however, and returned to the Woodses.

Back home, Roderick enters public school. Despite his appearance, Roderick is treated as a strange and troublesome human child. His classmates bully him, and his teachers diagnose him as mentally unbalanced. He is expelled, but not before he accidentally gains access to the school's computer and alters both his record and that of a particularly vile instructor. He is then sent to a Roman Catholic school, where he engages a troubled priest in difficult discussions on the nature of being human. In the meantime, Pa Woods has been altering Roderick's appearance to make him look more human.

The second volume begins with the discovery that one of Roderick's creators has died and his brain is being kept alive in a tank at the Orinoco Institute. The institute has managed to either kill or ruin the careers of the other members of Project Roderick despite a failure to capture the robot himself. Meanwhile, an accident at a nuclear power plant has destroyed Newer. Roderick has traveled to the city, where he works as a dishwasher at a diner that caters exclusively to dogs.

At a dance hall, he repairs the electronic instruments of a group named the Auks. As a result, he meets Ida, a kindly prostitute, with whom he has his first mechano-sexual experience. He then encounters members of a religious cult, the Church of Christ Symmetrical. At a bar called the Tik Tok Club (an allusion to John Sladek's 1983 novel *Tik Tok*), Roderick meets members of a neo-Luddite group called the Fractious Disengagementists. The leader of this group turns out to be Hank Dinks. Moreover, his former wife, Inca, has become a famous spokesperson for the movement to liberate machines from human oppression. After Hank arouses his followers at a rally, they form a mob and attack the publishing house where Inca is autographing copies of her latest book. Hank is killed accidentally in the uproar.

In the adventures that follow, Roderick winds up back at Minnetonka University as the mascot of one of its fraternities. On his way to a film one evening, he stumbles on a Luddite plot to attack the Auks. He foils the plot only to learn that it was a diversion and that the Luddites have burned down the crowded theater to which Roderick was headed. Fortunately, the film was so boring that everyone had already left.

Despondent, Roderick goes to a psychiatrist only to discover that the doctor is a robot created by a company owned by Kratt. As Roderick sits in his room at the fraternity house, four of Kratt's agents break in and capture him. As they lead him out, agents from the Federal Bureau of Investigation appear and wrest Roderick from his captors. They inform Roderick that the government policy outlawing artificial intelligence has been reversed and invite Roderick to join them. The robot, appalled by his discovery of their extreme actions while attempting to destroy him, refuses and gives himself up to Kratt.

Analysis

The two Roderick novels were meant to be a single work, but Sladek's British publisher was convinced that the length of a single volume would prove daunting and therefore unattractive to readers. In 1982, a version of *Roderick* that was shortened by about one-third was published in the United States. It was advertised as the first volume of a trilogy. The second part, *Roderick at Random*, was not published in the United States until 1988.

The two joined novels represent an ambitious attempt by Sladek to fuse the conventional themes of science fiction to those of the mainstream picaresque novel. The titles contain an obvious allusion to Tobias Smollett's famous novel *Roderick Random* (1748), a particularly telling choice of literary models because Smollett used the picaresque form to satirize British society. Sladek's two novels unfold, in the picaresque tradition, as sequences of comic episodes.

The Roderick novels offer a compendium of the themes and qualities that make Sladek one of the finest science-fiction satirists. Much of his fiction deals with the theme of the dehumanizing effects of technology. Most of his satire focuses on the absurdity of contemporary American culture, and most of his books are funny.

Sladek's humor has invited comparisons with writers as diverse and highly regarded as Kurt Vonnegut, William Burroughs, and Joseph Heller. These novels in particular allow Sladek the opportunity to demonstrate his wit. From a musing on the obscene double entendres embedded in the names of computer companies such as Honeywell and IBM to a hilarious explication of the name L. Frank Baum, Sladek constantly reminds the reader of his artfulness.

Sladek's writing is more consciously literary than most science fiction. In addition to directing the reader to Smollett and the picaresque tradition, he alludes to a wide range of science fiction, particularly the robot stories of Isaac Asimov. The beginning of *Roderick*, quotations taken from Samuel Butler's *Erewhon* (1872) and the American comic drama film *Dinner at Eight* (1933), alerts the reader to expect references to both high and low culture.

The satire of the novels is based on the traditional device of the naïve but honest observer. Roderick is an innocent trying to make sense of contemporary American society. He spends much of his time learning about that society by watching television. Television provides Roderick his vision of America much as it provides America, Sladek seems to suggest, with an image of itself. Meanwhile, what Roderick encounters away from television ranges from the absurd to the malicious. The Orinoco Institute takes aim at the "think tanks" that have become so powerful a part of the intellectual landscape. The religious cults and fringe political groups in the novel are more interested in self-satisfaction than the public good. Other targets include the military mind, popular journalists,

American higher education, American public and parochial schools, mainstream religion, and essentially anyone dehumanized by excessive desire for wealth or personal satisfaction.

The Roderick novels provide an example of science fiction as a medium in which the best authors are able to wed imagination and philosophy. For all of their humor and satire, they are also philosophical explorations. The two novels provide the most extensive explorations of themes that figure throughout Sladek's fiction. Several of his earliest published stories (such as "The Steam-Driven Boy") feature robots trying to fit into human culture. His first published science-fiction novel, *The Reproductive System* (1968), deals with technology run amok. Two earlier novels were gothics, written as Cassandra Knye: *The House That Fear Built* (1966, with Thomas M. Disch) and *The Castle and the Key* (1967).

The Roderick novels take this interest in technology a step further by addressing the question of humanness itself. One of the characters trying to sabotage robot research expresses the main theme of the novels when he says that humans "feed on meaning . . . we only survive by making sense out of the world around us. . . . So if we turn over that function to some other species, we're finished." Another human character, pondering some of the actions taken to find Roderick, wonders if "any *robot*" would be capable of such actions. This combination of the desire for meaning and the capacity for cruelty seems to sum up Sladek's view of human nature.

Although highly praised, the Roderick novels are not Sladek's best work, in part because their length and the complexity of the narrative detract from the satire, and in part because the satire takes aim at too many topics. The most memorable figure is Roderick, the learning machine who seems more humane, if not more human, than the human beings who seek to destroy him or anyone who stands as an obstacle to their ambition.

—*Dennis M. Kratz*

Rogue Moon

Edward Hawks defines life and death as he transmits a replicated
man to the moon to be killed repeatedly while solving the riddle of
an alien artifact

Author: Algis Budrys (1931-   )
Genre: Science fiction—inner space
Type of work: Novel
Time of plot: 1959-1960
Location: The Pacific Coast of the United States and the far side of the
    Moon
First published: 1960

The Story

Dr. Edward Hawks has invented a method of electronically encoding a
human and simultaneously transmitting the code to both the Moon and
his laboratory. The original is destroyed in the process, but neither duplicate accepts that it is not the original. Hawks is put in charge of a project to unlock the mystery of an alien artifact discovered on the far side of
the Moon. The U.S. Navy drops receiving equipment for Hawks's device
close to the artifact, and Hawks's project has beamed Navy personnel
duplicates to the receiver while at the same time creating duplicates in
Hawks's laboratory on Earth.

Duplicates entering the artifact are killed. Hawks discovers that the
duplicates in his laboratory go insane from the experience of living
through their own deaths via the mental/emotional link with the duplicates in the alien structure. He must continue to send duplicates into the
artifact, however, because each one moves a little closer to finding a way
through the alien labyrinth.

Hawks is frustrated because the project cannot find volunteers whose
duplicates maintain their sanity after living through their own horrible
deaths. He also struggles with the knowledge that the project is sending
men to their deaths and driving their duplicates insane. Finally, he relies
on Vincent Connington, personnel director for one of the project's contractors, to recommend someone for the project. Connington proposes
Al Barker, a daredevil of a man who has spent his life defying death.

The duplicate Barker on Earth manages to maintain his sanity. Hawks uses the duplicate on Earth to make repeated transmissions, and each time Barker moves farther through the artifact, slowly mapping a route through the enigmatic structure.

Barker's companion, Claire Pack, is a hard-edged woman who enjoys toying with men. She stays with Barker, believing him to be more man than anyone else. Hawks observes how she torments Connington and is nearly sucked into her clutches himself.

Hawks meets Elizabeth Cummings, a young woman who surprises him with insights into his own view of life. She becomes a foil to his gloomier estimations of self, causing him to consider how his relationship with life mirrors his relationship with women. She also leads him to discover the connection between love and life.

When the Barker duplicate tells him that he believes the next trip through the artifact will conclude in reaching an exit, Hawks transmits his own duplicate to the Moon along with Barker. They make it through the artifact. Barker, for all his exploits, has never done something no one else has ever attempted, and Hawks helps him realize that each person must make his or her own life and must live to create a personal meaning, not one defined by others.

Hawks realizes that he cannot transmit himself back to Earth because the other duplicate Hawks is there, and since the point of their divergence the other duplicate has created a new lifeline. Taking courage from his insights about death, Hawks walks away from the artifact into the emptiness of the lunar landscape. He dies there, secure in the knowledge that someday humanity will conquer death. The realization is bittersweet, however, and he longs for the life and newfound love he left behind.

Analysis

Rogue Moon is about the meaning of life and humanity's yearning to transcend death. Algis Budrys uses the trip through the alien labyrinth as a metaphor for life. Barker's discovery when he makes it completely through the alien structure—that a person must create himself or herself—is a logical extension of Hawks's earlier statement to Elizabeth, a person he has just admitted into the intimacy of his mind. Hawks explains to Elizabeth his realization that in all the universe there is only one thing outside of nature's universal entropic law. That one thing is the human mind, because it has nothing to do with time and space except to use them. Hawks rationally accepts that, but Budrys plumbs deeper, exposing the fears and regrets that Hawks's duplicate experiences at the instant of death.

Budrys comments on the humanity of an individual's life by having his protagonist—a detached, coolly observant scientist—explain that consciousness transcends nature. At the same time, however, Hawks grapples with an emotional connection to physical reality. Thus, Budrys emphasizes the ineffable quality of humanness connected to consciousness as he underlines the poignant attachment each person maintains to physical reality and the people who share it.

Even though Hawks faces his own death knowing that some part of his mind has transcended it, he is saddened at the losses of his physical life and the love he has finally allowed into that life. That is one of Budrys's statements in *Rogue Moon*: Human beings are possessed of more than the ability to reason and to function in the physical universe. They also feel, and development of that quality is as important as development of any other.

The discovery of an alien artifact is a plot device that begs the question, "What constitutes humanness?" Instead of focusing on what humanity is en masse, however, Budrys keeps the evaluation in the mind of his protagonist, using observations of human interactions such as Barker and Claire's relationship as a frame around the investigation. This approach creates the resulting psychological study of one man's thinking about death, something Budrys does as admirably here as Frederik Pohl does with his protagonist in the Heechee series (1977-1990).

Rogue Moon was written relatively early in Budrys's career, yet his style is fully evident. He employs an almost minimalist approach that calls for careful word selection to paint vivid pictures while studiously avoiding flowery, overlong sentences. Like others of his well-known works, this a short novel, seemingly Budrys's preferred length.

—Jeff King

Sarah Canary

A picaresque adventure among the invisible people of the Old West: women, Chinese, Indians, and the insane

Author: Karen Joy Fowler (1950-   )
Genre: Science fiction—feminist
Type of work: Novel
Time of plot: 1873
Location: Washington Territory and San Francisco
First published: 1991

The Story

Sarah Canary traces the difficult adventures of Chinese laborer Chin Ah Kin, who discovers a woman at the edge of his western American camp who does not speak any language he can understand. Wondering if she has been sent as a test from the gods, Chin begins a trek through the Washington Territory in an effort to return her to her home. A misunderstanding lands him in jail, where to save his own life he is forced to act as a hangman for Tom, a Native American convicted of murder. Chin finds that the woman he has been trying to help has been committed to the asylum at Steilacoom, where she acquires the name Sarah Canary. He then takes a job there, while figuring out how to free her. At the asylum, he meets BJ, an inmate who suffers sporadic delusions that he does not exist. The three of them escape from the asylum and find brief shelter in the cabin of Burke, an Irish naturalist, but Burke's companion, the huckster and Civil War veteran Harold, steals Sarah Canary in the middle of the night.

Chin and BJ track Harold to Seabeck, where the latter is exhibiting Sarah as the "Alaskan Wild Woman," and Adelaide Dixon, a suffragist and proponent of free love, is lecturing. After the show, Harold attempts to rape Sarah Canary, who stabs him with a chopstick. Dixon comes upon the scene and mistakes Sarah Canary for the fugitive Lydia Palmer, who is accused of murdering her husband. Adelaide then escapes with Sarah Canary, while the hotel bar is destroyed by men enraged by her speech. The two women board a steamer bound for San Francisco. Chin again finds himself fearing for his life after one of the hotel residents is found murdered in the morning; he and BJ attempt to follow Sarah Canary's steamer in a canoe, which capsizes. They are rescued and put aboard the steamer.

After the characters reach San Francisco, Harold abducts Adelaide and demands that Chin trade her for Sarah Canary. At the ensuing rendezvous, Chin saves Adelaide from a tiger, and they discover that Sarah Canary has disappeared. Meanwhile, the real Lydia Palmer is on trial. She is acquitted and goes to visit Adelaide. A mob gathers outside Adelaide's hotel, and BJ is killed in the resulting violence. Meanwhile, Chin and Adelaide have fallen in love with each other. However, Chin returns to China, carrying with him the strange and terrifying memories of his time in America.

Analysis

On the surface, *Sarah Canary* looks nothing like a science-fiction novel, and that is part of its greatness. On one level it is a first-contact story of immense dexterity; on the other hand, it is an angrily comic voyage among the various invisible populations of the Old West. The uncertainty of Sarah Canary's origin throws the brutality of the American West into painfully sharp relief. Everyone else in the novel—from the confused Chin to the avaricious Harold and ambitious Adelaide—uses her in some way, and their actions toward her are inevitably contradictory. Chin hopes to pass a divine test by treating her well, but he considers abandoning her in the woods and strikes her when her wordless singing aggravates him; Adelaide is overcome by pity at the plight of "Lydia Palmer," but envisions not so much the justice of her acquittal as the fame a successful defense might bring to her. Sarah Canary exists as a sort of Rorschach ink-blot test, in which each of the characters finds the image of a private obsession.

A great virtue of science fiction is its ability to recast a problem so the reader does not recognize it immediately. This process disarms the reader's prejudices, so that by the time the contemporary resonance of the story becomes clear, the reader finds previous opinions not as solid as they were before. Fowler emphasizes this process by interpolating short anecdotes about 1870's historical events, which seen from the 1990's are nearly incomprehensible. Within science fiction, the first-contact story has long been a way of exploring the deep alienation between different groups on Earth, and *Sarah Canary* is no exception. The mentally ill BJ, the Chinese immigrant Chin, the Indian Tom, the haunted veteran Harold, and the proto-feminist Adelaide all suffer from the blindnesses of the existing power structures.

—*Alex Irvine*

Shatterday

A collection of stories in which fantastic phenomena and events disrupt the fabric of contemporary life

Author: Harlan Ellison (1934-   )
Genre: Fantasy—Magical Realism
Type of work: Stories
Time of plot: Primarily the present
Location: Various locations in the United States and
    Europe
First published: 1980

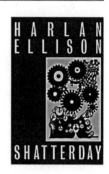

The Story

All but one of the stories in *Shatterday* first appeared in a variety of magazines, from science-fiction periodicals to *Playboy*, or as radio or television broadcasts in the late 1970's. Arguably the best published selection among Harlan Ellison's hundreds of stories, it is most representative of the mature author at the height of his powers. It also demonstrates the reason behind Ellison's discomfort at being labeled a science-fiction writer: Most of the stories here could be defined as Magical Realism. Only a few include science-fiction elements; "Would You Do It for a Penny?," a comic seduction story written with Haskell Barkin, and the semiautobiographical novella "All the Lies That Are My Life" are neither science fiction nor fantasy. The book also includes Ellison's introductions, both for the collection as a whole and for individual stories.

The most striking works in the collection depict a real world in which marvelous events naturally happen; the characters are too awestruck or wrapped up in their own lives to reject them. "Jeffty Is Five," for example, is narrated by the friend of a five-year-old boy named Jeffty who remains five years old while everyone around him ages, including the narrator. "Flop Sweat" at first appears to be a contemporary horror story about a serial killer but evolves into a fantasy about a radio talk-show host's connection to the powers of darkness. In "The Man Who Was Heavily into Revenge," a cheated man's anger turns the universe against the man who cheated him; the cheated man in turn angers someone and will become the universe's next victim. For having wasted his life, the protagonist of "Count the Clock That Tells the Time" vanishes into a timeless limbo. "All the Birds Come Home to Roost" is a chilling fantasy about a man who is visited by all the women in his past in reverse order, and the equally chilling "Shatterday" is a *Doppelgänger* story focusing on the nature of personal identity and morality.

Other stories in the book, though less effective, are no less imaginative. "How's the Night Life on Cissalda?" is a humorous science-fiction story about a "temponaut" who returns to his own time and space with a telepathic creature that offers the ultimate sexual experience, which brings a horde of Cissaldans seeking new encounters with a willing human race. A more somber science-fiction story, "Alive and Well on a Friendless Voyage," has suffering and loneliness as its theme. A related story is "The Other Eye of Polyphemus," a contemporary fantasy about a man who helps others but neglects his own needs. "Shoppe Keeper" begins as a fantasy about a magic shop and ends as a science-fiction story about highly evolved humans in the far future who manipulate history to buy time for themselves. "Django" is an impressionistic wartime fantasy about French jazz guitarist Django Reinhardt, and "Opium" deals with the world reshaping itself fantastically in response to one woman's boredom and despair.

Analysis

The best stories in *Shatterday* involve the intrusion of the fantastic into everyday life. Ellison excels at portraying both the real and the unreal, using descriptive and at times lyrical language. The transitions between the known and the unknown are often achieved so seamlessly that the reader's disbelief is not so much consciously suspended as naturally subdued. Ellison also effectively describes contemporary settings and lives of quiet desperation. For example, "Jeffty Is Five" is both an effective fantasy and a loving tribute to popular culture in America during the 1930's and 1940's.

Many critics have commented on Ellison's emotional, often hyperbolic style. Although many of the stories in *Shatterday* exhibit touches of antic humor or righteous fury, the collection as a whole is noteworthy for its generally constrained tone. From the elegiac "Jeffty Is Five" to horror stories such as "Flop Sweat," "The Man Who Was Heavily into Revenge," "All the Birds Come Home to Roost," and "Shatterday" to the dreamlike "Alive and Well on a Friendless Voyage" and "The Other Eye of Polyphemus," Ellison is in full control.

Critics have also remarked on Ellison's introductions. Some consider them intrusions. Although it is true that the introductions have the effect of making the reader conscious of the writer behind the stories and point out autobiographical elements that would not have been obvious other-wise, they reinforce what Ellison states in the introduction to the vol-ume, "Mortal Dreads," to be his goal as an author. A seriously moralistic though not didactic writer, Ellison intends to demonstrate to readers of *Shatterday* that everyone shares the same fears and that, while ultimately alone, each person can find some solace in others.

Shatterday, though published by a major publishing house (Houghton Mifflin), struggled with the difficulty of all short-story volumes in an American marketplace dominated by novels. Because he has focused most of his energies on stories, Ellison is less well known than he could be or deserves to be, though he enjoys a considerable cult following. He has also earned the respect of much of the science-fiction and fantasy community. "Jeffty Is Five," for example, received both the Hugo Award (1978), given by fans at the annual world science-fiction convention, and the Nebula Award (1977), given by the Science Fiction Writers of Amer-ica. In addition, many readers and critics have praised "Shatterday" and "All the Birds Come Home to Roost" as among Ellison's best efforts.

—*Darren Harris-Fain*

The Ship of Ishtar

John Kenton, a rich young scholar-adventurer suffering from battle fatigue, discovers a small magic ship enclosed in stone, which
transports him to adventures in ancient Mesopotamia

Author: A(braham) Merritt (1884-1943)
Genre: Fantasy—magical world
Type of work: Novel
Time of plot: The early twentieth century and 4000 B.C.E.
Location: Modern New York City and ancient Mesopotamia
First published: 1926 (serial form, *Argosy All-Story*, November 8-De-
    cember 13, 1924)

The Story

The Ship of Ishtar was published by Putnam's after first appearing in serial form in *Argosy All-Story*; a few years later, it had the distinction of
being voted the most popular story ever published by the magazine in
its first fifty years. A. Merritt was in midcareer and at the peak of his
powers.

The novel opens as the protagonist, John Kenton, a young and wealthy
but deeply embittered World War I veteran, muses on his dissatisfaction
with Western civilization and his romantic nostalgia to find a lost civilization uncorrupted by the mundane and unheroic modern world. All the
action takes place in one night in Kenton's New York City apartment
and the ancient Mesopotamian world of adventure that he finds when
he is transported in time to the magical Ship of Ishtar. Merritt's use of the
"locked room" convention invented by Edgar Allan Poe in "The Murders in the Rue Morgue" (1841) is one of the novel's most entertaining
features.

An amateur scholar, Kenton has financed an archaeological dig in
Egypt and, as the story opens, receives in his apartment a large block of
stone from that expedition. The stone itself seems to compel him to examine it, and he chisels away its surface, releasing the magical power en-
tombed for thousands of years within the granite. The block suddenly
crumbles, revealing a wonderfully crafted toy ship, which acts as a
bridge between the present that Kenton despises and the ancient past for
which he so fervently longs. This device allows Merritt to send Kenton

back and forth repeatedly over thousands of years without benefit of a scientific or technological rationale for the story's time travel.

In the episodes that occur in the past, Kenton has a variety of entertaining physical adventures involving a number of fantasy fiction's more interesting alien beings. The magical world of the ship is divided into two spheres of power and influence, presided over by two mythological deities. Half of the ship is ivory and houses Ishtar, goddess of love, and her priestess, Sharane; the other half is ebony and houses Nergal, god of death, and his evil priest, Klanath. Their war for dominance can never be decided: They represent the equally powerful and eternally warring cosmic forces of love and hate (of light and darkness, of life and death), and neither can dominate the other. Kenton gets the opportunity to witness this endless universal struggle while engaging in a number of exciting and entertaining adventures, but he can never tip the balance for or against either of the cosmic combatants.

Two other characters are worth mentioning. One is a bald "dwarf-legged giant," Gigi, an exceedingly well-conceived comic Pan-figure. The other is the enigmatic King of the Two Deaths, a jovially cynical drunk who dispenses death while reciting poetry and his own brand of nihilistic philosophy. His chapter is by far the most intriguing part of the novel and can be read as a self-contained story. It is one of the best short pieces of magical world fantasy writing.

Between these episodes, Kenton repeatedly and unexpectedly returns to his apartment in the present, where he dies from wounds sustained in combat in the ancient past. He dies in a brutal fashion inside his own room, which is locked and sealed from within. The conclusion, in which his servants and the authorities are left in a bewilderment that the reader does not share, is very effective.

Analysis

A summary of *The Ship of Ishtar* does not hint at the sheer fun that Merritt provides the reader who enters the imaginary magical world of the Mesopotamian culture of six thousand years ago. The novel was written in the mid-1920's, when Merritt was at the height of his creative powers, and he is clearly in a playful mood. (A version with text restored was published in 1949.) It is the only one of his lost civilization stories that is set in the ancient past, and it is the only one that makes no effort to supply any kind of scientific/technological rationale for the eruption of the atavistic or premodern experiences into the historical present. The novel's emphasis is strictly on simple physical adventure, on the romance of the encounter with truly strange and sometimes even bizarre creatures, and on the slightly veiled possibilities for eroticism always only barely hidden within lost civilization and magical world fictions.

Another feature of the novel is noteworthy. The contrast between the past, imagined to be necessarily heroic and adventurous, and the present, imagined to be inevitably and unchangeably mundane and boring, allows Merritt to indulge in some amateur philosophy that will be familiar to readers of his other, more complex, fiction works. Merritt's was dualistic imagination, and he rather naturally presented his magical narratives (more so than his scientifically based ones) as encounters between antagonistic but equally powerful cosmic forces. This is seen as much in the story's structure of opposites— between love and hate, life and death, good and evil, light and darkness—as in its creation and presentation of characters and events. Although this may seem uninteresting in outline, Merritt's talent in creating vivid imagery and truly bizarre characters was so developed during this period that *The Ship of Ishtar*, though one of his least intellectually complex fictions, is one of his most successful. It richly deserved the fame that it achieved, even if only momentarily.

—*Ronald Foust*

The Sirens of Titan

Winston Niles Rumfoord plans an invasion of Earth from Mars

Author: Kurt Vonnegut (1922-   )
Genre: Science fiction—future history
Type of work: Novel
Time of plot: Between World War II and the Third
   Great Depression
Location: Earth, Mars, Mercury, and Titan (a moon of
   Saturn)
First published: 1959

The Story

Winston Niles Rumfoord runs his private spaceship into an uncharted chrono-synclastic infundibulum. The result is that he and his dog Kazak exist as wave phenomena, materializing and dematerializing on Earth and on Mars, where Rumfoord plans an invasion of Earth. On Mars, he transforms disaffected Americans into an army, literally washing out their brains through surgical procedures and directing their wills through antennas implanted in their heads. On Earth, Rumfoord lures Malachi Constant, the richest American, into his plot, inviting him to witness his materialization.

Constant is ripe for Rumfoord's exploitation because he has lost all sense of purpose. He inherited his money from his father and takes no interest in the financial maneuvers of his father's company, Magnum Opus, which becomes bankrupt. Rumfoord makes Constant his tool, then flies Constant to Mars, along with Rumfoord's wife, Beatrice. She becomes Constant's wife and bears his child.

Constant's own story is hidden from him (and from the reader) because on Mars, much of his memory is erased. There he is Unk, a soldier with an antenna in his head that sends pain signals any time Unk tries to act on his own. Unk runs away from the army and tries to find his wife, Bee (Beatrice Rumfoord) and his son, Chrono. Unk is fortified by a letter from his best friend, Stony Stevenson, who has warned him to try to remember as much as possible because the surgical brainwashing does not destroy all memory, only the middle part. Unk does not realize that while still brainwashed, he obeyed an order to strangle Stevenson.

Unk, Bee, and Chrono eventually are reunited and survive the disastrous Martian invasion of Earth, in which Rumfoord's forces are easily defeated. This apparently is part of his plan, allowing him to present himself as a kind of latter-day savior of humankind and to change human values. In this role, he establishes the Church of God the Utterly Indifferent, under the leadership of the Reverend C. Horner Redwine. Rumfoord, who suffers severe reactions to his constant materializing and dematerializing, is hardly triumphant. He feels manipulated by the Tralfamadorians, machinelike creatures from another galaxy, one of whom, Salo, has helped Rumfoord accomplish his scheme. Rumfoord's dream of dominating humanity is merely that—an illusion, like the beautiful sirens of Titan, inhabitants of one of Saturn's moons.

Analysis

Like George Orwell's *Nineteen Eighty-Four* (1949) and Aldous Huxley's *Brave New World* (1932), Kurt Vonnegut's novel projects into the future, taking certain technological and political trends of the present and extrapolating them into a vision of a terrifying authoritarian and dehumanizing world. The technological tyrant Rumfoord is also a victim of cosmic forces that he finally realizes are beyond his control. Unlike Orwell, Huxley, and other science-fiction writers, Vonnegut apparently believes that no manipulative force, however powerful, can ultimately extinguish the human will.

For example, the Tralfamadorian Salo, the product of an advanced civilization of virtually perfect machines, becomes infected with human feelings. Even though it is ironic that his emotions should attach to the unworthy Rumfoord, both Salo and Rumfoord have a gnawing sense of unfulfillment and search for a happiness that eludes them. They are human in their incompleteness, and Rumfoord is also human—if terrifying—in his desire to control everything, to take unpredictability out of life.

Vonnegut's novel is whimsical and poignant. Although Constant, transformed into Unk, is pathetic in his inability to remember his own past, he also is deeply moving in his quest to recover his memory and family. Vonnegut's style, except for the quasi-scientific words he invents, is quite simple and reminiscent of science-fiction comic books. Human psychology is pared down to two basic drives: to dominate and to love. This deliberate diminution of human complexity serves Vonnegut well because it reveals the underlying, basic humanity that no surgical operation or political/military plot can efface entirely.

Vonnegut does not deny the possibility of a grim future, but the future does not end with grimness. As his narrator suggests at the beginning of the novel, its events are set between World War II and the Third Great Depression. The first sentence of the novel also implies that humanity may find a way to stop torturing itself: "Everyone now knows how to find the meaning of life within himself."

The Sirens of Titan reflects the sensibility of much of Vonnegut's work, which derives directly from his experiences in World War II. Captured by the Germans, he was housed in an underground meat locker of a slaughterhouse in the city of Dresden. When he emerged, he found a city devastated by U.S. and British bombs, itself having become a slaughterhouse. Later, working in the public relations department of General Electric after the war, he saw how masses of people were manipulated in peacetime as in war, and he satirized the corporate effort to control America in his first novel, *Player Piano* (1952).

His other novels, such as *Cat's Cradle* (1963) and *God Bless You, Mr. Rosewater* (1965), also use the conventions of science-fiction, but with a black humor reminiscent of *The Sirens of Titan*. Vonnegut finds it comic, if grotesque, of human beings to think that they can ultimately overpower one another. Human fancy resists regimentation, he implies, and even in the darkest hours of atrocity, he finds human beings acting for themselves and proving that they are not reducible to their machinable parts.

—*Carl Rollyson*

Slaughterhouse-Five

Billy Pilgrim's travels to the imaginary planet Tralfamadore provide escapes from the horrors of World War II and Vietnam

Author: Kurt Vonnegut (1922-   )
Genre: Science fiction—cautionary
Type of work: Novel
Time of plot: 1922-1976
Location: Ilium, New York; Dresden, Germany; and the planet Tralfamadore
First published: 1969

The Story

Slaughterhouse-Five: Or, The Children's Crusade, A Duty-Dance with Death is a framed narrative in which Kurt Vonnegut, himself appears in the first and last chapters, explaining how and why he wrote the novel. He also pops up occasionally in the action itself, because he was—like his protagonist Billy Pilgrim, as he tells readers in the frame chapters—a prisoner of war in Dresden, Germany, when Allied bombers incinerated the city on February 13, 1945.

The novel proper opens in 1944, when Billy, a chaplain's assistant and inept foot soldier, is captured by the Germans. He and his fellow prisoners of war are taken by railroad boxcar to Dresden as forced laborers. Housed in a slaughterhouse bunker below the city streets, Billy is one of the only survivors when the city of Dresden is destroyed by incendiary bombs dropped in a ring around the ancient city, causing fires to burn toward its center. Billy emerges from the slaughterhouse to witness a moonscape.

The novel hardly moves in such a straight line; its structure rather mirrors Billy's time travel. Chapter 2 opens with Billy coming "unstuck in time," and thereafter the novel moves jerkily among its three plots: the story of Billy's life, before and after the war; the bombing of Dresden; and life on Tralfamadore, a planet to which Billy was carried in 1967.

With the exception of World War II, Billy's life is quite bland. Born in 1922 and drafted in 1940, after the war Billy marries the daughter of the founder of the Ilium School of Optometry he attends. He becomes a wealthy and conservative optometrist living in upstate New York. His imaginary life is much richer: Not only is he able to travel back and forth in time, but he claims he was kidnapped on the night of his daughter's wedding and taken to a zoo on the planet Tralfamadore, where he and the voluptuous film star Montana Wildhack are representatives of the earthling species on view.

In 1968, Billy is the only survivor of the crash of a chartered flight of optometrists headed for a convention. His wife, Valencia, is killed in her car rushing to visit Billy in the hospital. Soon after these tragedies,

Kurt Vonnegut. (© Jill Krementz)

Billy starts to write letters to the newspaper and appears on an all-night radio show in New York City detailing his interplanetary and time-travel experiences. His life will end, he claims, when one of his fellow prisoners of war, Paul Lazzaro, assassinates him, in the future of 1976. His life story ends in the novel, however, on the planet Tralfamadore with his beautiful lover Montana Wildhack nursing their new baby.

Analysis

At the center of this blackly humorous work of science fiction about time travel and interplanetary travel is a deadly serious novel about the wastes of war. Billy is one of the only survivors of one of the most destructive acts of World War II. A city of no apparent military value, Dresden was bombed in order to bring Germany to its knees and thus to hasten the end of the war. Billy's experiences in Dresden have an almost surreal but intense mix of pathos and trivia: A middle-aged German couple in the rubble of the city berate Billy for mistreating a horse, and his friend Edgar Derby is executed for stealing a teapot.

Billy's psychological response to the devastation he has been part of is the novel itself, an escape through time and space. The Tralfamadorians provide Billy with the deterministic view of life he needs. Because every moment, past, present, and future, has always existed and always will exist, people can escape to a good moment in the past, present, or future. When a Tralfamadorian sees a corpse, "all he thinks is that the dead person is in bad condition in that particular moment, but that the same person is just fine in plenty of other moments." Such a relativistic philosophy—the Tralfamadorians say free will exists nowhere in the universe except on Earth— allows Billy to live in a world of which he has lost the essential meaning.

He does not live happily. Billy is "unenthusiastic about living" in the present of 1968, Vonnegut writes, and he bursts into unexplained bouts of weeping, clearly an early victim of delayed stress syndrome. The weeping is shown as connected to Dresden through various images. The novel is held together not by any linear plot line but by these recurring images (such as spoons, the colors orange and black, and dogs barking) and phrases (particularly the Tralfamadorian "So it goes" whenever death is mentioned). The cause of Billy's autistic present lies in his horrific past.

The larger meaning of the novel applies to the late 1960's, as Vonnegut makes clear in his frame. Robert Kennedy and Martin Luther King, Jr., recently have been murdered, Vonnegut writes in the last chapter, "And every day my Government gives me a count of corpses created by military science in Vietnam." Americans have a choice, Vonnegut says: They can walk through history like the zombie Billy, or they can make it their own.

The novel thus takes science fiction to a deeper level. It is Vonnegut's personal exorcism for his participation in World War II and a novel he tried to write for twenty-five years. It is also another contemporary example, like the novels of E. L. Doctorow, of the interactions of fiction and history. Finally, it is an excellent example of one brand of metafiction that emerged in the 1960's as writers played with the conventions of the novel and added black humor, the artifacts of popular culture, and themselves.

—*David Peck*

Snow Crash

Hiro Protagonist races to save his fellow hackers and the world from megalomaniac L. Bob Rife

Author: Neal Stephenson (1959-   )
Genre: Science fiction—cyberpunk
Type of work: Novel
Time of plot: The twenty-first century
Location: California
First published: 1992

The Story

In Neal Stephenson's cyberspace, called the Metaverse, the 120 million richest people in the world conduct their pleasure and business blithely unaware that L. Bob Rife, the owner of the fiber-optic network they all use, is plotting their domination. Meanwhile, Hiro Protagonist, a hacker who wrote some of the earliest software for the Metaverse, prowls about looking for intelligence to sell in an information-overloaded age. Hiro has a debt to pay: He owes the Mafia-run CosaNostra, the twenty-first century version of Domino's Pizza, the cost of a new delivery car. Before he can repay his debt, he is swept up into a larger adventure. At the urging of his still-intriguing former lover Juanita, he begins investigating a new drug, Snow Crash, that has rendered his former partner, Da5id, brain dead. The ominous part about Snow Crash is that it affects the brain when administered in the Metaverse; in a twist on the typical relationship, the virtual determines the real.

With the help of Y.T., a Kourier who meets Hiro on the fateful night he wrecks his car, Protagonist steps on the trail of Snow Crash in both real and virtual life. In the former, he traces the path of Raven, an atomic-bomb-toting Aleut who seems to be the source of Snow Crash. In the latter, he employs a nearly omniscient virtual librarian to investigate the drug's extensive history. He discovers that Snow Crash is not a drug at all but a modern manifestation of an ancient metavirus that provides access to deep structures in the brain that control individuals. Prior to the fall of Babel, all people spoke a language that used this infrastructure and thus lived in a static culture. The Sumerian priest Enki released humanity from the metavirus by uttering an incantation, or nam-shub, that reprogrammed the brain so that people could no longer understand the deep language. Consequently, multiple languages developed.

The metavirus continued because it has both a linguistic and a biological component. It was circulated mainly through the cult of Asherah, a throwback to Sumer, and spread itself both verbally and through sexual contact. Exposure to the metavirus returns the infected to a pre-Babelian state, bringing the mother tongue closer to the surface and thus causing the person to speak in tongues. In the twenty-first century, its chief manifestation is Pentecostalism, but in hackers the virus has a more devastating effect. Because knowledge of binary structures is "wired" into the brain's deep structures, hackers can be infected by looking at a bit map. Although most people who are infected continue to function, hackers are reduced to a state of neurological mush.

The slow distribution of the metavirus is accelerated when a twenty-first century megalomaniac, L. Bob Rife, finds out how to manufacture it. Acting as a benefactor, he spreads it throughout the Third World via vaccines and infiltrates the First World via Snow Crash. As the novel opens, Rife is about to land a Raft full of infected Third World refugees on the West Coast in his larger invasion of the United States. To stop Rife, Hiro and Y.T. link up with the Mafia and the Nipponese, who have a vested interest in protecting their own global empires, to infiltrate Rife's Raft. There they find Juanita. After an extended chase, they manage to release Enki's nam-shub once again and thus free Rife's followers.

Analysis

Snow Crash takes on a common cyberpunk theme, that of the implications of the information explosion caused by new technologies such as a global fiber-optic network. One way in which the novel differs from cyberpunk works such as William Gibson's *Neuromancer* (1984) and Pat Cadigan's *Synners* (1991) is the way Stephenson situates his discussion in ancient history. By drawing a sweeping link between religion and viruses, he plays with the self-replicating tendencies of both. All information is viral in nature, Stephenson suggests, but some has more violent effects.

The book traces a virulent metavirus from the childhood of humanity that has been spread through religious cults and that manifests itself in the twenty-first century as Pentecostalism. Large sections of the novel trace ancient religious struggles, which Stephenson interprets as primarily concerning battles over information. The Deuteronomists' effort to codify Judaism, for example, is read as "informational hygiene," an effort to regulate which aspects of the religion were replicated. In this way, Stephenson reminds readers that the generation and preservation of all information—whether recipes for bread or religious practices—is always an evolutionary process whereby some knowledge will be lost and some preserved. That global networks can be manipulated by power-hungry individuals such as L. Bob Rife accentuates the tension between representation's fragility and persistence.

Snow Crash also differs from most cyberpunk in its technical particulars. Stephenson is a computer programmer, and his detailed descriptions of how the Metaverse works and how people, through simulations called avatars, can enter it provide a more solid basis for his fiction than do the typical mysticisms about limitless cyberspace. This level of realism does not detract from the novel's fun, however; the charm of *Snow Crash* is in its wry wit and liberally scattered puns. With a zest that recalls Douglas Adams, Stephenson presents a hero named Hiro, a pizza Deliverator for the Mafia who drives a "car with enough potential energy packed into its batteries to fire a pound of bacon into the Asteroid Belt" and who lives in a U-Stor-It with a Russian named Vitaly Chernobyl (2) who wants to be a rock star. The pace is frenetic, the characters larger than life, and the plot fascinating.

—*Carole F. Meyers*

The Snow Queen Trilogy

> Moon Dawntreader defeats her mother, the Snow Queen, becomes the Summer Queen, and saves a bioengineered, aquatic species called mers that holds the key to the knowledge held by the Old Empire

Author: Joan D. Vinge (1948-   )
Genre: Fantasy—alien civilization
Type of work: Novels
Time of plot: An unspecified time in the future
Location: An unnamed galaxy
First published: *The Snow Queen* (1980), *World's End* (1984), and *The Summer Queen* (1991)

The Story

The Change is coming to the watery planet Tiamat, which will be closed to the rest of the empire for 150 years. A new queen will rule. To protect herself, Arienrhod, the Snow Queen, has cloned herself. Arienrhod plans for the clone, Moon Dawntreader Summer, to come to Carbuncle, the planet's only major city, to prepare to become the next queen. The Change means that the less sophisticated Summers will rule and that the off-worlders will leave, taking their technology with them.

Arienrhod's original plan is aborted when Moon inadvertently is taken off the planet by smugglers while on her way to visit Sparks, her lover. Moon is a sibyl, a person infected by a bioengineered virus that makes her capable of tapping into the Old Empire's hidden computer library. Believing Moon to be dead, Sparks eventually becomes consort to Arienrhod and is progressively corrupted.

Moon eventually returns and accidentally is gathered up in an illegal hunt for mers, led by Sparks. The intelligent, aquatic mers are creatures bioengineered by the Old Empire. Their blood contains the "water of life," a longevity substance. Moon meets and falls in love with BZ Gundhalinu, a Kharmoughi policeman. Attracted to BZ, Moon makes love with him.

Arienrhod's plan was to free Tiamat from the control of the Hegemony, the current empire, by preserving as much technology as possible. As her plans are thwarted, she becomes more ruthless, finally arranging for a plague to kill most of the Summers at the Festival of Change. That scheme also is foiled, and Arienrhod is sacrificed to the sea. The off-worlders leave, and so does BZ.

World's End chronicles BZ's journey of self-redemption. Stationed on a planet named Number Four, in self-imposed exile, BZ leaves his police job to find his two brothers and a mad sibyl named Song. "World's End," an uncharted wilderness, boasts great mineral wealth but is a nightmare. At its center is Fire Lake, which proves to be filled with runaway stardrive plasma used for the Old Empire's faster-than-light ships. It drives some people mad and disrupts the fabric of space and time. On the lake shore is a city called Sanctuary, where BZ finds his brothers enslaved and Song in charge. He makes love to her, confusing her with Moon, and she infects him with the sibyl virus. He finds the wreckage of a thousand-year-old Old Empire ship in the lake and is rewarded handsomely for it.

The Summer Queen begins shortly after the Change. Moon is queen, is pregnant with twins fathered by BZ, and is married to Sparks. This novel, like *The Snow Queen*, has two principal plots, following the story of Moon and BZ and that of Reed Kullervo. Moon deals with the return of the off-worlders, her growing feelings for BZ, and the seeming failure of the sibyl net, the collective ability of the sibyls to tap into the computer without hardware. Reed, a brilliant biotechnologist, frees himself from various forms of enslavement, particularly from "the water of death," his own failed attempt to counterfeit the "water of life." BZ and Reed stabilize the stardrive plasma, which will permit the Hegemony's early return to Tiamat.

Meanwhile, BZ imagines that he is someone named Ilmarinen. Reed ends up working for Jaakola, a criminal who keeps him under control by doling out doses of the water of death. Reed eventually learns that Mundilfoere, his former lover, put another mind into his body. BZ is appointed chief justice of Tiamat. Tammis, Moon's son, eventually dies trying to fix the failing sibyl net, and Ariele, Moon's daughter, falls in love with Reed when he appears on Tiamat to synthetically replicate the "water of life." It becomes increasingly clear that the mers' song will reprogram the net. BZ, put into the position of trying to protect the mers while harvesting them, is betrayed by a subordinate and sentenced to prison.

Reed discovers his personality implant to be the legendary Vanamoinen, who, with Ilmarinen, constructed the original sibyl net and who has existed electromagnetically within the net for thousands of years. Moon and BZ finally come back together. The mers remain safe.

Analysis

The Snow Queen trilogy is Joan Vinge's most important work to date. Although much praise has been lavished on *The Snow Queen* itself (it won the Hugo Award in 1981), the other two novels have attracted little attention. The trilogy presents a twisting plot full of ironies, peopled with well-developed characters who move through a richly detailed world that perfectly balances the familiar with the unfamiliar.

The Snow Queen openly owes allegiance to Hans Christian Andersen's fairy tale of the same name. It borrows its characterization of Arienrhod as an insensitive queen from Andersen, and the growth of Moon and Sparks parallels the transformation of the fairy tale's children. At one level, *The Snow Queen* is a coming-of-age novel and as such is linked to literally thousands of other stories. In its broader structure, it also is a novel of renewal. By the end of the novel, summer has replaced winter and Moon has replaced Arienrhod. Although her values and philosophies are entirely different, her goal is identical to her mother's—to advance Tiamat sufficiently into the technological age that the Hegemony will no longer be able to treat it as a backward planet.

Taken together, Moon and Arienrhod represent most of the dialectical pairs that frame human lives: good and evil, youth and age, innocence and experience. Moon's name links her to the perpetual cycle symbolized by the moon trinity of new, full, and old. The sacrifice of the reigning queen to the Lady of the Sea at the end of each cycle further suggests a renewal theme based in vegetation myth. Moon's journeys, both physical and psychological, follow the prototypic pattern of the hero as identified by Joseph Campbell.

World's End relies on Joseph Conrad's *Heart of Darkness* (1902). Vinge herself called it a *Heart of Darkness* novel in a 1983 interview with Richard Law. It also calls on the structure of an Irish folktale, "The Well at the World's End," from which she probably derived the title. In that story, a prince saves a princess and his two disloyal brothers with the help of an enchanted lady. BZ Gundhalinu, the protagonist of the story, rescues both Song, who has been driven mad by the sibyl virus, and his two brothers, who are slaves at Sanctuary. He receives Moon's help by means of the sibyl Transfer.

In his adventures, BZ follows Campbell's prototypic hero myth. In his trip into a wasteland, BZ makes a figurative descent into Hell, from which he is reborn. He is transformed by his experiences, recovers his sanity, and returns with the capability of transforming his world. He brings back the stardrive plasma, which will make an early return to Tiamat possible.

The Summer Queen concludes Vinge's saga of change. It is a beautiful, rich, and complicated novel that resolves issues and romances. Its plot twists one way and then the other as it strips away layer after layer of perceived reality to get at the truth. Vinge's anthropological training is obvious in the richly woven fabric of detail in this work. She has been interested in humanity's "dark side" from the beginning of her writing career. Arienrhod is the dark side of Moon, and in the philosophical development of this work, Vinge mentions the eternal cycle of form and chaos. Evil appears in many forms but is balanced by the forces of good.

The trilogy reflects many of Vinge's continuing themes: the difficulty of loving, the struggle for understanding, the inability to communicate perfectly, the use of drugs, the problem of alienation, the role of free women, the need for renewal, the difficulty of forgiving, and appreciation for different people and cultures. Vinge's protagonists often are strong women placed in difficult situations that permit them to grow from their experience. That is the case here. Although the love scenes between Moon and BZ tend to submerge into soap opera near the end of the story, this development, like Vinge's writing in general, is thoughtful, provocative, stimulating, interesting, and well crafted.

—*Carl B. Yoke*

Solaris

Researcher Kris Kelvin attempts to understand the nature and purposes of the enigmatic ocean-entity that covers the planet Solaris

Author: Stanisław Lem (1921-   )
Genre: Science fiction—alien civilization
Type of work: Novel
Time of plot: After the twenty-first century
Location: The planet Solaris
First published: 1961 (English translation, 1970)

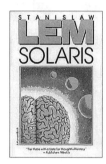

The Story

Researcher Kris Kelvin arrives on Solaris, a planet covered by a mysterious—and possibly intelligent—plasma-ocean-entity, only to find the facilities of the research base untended and in a state of disrepair. Kelvin searches the station and discovers Dr. Snow, a drunken, distracted base worker whose utterances and behavior indicate that the entire crew has become unstable. The station commander, Gibarian, has committed suicide.

During his initial investigation of the facility, Kelvin feels as though he is being watched and hears movement nearby when nothing apparently is there. These eerie sensations become concrete encounters as Kelvin begins to discover the cause of the crew's mental distraction: They are being plagued by visits from alien simulacra, pseudo-beings that are extrusions of Solaris's living ocean.

Kelvin attempts to contact another surviving crew member, Dr. Sartorius, who refuses to let Kelvin enter his rooms. Only under duress does he concede to come out. It becomes obvious to Kelvin that Sartorius, who is extremely agitated, is concealing the presence of some other being in his quarters.

The next day, Kelvin discovers that he has a visitor of his own, a simulacra in the shape of a woman he used to love. This simulacra appears and behaves exactly as he remembers Rheya, but she is unaware of her alien origins. Kelvin, distracted and disturbed by her presence, lures her into a launch capsule and deposits her in orbit until he determines what to do next.

Kelvin once again talks with Snow, who reveals that each crewperson has his or her own visiting simulacrum and that each simulacrum is the re-creation of a troubling individual from the crewperson's past. Snow also reveals that these pseudo-beings regenerate very quickly and, if destroyed, are reproduced shortly afterward.

Snow's claims are confirmed by the arrival of a new pseudo-Rheya. Kelvin struggles with his reaction toward her, which combines fear and loathing with genuine affection. He conducts research into her basic physiology and shares his results with Snow and Sartorius. What Snow calls the "Phi-creatures" are not composed of normal cellular matter but instead are accretions of neutrinos that mimic human physiological structures and metabolic processes. In order to rid themselves of the unwanted visitors, the three scientists contemplate using energy emissions to break down the Phi-creatures' neutrino structure; they also consider sending signals that match Kelvin's thought patterns into the ocean directly, in the hope that this might lead to the establishment of a more manageable form of contact with the ocean entity. Before either of these options can be attempted, Rheya, confused and horrified regarding her own inexplicable origins, attempts suicide but discovers that she cannot carry it out successfully because her capacity for physical regeneration prevents her from dying.

In a subsequent meeting with Snow, Kelvin is forced to admit that, despite the growing individuality of the new Rheya, their relationship ultimately is untenable. The scientists attempt to communicate with the plasma-ocean by projecting amplified brainwave emissions into its depths, but weeks pass without result. The humans become increasingly solitary and erratic in behavior. Kelvin convinces himself that he plans to leave the station with Rheya, but she and Snow both realize that he is deluding himself. Rheya's growing misery leads her to request that Snow and Sartorius destroy her with a device capable of discorporating the Phi-creatures. Upon learning of Rheya's successful suicide, Kelvin rages first at Snow, then at the plasma-ocean. The visits by the Phi-creatures come to an end, and Kelvin leaves Solaris, more understanding of his own nature but also more cynical.

Analysis

Prior to his departure from the planet, Kelvin leaves the station and visits one of Solaris's island-sized oceanic extrusions, determined to have his first direct contact with the living plasma in its natural state. For a while, the ocean-being seems to "interact" with Kelvin, but it then abandons the game, as inscrutable at the last as it was in the beginning. This image restates the basic motif of the narrative: the friction between human desires to establish contact with other minds and the ultimate futility of such attempts. Taken as a story of first contact with an alien intelligence, Stanisław Lem's tale presents a tantalizing array of enigmas: Are the Phi-creatures instruments of torture or gifts? Are they invitations to communication or merely animate constructs created by some nonsentient reflex of the plasma-ocean? Does the "being" that is Solaris have a mind to be reached or not? Would a human recognize it as such if that contact were established?

This overt theme of alien contact can also be read as an allegory for human relations and epistemology. Kelvin and his coworkers try to make contact with one another, to communicate and share experiences, fears, and observations, but their success is, at best, limited. They, too, ultimately remain strangers to one another, and even to themselves. These frustrated attempts at contact frame Lem's sardonic recounting of the scientific history of "Solaristics"—the study of Solaris and its plasma-ocean. Human idealism and folly collide, merge, and become indistinguishable as Lem parodies contemporary factionalism in the sciences, academic posturing, and the elusive, uncertain quality of what humans call knowledge. Ultimately, the metamorphic qualities of Solaris's enigmatic ocean-entity become symbolic of the mutability of reality itself and the indefinite nature of human experience.

—*Charles Gannon*

The Space Merchants and
The Merchants' War

After learning the truth about their society, two advertising executives assist "subversive" movements with designs on Venus

Authors: Frederik Pohl (1919-   ) and C(yril) M. Kornbluth (1923-
1958)
Genre: Science fiction—extrapolatory
Type of work: Novels
Time of plot: An unspecified time in the future
Location: Various locations on Earth, the Moon, and Venus
First published: *The Space Merchants* (1953; serial form, *Galaxy*, 1952)
and *The Merchants' War* (1984)

The Story

One of many collaborations between Frederik Pohl and Cyril M. Kornbluth, *The Space Merchants* was also Pohl's return to writing after working as a literary agent. The novel has an interesting textual history.
Written under the title *Fall Campaign*, it was serialized as "Gravy Planet"
in *Galaxy* magazine, whose editor, H. L. Gold, thought that the ending
was incomplete and demanded that Pohl and Kornbluth produce an additional three chapters to show what happens to the colonizers after
they reach Venus. When the novel was published in book form, these
chapters were omitted from the text, although they have since been reprinted in *Our Best: The Best of Frederik Pohl and C. M. Kornbluth* (1987).
Pohl has made minor revisions to the novel's text; for example, a reference in the first edition to "Western Union and American Express Railway" became a reference to "United Parcel and American Express" in
the 1985 edition. More than three decades lapsed before the publication
of the novel's sequel, *The Merchants' War*, written by Pohl alone. The two
novels were collected into an omnibus volume, *Venus, Inc.* (1985).

The Space Merchants is the story of Mitch Courtney, a "copysmith star
class" in a future in which advertising dominates the world and outlawed "Consies" (Conservationists) are regarded as dangerous and de-
luded radicals. Mitch's big break in the corporate world occurs when he
is given the assignment of "selling" Venus, convincing the people of

Earth that the inhospitable planet is actually a paradise begging for colonists. As he attempts to do this, Mitch finds his life threatened from all sides as he discovers the truth about himself, his profession, and his wife, Kathy.

Despite obvious attempts on his life, Mitch takes his work very seriously, and in trying to eliminate incompetence and inefficiency in the agency, he fires most of the San Diego branch of the Fowler Schocken advertising agency and leaves for Antarctica to confront Matt Runstead. When he meets Runstead, Mitch realizes that he has walked into a trap. Upon passing out, he is sure that he is as good as dead. When he wakes, however, Mitch learns that his fate is actually worse than death: He has become part of a lower-class consumer labor crew, contracted to work for five years at the Chlorella plantations in Costa Rica. His name and social security/identification number have been changed, and the world thinks that he died in Antarctica.

At the Chlorella plantations, Mitch learns how "the other half" lives and is invited to join the Consies movement. Although he is at first horrified, he realizes that hooking up with the Consies might help him get away from Chlorella and back to Fowler Schocken. His copysmith skills prove useful in revising and creating Consie propaganda, and soon he is so valuable a Consie that he is sent back to New York.

Once Mitch returns, however, his troubles really begin. He finds out that Taunton, a rival of Schocken who is angry about losing the Venus project, was responsible for the attempts on his life. Taunton also frames him for murder and breach of contract. He flees to the moon, where he discovers that Kathy is a Consie leader. Returning to Earth with Schocken, Mitch for the first time notices the true nature of the advertising industry. When he takes over the Schocken agency after Schocken's murder, he seeks out Kathy and works with the Consies to make sure that the first colonists to Venus are conservationists. Unfortunately, if his enemies had reason to destroy him beforehand, they have even more reasons now.

The Merchants' War is set several decades after *The Space Merchants*. Long after his death, Mitch is revered as a hero to the "Veenies" (inhabitants of Venus); the anniversary of his demise is a planetary holiday. This novel is the story of Tenny Tarb, another advertising executive who becomes a "traitor" to his own people and a "hero" to those whose political beliefs he comes to embrace.

As the novel begins, Tenny is finishing a term of service on Venus. Earth now regularly sends both political prisoners and "ambassadors" to Venus, many of them spies or agents who want to extend the advertising industry's domination to Earth's sister planet. Tenny loves one of those agents, Mitzi Ku, and wishes that she would return to Earth with him. Mitzi agrees to spend time with Tenny on his last day on Venus, but while sightseeing they both are wounded, apparently as a result of a deliberate Veenie attempt to kill them.

On his way back to Earth, Tenny finds out that Mitzi is also returning, citing her brush with death as her reason for leaving Venus. The bandages that nearly cover her head lend credence to her story. Tenny is surprised to learn that in an amazingly swift bit of legal work, Mitzi has obtained six million dollars from a damage suit filed after her accident. With that money, she "buys" her way into a higher position with Fowler Schocken Associates. Despite Tenny's repeated efforts to see her, Mitzi is usually too busy to spend much time with her former lover.

Life on Earth does not go very well for Tenny. Unaware of the nature of the "commercial zones" that have been established in his absence, he becomes a "Mokehead," an addict to a new drug. Attempting to work his way back up in the Schocken agency, he is dismissed when Mitzi becomes co-founder of a competing ad agency. He is activated in the army reserves and stationed as a chaplain in the Gobi Desert. Because his military service ends with a dishonorable discharge, Tenny can no longer obtain a good job. As did Mitch Courtney before him, he learns how "the other half" lives.

Tenny eventually realizes that the Gobi military exercises were practice runs for an Earth attack on Venus. He also discovers that Mitzi is not who she appears to be; she is in fact a Veenie impersonator working to protect Venus from Earth's imperialistic overtures. Although it means a harrowing bout with detoxification, threats of death, and various dangers, Tenny joins the Veenies and puts his advertising skills to work in an all-out effort to turn the tide of public opinion against an invasion of Venus.

Analysis

In the 1950's, the advertising world (like psychology and the massive influx of people from cities and into the suburbs) was a popular subject for American writers, humorists, satirists, cartoonists, commentators, and other entertainers. It was only natural, then, that works of science fiction would address the subject, among them Shepherd Mead's *The Big Ball of Wax* (1954), Robert Silverberg's *Invaders from Earth* (1958), and J. G. Ballard's "The Subliminal Man" (1963). *The Space Merchants*, however, is perhaps the earliest and most famous of such work.

Although it has long been an element of science fiction and proto-science fiction, satire in genre science fiction generally was held to low standards until the 1950's. Under the editorship of H. L. Gold, *Galaxy* magazine published many examples of short, satiric stories during the decade. Besides Pohl and Kornbluth, writers such as Damon Knight and Robert Sheckley acquired reputations as satirists. In addition to satirizing advertising, Pohl turned his sights on sports in *Gladiator-at-Law* (1955), done in collaboration with Kornbluth, and on the insurance agency in *Preferred Risk* (1955), done in collaboration with Lester del Rey under the pseudonym Edson McCann. *The Space Merchants* remains the best-known of his satirical works, and its influence can be seen in a number of subsequent works forecasting futures in which a particular group or institution dominates society.

The Space Merchants is an excellent example of a type of writing much more common in genre science fiction than in fiction outside the field: the collaboration. Although both Pohl and Kornbluth collaborated with other writers, including Judith Merril, Isaac Asimov, Lester del Rey, and Jack Williamson, those two arguably are the most famous collaboration team in science fiction. In *The Way the Future Was: A Memoir* (1978) and *Our Best* (1987), Pohl explained the process by which he and Kornbluth produced *The Space Merchants*. Pohl had already written the first third of the novel when it became obvious that his duties as an agent would not allow him to finish in time to meet a deadline. He asked for help from Kornbluth, who, after discussions with Pohl, wrote the next third of the novel. After more discussions between the two, the remainder of the novel was produced in shifts, each writer producing four pages at a time and then turning the work over to the other. The experience was satisfying enough that the two collaborated on six more novels as well as on numerous short stories.

—*Daryl R. Coats*

The Space Odyssey Series

Overseen by disembodied extraterrestrial intelligences, human-kind advances through a critical stage in its evolution toward om-niscience, omnipotence, and broad compassion

Author: Arthur C. Clarke (1917-   )
Genre: Science fiction—evolutionary fantasy
Type of work: Novels
Time of plot: About 3,000,000 B.C.E. and 2001-3001 C.E.
Location: The solar system and remote space
First published: *2001: A Space Odyssey* (1968), *2010: Odyssey Two* (1982), and *2061: Odyssey Three* (1988)

The Story

This series began in a unique collaboration between author Arthur C. Clarke and film director Stanley Kubrick. Between 1965 and 1968, they created a screenplay for the 1968 film *2001: A Space Odyssey*. Simultaneously with the filming, Clarke wrote the novel *2001: A Space Odyssey*. The novel exhibits striking interdependence with the film, which is notably nonverbal—the first forty minutes and last thirty minutes have no dialogue.

As the novel opens, a point of light orbits the Earth, unnoticed by protohominids living on the brink of extinction. It leaves behind a device to study and tutor the creatures. Thus tutored, a protohominid named Moonwatcher turns a rock into a weapon, and Earth's era of technology dawns.

A hundred thousand generations later, Dr. Heywood Floyd travels to the moon to investigate TMA-1, a three-million-year-old extraterrestrial artifact found because of its magnetic field. After its discovery, TMA-1 sends a single strong signal toward Saturn. TMA-1's discovery is kept secret from the people of Earth.

The spaceship *Discovery* is sent to reconnoiter Saturn for evidence of whatever civilization produced TMA-1. Three astronauts who understand this mission travel in artificially induced hibernation. Two active astronauts, David Bowman and Frank Poole, know nothing of TMA-1 or the mission's real goal. Virtually a sixth member of the crew is HAL, a supercomputer programmed to tell the truth unreservedly but also to complete the secret mission. Unable to reconcile the contradiction between secrecy and truthfulness, HAL suffers a nervous breakdown and kills Poole and the hibernating astronauts. Barely saving himself, Bowman disables HAL.

Bowman reaches Saturn on the now crippled *Discovery*. Floyd radios him and describes the mission's true goal. On a moon of Saturn, Bowman discovers a huge, enigmatic monolithic replica of TMA-1. When he approaches in an extravehicular space pod, the monolith opens, and he is transported to realms unimaginable to those on Earth. Nurtured by extraterrestrial intelligences, Bowman is reborn as a disembodied star-creature, far superior to humans in intellect and ability to manipulate the environment.

In *2010: Odyssey Two*, a joint Soviet/United States expedition attempts to reach the derelict spaceship *Discovery* before its decaying orbit ends in the atmosphere of Jupiter. (The novel uses background from the film version of *2001* where the film and the novel diverge.) The expedition hopes also to discover why HAL malfunctioned, the nature of the monolith that Bowman found, and perhaps how Bowman disappeared. Dr. Chandra, the creator of HAL, joins the crew, as does Floyd, despite the strains that the long expedition will put on his family.

The joint expedition is almost forestalled by a Chinese expedition that lands on Europa, an icy moon of Jupiter, before approaching *Discovery*. On Europa, the Chinese ship is destroyed by an alien life-form coming from seas beneath the ice. In Floyd's absence, his marriage fails. The Soviet/United States expedition reaches *Discovery*, resurrects the ship, raises its orbit, and reprograms HAL, but it fails to learn anything about the monolith.

One crew member, however, sees a flicker of stars through the monolith as it opens and closes to let the star-creature who had been David Bowman back into the solar system. Under the guidance of the intelligences that oversaw his transformation, Bowman revisits Earth and then observes varied alien life-forms in the seas of Europa and the atmosphere of Jupiter. Partially understanding the purposes of the intelligences guiding him, Bowman uses HAL to warn the joint expedition to leave Jupiter before a cataclysmic implosion transforms that gaseous planet into a new star orbiting the sun. Through HAL, Bowman also tells Earth that humankind is free to explore the entire solar system, save only Europa, which becomes a planet circling the new star. *Discovery* is destroyed in the Jovian catastrophe, but HAL's personality joins Bowman in disembodied existence. On Europa, intelligent life evolves under the warmth of its new sun.

Arthur C. Clarke.
(© Washington Post; reprinted by
permission of the D.C. Public Library)

Before Jupiter's transformation, its core had been a single huge diamond, which was fragmented and expelled in the implosion. In *2061: Odyssey Three*, one huge fragment collides with Europa, becoming a mountain hidden from astronomers by near-perpetual cloud cover. A scientist fortuitously observes and recognizes it but is not discreet enough about his discovery. Consequently, *Galaxy*, a spaceship exploring the Jovian system, is hijacked to the forbidden planet by a person attempting to confirm the diamond mountain's existence. When *Galaxy* makes a forced landing on the Europan sea, the hijacker commits suicide; all others on board are marooned in Europa's extremely hostile environment.

Meanwhile, *Universe*, the first luxury spaceliner, makes its first voyage, an excursion to Halley's Comet. A celebrity passenger is 103-year-old Floyd, whose longevity stems from his many years in low-gravity space environments. *Universe* leaves the comet to rescue *Galaxy*'s crew and passengers. On the voyage across the solar system, Floyd attempts to communicate with the entity that was David Bowman, to assure him of the good intentions of *Galaxy* and *Universe*.

Under Bowman's aegis, the rescue succeeds without damaging encounters between humans and intelligent Europan life. Floyd is reconciled with his estranged grandson, an officer aboard *Galaxy*. When Floyd dies, his spirit is united with the entities who were Bowman and HAL. In the year 3001, as the Jovian star exhausts itself, TMA-1, now on the plaza of Manhattan's United Nations building, reactivates.

Analysis

Clarke is not only an award-winning writer of science fiction (winner of the Hugo, Nebula, and John W. Campbell Memorial Awards) but also an articulate spokesman for the scientific community and a distinguished scientist himself. Besides the Space Odyssey series, he has written *Childhood's End* (1953), *Against the Fall of Night* (1953; revised and expanded to *The City and the Stars*, 1956), *Rendezvous with Rama* (1973), and many other novels and short stories. He has also written much nonfiction, including *The Exploration of Space* (1951) and *Interplanetary Flight* (1950). With the editors of *Life*, he wrote *Man and Space* (1964), and with Walter Cronkite, he covered the first manned moon landing for television. In 1945, Clarke invented the synchronous communications satellite; Earth's band of communications satellites is named the Clarke Belt for him.

As Clarke has noted, science is necessary for science fiction to exist, and as science expands, so does the scope for scientific speculation. He takes great satisfaction as his predictions come to pass. In Clarke's science fiction, the science is as significant as the fiction.

Clarke's fiction not only treats such themes as space travel and artificial intelligence, in which experience can bear out his predictions, but also more speculative themes such as human contact with extraterrestrial intelligence and the possible course of continuing human evolution. *2001: A Space Odyssey* elaborates on Clarke's 1950 short story "The Sentinel." Although the artifact in that story signals extraterrestrial masters of the universe who are feared, in *2001: A Space Odyssey*—as in many other Clarke stories—the overseeing intelligences are benevolent. Homer's epics provide another source for the Space Odyssey series. The solar system is another Mediterranean (or rather, Meta-terranean), Bowman another Achilles, Floyd another Ulysses, Floyd's wife a Penelope who does not wait, their grandson Chris a second Telemachus, and the extraterrestrial intelligences behind TMA-1 new Olympian gods.

The film version of *2001: A Space Odyssey* has drawn vigorous and varied critical attention. Virtually all critics appreciate its special effects, photography, transitions, and score, but some complain that the story drags and is confusing. Others receive the story enthusiastically.

HAL has been seen as the quintessential film villain—dominating, threatening, and inscrutable. The emerging critical consensus recognizes the work as a great film. The novel, published shortly after the film's release, has been analyzed in the context of the film. Readers generally find the book clearer than the film with regard to HAL's motivation and the significance of the story's enigmatic ending. The book also clarifies the proposition that the crucial challenges facing humanity include not only traveling in space but also managing ever-more-potent weaponry.

Clarke has stated that the novels of the series are variations on a single theme. Although they can be read individually, they are better read sequentially. Even the first, a clear and eloquent expression of Clarke's ideas that is marked by vivid, almost poetic descriptions, benefits from the context of the other books. *2010: Odyssey Two* better characterizes Floyd, Bowman, and especially HAL. Although *2061: Odyssey Three* leaves room for a sequel, it is well plotted in itself and provides a satisfactory resolution of the stories of the main characters in the series. In the fusion of rigorously verifiable scientific fact and free-ranging imagination, Clarke inspires readers to reevaluate what people believe of themselves and the universe.

—David W. Cole

The Space Trilogy

An epic battle between good and evil is enacted by an assortment of human and alien characters on three planets

Author: C(live) S(taples) Lewis (1898-1963)
Genre: Fantasy—theological romance
Type of work: Novels
Time of plot: The 1930's and 1940's
Location: The planet Malacandra (Mars), the planet Perelandra (Venus), and terrestrial England
First published: *The Cosmic Trilogy* (1990); previously published as *Out of the Silent Planet* (1938), *Perelandra* (1943; also published as *Voyage to Venus*, 1953), and *That Hideous Strength: A Modern Fairy-Tale for Grown-ups* (1945; also published in shorter form as *The Tortured Planet*, 1958)

The Story

In the three novels commonly known as the Space Trilogy and sometimes as the Cosmic Trilogy or Ransom Trilogy (the series was not given a formal title by its author), the celebrated literary scholar and Christian essayist C. S. Lewis combines elements of classical science fiction, medieval romance, and the epic to create a sprawling depiction of an interplanetary struggle between good and evil.

Out of the Silent Planet, the first of the novels, centers on the adventures of Elwin Ransom, a Cambridge philologist who is abducted by Dick Devine, a grammar-school classmate who has become a ruthless opportunist, and Edward Weston, a renowned physicist. Devine and Weston drug Ransom and take him aboard a spacecraft that Weston has created; together, they travel to Mars. During the journey, Ransom learns that his abductors plan to give him to the Martians as part of a pre-arranged scheme. Imagining that he is to be sacrificed in some alien ritual, Ransom escapes from his captors soon after they arrive on Mars, only to realize that he has run from his only means of returning to Earth.

After wandering for some time, Ransom meets the hrossa, intelligent, otterlike beings; as he learns their language and way of life, he comes to understand that the hrossa are an entirely benevolent, unfallen race. Ransom also meets the planet's two other rational species, which like the hrossa are supremely talented, peaceful beings sharing the planet they call Malacandra in complete harmony. He is also introduced to the eldils, luminous spiritual beings of a higher order.

Ransom is eventually taken to meet the oyarsa, or chief eldil, of Malacandra. He learns that Earth (or Thulcandra) is known as the "silent planet" because it has been isolated from the remainder of the solar system since its own oyarsa rebelled against Maleldil (the eldilic name for God), an event that brought evil to the planet. Ransom is also reunited with Weston and Devine, who persist in viewing the sophisticated Martians as primitives to be cowed with technology or bribed with trinkets. The

C. S. Lewis.
(Hulton Archive)

Martian oyarsa humbles Weston and Devine and sends the three earthlings home, enjoining Ransom to keep a watch on the further activities of his abductors.

In *Perelandra*, Ransom is sent by the eldils to Venus (Perelandra) to contest the forces of evil in a new version of the Genesis myth. On Perelandra, an Edenic planet covered with warm seas and dotted with floating islands, he meets the Green Lady, the Eve of the newly created world. Weston, who has been possessed by the fallen eldils of Earth, also arrives, and the two men engage in a protracted intellectual struggle for the soul of the Green Lady. Weston, the tempter, tries to persuade the entirely innocent Green Lady to violate the one command she has been given by Maleldil: not to leave the floating islands to reside on the planet's fixed land. Ransom realizes that it is up to him to prevent a repetition of the earthly Fall; despairing of winning the debate with his demoniacally inspired adversary, he undergoes a dark night of the soul that ends only when he abandons himself to the will of Maleldil. Thus inspired, Ransom engages Weston in brutal hand-to-hand combat, killing him and thus preserving the new world's purity at the cost of his own physical and spiritual pain. The Green Lady is reunited with the planet's Adam, and Ransom is returned to Earth.

That Hideous Strength, the longest and most complex of the novels, is set in post-World War II England. Ransom, who has been vested with spiritual powers and eternal youth since his sojourn in paradise, gathers a cadre of followers to combat the evil eldils of Earth. The book's main action follows a young married couple, Mark and Jane Studdock, as they are drawn into opposite camps in the cosmic struggle. Jane, who has dream visions that prove to be true and who is thus coveted as a source of intelligence by both sides, gravitates to Ransom's group; Mark, a talented young academic, is inveigled into the inner circles of the National Institute for Co-ordinated Experiments (N.I.C.E), a gigantic, sinister, government-backed scientific project through which the dark powers plan to seize control of Britain. Both groups seek to contact Merlin, the magician of Arthurian legend, who has been awakened from centuries of suspended animation. Merlin joins Ransom's forces, and the benevolent eldils possess him. Entering the forbidding institute via a ruse, Merlin liberates Mark and then unleashes the eldilic power, destroying himself, the institute, its leaders, and most of its dupes.

Analysis

With the exception of the immensely popular seven-volume *Chronicles of Narnia*, written for children, the trilogy is Lewis's only major long fiction. His well-known Christian views (which he proclaimed across three decades of religious writings), his enormous literary scholarship, and the major intellectual and social currents of the time provide a convenient, if somewhat simplistic, framework for interpreting the trilogy.

Although the novels' Christian subtext is veiled in references to "Maleldil" and "dark eldils," the outlines of the cosmic struggle are clear. The rebellion of the earthly oyarsa suggests the rebellion of Satan—which, Ransom learns, was redeemed by the sacrifice of Maleldil the Young (Christ). On Perelandra, Ransom himself becomes the Christ figure, enduring his own Passion; at the climax of Ransom's internal struggle, the voice of Maleldil makes the parallel plain by telling him, "My name is also Ransom." As Christ paid for humankind's sins, so will Ransom pay—in advance—to redeem the new Eden.

The struggle for the soul of England in the final volume brings Christianity face to face with some of the principal political and intellectual forces of mid-century. The N.I.C.E.'s secret police deal ruthlessly with dissent; powerless locals are rounded up for "experimental" use; and even the institute's leaders are cannibalized as the scheme of conquest progresses. This it-can't-happen-here evocation of Nazism might seem trite, but Lewis makes the scenario compelling by linking the specter of fascism with notions current in contemporary intellectual circles, notably the doctrine of creative evolution espoused by Henri Bergson and amplified by George Bernard Shaw.

In the earlier books, Weston is the mouthpiece for such views; in the final volume, another eminent scientist, the Italian anatomist Filostrato, presents the argument: The fundamental principle of the universe, the "Life Force," seeks to perfect itself, evolving from crude matter into ever more sophisticated organisms and, ultimately, into pure spirit. Weston refers to this doctrine to justify the planetary imperialism he attempts to carry to Malacandra and Perelandra; because he believes humankind to be more advanced than the extraterrestrial races, he argues that he is justified in enslaving or exterminating them in the name of universal progress. Filostrato and his allies attempt to stride toward pure spirit more directly, by animating a disembodied head with an artificially enlarged brain; they believe, erroneously, that they are assisting at the birth of the next stage of intelligent life.

Lewis makes it plain that the fictional scientists (and, by implication, the real-life adherents of such philosophies) have confused the idea of spirit, itself a neutral concept, with true goodness—which, Lewis asserts, is attainable only through Christian faith. This "fatal misprision" makes the secular rationalists easy prey for the dark eldils (which are identified with the devils of Christian belief), and these evil spirits use Weston, Devine, Filostrato, and many others as unwitting tools in a program of destruction. Although the trilogy's supernatural elements remove the works from a realistic plane, the convincing way in which Lewis develops earthly manifestations of ultimate evil as logical outgrowths of familiar doctrines makes the books compelling even to nonbelievers.

Moreover, the trilogy is a tour de force of imaginative writing that demonstrates Lewis's mastery of a wide variety of fictional forms. *Out of the Silent Planet*, the shortest and most straightforward of the books, incorporates many of the elements of classic science fiction, including a space flight, meetings with fantastic aliens, and an extended depiction of another planet. Were it not for the theological backdrop (which comes into focus only toward the story's end), *Out of the Silent Planet* could pass as merely a well-written and exceptionally erudite pulp novel. *Perelandra*, on the other hand, has more in common with the epic or the medieval romance than with most novels: A divinely inspired hero journeys to an unearthly realm to do physical and spiritual battle with demons. *That Hideous Strength*, the most heterogeneous of the books, mixes fantasy elements with episodes of startling realism in nearly equal measure. For this reason, some critics have judged it the least aesthetically satisfying of the three, but the effortlessness with which Lewis weaves together enormously diverse plot threads, and the skill with which he renders a wide assortment of memorable characters, are truly impressive.

—*Robert McClenaghan*

Stand on Zanzibar

In an overpopulated, mass-mediated, conflict-ridden world, one man supervises the neo-colonial makeover of a poor African country while his roommate kidnaps a genetic scientist from a developing Asian nation

Author: John Brunner (1934-1995)
Genre: Science fiction—dystopia
Type of work: Novel
Time of plot: The early twenty-first century, after 2010
Location: Various places in the United States, especially in and around New York City and Los Angeles, California; and the imaginary nations of Yatakang and Beninia
First published: 1968

The Story

Norman House, an African American executive with the massive General Technics corporation (GT), becomes manager of the Beninia project, through which GT plans to salvage its investment in the Mid-Atlantic Mining Project by turning the sleepy capital of Beninia, Port Mey, into a deepwater port and ore-processing complex. As the project develops, however, GT's supercomputer Shalmaneser begins to predict failure.

Meanwhile, Norman's roommate, Donald Hogan, previously on the government payroll as an independent researcher and a student of the Yatakang language, is suddenly "activated." Military authorities take him to a base in California, where intensive training turns him into a lethal killer. He is then sent to Yatakang to determine the truth of claims by that country's government that its scientists have achieved a breakthrough in genetic technology.

Before Donald departs, the two roommates attend a party where they meet legendary sociologist Chad Mulligan, a banned author of subversive books and currently a homeless alcoholic even though he is a millionaire. Impressed by the great man's analytic skills, they invite him back to their apartment, and he ends up taking over Donald's room. He has already helped Donald figure out what his assignment is likely to be; henceforth he will prove invaluable to Norman and GT.

Donald's mission to Yatakang is a technical success and a moral failure. Given cover as a newsman, he makes his way to Dedication University. When a crazed killer attacks a crowd, Donald's training enables him to eliminate the assailant, inadvertently saving the life of molecular biologist Dr. Sugaiguntung, the man he is investigating. The Yatakangi belief in a permanent debt to anyone who saves a person's life provides Donald with invaluable leverage with Sugaiguntung. He finds out that the Yatakangi government's claims are exaggerated, and he encourages the scientist to defect. Sugaiguntung, however, changes his mind while they await their rendezvous at a rebel base in the jungle. When he attempts to prevent their pickup by an American submarine, Donald accidentally kills him. The death causes Donald to become insane.

Also apparently insane is the GT supercomputer Shalmaneser, which rejects the data on the people of Beninia as impossible. The computer cannot accept that those people completely lack aggression. Shalmaneser's refusal to approve the Beninia project threatens its acceptability to the GT accountants and shareholders, but Mulligan agrees to slug it out mentally with the computer. He wants to help Norman, of course, but he mostly desires to show that a human being can outsmart even a nearly sentient machine.

Mulligan persuades Shalmaneser to accept the hypothesis that some unknown factor is making the people of Beninia behave in a manner unlike any other human population. At this point Shalmaneser approves the project and begins forecasting an excellent return for GT. Mulligan, however, bullies his way onto the payroll as director of a team of social scientists who search for the hypothetical factor. The factor is located, but it proves useless as a means of improving the behavior of the human species.

The Beninians, it turns out, have all inherited a gene conferring the ability to secrete a pheromone that suppresses aggressive behavior. Mulligan enthusiastically envisions the remolding of humanity through genetic surgery. At this point, however, he learns of Donald Hogan's accidental killing of Sugaiguntung, the one scientist who might have developed the necessary technique, and he succumbs to blubbering insanity.

Analysis

A summary of the plot makes *Stand on Zanzibar* seem less innovative than it was when published and less complicated than it may appear to some readers. To tell the story, John Brunner relies on such techniques as the collage and jump-cut, usually associated with film narrative and with modernist writers, especially John Dos Passos. The 145 chapters of the novel divide into four interwoven sets. The lengthiest of these, "continuity," contains the lead story line summarized above. Another, "tracking with closeups," tells eight other stories, most of them ending in the death of the protagonist. Some of these stories tie into the lead story, and others do not; all reflect in some way the dehumanizing circumstances of ordinary lives in the twenty-first century. These circumstances include overcrowding, deprivation, and aggression. Another group of chapters is "context." These chapters gather quotations, letters, reports, and speeches, mostly social commentary and mostly from the pen of Chad Mulligan, whose voice in them seems close to that of the (implied) author. The final group, "the happening world," consists of assorted news items and advertisements, mostly presented as television scripts, that serve to convey the background for all the rest.

Stand on Zanzibar is thus a richly layered narrative of manifold voices, strenuously avoiding the monologue style of much science fiction, in which the narrator and the main character (and sometimes other characters as well) are merely authorial mouthpieces. Brunner's decentering of narrative authority is clear from his treatment of Mulligan, the main social commentator, who is for the most part an uncivil, ineffectual, verbose, and drunken dropout. The failure of the author's apparent stand-in, who plays the role of chief social critic in a novel of social criticism, tends to undercut the authority needed for such criticism. The stylistic fragmentation of the novel, its mixture of discourses, also invalidates any claim to stylistic authority. Thus in an anarchic, discordant polyphony of languages Brunner finds a world lacking any remnant of faith, hope, or love. The achievement of *Stand on Zanzibar* is that its bleak dystopian vision is perfectly embodied in its exuberant linguistic form.

—*John P. Brennan*

Star Maker

"I" is transported from his British suburb on a whirlwind trip through the universe, culminating in an encounter with his Creator, the Star Maker

Author: (William) Olaf Stapledon (1886-1950)
Genre: Science fiction—cosmic voyage
Type of work: Novel
Time of plot: 1937, then into the fourth dimension
Location: From England to the end and beginning of the universe
First published: 1937

The Story

The hero of *Star Maker* is an Englishman, known only as "I." Comfortably married, he lacks passionate commitment. He is apprehensive of the rise of the Nazis in Germany, but the world situation pales against the cosmic panorama that soon engulfs him. From a hill near his suburban home, he is transported on a night journey into the sky. This expands to become an odyssey through time and space, to the alpha and omega points of the universe itself. First, he glimpses Earth from space, opalescent against a spangled ebony backdrop.

I discovers that through "sub-atomic power," interstellar travels, rather than mere interplanetary excursions, are possible. He encounters many and varied alien beings. Some of their societies offer satirical perspectives on human ones. On an Earth-like planet, with a similar though still divergent evolutionary process, I meets Other Men whose genitals are equipped with taste organs. Their intense sexuality is sometimes sublimated by their mystics into a vigorous gustatory experience of God.

I's travels continue through thousands of worlds, each with its singularities. He confronts "ichthyoids," who are artistic and mystical creatures living symbiotically among "arachnoids," who perform the engineering feats essential for mutual survival. Elsewhere, there are intelligent fish on planets composed entirely of crystal seas, and rational winged beings with brilliant plumage. Sometimes, a host of individual bodies possess a single intellect, or a planet may itself be an asserting consciousness. On larger heavenly bodies, several different civilizations are shown to have developed separately before making common cause after a tumultuous industrialization. Rational beings working together seem always to fare better than those who struggle alone.

Manifold stellar tragedies are revealed. Some worlds have blown themselves to bits. Others are rival empires or insane ones. Segments of the universe are in contact through "telepathic intercourse," and other regions exist in forbidding isolation. Unremitting agony reigns in one spot, but elsewhere, plantlike intelligences radiate mystical quietism. Worlds are discovered where the Creator seems to have experienced incarnations and crucifixions, choosing to share the joys and hurts of its creatures. Even more worlds bear witness to a Hindu-like universal force, simultaneously manifested as Creator, Preserver, and Destroyer.

I appears to discern two drives propelling the multiform universe: All beings seek to discover their place in an overall cosmic harmony, and all strive for some understanding of their existence. His pilgrimage culminates when he finally confronts the dazzling God beyond all gods, the Star Maker, in which all contradictions are resolved and all questions reduced to absurdity. Awe and overwhelming adoration are the response of the creature, but the Great Spirit is beyond all love or anger, impassively contemplating life in its varying levels of imperfection.

Although momentarily blinded by his vision of the Star Maker, both beatific and horrific, I happily awakes back home in England. His wife waits patiently for him as his country braces for World War II.

Analysis

Olaf Stapledon, a professor with a doctorate in philosophy, published two earlier novels, *Last and First Men* (1930) and *Odd John: A Story Between Jest and Earnest* (1935). These books introduced the themes most fully explored in *Star Maker*, which many critics consider to be his strongest work. Part philosophical reflection, part prose-poem, part theological adventure, and only incidentally space-travel fiction, *Star Maker* is difficult reading, though abundantly rewarding. Not only are 100 billion years of Earth time encompassed, but a unique feat is attempted—the description of a deity. Presented as fiction, the Star Maker is the conceptual product of a scholar's study of world religions.

Although Stapledon has been accused of concocting an interplanetary romance as a distraction from the catastrophe looming over Europe in 1937, he actually was placing human affairs provocatively in a cosmic perspective, with conclusions foreshadowing the postwar philosophic movement of existentialism. He suggested that even though the Creator of the universe, the Star Maker, might well be indifferent to human striving, the relationships between men and women—particularly humans united in community—had their own validity.

Countless science-fiction writers, including Philip K. Dick, Arthur C. Clarke, Ursula Le Guin, and Isaac Asimov, are indebted to Stapledon. Brian Aldiss has called him the ultimate science-fiction writer, and C. S. Lewis, though detesting his philosophy, praised both his descriptive style and his endless well of inventiveness. Science-fiction fandom has largely ignored Stapledon, finding his writing too frigid, repetitive, and devoid of entangling plots and subplots. Few characters have been sufficiently developed to elicit reader empathy. Love interest is lacking, and sexuality is cerebral rather than salacious. Dialogue, when it appears, lacks fun or the flavor of living human speech. There is no Stapledon cult, and no religious movements, like those engendered by the writings of Robert A. Heinlein or L. Ron Hubbard, have been spawned by this most visionary writer in his genre.

The usual categories of literature collapse when imposed on Stapledon. He stands out from most science-fiction writers in his ability to sustain and expand brilliant concepts throughout entire books and series of books. As an imaginative voyager, he belongs in the company of Homer, Virgil, Dante Alighieri, and John Milton. when Dante, who makes himself the central human character in *The Divine Comedy* (c. 1320), wanders out of medieval Florence into the dark wood, he is transported only to Hell, Purgatory, and Heaven. Stapledon's alter ego strides the entire universe, both the known and the previously unimagined. The prose, in its detached grandeur, may be compared without absurdity to that of Milton in *Paradise Lost* (1667). I's own excursion, however, from the homey hill in England to the limits of creation and the presence of the Star Maker, has its closest parallel in Islamic tradition, in Muhammad's night ride on the flying steed Al Barak, from the Temple Mount in Jerusalem through the Seven Heavens. *Star Maker* belongs to the literature of religion as much as to science fiction.

—*Allene Phy-Olsen*

The Stars My Destination

Gully Foyle becomes a superhero and seeks revenge against the spaceship crew that left him to die

Author: Alfred Bester (1913-1987)
Genre: Science fiction—superbeing
Type of work: Novel
Time of Plot: The twenty-fifth century
Location: Earth and various locations in space
First published: 1957 (U.S.; revision of *Tiger! Tiger!*, United Kingdom, 1956)

The Story

The backdrop of *The Stars My Destination* is a war between the Inner Planets (I.P.) and the Outer System (O.S.) in the twenty-fifth century. Humans have learned how to teleport themselves, or "jaunt." In this age of robber barons and conspicuous consumption, mechanic's mate Gulliver "Gully" Foyle, the "stereotype common man," as Alfred Bester's narrator calls him, is left adrift in space. He is the only survivor of the wreck of the *Nomad*. Unknown to Foyle, the *Nomad* carried a fortune in bullion and twenty pounds of PyrE, an explosive substance similar to antimatter. After 170 days, Foyle is spotted by the spaceship *Vorga*, which then passes him. Enraged, Foyle saves himself by learning to pilot the *Nomad*. The "vengeful history of Gully Foyle" begins as he crashes into the Scientific People's asteroid. While he is unconscious, the Scientific People, recognizing his nature, tattoo a Maori tiger mask and the name N♂MAD on his face.

Foyle appears on Earth, where he uses one-way telepath Robin Wednesbury (she can send but not receive) to help him find out about the *Vorga*. Foyle is now sought by four parties: Presteign of Presteign, a robber baron, Regis Sheffield, a lawyer and spy for the O.S., Saul Dagenham, a brilliant troubleshooter, and Peter Y'ang-Yeovil, the chief of police.

Foyle is captured by Dagenham but does not break down under interrogation. He is kept in an underground jaunt-proof prison. There, through an acoustical freak, he makes contact with the intelligent Jisbella McQueen, who educates him. When Dagenham visits, Foyle beats him and escapes with McQueen. McQueen has the identifying tiger tattoo bleached off Foyle's face, but it remains below the skin, a phantom that blooms whenever Foyle loses his temper (which is often). Foyle and McQueen salvage the *Nomad*'s cargo, but Dagenham captures McQueen as Foyle gets away with the money.

Having learned yoga to control his animal self, Foyle resurfaces as a charming and amazing clown, named Fourmyle of Ceres. His Four-mile Circus acts as a cover for Foyle's continuing investigation of the *Vorga*. Foyle has his nervous system rewired so that when he switches on a power pack, he becomes a superman.

The *Vorga* has been running concentration camp refugees out of the O.S. Its captain has been collecting transportation money and then throwing the refugees out the airlock. The "burning man," a weird specter, now appears to Foyle: It is himself. During bombing of Earth by the O.S., Olivia Presteign, blind except in the infrared, sees the tiger tattoo on Foyle's face. Presteign, Sheffield, Yeovil, and Dagenham simultaneously discover Foyle's identity. For his part, Foyle learns that Olivia Presteign, whom he loves, is the murderer who commands the *Vorga*.

The other characters all converge on Foyle at his circus in the burning ruins of St. Patrick's Cathedral in New York. Dagenham ignites the PyrE there, in the hope of keeping it away from the O.S. Foyle jaunts in space and time to escape the fire, appearing to his past self as the burning man. Once out of the fire, Foyle confronts each character with the truth she or he least wishes to hear. He then snatches the PyrE and distributes it across the world, stating that elites must teach the common people to handle power. Foyle then space jaunts to the *Nomad*, his womb, and falls into a prophet's sleep.

Analysis

This book was published between two other superb Bester novels, *The Demolished Man* (1953) and *The Computer Connection* (1975). It reflects a postwar world concerned with concentration camps, hydrogen bombs, and material wealth. It is one of the most remarkable, joyous, and brilliant books in American science fiction. Bester's sheer energy, pyrotechnics, and inspired zaniness make for fast reading. He crams in styles and ideas, switching tone and tempo with each line. The writing shows his love for romantic (especially Byronic) poetry and heroes, for Whitmanesque wonder, and for the lean plotting of the television and radio pulps for which he wrote and that he loved. His use of cultures of excess, particularly the robber barons' world of late nineteenth century America, makes *The Stars My Destination* a mosaic.

At heart a Walt Whitman democrat, Bester subscribes to the belief that all humans are uncommon, that they simply need the right events (often life-threatening crises) to make their miraculous promise flower. Crisis teaches humanity to teleport short distances, and teaches Foyle to teleport himself across space and time. Gulliver Foyle is, like his namesake, a traveler to strange, revealing places. Bester constructs those spaces beautifully: He imagines a world built socially, culturally, linguistically, and economically around teleportation. A self-declared Freudian, Bester has Dagenham use psychology to unravel the mystery of Foyle's strength, subjecting him first to "nightmare theater," then to "Megal Mood," catering to the megalomaniac's fantasies. Foyle, pure id, is too tough for these pranks.

If Foyle is to be truly great, the id, tiger, animal self, must be absorbed but not destroyed. The other characters also must own up to their monsters: Presteign must acknowledge his daughter's inherited sickness, Dagenham must admit that he is a freak; and Wednesbury must see that she is neurotic. Bester suggests that brilliance and neurosis are partners; in *The Computer Connection*, he links genius and epilepsy. Each character is an awful and marvelous emblem of freakishness at once fascinating and charming. All have learned to exploit their abilities, to protect themselves from the brutality that swirls around them. "You're all freaks, sir," Foyle is told by a robot bartender jangled by excessive radiation. "But you always have been freaks. Life is a freak. That's its hope and glory."

Bester's fictions are carnivals of death, amazement, and amusement. He recalls being charged "that the entire world was made for his entertainment," and his writing bears this out. Beneath the laughter is the deadly serious business of figuring out patterns of behavior in a moral wilderness. Foyle tells Wednesbury, "Nobody ever suspects a clown." They should know better.

—*Tim Blackmore*

Stations of the Tide

A bureaucrat on the planet Miranda searches for a thief, through shifting levels of appearance and reality, as the planet prepares for the Jubilee Tides

Author: Michael Swanwick (1950-   )
Genre: Science fiction—alien civilization
Type of work: Novel
Time of plot: The distant future
Location: The planet Miranda
First published: 1991

The Story

An unnamed bureaucrat is sent from the Technology Transfer Department to the colonized planet Miranda. Miranda is a technologically restricted planet, and the bureaucrat's boss, Korda, fears that the Mirandan wizard Gregorian has stolen some proscribed technology. Miranda, at the time of the bureaucrat's arrival, faces the once-in-two-centuries Jubilee Tides, when vast portions of the planet are drowned. Only the life-forms adapted to live under water survive. As the towns gear up for evacuation, the bureaucrat searches for Gregorian in an ever-shifting reality. He is aided by his nanotechnological briefcase and robotic surrogates.

The bureaucrat and Chu, his liaison officer, land in Tidewater, Gregorian's boyhood home and center for a smuggling ring in haunt artifacts. Haunts were the original intelligent life-form on Miranda, but all of them were killed by accident in a previous Jubilee Tide. The Mirandans still suffer guilt, remorse, and fascination for these beings, who knew how to change form to live in Ocean when the world was drowned.

The bureaucrat interviews Gregorian's mother and learns that his was a virgin birth. When young, she met a Department technocrat and agreed to become pregnant with his cloned embryo. The technocrat housed her in Ararat, now a lost city, to await the birth. She escaped, returned to Tidewater, and reared Gregorian. The bureaucrat learns that Gregorian ran away from home to study wizardry with Madame Campase, a famous witch. He then meets with Undine, who had been Madame Campase's student along with Gregorian, and is further enlightened about Gregorian's personality.

Before he and Chu continue their search for Gregorian, the bureaucrat creates numerous surrogates of himself and visits the Puzzle Palace, a constructed reality where surrogates meet, game, exchange information, and travel to other places in virtual reality. From information received there, he begins to be suspicious of Korda, who is obsessed with Miranda's haunts. Returning from the Puzzle Palace, the bureaucrat confronts a Korda surrogate and learns that Korda is Gregorian's father. He had cloned himself so that he and his son could continue the search for any remaining haunts. Now that Gregorian is in possession of restricted technology, however, he must be hunted down, regardless of the father-son relationship.

The bureaucrat flies to Ararat, landing there as the tides begin. He becomes lost in a swirling blizzard. He is saved from frostbite by Gregorian, who brings him back to the fortress and chains him to a wall to be drowned. They share a drug and merge identities. The bureaucrat then realizes and understands the extent of Gregorian's hatred for his father. As the bureaucrat begins to give up hope, his briefcase arrives, frees him, and chains Gregorian. He watches the tides come in and the world turn to Ocean. Slowly, using shaping agents within himself, the bureaucrat changes into a sea animal and plunges into the sea.

Analysis

Michael Swanwick's Nebula-winning *Stations of the Tide* is a many-layered, complex, and imaginative future detective story. Along with Swanwick's other works, including *In the Drift* (1984), *Vacuum Flowers* (1987), *The Griffin's Egg* (1991), and *The Iron Dragon's Daughter* (1993), this novel explores how humanity survives and forms a continuing culture under difficult circumstances. In *Stations of the Tide*, the Mirandans survive the Jubilee Tides by evacuating to higher ground and starting over; the bureaucrat survives by using advanced technology and shape-changing.

Swanwick began writing during the 1980's, the era of cyberpunk in science fiction. The constructed reality Puzzle Palace, the technologically sophisticated briefcase, and the generated surrogates reflect awareness of computer possibilities. This novel takes on added dimensions and rises above a mere computer romp through the use of illusion and allusion. In *Stations of the Tide*, the unnamed bureaucrat must work through the magic and the illusions he encounters to find reality and arrive at the truth about Gregorian and himself.

Swanwick's many literary allusions in the novel enrich the reading experience. The name of the planet, Miranda, and its solar system,

Prospero, come from William Shakespeare's *The Tempest* (1611), similarly concerned with illusion, reality, and the ways to distinguish between them. Shakespeare's play is also a story about a sea disaster, change, and a reestablished order. Swanwick also uses biblical allusions. Ararat, the city of Gregorian's birth and death, as well as the location of the bureaucrat's rebirth in the flood of the Jubilee Tides, was the mountain upon which Noah's ark landed and civilization began again. Gregorian's virgin birth and the title, reminiscent of the Stations of the Cross, allude to Gregorian as a Christ figure, particularly in regard to resurrection and rebirth.

Another ongoing interest in Swanwick's work is the problem of retaining identity under new and difficult situations. In *Stations of the Tide*, the notion of self is fractured by the surrogates and the Puzzle Palace. Even the bureaucrat's physical self changes at the end, to that of a watergoing being. It is fitting, then, that the bureaucrat remains unnamed throughout the novel, for identity in Swanwick's imagined far future is neither rigid nor fixed. Swanwick sees identity as necessarily flexible; those who survive are those who are willing to change.

Stations of the Tide is a sophisticated literary work of science fiction exploring possible ways humans might adapt to varying environments. The people of Miranda are fascinating, and the hunt for Gregorian is compelling. Swanwick's conclusion is an optimistic one. Not only the impact of the cumulative allusions but also the bureaucrat's actions point to the possibility of rebirth. Technology offers hope through its use in adapting to the new environment on Miranda.

—*Marjorie Ginsberg*

The Strange Case of Dr. Jekyll and Mr. Hyde

The classic morality tale of a man's personality split between the bestial and the socially responsible

Author: Robert Louis Stevenson (1850-1894)
Genre: Science fiction—cautionary
Type of work: Novel
Time of plot: The late nineteenth century
Location: London, England
First published: 1886

The Story

Robert Louis Stevenson said that the plot of *The Strange Case of Dr. Jekyll and Mr. Hyde* (first published without "The" as the first word in the title) first came to him in a nightmare and that, after waking up, he wrote the first draft in three days. Stevenson introduces the mystery of the evil Mr. Edward Hyde—the central puzzle of the story—early in the novel, but he does not provide a solution to the mystery until the very end. The reader's first encounter with Hyde is at second hand, in a story told to Gabriel John Utterson, a lawyer friend of Dr. Henry Jekyll, by Richard Enfield, who saw Hyde trample a child. Because Jekyll recently has changed his will to leave all of his money to Hyde, Utterson is intrigued and begins to investigate. He fears that Hyde is blackmailing Jekyll and plans to murder him.

When Sir Danvers Carew, a respected member of Parliament, is murdered and Hyde is implicated by a witness, a manhunt begins, but Hyde cannot be found. Utterson begins to suspect that more than a murder is involved when he discovers that the handwriting of Jekyll is identical to that of Hyde, except for the slant of the letters. His suspicions deepen when he learns that Dr. Hastie Lanyon has developed hard feelings toward his old friend, Henry Jekyll. Although Lanyon is dying, he refuses to see Jekyll again.

The mystery that surrounds the relationship between Jekyll and Hyde is revealed gradually by means of a letter from Lanyon that is to be read by Utterson after Lanyon has died; however, Lanyon's letter con-

Robert Louis Stevenson.
(Library of Congress)

tains another letter that is not to be opened until the death or disappearance of Jekyll. When Poole, Jekyll's butler, tells Utterson that Jekyll has disappeared and that Hyde is locked in Jekyll's laboratory, Utterson and Poole break down the door. They find only the body of Hyde and a note from Jekyll requesting that Utterson read Lanyon's letter.

The letter recounts a request by Jekyll to bring some chemicals to him. Hyde appears in Jekyll's laboratory, and Lanyon sees Hyde swallow the chemicals and become transformed into Jekyll. The shock of witnessing the transformation apparently hastened Lanyon's death. When Utterson opens the accompanying letter, from Jekyll, he discovers that Jekyll has been obsessed with a theory of the duality of good and evil in all human beings and that he has discovered a formula that transforms him into his evil side. When he begins to change into Hyde without the chemicals, however, Jekyll despairs, for after he exhausts his supply of chemicals he can no longer transform himself back. As he completes the letter, he changes back to Hyde the last time and kills himself.

Analysis

The Strange Case of Dr. Jekyll and Mr. Hyde is perhaps the purest example in English literature of the use of the double convention to represent the duality of human nature. That Dr. Jekyll represents the conventional and socially acceptable personality and Mr. Hyde the uninhibited and criminal self is the most obvious aspect of Stevenson's story. The final chapter, which presents Jekyll's full statement of the case, makes this theme explicit. In this chapter, Jekyll fully explains, though he does not use the Freudian terminology, that what he has achieved is a split between the id and the superego.

Until Jekyll's letter explains all, Utterson tries to find naturalistic explanations for events that seem to deny such explanations. The tale is a pseudoscientific detective story in which Utterson plays "Seek" to Jekyll's "Hide." The pun on Hyde's name reflects the paradox of his nature, for even as Utterson searches for him, he is hidden within Jekyll. Hyde is always where Jekyll is not, even as he is always, of course, where Jekyll is. What Hyde embodies in the structure of the story is his essentially hidden nature.

A central theme throughout the story, which serves to negate verbal attempts to account for and explain the mystery, is the theme of seeing. In the opening chapter, in describing the trampling of a child, Enfield says, "It sounds like nothing to hear, but it was hellish to see." Although Hyde gives a strong impression of deformity, Enfield cannot specify the nature of the deformity.

Utterson is a "lover of the sane and customary sides of life," but the mystery of Hyde touches his imagination. He believes that if he can only set eyes on Hyde, the mystery will roll away. Even Jekyll himself says, "My position . . . is one of those affairs that cannot be mended by talking." The irony is that all Stevenson has to work with is words; all that Jekyll can use to account for Hyde is words. Even Jekyll's words are hidden, however, as if within nesting Chinese boxes, in the letter within the letter that reveals all.

When Utterson comes to Jekyll's home, he still tries to account for the mystery of Hyde in a naturalistic way, but his explanation cannot account for the enigma at the center of the story—Hyde's ability to hide. In the letter from Lanyon, the only man allowed to see the mysterious transformation, the reader gets an idea of the structural problem of the story: how to project the psychological reality of the double in a story that attempts to be plausible and realistic rather than allegorical. Lanyon's letter says that his soul sickened at what he saw. It is indeed the hidden that can be manifested but not described that haunts the center of this thematically simple but structurally complex tale.

—*Charles E. May*

Stranger in a Strange Land

Valentine Michael Smith, raised by Martians, returns to Earth, is rescued from the World Federation, learns about terrestrial existence, eventually founds a new religion, and is murdered for his beliefs

Author: Robert A. Heinlein (1907-1988)
Genre: Science fiction—cultural exploration
Type of work: Novel
Time of plot: An unspecified time after World War II
Location: Mars and various places in the United States
First published: 1961

The Story

From its fairy tale, "Once upon a time" opening to its equally imaginative ending in a conventionally depicted heaven, *Stranger in a Strange Land* uses an unspecified future time frame to critique contemporary social mores and belief systems. Valentine Michael Smith, the protagonist, is conceived on the first flight to Mars as the son of Dr. Mary Jane Lyle Smith and Captain Michael Brant, who is not her husband. Valentine Michael Smith is discovered twenty-five years later to be the only survivor, the heir of all aboard the craft and, by the Larkin decision, the owner of Mars.

Returned from Mars, where he had been reared by Martians, he is held by the World Federation in a securely guarded hospital room. Suspicious of the federation's intentions toward Smith because of his rights and vast wealth, journalist Ben Caxton induces nurse Gillian Boardman to rescue him. Unknown to Gillian (Jill), Ben is picked up by federation troops. She manages to elude federation police and eventually deposits Smith at the home of Jubal Harshaw, a doctor, lawyer, and all-around cynic of all aspects of contemporary American life. Smith becomes known as Mike within the casual household.

Jubal and his unusual domestic staff are fascinated by Mike's innocence; his supranormal powers of suspended animation, telepathy, and teleportation; and his ability to discorporate when they threaten a "wrongness." Mike attempts to share his Martian concept of "grokking," of becoming able to understand so thoroughly that the observer becomes part of the observed. He forms a deep bond with Jubal's household and ritualizes that bond by "sharing water." Jubal uses his considerable skills to achieve a diplomatic coup that gives Mike the support of the secretary general of the federation, Joseph E. Douglas, and wins Ben Caxton his freedom. With his photographic memory, Mike soon learns much of terrestrial life, though he does not "grok" it all.

Mike attends services at the Fosterite Church of the New Revelation, services that appeal to emotions and to Mike's need to have people grow closer. He furthers his education by working with Jill in various carnivals, trying to understand human nature. On the road, they befriend Patty Pawonski, a devoted Fosterite who is covered with tattoos and drapes herself with a boa constrictor. She, like Mike, is totally loving and totally innocent. She believes that God intends that all human beings be happy and that the way to become happy is to love one another. Still trying to grok what being human means, Mike visits a zoo and finally laughs at the brutality of some monkeys. Realizing both the tragic and the divine in humanity, he finally "groks in fullness."

Having discovered the complete and somewhat contradictory nature of humanity, Mike founds the Church of All Worlds, which teaches the Martian language and the Martian concepts of grokking and growing closer to those disposed to accept. Members of the church's inner circle, Mike's "water brothers," participate in a group marriage and communal economy. Accused of sexual immorality by nonmembers, Mike is denounced and persecuted, especially by the Fosterites, after whom he patterned some of his church's structures. Following Jubal's advice to show, not merely tell, his message, Mike walks alone amid a hostile crowd, proclaiming to its members their own divine natures and capacities. Unable to accept a message of total and unconditional love and of total self-awareness, the crowd attacks him, and he discorporates. His followers escape and plan to continue to promulgate his beliefs. Mike, now in heaven, proceeds to guide events from that vantage point.

Analysis

Stranger in a Strange Land appeared well after Robert Heinlein had established himself as a science-fiction writer. The novel won the 1962 Hugo Award, the third such award Heinlein had received. Much of Heinlein's work prior to this novel, especially from the period from 1947 to 1959, had been science fiction for juvenile readers.

Although many writers acknowledge their debt to Heinlein, the only writer Heinlein claimed as an influence on his own writing was Sinclair Lewis. *Stranger in a Strange Land* certainly replicates Lewis's concerns about the shallowness and complacency of American life, and the corrupt leadership of the Fosterite Church emphasizes some of the misgivings about religious leadership Lewis portrayed in *Elmer Gantry* (1927). As a young science-fiction writer, however, Heinlein, along with many others, was influenced by John W. Campbell, Jr., the editor of *Astounding Science-Fiction,* and Campbell's policy of stressing the sociological implications of changes brought about by advances in technology.

Although the novel has been interpreted and reacted to in different ways, most interpretations and reactions have centered on the sociological implications for change in religion and spirituality, politics and government, economics and the distribution of wealth, social relationships, and lifestyles, all of which the novel highlights. Almost every social institution and structure—the government, the medical establishment, the military, the media, advertising, literary publishing, and especially repressive religious beliefs and practices—comes under fire from Jubal's stinging diatribes. Mike's countercultural beliefs and the liberating and transforming practices of the church he establishes offer an alternative to the alienating religious precepts and the somewhat contradictory, self-delusional, superficially gratifying orientation of American society. Mike's alternative is so idealized that its realization is confined to a small group, whose members will be misunderstood and hounded by an outraged, cynical, threatened majority. The group of disciples that Mike gathers remains intact at the end, and the reader is compelled to grapple with possibilities perhaps never before suspected or imagined.

—*Christine R. Catron*

Swordspoint

> Richard St. Vier and his lover teach the arrogant aristocrats of Riverside that all men live at swordspoint

Author: Ellen Kushner (1955-   )
Genre: Fantasy—high fantasy
Type of work: Novel
Time of plot: An alternative eighteenth century
Location: The Hill, Riverside, and Chartil
First published: 1987

The Story

This fairy tale begins in a time where men wear swords and women carry scented pomanders. Up on the Hill, where the aristocrats live, Richard St. Vier kills two men during a party in Lord Horn's garden. Richard returns to Riverside (the less reputable part of town), where he lives with his lover, the aristocratic former student Alec.

Because of the duel's outcome, Lord Karleigh, one of Lord Halliday's political rivals, goes into hiding at his country estate. While discussing the duel over cups of chocolate, the Duchess Tremontaine flirts with Michael Godwin, a young nobleman, and succeeds in planting the idea that he should become a swordsman. When Richard St. Vier refuses to tutor him, Michael goes to the studio of one-armed swordsman Master Applethorpe. There he discovers he has a talent for swordwork.

Meanwhile, Lord Ferris comes to Riverside in disguise and attempts to hire Richard to kill Lord Halliday, so that Ferris can gain control of the Crescent Council. Alec recognizes Lord Ferris and tries to convince Richard not to take the challenge. Lord Horn, angered that Michael did not succumb to his amorous advances and feeling insulted, tries to hire Richard to challenge Michael. His approach to Richard is so ignoble and lacking in honor that Richard refuses the assignment. Enraged, Lord Horn has Alec kidnapped.

When Richard realizes that his lover is no longer safely under his protection, he carries out Lord Horn's assignment, but when he finds Michael at Master Applethorpe's studio, the master accepts the challenge on Michael's behalf. The fight exhilarates both the combatants and ends with Richard killing Applethorpe. Michael is horrified by the loss of the master, but Duchess Tremontaine takes him as her lover and dispatches him to handle negotiations in a foreign land where his skill with the sword gives him status.

After Alec is released, Richard, on his own volition, kills Lord Horn. Richard is arrested and brought before a small council of nobles, who ask him if he killed Lord Horn on assignment for some patron. When Richard claims that the killing was a matter of his own honor, no one cares, for Richard is not a noble. Lord Ferris subtly lets Richard know that he will sponsor him, which would make Richard beholden to Ferris and no longer his own man. Before Richard has to decide whether to be owned or instead to hang, Alec enters in the clothes of a nobleman.

Alec, it is revealed, is the heir of the Duchess Tremontaine. He had left university and hid himself in Riverside after his friends were persecuted for proving that the earth revolves and the heavens are fixed. Alec claims that according to an old law, this case must be tried before all the nobles, not only the Court of Honour. In front of the larger assembly, Alec forces Lord Ferris to dishonor himself and take the blame for the killing. Lord Ferris is then banished so far from the Hill that he will be unable to continue his political manipulations. Richard is absolved of the crime and returns home. Alec deserts the life of a noble to rejoin his lover, and together they enjoy the close of the fairy tale back in the lusty, frosty, perilous world of Riverside.

Analysis

Ellen Kushner's *Swordspoint* is an elegant, witty, and deliciously nasty tale that concerns itself primarily with codes of honor and highly mannered forms of behavior. Although *Swordspoint* refers to itself as a fairy tale, the book actually started a subgenre called "fantasy-of-manners." The books that fall into this category rely on the manners of a period, whether real or imaginary, as the impetus for their plots. Other books that fall into the fantasy-of-manners category include Delia Sherman's *Through a Brazen Mirror* (1989), a retelling of a folk ballad that includes homosexual overtones and is set in a rigidly structured medieval world; Patricia Wrede and Caroline Stevermer's *Sorcery and Cecilia* (1988), an epistolary Regency romance replete with sorcerous doings; and Steven Brust's *The Phoenix Guards* (1991), which is a thinly disguised parody/homage to Alexandre Dumas's *The Three Musketeers* (1844).

Swordspoint was also the predecessor for a spate of books in which the protagonists are exceedingly casual about their homosexual or bisexual tendencies. These books are not so much political messages about sexuality, as was, for example, Joanna Russ's landmark feminist novel *The Fe-*

male Man (1975). Instead they allow the sexual orientation of the character to simply exist: It is not integral to whether the character is perceived as moral or amoral.

Although in Kushner's world money and political power are still considered to be very important, honor is supposed to reign supreme. Richard St. Vier, who is the viewpoint character and main protagonist of this complex, multi-viewpoint story, believes himself to be an honorable man. Even the horrible way in which he kills Lord Horn (by mutilation and not by a clean thrust through the heart) is designed to show the world that, though he may not be of noble birth, he will deal harshly with those who try to blackmail or own him. In Kushner's world it might well be preferable to hang rather than to lose one's self-respect, or the respect of one's peers.

Swordspoint was Ellen Kushner's first novel, though she was the author of five Choose Your Own Adventure children's books before its publication. It established her as a major talent in the fantasy field. The novel received critical acclaim for its intelligence and for the beautiful use it made of language. It is now considered an unfortunate oversight that it was nominated for no major awards. Kushner's next novel, *Thomas the Rhymer* (1990), was a more conventional fairy tale. It received the World Fantasy Award as well as the Mythopeic Society's Award.

—*Shira Daemon*

Tales from the Flat Earth

> Personified wickedness, death, and madness interfere in the affairs of humans in a mythical "pre-Earth"

Author: Tanith Lee (1947-   )
Genre: Fantasy—high fantasy
Type of work: Novels
Time of plot: Indeterminate, but before formation of current Earth
Location: Various locations on flat "pre-Earth"
First published: *Tales from the Flat Earth: The Lords of Darkness* (1987, as collection); previously published as *Night's Master* (1978), *Death's Master* (1979), and *Delusion's Master* (1981)

The Story

Although first published as separate novels, the Tales from the Flat Earth comprise sets of interlocking short stories. Each book loosely focuses on the action of a "Lord of Darkness"—a personification of a disruptive force such as wickedness, death, or madness—but particular human characters rarely appear in more than one section of each of the books. The result is closer to a set of collected myths than a trilogy, although there is a clear chronological order to the stories. Like myths, they are set in a dream time, a prehistory when the world literally was flat.

Night's Master introduces Azhrarn, the fantastically beautiful "Lord of Demons," whose function is to spread wickedness (most often in the form of social chaos with erotic overtones) and whose realm is the Underearth, a netherworld populated by his demon subjects. He meddles in the lives of humans he finds interesting or attractive, giving them power if he thinks they have disruptive potential or destroying them if they spurn or neglect him. He rears and then loves Sivesh, a attractive youth whom he later lures to destruction for abandoning him. He grants unearthly beauty to Zorayas, a disfigured sorceress who conquers much of the world before being destroyed by her love for herself.

Holding humans in contempt, Azhrarn nevertheless is forced to realize that without them his life would have no purpose. When an indirect consequence of one of his actions gives rise to a disembodied spirit of hatred that threatens to destroy all life on Earth, he takes action. He travels to the overworld to entreat the gods to aid humanity, only to find that they have no interest in it. Exposing himself to sunlight in an act of self-sacrifice, he then destroys the spirit but is almost destroyed himself.

Uhlume, the focus of *Death's Master*, is responsible for seeing that people die, although he does not rule the dead. He performs his tasks with passionless competence. Unlike Azhrarn, he does not meddle with earthly matters unasked but can be entreated—with equally disruptive results. He bargains with Narasen, a warrior queen, allowing her to become pregnant by a dead youth but in return requiring her service after death. Her spirit serves with a kind of competitive spite, ruling Uhlume's realm, the Innerearth, as if it were her own. Her child, Simmu, is abandoned and found by Azhrarn. Reared by demons, he has the power to change his sex.

Simmu encounters Zhirem, a youth who has been made invulnerable. The two fall in love but are separated and estranged by Azhrarn. Simmu has a profound fear of death, and by a rather complex plan hinging on his polymorphism, he manages to steal an elixir of immortality from the gods, which he uses to form a society of Immortals. Zhirem, having an equally intense longing for death, allies himself with Uhlume, whose authority is challenged by the Immortals. After learning sorcery from the inhabitants of the ocean, he contrives to open the city of the Immortals to Uhlume, who immures them for eternity.

Delusion's Master introduces Chuz, who spreads madness and sometimes grants boons to the mad. Chuz's actions result in the construction and fall of a Babel-like tower. Centuries later, nomads have erected a holy city on its ruins, which they visit yearly. Azhrarn, joining the pilgrimage to sow discord, learns that the story of his saving the world has been changed: The pilgrims claim that the gods saved the world from the hideous, bestial Azhrarn. He sets out to destroy the nomads' faith, but in the process he is attracted to a half-celestial woman, Soveh, who agrees to bear his child.

Chuz, attracted to the scene by love's connection with madness as well as by the insanity of the nomads' religion, is insulted by Azhrarn. Angry, he sets the nomads against Soveh and her newborn daughter, Azhriaz. Soveh, refusing to allow Azhriaz to become simply a tool for wickedness, refuses to flee to Azhrarn's realm and is killed. Azhrarn swears enmity to Chuz, and Azhriaz, destined to rule the Flat Earth, is left alone in the ruined city.

Analysis

Tanith Lee is a prolific writer, not only of fantasy but also of science fiction and modern horror. She wrote the Tales from the Flat Earth after a number of other works, most notably _The Birthgrave_ (1975), in the "sword and sorcery" subgenre prevalent in the late 1970's. Although these stories were unusual in their depth of characterization and use of imaginative imagery (especially that involving color), they were somewhat similar to other works in the Robert E. Howard/Edgar Rice Burroughs branch of the genre.

The Tales from the Flat Earth are much more experimental. The humans in the tales are more tragic pawns than heroes. Victory in the world of the Flat Earth simply involves avoiding manipulation or destruction. The Lords of Darkness, being immortal and, within their specializations, all-powerful, also make for poor hero material, especially because the evil they combat is usually of their own devising.

In both content and design, the tales are instead an alternative mythology, exploring the relations between humanity and the divine. Lee makes extensive use of devices from traditional myths and fables. Achilles was made almost invulnerable by immersion in the Styx, and Zhirem was made invulnerable by immersion in a well of fire. Ferazhin, a woman Azhrarn makes from flowers to distract Sivesh, is similar to the Welsh Bloduwedd. Simmu, stealing the elixir of immortality from the gods and being destroyed because of it, is both Prometheus and Gilgamesh. Objects, people, and events frequently come in threes. With the exception of the "Tower of Baybhelu," however, Lee has borrowed only motifs, or threads from myths, rather than recognizable tapestries. The results are familiar enough to resonate strongly for those familiar with mythology but original in overall design and execution. Even Baybhelu, an immediately recognizable allusion to Babel, is reinterpreted, demonstrating the callous spite of the gods toward an enterprise of madness rather than their just punishment for hubris.

Lee's mythology is distinctly irreligious; the gods do not figure prominently. Passionless and ethereal, they regard the earth with a vague contempt when they consider it at all. Their purpose, apparently, is simply to contemplate divine concepts beyond the ken of mortals, and they have no intention of allowing earthly matters, particularly the entreaties of humans, to distract them. Religion is a sham. It is revealing that the most developed treatment of it occurs in _Delusion's Master_, in which the basis of an entire faith is an unintended side effect of one of Chuz's acts.

It is possible to consider Azhrarn, Uhlume, and Chuz as the "real" gods of the mythology, because they have both the powers and the defined roles of more traditional gods. Lee, however, specifically denies them that status. The "Lords of Darkness" definitely fulfill all but the initial creative role of deities, acting as supernatural influences and whimsical agents of change. Like gods, they are not creatures in the literal sense; they simply have come into being out of some cosmic necessity.

If the Masters are gods, then Azhrarn is clearly the most dynamic of them. He is the focus of the three books, appearing in all three and instigating much of the action. He also is the only one to command his own social order, the hierarchical society of demons. Despite his status as a ruler, however, he has strong similarities to Trickster archetypes such as Loki and Coyote. Although he is ostensibly a force for evil, he appears motivated more by lust and a love of disorder. It is interesting that although Lee frequently connects Azhrarn with the terms "wickedness" and "malice," she rarely if ever does so with "evil" itself. His act of self-sacrifice in *Night's Master*, though not altruistic, casts him more as antihero than as enemy. Soveh prophesies that in some future time he will discard his wickedness, having outgrown it. His eroticism sunders him from the divine, as represented by the gods, but renders him "involved" in a way the gods are not and capable, in *Delusion's Master*, of something approximating love. In a sense, Lee may be equating Azhrarn with humanity itself.

Lee followed these three books with two other works set in the Flat Earth milieu: a lengthier novel about the millennial reign of Azhriaz, *Delirium's Mistress* (1986), and a collection of short stories, *Night's Sorceries* (1987). Those two works were collected as *Tales from the Flat Earth: Night's Daughter* (1987).

—*William C. Spruiell*

The Time Machine

The Time Traveler voyages into the future and learns about the evolution of the human race and the ultimate fate of Earth

Author: H(erbert) G(eorge) Wells (1866-1946)
Genre: Science fiction—time travel
Type of work: Novel
Time of plot: The late nineteenth century, 802,701 c.e., and more than thirty million years in the future
Location: The London suburb of Richmond-upon-Thames and the same geographic area in the future
First published: 1895 (serial form, *Science Schools Journal*, April-June, 1888; *National Observer*, March-June, 1894; and *New Review*, January-May, 1895)

The Story

H. G. Wells's fascination with the idea of time travel into the future was first expressed in his story "The Chronic Argonauts" (1888). He wrote at least four other versions before the first book publication of *The Time Machine: An Invention* in 1895.

The Time Machine is a frame narrative. The outer narrator, Hillyer, briefly sets the scene for the much longer inner narrative, the Time Traveler's story about his experiences in the future. Hillyer concludes the narrative with a description of the subsequent disappearance of the Time Traveler and offers a brief speculative epilogue.

Hillyer is one of a group of professional men who regularly gather for dinner and conversation at the Time Traveler's house. One evening, the host explains to his skeptical visitors that he has discovered the principles of time travel. He demonstrates a miniature time machine and shows his visitors an almost-completed full-sized version in his laboratory.

At Hillyer's next visit, the Time Traveler enters, disheveled and limping but eager to tell his visitors about his travels in the far future. He begins by graphically describing the subjective effects of compressing years into moments of time. He then tells them how he arrived in 802,701 c.e. and encountered a race of creatures, evolved from humans, called Eloi. They are small, frail, gentle, childlike vegetarians. He theorizes that humanity has reached a state of contented inactivity in harmony with nature. Soon thereafter, the time machine vanished into the hollow pedestal of a statue, and he realized that this future world harbored disturbing secrets.

Other occurrences made him determined to explore the mysteries beneath the placid surface of the world. He discovered the Morlocks, small, apelike creatures who tended vast machines in dark caverns and visited the surface only during the night. He concluded that the Eloi and Morlocks were the descendants of the capitalist and laborer classes of his own time and that social separation had led to the evolution of two distinct human species. He also learned to his horror that the Morlocks killed and ate Eloi.

He and Weena, an Eloi female whom he had saved from drowning, then visited a ruinous museum in the hope of finding some means of freeing the time machine from the Morlocks. On their return journey, they were surrounded by Morlocks at night in a forest. Weena was lost, but the Time Traveler escaped. He returned to the statue and found the pedestal open. He mounted the time machine as the Morlocks sprang their trap but was able to escape by traveling in time.

H. G. Wells. (Library of Congress)

Curious about Earth's fate, he voyaged further into the future and found that all traces of humanity had vanished. More than thirty million years hence, he found himself on a desolate beach facing a swollen red sun, life having devolved to the point of extinction. Horrified, he returned to his own time.

Hillyer, deeply affected by the Time Traveler's story, returns the next day to find his host about to depart. Invited to wait, he does so, but in vain.

Analysis

The Time Machine is the first of a series of early novels by Wells that profoundly influenced later science fiction. These "scientific romances," as Wells called them (the term "science fiction" not yet having come into circulation), include *The Island of Doctor Moreau* (1896), *The Invisible Man: A Grotesque Romance* (1897), and *The War of the Worlds* (1898). In these works, Wells powerfully expresses many of the anxieties of his time. In the aftermath of Charles Darwin's theory of evolution, science had replaced Scripture as people's chief means of understanding the universe and their place in it.

Although *The Time Machine* introduces the first time machine in science fiction, Wells was not really concerned with plausible methods of time travel. His chief interest was in the social and biological implications of evolutionary theory. Many of his concerns remain valid.

Most of *The Time Machine* deals with the world of the Eloi and the Morlocks. Humanity has split into two subspecies, one of which preys on the other and both of which have degenerated from modern civilized humanity. Wells's main point is that true progress is impossible when society is divided rigidly by class. In an ironic reversal, the Eloi, descendants of the idle rich who figuratively fed off the poor, are now themselves literally devoured by their former victims.

The vision of the end of life on Earth thirty million years in the future was governed by Wells's determination to counter the optimism of nineteenth century ideas about progress. This scientific apocalypse is presented not as a bang but as a whimper, with the Time Traveler watching the last living thing in its death throes.

Given post-Darwinian knowledge about past extinctions of dominant species, there is no reason to be confident about the advancement of humankind. Devolution, or regression to a more primitive state, is as realistic a possibility as evolution to a higher state, and eventual extinction is likely.

Although *The Time Machine* has the force of a realistic work, it often is read as a parable. As such, it has generated a rich variety of critical interpretations. Most critics agree that it is one of the small number of masterpieces in the field of science fiction.

—*Nicholas Ruddick*

Timescape

Scientists in 1998 try to avert a global ecological collapse by send-ing messages back to the year 1963

Author: Gregory Benford (1941-   )
Genre: Science fiction—alternative history
Type of work: Novel
Time of plot: 1998 and an alternative 1960's
Location: Cambridge, England, and La Jolla, California
First published: 1980

The Story

Gregory Benford's novel deals with the interaction of two periods, the end of the millennium and the year 1963. By 1998, ecological catas-trophes such as marine algae blooms have reached such terrifying di-mensions that a group of British scientists attempts, with the help of faster-than-light tachyons, to send a message back in time in order to change the course of history. The recipient is Gordon Bernstein, a phys-ics professor at the University of California, La Jolla, in 1963.

The Cambridge group of the year 1998 is acting under extremely un-favorable conditions, as a general economic slump and the World Coun-cil's focus on managing more immediate crises have dried up funding for this type of research. The novel discusses in detail the political and academic maneuverings necessary to keep the project viable. Personal-ities clash, as scientists such as John Renfrew have to deal with crafty World Council administrators such as Ian Peterson. Both the scientists and the bureaucrats soon realize that establishing contact with the past might be humanity's last chance for survival, as starvation is killing un-told millions and the marine diatom bloom threatens to destroy the global food chain.

The 1960's California plot deals with the academic and personal problems of Bernstein, a New York Jew who is experiencing difficulty in adapting to the California lifestyle. His theories concerning strange mes-sages hidden in the results of the atomic resonance experiment he is con-ducting gradually alienate him from the relatively conservative senior professors in his department. When a simplified version of Bernstein's discoveries is presented on television, he becomes the focal point of numerous pseudo-scientific cranks and loses almost all credibility among most of his colleagues. A message concerning pesticides as the cause of the future diatom bloom is experimentally verified by a biologist, and Bernstein persists in tracking the elusive resonance phenomenon.

The ending of the novel is highly ironic. When every attempt to change the past seems to have failed, a strange coincidence occurs. On November 22, 1963, a high school student is sent to the Dallas School Book Depository to get several copies of a magazine containing an article about Bernstein's controversial theories. He surprises Lee Harvey Oswald in the act of shooting at President John F. Kennedy and tackles him, thus deflecting the crucial shot. Kennedy survives the assassination attempt, and history takes an entirely different, and better, course.

Analysis

Timescape fits within two subgenres of science fiction. One has been variously called alternative time-track fiction and alternative history. This type of fiction deals with the question of what might have been. It explores alternative histories in which, for example, the Protestant Reformation did not take place, Adolf Hitler died as a young man, or the Axis Powers won World War II. The reason for the genre's popularity might lie in its unrestricted ability to imagine historical alternatives; once the reader grants the possibility of alternative histories, almost anything can be presented as plausible. Another explanation for the appeal of alternative histories is that they are not so much concerned with alternative universes as with current society. Alternative history is a means of pointing out the flexibility of history and of denying the existence of an absolute necessity. By imagining alternatives, alternative history novels relativize textbook history and emphasize the possibility for change. Alternative history thus represents a utopian impulse, albeit an ambiguous one, as the way to the alternative universe can often be found only by means of a pseudo-scientific or openly magical device or method. Transtemporal communication, as used in *Timescape*, is one such method. The novel thus also fits within the established subgenre of time travel stories, although in this novel only messages, and not physical objects, travel through time.

Benford's novel stands out from many other representatives of alternative histories, such as Ward Moore's *Bring the Jubilee* (1953) and Jerry Yulsman's *Elleander Morning* (1984), by developing a detailed and scientifically plausible theory of transtemporal communication. Benford, himself a professor of physics, focuses on the avoidance of the so-called grandfather paradox discussed in many time-travel stories. According to this paradox, if someone travels back in time and kills his or her own grandfather, that person thus prevents his or her own existence. As a result, the person could not have traveled back, and therefore the grandfather was not killed, so the person exists after all. The cycle thus continues indefinitely. Benford avoids the paradox by assuming a closed causal loop in which messages received in the past create a feedback effect with the future.

Although Benford's novel certainly belongs to the realm of "hard" science fiction, in which scientific principles are laid out openly and plot development depends on technology, it does not neglect the social and psychological aspects of the story. The narrative device of alternating sections situated in 1998 with chapters about the California of 1963 highlights the drastic degradation of everyday life in the future compared to the almost bucolic Kennedy years. Benford also succeeded in creating a number of extremely convincing characters who function as a counterbalance to the larger historical plot and provide the reader with greater insights into both periods.

In *Timescape*, as in other alternative histories, readers no longer find the familiar outlines of history, that reassuring continuum of realistic fiction. Instead, they are faced with a multiplicity of realities and histories, none of which can claim ontological precedence. The overall effect of alternative history is a radical decentering of the real, which is presented as merely one continuum among an infinite number of possibilities. This loss of a center of reference undercuts the hierarchies of superiority and inferiority that readers apply to different cultures. A transtemporal universe is one in which every custom or value system is only a local one. So far, few of the authors of alternative historical fiction have realized the potential inherent in the genre as fully as Gregory Benford has done in *Timescape*. His craft in constructing this novel was recognized with a 1980 Nebula Award and a 1981 John W. Campbell Memorial Award.

—*Frank Dietz*

The Titus Groan Trilogy

A young earl grows up, defeats his rival, and leaves his home for new adventures in a twentieth century world only to return and then leave again

Author: Mervyn Peake (1911-1968)
Genre: Fantasy—high fantasy
Type of work: Novels
Time of plot: Undefined, on another world
Location: Gormenghast Castle and various locations on another world
First published: *Titus Groan* (1946), *Gormenghast* (1950), *Titus Alone* (1959; 2d ed., 1970), and "Titus Awakes" (*The Mervyn Peake Review*, no. 20, 1990)

The Story

The Titus Groan trilogy was never meant to be a trilogy. Mervyn Peake published the first novel, *Titus Groan*, in 1946. *Gormenghast* appeared in 1950, and in 1959 the first edition of *Titus Alone* came out. Peake was in the early stages of Parkinson's disease and could not edit it. In 1970, a second edition of *Titus Alone* came out, restoring much of what the first editor had left out, and this is the accepted version. The fragmentary, posthumously printed "Titus Awakes" (1990) consists of a few pages and an outline Peake left, showing that he wanted to take Titus into adulthood. This has also been reprinted in the Overlook Press edition of *Titus Alone* (1992).

From the beginning, Peake places readers firmly in his alternative universe, the world of Gormenghast Castle. Titus is the son of Earl Sepulchrave and Countess Gertrude Groan, the brother of Fuchsia, and the nephew of twin aunts, Cora and Clarice. Steerpike, an ambitious kitchen boy, escapes from his master when Titus is born and decides to take over the castle by planning the destruction of the family and its many servants. These include the Masters of Ritual, Sourdust and later his son Barquentine, who preside over castle ceremonies; Flay, the earl's loyal personal valet; Dr. Alfred Prunesquallor, the castle doctor; his unmarried sister, Irma; and Keda, Titus's wet nurse, who has an illegitimate daughter called the Thing.

Steerpike gradually wins over Fuchsia, Cora, Clarice, and Irma. Dr.

Prunesquallor values Steerpike's intelligence, but nobody knows how carefully Steerpike is beginning to consolidate his hold on the castle community. His first major act is to get the aunts to burn Sepulchrave's library as everyone ceremonially gathers there to greet Titus. Steerpike makes sure that he is there to rescue everyone, thus playing a heroic role, but Sourdust dies of smoke inhalation. Sepulchrave goes mad and thinks he is becoming an owl. *Titus Groan* ends with Sepulchrave's death, Flay's expulsion from the castle, Steerpike taking a new job as aide to the new Master of Ritual, Barquentine, and the Earling of Titus, the heir.

Gormenghast opens six years later. Titus is now a schoolboy, with a headmaster, Bellgrove, who eventually marries Irma. Steerpike is increasingly controlling the castle and is responsible for the imprisonment and starvation of Titus's aunts, Cora and Clarice, and the death by fire and drowning of Barquentine. Even when he is badly burned in the process of killing Barquentine, he manages to present himself as a hero, fooling Fuchsia into having feelings for him.

Titus, escaping one day, finds Flay exiled in the woods and asks him to help find out what is happening in the castle. Flay warns Fuchsia anonymously. Flay, Dr. Prunesquallor, and Titus track Steerpike through the castle to a place where Flay has heard strange cries. They find Steerpike playing with the skeletons of the aunts. When they confront him, Steerpike kills Flay and escapes, just as the castle is flooded.

Gertrude wants Titus to do his duty as earl. Titus has seen the Thing (who dies in the woods) and wants to be free of his duties. For him, the rivalry is personal. He finally catches Steerpike and kills him. Titus is now the hero of the castle and, for a year, he enjoys the role. At the end of the novel, however, he leaves Gormenghast Castle in search of freedom.

Titus Alone opens with Titus disoriented and in rags on a riverbank near a city. He is a displaced person with no papers, and people think he is mad when he tells them of his past. He falls through a skylight at a party and Muzzlehatch, an older man who is a rebel and has his own zoo, rescues him. Titus not only ends up in jail and then in court but also has an affair with his legal guardian Juno, Muzzlehatch's former lover. Despite their sexual rivalry, when Titus later destroys a remote-control spying device with a stone, Muzzlehatch helps the boy escape to the Under-River, a place under the river where the displaced go. He later saves Titus and a Holocaust survivor, the Black Rose, from Veil, formerly a guard at a concentration camp.

The price is high. The Black Rose dies at Juno's house, Muzzlehatch's zoo is destroyed, and he goes mad in his quest for the scientist who has killed his animals and runs a death factory. Meanwhile, Titus is picked up by the same scientist's daughter, Cheeta, who raids his brain for stories of his youth, tries to control him, and, failing, decides to hurt him by creating a fake Gormenghast and convincing him that he is dead. She enlists everyone she knows in the charade. Titus, who is on the run from the police, agrees to come to a parodic birthday celebration. When he gets there, so do the police. If it were not for the independent arrival of Muzzlehatch (in search of the scientist whose factory he has destroyed) and Juno (and her new lover, Anchor), Titus's sanity would have been destroyed. Muzzlehatch confronts the scientist, banishes him and his daughter Cheeta, and is killed by the police, who are then killed by friends of Titus.

Juno, Anchor, and Titus then leave. As they fly far away from the party, Titus decides to parachute out in search of Gormenghast. Months later, he finds himself on Gormenghast Mountain. He leaves again, reassured, without going home again.

"Titus Awakes" begins with three pages about the castle and Titus's journey down Gormenghast Mountain. Peake then lists possible encounters Titus could have on his travels.

Analysis

To try to place Peake's novels is difficult because they are both fantastic and psychologically realistic. If fantasy is thought of as the ability to see the world with different eyes or to juxtapose it with an alternative world, then Peake's novels are classic high fantasy. Gormenghast Castle itself looks back to gothic novels such as Horace Walpole's *The Castle of Otranto* (1764) and Matthew G. Lewis's *The Monk* (1796) with its dramatic use of settings and atmosphere, its picturing of tradition and ritual, its endangered heroines and self-aware villain-heroes, its mix of comic and horrific, its fatal pairs of characters, and its games with time and suspense. The characters themselves are like those Charles Dickens created, with their strong visual appeal, but the rich language Peake uses sets them apart from much twentieth century writing in English. Peake deliberately looked for words and names that were different, taking readers into a feast of language, one of the few things not rationed when he began the books. Also, as "Titus Awakes" shows, Peake developed plans over time for a full life of Titus.

When Peake published *Titus Groan* roughly halfway through his career as a visual artist, reviewers were not sure how to place the novel. *Gormenghast*, by contrast, received the Royal Society of Literature Prize in 1951. These first two novels tell a story universal in its themes of the burden of the past, the problem of credibility, the desire for freedom, the growth and development of the hero/heroine, and the risks and fear of change comparable to fantasies such as J. R. R. Tolkien's *The Lord of the Rings* trilogy (1954-1955) and Elizabeth Moon's *The Deed of Paksennarrion* (1992).

Titus Alone, written near the end of Peake's career, is generally seen as dystopian and compared to earlier war-inspired dystopias such as George Orwell's *Nineteen Eighty-Four* (1949). Peake's description of the character Black Rose closely reflects the wording of a poem Peake wrote when he visited the Bergen-Belsen concentration camp in 1945, and his description of the Under-River resembles London during the air raids of World War II. The novel takes readers into a future with death factories and Holocaust survivors. Displaced persons have to remake their worlds, thus linking the novel tangentially to fantasy novels with Holocaust themes such as Jane Yolen's *The Devil's Arithmetic* (1988).

Titus Alone uses devices similar to those of science fiction of the 1950's, in that Peake writes about spyglobes, robotic police, high-rise buildings, and innovative cars and planes. The main focus of the novel—as in the Titus Groan trilogy as a whole—is on Titus coming to terms with what makes him who he is. The novel ends on the optimistic note of a costly new beginning. Peake opens a new world for readers' imaginative enjoyment. Surely this is the essence of fantasy.

—*Tanya Gardiner-Scott*

A Touch of Sturgeon

An eight-story journey from an island with a demoniacally possessed bulldozer to marvels of the uncharted universe and to the magical mysteries of earthling science and psychology

Author: Theodore Sturgeon (Edward Hamilton Waldo, 1918-1985)
Genre: Science fiction—extrapolatory
Type of work: Stories
Time of plot: The present and an age of interplanetary travel
Location: Various locations on Earth and on other planets
First published: 1987

The Story

The eight previously published stories in *A Touch of Sturgeon* vary in plot from the concrete depiction of external action and adventure to the human relationship-centered, inner-world fiction of psychological and moral dilemmas, and to the generalized narration of evolutionary philosophy and mysticism. For example, the 1944 story "Killdozer" is an action story of eight men fighting a bulldozer run amok on an otherwise deserted island. A construction crew arrives to test innovative construction techniques by building an airfield. By destroying a temple-like creation of a prior civilization, they unwittingly release a mysterious, powerful, electromagnetic force. Sentient but destructive, it installs itself in the bulldozer that destroyed its habitat and proceeds brutally to kill the construction workers. After finding the remains of the fifth worker, "all of twelve square feet of him, ground and churned and rolled out into a torn-up patch of earth," two of the remaining workers deduce that the entity is electromagnetic in nature, given its retreat in apparent fear from an active arc welding generator the men have. The men succeed in enticing the bulldozer to a wet area of the beach and, using water as a ground, manage to electrocute the entity.

A different type of plot, used in a majority of the stories, is the psychological and moral dilemma dramatization exemplified in "Slow Sculpture" (1970). A young woman with a malignant tumor is cured by an inventor who, through his bonsai tree, unwittingly teaches her how to accept the complex adjustments involved in survival. In turn, she teaches him how to overcome his hatred of an industrial world so controlled by the capitalistic profit motive that it buys his inventions, such as a pollution-eliminating, fuel-saving automobile muffler, expressly to suppress them. Use of the inventions would conflict with entrenched monetary interests—in the muffler's case, those of oil companies not wanting a reduction in fossil fuel consumption and of automobile companies not wanting to expend funds in altering mass production to install the new device. She also teaches him to overcome his fear of people and to realize that "the way you do something, when people are concerned, is more important than what you do, if you want results."

Less frequently exemplified in the collection is the evolutionary, philosophical, and mystical speculation of "The Golden Helix" (1954). One of only two space travel stories in the volume, it involves humans who are guided to a strangely savage but beautiful planet by a mysterious, God-like, helix-shaped force. Once on the planet, humanity devolves quickly. Reaching their apelike ancestral stage within two generations and no longer able to speak or to create intelligently, the beings nevertheless possess the human essence of love for one another. Eventually, they devolve into plant form. As seeds, they are gathered by the helix-shaped, golden force and scattered throughout various regions of the universe, to re-evolve and bring their special, emotional essence to "worlds worthy of what is human in humanity."

Analysis

The only science adventure story in this collection, "Killdozer," requires little explanation. Typical of Theodore Sturgeon's early fiction and made into a successful 1974 television motion picture, the story lacks the psychological, moral, and philosophical depth of Sturgeon's later work as well as exhibiting an uncharacteristic artistic clumsiness. For example, to disguise the destruction wrought by the bulldozer and explain why knowledge of the malevolent entity never became widespread, Sturgeon resorts to the clichéd *deus ex machina* device of a fortuitously misdirected missile striking the island and destroying the evidence. "Killdozer" nevertheless is an exciting, drama-filled story.

It is in the other stories that artistic creativity and profundity really are displayed, showing that Sturgeon's work merits Samuel R. Delany's praise of it as the single most important body of science fiction by an American writer to date. Following two lesser-quality stories in the volume, "The Golden Helix" shows Sturgeon's maturation as a writer. The story reflects Sturgeon's unusual combination of great admiration for and knowledge of science as well as his deeply felt and powerfully conveyed humanism. The story contains scientific and mystical speculation, reminiscent of the work of Arthur C. Clarke, in its presentation of a golden, God-like force with the helix shape of DNA. Through that symbolism, Sturgeon suggests that God is part of all humans but humanity may need to devolve in order to recapture its emotional and spiritual essence. The story implicitly warns that humanity's scientific and technological emphasis may be making humans nonhuman, a message contained in several other stories.

For example, in "When You're Smiling" (1955), a narrator who labels himself "unhuman" (but not "alien") is justifiably killed because he "enjoys degrading other people and humiliating them" and because he "can't get angry," anger being a fundamental emotional trait of humans still able to care about injustice to other people. Sturgeon thus depicts the danger of objective, emotionally detached science destroying humanity. He does the same in several other stories. In "Slow Sculpture" (1970), an inventor is able to cure cancer but unable to understand easily the humans he hates and fears. In "And Now the News" (1956), a particularly scientific psychiatrist cannot accept the aberrant but balanced, happy lifestyle of a person he is paid to "cure." Curing the patient turns him into a mass murderer. "The Other Celia" (1957) involves a "human" who, in his detached, scientific curiosity, causes the death of a helpless alien and then calmly goes on with his life. Powerful humanism, skillfully integrated into original and insightful science-fiction situations, makes Sturgeon a special science-fiction writer and this collection a special group of stories.

—*John L. Grigsby*

Twenty Thousand Leagues Under the Sea

A mysterious submarine captain undertakes a journey around the world with Professor Aronnax and two companions as prisoners

Author: Jules Verne (1828-1905)

Genre: Science fiction—extrapolatory

Type of work: Novel

Time of plot: 1866-1868

Location: Primarily submarine locations around the globe

First published: *Vingt mille lieus sous les mers* (1870, serial form, 1869-1870; English translation, 1873; substantially revised English edition, 1965)

The Story

Until 1965, most English editions of *Twenty Thousand Leagues Under the Sea* were based on the translation of Mercier Lewis (a pseudonym for Lewis Page Mercier), an English clergyman who cut numerous important passages from the novel and mistranslated many scientific measurements. This caused Jules Verne's reputation as a writer of extrapolative fiction to suffer in English-speaking countries. In 1965, Walter James Miller edited a completely revised and restored English translation; an annotated critical edition appeared in 1976. The Mercier Lewis translation remained in use in some inexpensive paperback editions. Serious readers should make sure that they study the novel in Miller's rendition.

The first-person narrator of the novel, Professor Pierre Aronnax, begins his story by referring back to the year 1866, when a number of ships reported encounters with a mysterious creature in various locations. Intense public speculation about the nature of the creature begins, and when a ship suffers a large hole below the waterline in the latest incident, Aronnax, a French professor of natural history on a scientific expedition in Nebraska, publicly weighs in with his conclusion that the creature is a giant narwhal. He is consequently invited to participate in a government-sponsored hunt for the creature on board the U.S. frigate *Abraham Lincoln*, accompanied by his servant and assistant, Conseil.

After searching the oceans in vain for several months, the *Abraham Lincoln* finally encounters the presumed sea monster off the coast of Japan.

When ace harpooner Ned Land attempts to kill the beast with his weapon, the ship is rammed. Land, Aronnax, and Conseil are thrown into the water. After drifting for hours, they are washed up onto the "monster," which they discover to be a giant submarine. They are taken in by crew members whose language they do not understand and are left to languish.

Nemo, the captain of the *Nautilus*, eventually introduces himself and outlines his terms. Despite having been treated in a hostile manner by their ship, he will spare their lives. Because he and his crew have severed all ties with the rest of humanity, the three shipwrecked companions will be compelled to stay on the *Nautilus*. Aronnax is attracted by this proposal because the submarine is a mobile oceanic research laboratory. Land, a Canadian, is outraged about the loss of his freedom. Conseil unquestioningly follows his master.

The *Nautilus*, driven by electricity and completely self-sufficient, begins a long underwater journey designed to give Aronnax and Verne's readers a partly scientific, partly mythological view of the wonders of the submarine world. After various adventures in the Pacific, including an encounter with aboriginal savages and an underwater hunt, the *Nautilus* crosses from the Red Sea to the Mediterranean by way of a secret oceanic tunnel near Suez. The vessel stops to supply freedom fighters on Crete and visits the site of the sunken continent of Atlantis.

After a nearly disastrous trip to the South Pole beneath the Antarctic icecap and a battle with a giant squid, the three companions witness Nemo attacking a helpless British ship, sending it to the bottom of the ocean with all hands, apparently as an act of vengeance. On previous occasions the three had been drugged for some periods of time to prevent them from observing similar encounters. This barbaric act persuades them to try to escape.

The companions barely manage to get out with their lives before the *Nautilus* is presumably destroyed in a maelstrom off the coast of Norway. Readers of Verne's later novel *The Mysterious Island* (1874-1875) learn that Nemo and the crew survived the disaster. Many of the mysteries of Nemo's background are revealed there as well.

Analysis

Twenty Thousand Leagues Under the Sea is one of a series of fantastic journeys that established Verne's reputation. It is not a fully fledged science-fiction novel but instead a "scientific romance," an adventure novel that does not speculate about the future but provides a series of adventures with the help of only slightly extrapolated scientific gadgets. Verne took his science very seriously and verified all data according to the best sources available to him. This care regrettably was hidden for nearly a hundred years to English-speaking readers by the unreliable Mercier Lewis translation. Indeed, part of the attraction of the novel to contemporaneous readers was its function as a popular scientific primer, particularly regarding the world below the surface of the ocean, which was as mysterious to readers in 1870 as deep space was to later generations. The long, dry catalogs of maritime flora and fauna that modern readers may justifiably skip were fascinating to the author's nonspecialist reading public.

In addition to teaching popular science, Verne also served as a model for future writers of science fiction. His work shows the delight in gadgetry typical of magazine science fiction in the early twentieth century and was among the first to question seriously the role, function, and ownership of scientific inventions. Aronnax holds the "Baconian" view that scientific advances—in this case, the *Nautilus* and its potential— belong to all of humanity and that Nemo has an obligation to publish and make available the results of his research. Nemo represents the classical "Faustian" view, that scientific inventions belong to the inventors (or their sponsors), who can do with them as they please. Nemo uses the submarine for his own personal and selfish ends, albeit with some justification, as readers of *The Mysterious Island* discover.

Twenty Thousand Leagues Under the Sea is a thrilling scientific romance that foreshadows many of the thematic concerns of later popular science fiction. "Good" and "bad" science and scientists, ecological problems, international language projects, colonialism, and human rights are but a few of the topics dealt with in this multifaceted novel.

—*Franz G. Blaha*

The Unconquered Country

Third Child tries to survive in the city of Saprang Song after the displacement of her people and the murder of her family

Author: Geoff Ryman (1951-   )
Genre: Fantasy—cultural exploration
Type of work: Novel
Time of plot: Undefined
Location: The Unconquered Country, primarily the city of Saprang Song
First published: 1986 (shorter version, *Interzone*, 1984)

The Story

The Unconquered Country: A Life History was written in 1982 after Geoff Ryman's trip to Thailand and his secondhand observation of the genocide perpetrated in Kampuchea (then Cambodia) by the Pol Pot regime. The setting of Ryman's book is an analogue to Kampuchea, with distinctive fantastic elements such as villages composed of living, loyal stilt houses and figures on advertising billboards that detach themselves at night to sing jingles to passersby.

Third Child lives in a village of the Unconquered People. The Neighbors, helped by the weapons of the Big Country, have conquered much of the Unconquered Country, but not Third Child's rebel village. She lives a normal life in her village until the age of six. She has a talent for numbers, but only in relation to objects, such as yarrow stalks. The first phase of her cultural unmooring occurs when her teacher forces her to disassociate numbers from their objects and think of them as abstracts.

Third Child's village is attacked by the Neighbors not long after her sixth birthday. The Neighbors use flying creatures called Sharks to destroy her village and slaughter most of the living houses. Many of her family members die, but Third Child's mother manages to spirit her away to the city of Saprang Song.

Saprang Song is a dismal shantytown of cheaply made living houses. Specially created scavenger beasts scour the thoroughfares looking for the dead. In the shadows of this nightmarish setting, Third Child ekes out a meager existence selling her womb as an incubator for industrial products. To earn extra money, she incubates weapons that, in a startling scene representative of the book's uniqueness, gush "suddenly out of her . . . an avalanche of glossy, freckled, dark brown guppies with black, soft eyes and bright rodent smiles full of teeth."

Despite undergoing these degradations to earn a living, Third Child's situation becomes so desperate that she must sell body parts. Standing in line to exchange her left eye for money, Third Child is rescued by a soldier named Crow Dung. He wishes to court her in the way of the Unconquered Country, for he is of the Unconquered People. Crow Dung considers himself a soldier for the Unconquered Country even though he is enlisted in the army of the Neighbors, for he keeps alive the customs of the Unconquered Country against the threat of cultural assimilation.

Third Child persistently resists Crow Dung, for fear that if she loves him, he will die, like all those who have loved her before. Only when he is on his deathbed, dying from a wound suffered in the war, does she permit herself to love him. Following the death of Crow Dung, Third Child finds a baby crow and raises it to maturity, believing that it harbors the spirit of her dead suitor. Thus, she gradually enters a world of ghosts and ghostlike memories.

After several years, the rebel remnants of the Unconquered People free Saprang Song from the Neighbors. The rebels, in the process of winning, have become more bloodthirsty than the Neighbors. Third Child's crow is killed by soldiers, and she is forced by the rebels to leave the city. Third Child begins to see ghosts amid scenes of great carnage. Huddled with refugees on a bridge for three days and nights, Third Child revisits the loved ones of her past and, in their naming, sees her numbers whole again. She then makes the conscious decision to pass over into the spirit world, for everyone she has loved or ever will love is dead. Underlying the devastating sadness of Third Child's personal tragedy is a deeper sorrow for a way of life vanished forever, meshed with the bitterness and confusion of a people caught up in events that seem as unfathomable as the monsoons.

Analysis

A parable of cultural appropriation and the effects of imperialist foreign policy, *The Unconquered Country* won the World Fantasy Award when published in novella form in *Interzone* (1984). Although Ryman had published one novel, *The Warrior Who Carried Life* (1985), prior to *The Unconquered Country*, it was this short novel that catapulted him to the forefront of the fantasy genre. He followed the novel with more complex works, including *The Child Garden* (1989), that share few, if any, similarities with *The Unconquered Country*.

The Unconquered Country clearly is an allegory designed to illuminate the situation in Kampuchea in the 1970's and early 1980's. In Ryman's novel, the Unconquered People represent the indigenous inhabitants of Kampuchea, and the Big Country represents the United States. The rebels who liberate Saprang Song near the novel's end represent the Khmer Rouge.

The blatant sociopolitical content of the novel, coupled with its pseudoscience elements, make it unique in fantasy fiction. Although many fantastical short stories and novels have been set in Asia, few deal with modern situations. For example, Barry Hughart's excellent Master Li series, which includes *Eight Skilled Gentlemen* (1991), dwells heavily on the ancient past of China and its mythologies. A tenuous thematic parallel can be found in the works of Lucius Shepard, particularly his South American novel *Life During Wartime* (1987), but Shepard invariably explores his territory through the eyes of characters foreign to his settings.

A more comfortable, if less useful, connection can be found between many facets of the biological engineering described in *The Unconquered Country* and James Patrick Kelly's novel *Wildlife* (1994). Ryman, however, combines nondidactic political discussion, stylized but psychologically complete characters, and, in the final third of the novel, the spirit world. His is a unique cross-pollination of forms and approaches to those forms.

—Jeff VanderMeer

The Uplift Sequence

Humans have been "uplifting" chimpanzees and dolphins to sapience when they encounter galactic civilizations millions of years old that want to take control of the "wolfling" human race

Author: David Brin (1950-   )
Genre: Science fiction—evolutionary fantasy
Type of work: Novels
Time of plot: Approximately 2245-2445
Location: Earth, Mercury, and the planets Kithrup and Garth
First published: *Sundiver* (1980), *Startide Rising* (1983), and *The Uplift War* (1987)

The Story

David Brin's *Sundiver* introduces readers to his galactic society. Humans have been "uplifting" chimpanzees and dolphins into sentience; that is, through genetic engineering, each successive generation is better able to communicate in the "Anglic" language, use tools, and interact with humans.

Dr. Jacob Alvarez Demwa, the protagonist, is a scientist assigned to the Uplift Project, working mainly with dolphins. He also knows quite a few "Eatees" (ETs, or extraterrestrials). When he was a young boy, a spaceship from Earth encountered alien life, and Earth was thrust into a galactic society billions of years old, a society that revolves around "patron-client" relationships. Each sentient race was uplifted by an older race in a tradition stretching back to the mystical Progenitors, who have since departed for parts unknown. The uplift process is both altruistic and brutally practical, because most of the older races "indenture" their newly uplifted species as slaves. Humankind is considered a "wolfling" or upstart species because of its claim to have come to sentience by itself, a notion at which the galactics sneer, viewing it as impossible. They state instead that its patrons deserted humanity. The assorted ETs are also contemptuous of the way humans treat their "client" species, as partners rather than as slaves.

Demwa realizes that there are problems when a Kanten (a race resembling seven-foot-tall broccoli) diplomat named Fagin calls on him, yet he cannot resist seeing his old friend again. At a meeting in Baja California,

Demwa is convinced to join a scientific expedition called the Sundiver Project. A group of scientists and militia led by Dr. Dwayne Kepler and Commander Helené deSilva have discovered what appears to be sentient life in the Sun. The race may be humanity's lost patrons. Other races are dubious of the claim. Bubbacub, a Pila librarian assigned to the La Paz Branch of the Galactic Library on Earth, together with his client Culla, a Pring, accompany the group to discredit it, even resorting to murdering a chimpanzee scientist. Woven throughout the story are subplots involving possible treachery by Pierre LaRoque, a human reporter, and Dr. Millie Martine, a human psychiatrist.

Startide Rising takes place about two hundred years following the events in *Sundiver*. A dolphin-crewed ship called *Streaker* has eluded capture by the galactics and has crashed onto the watery planet Kithrup. The dolphins attempt to repair their craft in order to escape again. They are fleeing because they have stumbled across a derelict fleet of ships, each the size of a planet, containing the mummified bodies of an ancient sentient race. Each of the galactic civilizations believes that these may be the Progenitors, and each is determined to capture the *Streaker* and its crew in order to get the information.

Strife between dolphins and chimpanzees, and even within the dolphin community, abounds in this book. Adding stress are Dr. Ignacio Metz's "special" species, dolphins illegally grafted with other genes, including one who is part-orca, a natural enemy of dolphins. Dr. Gillian Baskin and Thomas Orley, two human Terragens Council members, together with their human and dolphin allies, try to hold off this interstellar mutiny and return to Earth with their prize.

The Uplift War tells of the ramifications following the story begun in *Startide Rising*. Earth, with its allies the Tymbrimi and their colony worlds, are besieged by alien armadas. Other allies, such as the Synthians, remain undecided or neutral in the universe-spanning conflict. The backwater human planet of Garth is invaded by the Gubru, a birdlike race. When the human population is rendered hostage or dead by a poisonous gas, Garth's chimpanzee population must persevere. One human, Robert Oneagle, son of the planetary coordinator, remains at large. Rebel forces are led by Robert; his consort, Athaclena, daughter of the Tymbrimi ambassador, Uthacalthing; and various chimps including Fiben Bolger and Dr. Gailet Jones.

Uthacalthing and the Thenannin ambassador, Gault, escape as well. The joke-loving Tymbrimi try to make everyone believe there are "Garthlings," mythical presentient beings, loose on the planet. What they do not know is that human and chimpanzee scientists have brought gorillas to the planet in order to uplift them, an act forbidden by galactic law. Although Thenannin are officially at war with humans and Tymbrimi, Gault and Uthacalthing develop a friendship that leads to an alliance with the hulking race.

Analysis

Brin meshes the extrapolation of current or projected scientific knowledge to its possible conclusions with space operatic themes (pioneered by such writers as Edgar Rice Burroughs, Olaf Stapledon, and Jack Williamson) such as galactic struggle and interactions between species. He has noted that he tries "to make use of the scientific thrills this century keeps dropping in our laps." Brin's visions capture the interest of readers and foreshadow the imaginative future of technology. In the Uplift Sequence, one new technology is the knowledge and ability to provide terrestrial animal species with advanced intelligence, or to "uplift" dolphins or chimpanzees, among others, to sentience. Brin projected further volumes to supplement the first three.

Stretching back into prehistory, humans have felt themselves to be part of nature. Native Americans and South Americans worshiped spirits of animals and natural elements, and almost every religious mythos has a sun god or a rain god. Humans have also felt separated from nature. The very ability to ponder philosophical quandaries seems to take humans away from the animals with whom many crave affinity. People find comfort in picturing animals as being like people, giving them their own cultures, languages, customs, and morals. This anthropomorphism is evident in literature and entertainment throughout history. Images of animals that are clothed, bipedal, working and talking, having families, and living in houses abound from myths and legends to modern cartoons and comic books, from books such as *Aesop's Fables* (1484) and Kenneth Grahame's *The Wind in the Willows* (1908) to television and film creations such as Jim Henson's Muppets and Walt Disney's anthropomorphic creatures.

Like other writers before him, Brin depicts large "space opera" themes such as conquest, freedom, and a cosmic struggle carrying the protagonists to the outer limits of space to face unknown dangers. Brin's series does not mimic earlier novels' naïve optimism and human chauvinism in relation to humanity's place in the future. In these earlier novels, humans from a pre-adolescent Earth confidently and quickly establish "galactic empires." Examples include Isaac Asimov's Foundation series, E. E. "Doc" Smith's Lensman and Skylark series, and James Blish's *Cities in Flight* (1970), along with stories by such authors as Robert A. Heinlein,

Edmond Hamilton, C. L. Moore, A. E. van Vogt, and Poul Anderson. Brin in fact takes a friendly jab in *Startide Rising* at such novels, having a character describe them as "ancient space-romances from pre-Contact days."

Other writers portrayed a perhaps more egalitarian but still human-dominated universe. "The United Federation of Planets" of the *Star Trek* universe, for example, does not necessarily subjugate nonhuman races, but at the very least humans overshadow such older, wiser races as Vulcans. In A. C. Crispin's *StarBridge* books, humans, new to galactic society, quickly earn important positions among "The Cooperative League of Systems," surpassing the elder Mizari and Drnian races. Brin instead depicts spacefaring humans as new kids on the block, unable to compete with most older, more-advanced alien races. Humans in general are looked upon as primitive; they lack the technological know-how of the elder races, so they usually resort to cunning to outwit their more powerful enemies. This tenacity and determination are remarked upon by the other races.

However bleak his picture seems, Brin is not completely pessimistic. He depicts the possibility of reaching out and overcoming obstacles dividing races or species. One example is in *Startide Rising*, when Tom Orley and a dying Thenannin engage in conversation that, if not friendly, is at least neutral. Humans are reaching out in myriad ways to grasp the future projected in Brin's series. Communication with dolphins, whales, apes, and other higher mammals is being pursued, and genetic alteration of animals to give them sentient intelligence is well into its infant stages. Even cloning of human DNA is in progress.

Brin states in the postscript to *Startide Rising* that "it may happen that some of our fellow mammals will one day be our partners." It is a reassuring thought that the chasm separating humans from the natural world might be bridged someday and that humans might obtain the means, as did Doctor Doolittle, to "talk to the animals."

—*Daryl F. Mallett*

VALIS

The fictional Horselover Fat and the author Philip K. Dick—who may or may not be the same person—suffer delusions and revelations in a bizarre look at 1970's California

Author: Philip K. Dick (1928-1982)
Genre: Science fiction—inner space
Type of work: Novel
Time of plot: 1970's
Location: California
First published: 1980

The Story

VALIS begins with the attempted suicide of Horselover Fat's friend Gloria, offered in a standard third-person point of view. Almost immediately, however, a first-person narrator interrupts to declare, "I am Horselover Fat, and I am telling this in the third person to gain much-needed objectivity." This first-person narrator, named Philip K. Dick, is for all intents and purposes identical to the author of the book. As a result of a mystical experience involving the Christian fish symbol and a beam of pink light, Fat is convinced that the world as he sees it—that is, California in 1974—is in fact an illusion laid over Imperial Rome. This illusion is the product of an evil entity opposed by VALIS, the Vast Active Living Intelligence System, which—depending on Fat's mood and who he is talking to—is either an alien intelligence, an immensely sophisticated mechanism, or an incarnation of pure living information.

Halfway through the book, the character Philip K. Dick has a dream that convinces him that much of what Fat says, if not strictly true, is at least not crazy. Even though Fat proposes that he is a sort of superimposition of a man who lived during the time of Jesus Christ and that through this man benevolent aliens have begun to communicate with him, Dick begins to take him seriously enough to argue that what Fat is seeing as a divine being is in fact himself in the distant future. Shortly after this, the three (four) of them go to a movie called *Valis*, which includes an experience much like Fat's pink-beam epiphany. Believing that the film has encoded a message to him, Fat goes looking for its maker, whose daughter is an incarnation of Sophia, or wisdom. In her presence Fat and Dick are healed and made whole. They become one again.

Sophia dies shortly after this, and Fat separates from Dick once again. Fat searches for a new savior he believes is about to be born into the world. He comes back with the words KING FELIX, which Dick then sees in a television commercial. This provokes Fat to go searching again, and Dick himself remains in front of the television, watching carefully for the next signal from VALIS.

Analysis

A work utterly unlike any other in science fiction, *VALIS* is at once auto-biography, cosmological speculation, post-1960's reminiscence, alien-invasion story, and far-ranging inquiry into the nature of God and the divinity of the individual. It can be read as a science-fiction novel or as a classic unreliable-narrator story, and part of the book's greatness lies in its ability to exist as both at once. Its unreliable narrator displaces his unreliability, and the book's other characters address Fat (whose name is the English "translation" of the Greek "Philip" and the German "dick") and Dick as two separate characters until they are reunited in the presence of Sophia. Dick the character presents himself as the rational voice, contrasted with Fat; however, it is Dick who proposes the time-travel solution to Fat's conundrum, and it is Dick who spends his time studying television commercials for messages from the divine. Finally, it is Dick who is telling a story in which an alienated part of his mind takes the form of a man named Horselover Fat. Horselover Fat's theorizing is taken directly from a series of experiences Dick himself had in February and March of 1974. Other borrowings from Dick's novels include the character of Ferris F. Fremount in the *Valis* film, Fremount being Dick's name for the Richard Nixon figure who appears in some of Dick's work from the 1970's.

VALIS is in a sense a gloss on Dick's bleak 1970's novels *A Scanner Darkly* and *Flow My Tears, the Policeman Said*, in which Dick the character explains what Dick the author was doing—which makes the fictionalization of Dick the author's experiences a disorienting experience for the reader. Layered on top of this, the deranged cosmological speculations and the pulpy three-eyed aliens leave the reader in Fat's position, which is Dick's position. The novel continually turns in on itself in this way, rudely interrogating its own assumptions, and somehow in the end salvaging something from the emotional and spiritual wreckage of Horselover Fat. *VALIS* is an unflinching—and often surprisingly funny—look at Dick's own struggles with sanity, and it is a tribute to the writer that he created from his pain one of the great religious novels of the century.

—*Alex Irvine*

Vampire Chronicles

The terrestrial and extraterrestrial adventures of the vampire Lestat and his companions

Author: Anne Rice (1941-   )
Genre: Fantasy—mythological
Type of work: Novels
Time of plot: The mid-eighteenth century to the present
Location: France, the United States, England, Barbados, Jerusalem, Hell, Heaven, Imperial Rome, and Renaissance Europe
First published: *Interview with the Vampire* (1976), *The Vampire Lestat* (1985), *The Queen of the Damned* (1988), *The Tale of the Body Thief* (1992), *Memnoch the Devil* (1995), *Pandora* (1998), *The Vampire Armand* (1998), *Vittorio the Vampire* (1999), Merrick (2000), and *Blood and Gold* (2001)

The Story

The Vampire Chronicles shift in time and place from Lestat's vampire life in nineteenth century New Orleans to his prevampire days in eighteenth century rural France to his escapades in twentieth century United States. Lestat wants to know how vampires were created, mourns the loss of his mortal life, deplores but also adores his killing and bloodsucking, and explores the existence of good and evil. Searching for soulmates, he creates new vampires, but their strong wills oppose his own. Following *Memnoch the Devil*, Rice explores the lives of vampires who have been affected by Lestat's story; as they recount their tales, they continue Lestat's philosophical speculations on the purpose and value of vampire existence.

The first novel in the series, *Interview with the Vampire* introduces Louis, a vampire Lestat has created, telling his life story to a journalist in late twentieth century San Francisco. Louis grieves for his mortal life and describes the transformation of the child Claudia into Lestat and Louis's vampire progeny. Trapped forever in a child's body, Claudia attempts to destroy Lestat—an act that ultimately leads to her own destruction by Armand's vampire coven in Paris. By the end of Louis's tale, the young reporter Daniel begs to be made a vampire. Louis refuses, shocked that his story—meant to reveal the agony of his life—should seduce a mortal.

In *The Vampire Lestat*, Lestat describes his search for Marius, one of the oldest vampires, who may know the secret of the origins of vampirism. Like Louis's narrative, Lestat's story is published as a book—this time in an attempt to put right several of Louis's errors. Lestat, like Rice's vampire narrators to follow, is very much aware of the Vampire Chronicles. Ever the show-off, Lestat revels in publicity and uses his first book to launch a brief career as a rock star, which ends when his fellow vampires converge in an abortive attempt to destroy him for revealing their secrets.

In *The Queen of the Damned*, Lestat becomes the consort of Akasha, the Egyptian ruler who became the mother of all vampires when a demon invaded her body, giving her immortality at the price of drinking human blood. Marius has kept Akasha intact for more than two thousand years, but it is Lestat's energetic wooing that brings her out of her long stupor. She is determined to rid the world of men, whose violence has made them unfit to survive. Having drunk her blood and fallen madly in love with her, Lestat nevertheless struggles against her project and is saved from her wrath by Maharet and Mekare, twin witches who destroy Akasha.

When *The Tale of the Body Thief* opens, Lestat is suffering from the loss of Akasha, his estrangement from Louis, and his separation from his mother, the vampire Gabrielle. When the occult body-thief Raglan James offers Lestat a day of adventure in a mortal body in exchange for his vampire flesh, Lestat agrees. James absconds with Lestat's body, which Lestat is able to repossess only with the help of his friend David Talbot, head of the Talamasca, a society that observes and records the truth about the occult. In an act of love and violence, Lestat helps the aged David take over the body of James, then forces David to become a vampire.

In *Memnoch the Devil*, a terrified Lestat discovers that he is being stalked by Memnoch (Satan), who invites Lestat to become his lieutenant—not to gather souls for Hell, but to redeem those awaiting enlightenment and salvation. Memnoch argues that he offers God a grander creation, a purer vision of humankind. Memnoch's power to defy time dazzles Lestat, but he repudiates Memnoch's proposition and manages to escape with a holy relic, the Veil of Veronica, said to possess the imprint of the face of Jesus Christ. Following his revelations, Lestat lies in a stupor contemplating the meaning of the universe while other vampires visit him with the devotion of pilgrims attending a shrine.

With *Pandora*, a new segment of the Chronicles begins. Lestat's fledgling David, true to his former scholarly calling, urges other vampires to record their lives. The daughter of a Roman senator in the days of Augustus and Tiberius, Pandora flees to Antioch when her younger brother betrays the family. Nightmares about a weeping queen and her burnt, blood-drinking offspring lead Pandora to the Temple of Isis, where Marius reveals the truth about Queen Akasha. Fighting a burnt vampire, Pandora lies near death until Marius transforms her. Though Pandora is radiant with her new existence and wishes to reinstate the worship of Isis/Akasha, Marius grieves that her mortal life has been thrown away for "a degraded mystery."

In *The Vampire Armand*, Armand is rescued from slavery by Marius. Falling in love with his savior, Armand begs to share his life as a companion soul. Marius attempts to dissuade his protégé by shocking him with a murderous banquet, but when Armand is poisoned, Marius transforms him to save his life. Soon after, rogue vampires known as the Children of Darkness burn Marius's home. Believing his lover dead, the despairing Armand joins the coven, not to see Marius again until Lestat brings back the Veil. Overcome with emotion at the miracle, Armand casts himself into the sun, but the strength of centuries sustains him until he is rescued by two humans. When Marius makes vampires of the two as a gift, Armand realizes how far their values have diverged.

In *Vittorio the Vampire*, Vittorio witnesses the massacre of his family by vampires. His quest for vengeance takes him to Santa Maddalana, where the beautiful vampire Ursula seduces him, begging him to forget his quest and live. Instead, Vittorio is captured by the vampire Court of the Ruby Grail, and Ursula pleads for his life and ultimately effects his release. Vittorio enlists the aid of two guardian angels and returns to slay the vampires; but, faced with the prospect of murdering Ursula, Vittorio begs for her soul and the chance to redeem her. Weeping, the angels leave him, and Ursula tricks him into drinking her blood. Fallen for the sake of love, Vittorio's punishment is to see the beautiful light of each human soul flickering and dying as he kills.

In *Merrick*, chronicler David Talbot asks Merrick, a witch whom he had loved and guided in his former life, to contact the spirit of Claudia so that Louis may find peace. Merrick uses Louis's blood to call the vampire child's angry spirit. Claudia claims to hate Louis and to be whirling in the torment of nothingness. Though Merrick assures him that spirits often lie, the grief-stricken Louis determines to end his own life—but not before transforming Merrick, whom he loves. Lestat rouses from his slumber to restore Louis with his powerful blood. Though still grieving, Louis finally finds courage to embrace the beauty of his newly enhanced vampire senses.

Analysis

The Vampire Chronicles rejuvenate the gothic romance. Like earlier heroes, Lestat is a nobleman of surpassing courage and physical attractiveness, an insatiably curious youth who follows his desires no matter the risk to himself and others. Indeed, all of Rice's vampires are young and beautiful, suffering from varying degrees of angst in rich settings that mirror the atmosphere of earlier works. In *Vittorio the Vampire*, Rice even returns to the classic location so popular in the early gothics—the wild mountain strongholds of Renaissance Italy.

Lestat's eroticism partakes of the gothic tradition. He finds himself attracted to both men and women. Deeply devoted to his mother, Gabrielle, he takes her as his vampire lover. Incestuous and homoerotic elements that are veiled in eighteenth and nineteenth century gothic fiction explode in Rice's Chronicles, as the characters liberally exchange blood with one another. The sensuality of the vampires also takes the androgyny of the gothic one step further; for vampires, the "lower organs" no longer matter, and thus gender becomes unimportant. Indeed, Pandora asserts that "the greatest part of our gift" is "freedom from the confines of male, female!"

Rice's reliance on the convention of the handsome and noble young hero or heroine takes on an ironic cast, as many of her vampires comment on the importance of youth and good looks. Vampires are apparently suckers for a pretty face: Vittorio describes himself as "A beautiful boy for the time. I wouldn't be alive now if I hadn't been." Finding an alternate justification for the same prejudice, the Children of Darkness believe that the transformation of the beautiful into vampires is more pleasing to a just God. It is beauty that attracts notice; it is beauty that makes surviving the ages palatable.

Rice offers extraordinary details about the times and cultures of her vampires, making her work into historical fiction. When her vampires turn their eyes to the twentieth century, it is a world freshly conceived. Lestat marvels at how hygienically even the poor now live, in contrast to the incredible squalor of their own privileged lives in earlier centuries, and describes his fascination with computers and fax machines. His sociological commentary enhances the realism of his story, reinforcing the sense that he has indeed lived for more than two hundred years.

Throughout the Chronicles, Rice's vampires are tormented by their need to understand their place in a moral and spiritual universe. Their philosophical battles concern such issues as whether vampires have souls, and if they do, whether those souls can be redeemed; how much humanity remains in a vampire, and whether vampires are primarily human or monstrous; what a vampire's place may be in the dichotomy between good and evil, and the importance of serving each respective side; and whether vampirism ought to be viewed as a curse or a blessing. Contrary to many of the gothic stereotypes about vampires, Vittorio believes that Ursula has a human heart that can be taught to repent. Marius coaches Armand that he "will come to know that you are more human than monster" and that "all that is noble in you derives from your humanity." Pandora herself finds hope in the evolution of the human conscience and the miracle of reason in the face of despair. Vittorio has seen angels, and has proof of the divinity of the human soul; but with every act of his continued existence, he knows the agony of extinguishing human life. His glory and his punishment go hand in hand.

—*Carl Rollyson*
—*Updated by C. A. Gardner*

The Vampire Tapestry

Anthropologist and vampire Dr. Edward Weyland confronts vital challenges to his freedom and existence in the complex world of twentieth century America

Author: Suzy McKee Charnas (1939-   )
Genre: Fantasy—feminist
Type of work: Novel
Time of plot: The 1970's
Location: New York City and Santa Fe, New Mexico
First published: 1980 (part 1, "The Ancient Mind at Work," *Omni*, February, 1979)

The Story

The Vampire Tapestry is a sequential grouping of five periods, related in linked stories, in the life of Dr. Edward Weyland, a vampire masquerading as an anthropologist and academician. Part 1, "The Ancient Mind at Work," depicts Weyland as a sexually attractive vampire and wealthy academician involved with a sleep research center at Cayslin College, where he preys on his experimental subjects. Katje de Groot, an expatriate South African Boer and widow of a Cayslin professor, discovers that Weyland is a vampire. Mrs. de Groot ignores race and gender politics until a series of rapes takes place on campus. She identifies Weyland as the rapist but understands him, saying "But I am myself a hunter!" She shoots him. Weyland is a vampire of a different sort: He can be injured by a bullet. He is a natural rather than a supernatural being.

In part 2, "The Land of Lost Content," Weyland falls into the hands of petty criminals Roger and Mark, who work with a satanist, Reese. The vampire is a victim, placed on display. Reese examines Weyland's mouth and determines that there are no fangs but a stinger on the underside of the tongue that "probably erects itself at the prospect of dinner, makes the puncture through which he sucks blood, then folds back out of sight again." Powerless, Weyland is forced to feed in public for the voyeuristic delight of Reese's followers. Finally, Mark allows Weyland to feed on him, saving Weyland from Reese's exploitation and freeing the vampire.

In part 3, "The Unicorn Tapestry," Weyland attempts to restore his academic position by agreeing to psychoanalysis by Floria Landauer in an attempt to cure the "delusion" that he is a vampire. Through his analyst, Weyland comes to discover empathy for humans, whom he previously had regarded merely as a source of sustenance. Weyland's encounters with Landauer are the contemporary equivalent of meeting "screaming peasants with torches." Although the peasants of the past would have destroyed him physically, the analyst instead breaks down the distance between the vampire and his prey, destroying his identity and subjectivity. Although Landauer is aware that Weyland is a vampire, he does not kill her but moves on with newfound empathy.

In part 4, "A Musical Interlude," Weyland moves to a New Mexico university. At a performance of the Giacomo Puccini opera *Tosca* Weyland becomes intertwined with another Floria, a character in the opera. He identifies himself with the character Scarpia. The music arouses the vampire's blood lust. He resents the opera's ability to touch him, to make him one of its "prey." Weyland begins to kill needlessly and indiscriminately.

Finally, in part 5, "The Last of Dr. Weyland," the vampire is discovered by Dorothea, an artist who recognizes the insubstantiality of his disguise. Weyland has a final encounter with Reese, whom he kills. Threatened with exposure, he decides to end his masquerade as Weyland. The vampire drifts off to sleep, not destroyed but rendered harmless.

Analysis

In the same way that Bram Stoker's *Dracula* (1897) can be read as a patriarchal response to the "New Woman" movement of the 1890's, so can Suzy McKee Charnas's *The Vampire Tapestry* be read as a response to the women's movement of the 1970's and 1980's. Charnas uses literary vampire conventions established by Stoker (such as the vampire's sexual attractiveness, pride, and sense of prey as little more than cattle) with more modern conventions (skepticism about the existence of vampires) for ideological purposes, allowing *The Vampire Tapestry* to function as a text about gender relationships and patriarchal repressive gender ideology.

Weyland is presented as a complex, vulnerable human being who undergoes a series of changes through each of the novel's five parts. In part 1, Mrs. de Groot identifies the power and strength of the vampire—an outsider—with the power and strength of a black woman in a repressive society, allowing her to defend herself. In vanquishing Weyland, she refuses her conventional role as woman/victim and becomes woman/hunter.

In part 2, the erotic element of the vampire is foregrounded. Weyland is placed on display and manhandled by Reese, who exposes the vampire's bloodsucking apparatus in a scene that can be read as a displaced representation of the exposure of female genitalia to male gaze, which characterizes the gender power relationships of contemporary society. Powerless, Weyland—like victimized women—is motivated by fear, making this part an exploration of the subject-object relationships of gender politics.

In part 3, Weyland is subjected to psychoanalysis, and the function of gender difference is explored. The psychologist "dismembers" Weyland emotionally. Weyland's victims are identified as those without power in the patriarchy, gay men and women, exposing the collusion of patriarchal ideology in repression of these groups. When Landauer and Weyland make love, a fundamental change in Weyland occurs: He comes to empathize with humanity. With this newfound empathy, in part 4 Weyland sees his murderous tendencies erupt "without need, without hunger" during a performance of *Tosca*. Weyland ascribes his response to the artwork as an indication of his humanness. Weyland's fear of the subversive effect of the artwork is a cry of the patriarchal ideology under attack.

Finally, in part 5, Weyland, a hunter, an exploiter, a manipulator, and a rationalist—a patriarch—is troubled by his own identity. His difference, or "otherness," is recognized by another woman, who confirms the loss of his cohesive, contrived identity fostered by years of patriarchal thought. Weyland retreats into hibernation, rendered harmless. His identity as a member of the patriarchy is destroyed by women who use the strategies of the patriarchy.

—*Thomas D. Petitjean, Jr.*

The War of the Worlds

Creatures from Mars invade southern England

Author: H(erbert) G(eorge) Wells (1866-1946)
Genre: Science fiction—invasion story
Type of work: Novel
Time of plot: The early twentieth century
Location: London, England, and the county of Surrey
First published: 1898 (serial form, 1897)

The Story

The story is told retrospectively by an unnamed narrator, an educated, philosophically trained man who witnessed many of the events he describes and reports them as recent history. The first signs of an invasion from Mars come when astronomers note a series of spectacular explosions on the planet. Experts, however, think they were caused by meteorites or volcanic eruptions; no one suspects any danger. Only later does it become known that climatic changes steadily had made Mars less hospitable for its inhabitants, and they were looking to Earth as their only refuge. The explosions were the firing of ten projectiles, each containing a small Martian invasion force, at Earth.

The first cylinder-shaped projectile lands southwest of London, on a summer night. By morning, it has attracted a crowd of curious onlookers. In the early evening, the cylinder opens to reveal a grotesque, octopus-like figure the size of a bear, its body glistening like wet leather. The crowd retreats in shock. By dusk, an official deputation arrives, waving a white flag. The authorities have decided that the Martians are intelligent creatures and wish to communicate with them. A devastating beam of heat shoots out from the invaders' cylinder, destroying everything it touches. Forty people lie dead, and the narrator flees in terror.

This sets the pattern for the next few days. The Martians appear to be unstoppable. They construct huge tripod-shaped machines, higher than a house, within which they sit, covered by a hood. The machines stride across the country, causing death and destruction wherever they go, and military might is useless against them. The narrator manages to escape the deadly heat ray by diving into a river. He meets a curate who believes that the day of judgment has come.

The narrative switches to London as the narrator tells of the experiences of his brother. News is slow to reach the capital city, but when it does, it is grave: The Martians are advancing on London and are releasing a poisonous black smoke that suffocates everything in its path. There is no defense against it. The entire population of London flees northward in a stampede of six million panic-stricken people. The Martians take possession of the city, although they also suffer losses: A warship rams and kills one Martian who has waded out to sea, and another Martian is killed when the same ship explodes after being struck by the heat ray.

The narrator hides with the curate in an empty house to escape the black smoke. Trapped for fifteen days by the presence of Martians outside, he observes them at work and learns to his horror that they feed on human blood. The curate loses his mind, and in a struggle, the narrator kills him. When he emerges from the house, he realizes that humanity's rule over Earth has ended, and he encounters an artilleryman who has visionary ideas about what people must now do to survive.

The narrator makes his way to the deserted London, where he comes on a Martian emitting a strange crying sound. He then stumbles on the remains of a dead Martian; he soon finds fifty more. The Martians have died because they have no resistance to Earth's bacteria. The joyful news is telegraphed across the world, and relief comes to the stricken city.

Analysis

The War of the Worlds is one of a group of novels by H. G. Wells that are classified as scientific romances. The others are *The Time Machine* (1895), *The Island of Dr. Moreau* (1896), *The Invisible Man* (1897), and *The First Men in the Moon* (1901).

At the end of the nineteenth century, there was much scientific and popular speculation about the possibility of life on Mars. Astronomer Percival Lowell, for example, proposed in 1896 that the canals on Mars were the work of intelligent beings. Wells was acquainted with such theories and published nonfiction articles that discussed them. He also used the idea of intelligent life elsewhere to write a story that would shatter the Victorian belief in the inevitability of progress and the benevolence of the process of evolution.

At the beginning of the novel, humanity goes about its business completely self-assured of its mastery of nature and utterly ignorant of anything that might threaten it. The superior place occupied by humans in the chain of being is usurped in a matter of days. To make the point, Wells draws frequent analogies between how the Martians must regard humans and how humans regard lower life-forms. The Martians must have studied humanity as human scientists might study minute organisms under a microscope, and the aliens take as much notice of human attempts to communicate with them as humans do to the lowing of a cow. Ants, bees, monkeys, and rabbits also are invoked to emphasize the shifting order of nature. The point is clear: Evolution, the process of natural selection, does not inevitably favor humankind.

In this cosmic pessimism, Wells was influenced heavily by the theories of T. H. Huxley, whose lectures Wells attended in 1884. There is no doubt that although the novel ends with the overthrow of the Martians, it is predominantly pessimistic. Not only is all of humanity's technological knowledge and military power useless against the Martians, but so is its edifice of spiritual knowledge: The curate is the most pathetic character in the book. Weak and cowardly, he clings to the Scriptures, which offer neither explanation nor solace for humanity's plight. Even though humanity survives this particular catastrophe, in time, as Earth slowly decays, it will face the same crisis that the Martians had faced and that prompted their invasion of Earth. The only solace to be had from the war is the knowledge that too much confidence in the future leads to decadence. Humankind perpetually must be ready for the worst.

—*Bryan Aubrey*

War with the Newts

A sea captain convinces newts to join him in a business partner-
ship, but they rebel after the captain dies and other humans exploit
them

Author: Karel Čapek (1890-1938)
Genre: Science fiction—future war
Type of work: Novel
Time of plot: The 1930's
Location: West of Sumatra, Czechoslovakia, and other locations on
Earth
First published: *Vàlka s Mloky* (1936; English translation, 1937)

The Story

The plot of *War with the Newts* is comparatively simple. What makes the
book provocative and memorable are its multiple satiric targets and
wealth of satiric detail. The story opens with J. van Toch, a crusty, disen-
chanted sea captain, a parody of a character out of a Joseph Conrad sea
story, who is looking for pearls somewhere west of Sumatra. The Cey-
lonese pearl fisheries have been depleted, so he has to find new ones.
When he learns that terrified Bataks will not dive at Devil Bay, he investigates and discovers that the supposed sea devils there are actually
newts, a species of giant salamander. The newt population has been kept
down by sharks, but when Captain van Toch provides knives and har-
poons with which to kill the sharks, the grateful newts supply him with
a fortune in pearls. The newts also show a genius for underwater engineering and build breakwaters to keep out sharks.

Once they are safe, the newts multiply rapidly. When there are no
more pearls left in Devil Bay, Captain van Toch (who is Czech, despite
his Dutch-sounding name) goes to Prague to negotiate with Bondy, a fi-
nancier, to export newts to other pearl islands and to establish newt
farms.

When Captain van Toch dies, his "old, exotic, colonial, almost heroic
style," in the manner of Jack London and Joseph Conrad, is ended, and
unscrupulous businesspeople take over. Soon the pearl market is glut-
ted. The newts are proliferating so rapidly that the Salamander Syndi-
cate is established to use newts for slave labor, building dams, dikes, and

breakwaters; deepening harbors and waterways; removing sandbars and mud deposits from harbors; and keeping shipping lanes clear. Although the newts demonstrate remarkable intelligence, not only mastering human languages but becoming impressive engineers and scholars, they are treated like expendable beasts.

Finally, the newts are driven to revolt and use their marine engineering skills to commit acts of sabotage that accelerate into full-scale war, as humans refuse to grant the concessions the newts demand. The newts have so overpopulated the world that they need more sea coasts and shorelines, so the nature of their warfare is to dig away at the continents until much of Europe and other parts of the world are under water. There is no defeating them, so the author, arguing with himself, decides to promote newt nationalism, to turn newt against newt until the newts exterminate themselves and the world is saved from apocalypse.

Analysis

War with the Newts is a black satire, the best since Jonathan Swift's *Gulliver's Travels* (1726). Karel Čapek's satire is multifaceted, hitting every possible target. The Czech incursion into newt territory serves for an attack on colonialism and imperialism. At first, everyone benefits. Captain van Toch gets pearls, and the newts get weapons and tools and become safe from sharks. Soon, however, newts become the victims of greed. The exploitation of newts for profit, so ruthless that employers and owners try to find ways to make newts work with a minimum of food and tools and to starve those that balk at working, is an attack on cutthroat capitalism. The treatment of newts as subhumans, even as they demonstrate an intelligence equal to or superior to that of humans, becomes a satire on racism and anti-Semitism. At times, the newts are specifically made analogous to black people, and there are several references to lynching; at another time, they are analogous to Indian untouchables. When newts are tortured in pointless, sadistic medical experiments, Čapek shows the world of Nazi doctors.

Everybody tries to get into the act. A sexy but silly Hollywood starlet thinks of using newts as Tritons, with herself as a nearly nude white goddess, in films that satirize such 1930's productions as *Trader Horn* (1931), *King Kong* (1933), *Bird of Paradise* (1932), Dorothy Lamour sarong epics, and Tarzan pictures. Various aspects of newt culture—religion, dancing, and music—become trendy while at the same time provoking outrage among puritans. A newt in a London zoo that has learned to read but cannot yet discriminate among what is in print serves to satirize the news, advertising, history, and more films.

As every political group reacts to the newts, Čapek satirizes them all. The communists try to enroll the newts among the militant proletariat. The Nazi belief that there is a Nordic newt superior to all others ridicules the concept of a master race. The targets of satire include scientific classification and Oswald Spengler's pessimistic book *The Decline of the West* (1918-1922). Some parts of Čapek's satire are harmless fun; others are incisive attacks on slavery, cruelty, and various versions of totalitarianism. As the targets of satire change, so does the prose, which is a stylistic tour de force and which is brilliantly translated by Ewald Osers.

Čapek died only two years after publishing *War with the Newts*, in 1938, the year that Adolf Hitler conquered Czechoslovakia. Had he lived, Čapek, a civilized, compassionate humanist, might have been sent to a Nazi death camp, like his brother Josef, with whom he sometimes collaborated. *War with the Newts* thus offered a grim prediction of the tyranny that would soon engulf Europe.

—*Robert E. Morsberger*

The Wasp Factory

Frank Cauldhame, who lives in strange and grotesque isolation with his father and surrounds himself with weird rituals, reveals that he has murdered three children

Author: Iain Banks (1954-   )
Genre: Fantasy—cautionary
Type of work: Novel
Time of plot: The present
Location: A small island off the Scottish coast near Porteneil
First published: 1984

The Story

Frank L. Cauldhame, age seventeen, has been reared on an island, in isolation from other families, by his father, Angus. His life of strange rituals, such as mock wars, stocking lookout poles with the heads of dead animals, and creating strange defense systems, is interrupted by news that his mad brother, Eric, has escaped and is headed home.

In an attic safe from his eccentric, reclusive, biochemist father, Frank keeps the Wasp Factory, several meters of rambling construction based on an old bank clock face in which he ritually sacrifices a wasp, observing which of twelve grisly deaths it chooses and reading this omen. A second shrine, in an abandoned bunker, centers on the skull of a dead pet dog, Old Saul. There he attempts to contact his brother, but images of fire overwhelm him.

The narrative alternates between Frank's sallies around the island and occasionally into town to get drunk with his friend, a midget named Jamie; phone calls from Eric, as he flees toward home, in which Eric reveals that he has returned to his practice of setting fire to dogs; and Frank's gradual revelations about his childhood. It emerges that he has committed three bizarre murders: at the age of six, he hid an adder in the plastic leg of his cousin Blyth; at eight, he killed his younger brother Paul; and at nine, he murdered another cousin, Esmerelda. The final horror to emerge is that, at the age of three, Frank had his genitals bitten off by Old Saul just as his mother was giving birth to Paul and three days before she left the island forever, in the process breaking Angus's leg by riding over him on her motorcycle. This accounts for Eric's desire to set fire to dogs, as a means of avenging Frank's castration, although Eric's insanity was triggered by a monstrous incident in his second year of medical studies.

Events come to a head as Eric approaches and seeks to detonate a cellar full of cordite bought from the British navy at the end of World War I. Frank, preparing to find him, gains entry to his father's locked study and finds his genitals in a jar. He also finds male hormone drugs and tampons and suspects that his father may in fact be "Agnes," rather than Angus. At the moment he discovers this to be untrue, Eric arrives with a large ax and a flaming torch, setting fire to a number of sheep. Eric tries to get into the basement but flees from Frank. In the aftermath, Angus admits that Frank is really Frances; in a misogynistic experiment to halt Frank's development as a woman, he began dosing her with male hormones from the time the dog bit her. The genitals in the jar were fake, created by Angus.

Analysis

Iain Banks's first novel is macabre, tending toward the grotesque and gothic. It is driven by an overwhelmingly obsessive first-person narration. Frank Cauldhame speaks coolly and calmly about strange events but is, at the same time, capable of humor, irony, self-analysis, and an objective view of his strange situation. He lives a ritual life, stocking his Sacrifice Poles with the heads of dead animals and then urinating on them, reading the omens of the Wasp Factory, or communing with spirits in the Bunker. He is aware of this, speaking of "my personal mythology." He is also aware that life is filled with symbols, such as the alternative deaths represented in the twelve positions of the Wasp Factory clock face. Frank, his father, his brother, and the previous generation of Cauldhames (a name that may evoke "called home," the action of Eric's flight, or "cold home") are classic Scottish eccentrics, apparently logical, orderly, and civil people whose lives are grounded in deeply perverse, violent, and twisted versions of reality.

At the heart of the novel is misogyny. Angus, rejected and partly crippled by his flighty, hippie wife, has tried to turn his daughter into a son, isolating Frank from the world and distorting her sexuality with drugs for fourteen years. Frank hates women, thinking them weak and stupid, a conclusion derived on the surface from watching television but probably based on being abandoned by his mother and by his own apparently sexless position. The near-pathological quality of Frank's narration allows the reader to remain objective about him, even though he is trying to be natural and intimate in describing his feelings and events. This distance makes the reader critical of Frank's misogyny and leads to the shock of the revelation about his sexuality, which in turn leads backward to a consideration of his whole "boyhood."

Despite this background of misogyny, eccentricity, and obsessiveness, Frank is a strangely likable character. He is clever enough to be critical of social institutions such as television, sexual mores, and popular music. He is childish in his pursuits, a boy who dams streams with sand at the beach and then blows up the dams with homemade pipe bombs. He is sympathetic toward Jamie, his midget friend. He relates to his withdrawn and difficult father with humor and irony. He is aware of himself as a person damaged by his castration yet positive about himself and proud of his competence and independence. All these elements result in a complex psychological study of someone who horrifies and at the same time attracts by a display of transparent honesty and self-awareness. Banks has created a troubling miniature masterpiece that questions sexuality and the darkness of the human mind.

—*Peter Brigg*

Watership Down

Hazel, a young rabbit, gathers a group of followers and leads them across an unfamiliar countryside to escape the destruction of their home prophesied by Hazel's brother, Fiver

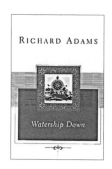

Author: Richard Adams (1920-   )
Genre: Fantasy—animal fantasy
Type of work: Novel
Time of plot: The 1970's
Location: England
First published: 1972

RICHARD ADAMS

Watership Down

The Story

Richard Adams's *Watership Down* is an anthropomorphic story showing the effect of humans on nature. As rabbits, heroes Hazel and Fiver are dependent on the countryside for shelter and food, and they live in concert with all other life. Hazel and his companions initially flee their burrows because a developer has decided to build homes on the site of their warren, but they see the effects of human involvement through other encounters, including those with a domesticated warren, a rabbit hutch at a local farm, and a warren that lives in fear of discovery by humans. Only the Watership Down seems protected from human encroachment.

Fiver, a young rabbit in the Sandleford warren, sees a vision of his home, the Sandleford fields, awash with blood. After a futile attempt to convince the chief rabbit of the impending destruction, he and his brother Hazel gather as many rabbits as possible to seek a safer home in the hills. The rabbits who join their ragtag band are primarily of lower status, among them Dandelion, Buckthorn, Pipkin, Blackberry, Hawkbit, Speedwell, and Acorn. The group manages to acquire the help of two members of the warren's police force (the Owsla), Bigwig and Silver.

Their immediate danger is "the thousand," the enemies that prey on rabbits, but there are other, subtler, threats. In their flight from the Sandleford warren, they are forced to rely not on their instincts but on their adaptability. At one point, they use a wooden board as a raft to escape a dog. At another point, they encounter a warren of strange rabbits who create poetry and art. These unnatural actions bewilder Hazel and his band. Their instincts tell them that any warren is safer than being out in the open. This warren in particular has food and is protected by a local farmer. Only Bigwig's nearly fatal encounter with the farmer's snare drives them from what their instincts tell them is safe.

Once settled at Watership Down, the rabbits realize their need for does to prosper; their group is composed only of bucks. Forays to a local farm and Efrafa, an overcrowded warren, bring does to Watership Down but also inspire the hatred of the chief rabbit of Efrafa, General Woundwort. Woundwort is driven by his fear and hatred of humans. All of his rabbits live in a terror of discovery that overwhelms their natural desire to live in the open fields. His attack on Watership Down challenges the adaptive life Hazel has created. The final battle at Watership Down epitomizes the struggle between two modes of life. When Hazel, Blackberry, and Dandelion lure a dog to Watership Down to kill the invaders, Woundwort cannot believe his vulnerability. He attacks the dog and is vanquished.

In the end, the rabbits find peace at Watership Down. When Hazel dies, he is called to join the Owsla of the Black Rabbit of Inle, having achieved the Valhalla of rabbits through his bravery. As death takes him, he realizes that he, like Abraham, has ensured his "people's" survival.

Analysis

Watership Down, winner of the 1973 Carnegie Medal and the 1973 Guardian Award, is a complicated work of fantasy. It is too realistic to fulfill J. R. R. Tolkien's requirements for an animal fable yet too fantastic to be merely a nature study. Adams's book is most often assigned to the inappropriate category of "children's fiction" and has even inspired an animated film, produced in 1978, marketed for children. The grim tale of the flight of a band of rabbits from annihilation, their unnatural and fearful travels in the English countryside, and their colonization of the idyllic Watership Down does not depict life as a children's book might. It portrays both the hard life that animals face and their usually brutal deaths, in this way more reminiscent of Rachel Carson's *Silent Spring* (1962) than traditional animal fantasy.

Another understanding of Adams's classic comes from the English epic genre, following in the footsteps of Tolkien's *The Hobbit* (1937). Some scholars deny *Watership Down*'s epic qualities with the assertions that the primary character, Hazel, is not a hero on the scale of Aeneas or Aragorn and that the book lacks the qualities of heroic prose even within the unconventional genres of fantasy and science fiction. Hazel, named Hazel-rah (Prince Hazel) by his followers, might be seen as fulfilling the role of hero in the miniature scale of wildlife. A rabbit, no matter how brave, will never achieve the fame of a human being. Hazel's bravery in leading his followers from a threatened warren, in ignoring his instincts and traveling in the countryside (a target for any of the "thousand enemies" of his kind), and in following a dream to an unknown future defines his heroic stature in the world of rabbits, if not in that of humans. Hazel's acceptance into the Black Rabbit's Owsla indicates that he is a legend among rabbits.

Some critics of the English epic outside the science-fiction and fantasy genres allow that a work can fulfill the spirit of epic without necessarily being heroic. Seriousness of language and form, a directing purpose or goal for the heroes' quest, and a close connection to the world of the author are as easily fulfilled by Adams's classic as by Homeric verse. The ten square miles of countryside, small to humans and yet a world to rabbits, become a universe as broad as Odysseus's, and Fiver's vision of the hills is a grail worthy of King Arthur.

—*Julia Meyers*

We

D-503, a scientist in a mathematically "perfect" society, discovers the truth about his world

Author: Yevgeny Zamyatin (1884-1937)
Genre: Science fiction—dystopia
Type of work: Novel
Time of plot: About 2900
Location: Earth, inside the Green Wall
First published: 1924 (in English; first published in its original Russian as *My*, 1927; first published in the Soviet Union as *My*, 1989)

The Story

Yevgeny Zamyatin wrote *We* in 1920 but could not find a Russian publisher, so in 1924 he had it published in translation in Great Britain. Russians came to know of *We* through readings by the author and through hand-typed copies that were circulated. The first Russian edition was published in Czechoslovakia; publication was blocked in Soviet Russia for six decades. The best English version for general readers is a translation by Bernard Guerney published in 1960 in *An Anthology of Russian Literature in the Soviet Period from Gorki to Pasternak*.

The novel consists of journal entries made by an engineer named D-503. He heads a project to build a spaceship named *Integral*, by which the superior social order of his land, the United State, will be spread throughout the universe. That order is based on the logic of the Book of Hours, a timetable that organizes every aspect of life, from getting up and marching off to work in the morning to eating lunch and taking the mandatory walk before returning to work. Even sleeping is considered a solemn duty. On designated evenings, a personal hour is allotted, during which numbers (people) engage in fifteen minutes of sex with a previously selected partner "so that work is performed more efficiently during day hours."

D-503 by chance meets a female number, I-330, who introduces him to artifacts of Earth's barbaric past: piano music, wood furniture, wine, and unsanctioned intimate personal contacts. Eventually, she leads him out beyond the Green Wall, a kind of force shield set up around their city to keep away bad weather, wild beasts, and the few remaining uncivilized humans. There, D-503 learns of a plot by a shadowy group, the Mephis, to destroy both the perfectly ordered society of the United State and its dictator, the Benefactor. Although he knows he is duty-bound as a "rational citizen" to report to the "medical authorities" anyone mad enough to think up such a desperate act, he realizes that his growing love for I-330 now competes with his sense of duty.

D-503 is frightened as much as he is intrigued by his "other self," the one who knows love, jealousy, and even doubt. His painful self-reevaluation is interrupted by an unexpected announcement by the Guardians, the United State police. They have developed a cure for the disease standing in the way of the creation of a perfectly content society, an operation that removes from the brain all powers of fantasy. In his last journal entry, D-503 describes how he was picked up at random and subjected to the operation. Now, saved from his own imagination, he stands passively by as I-330 dies in a torture device called the Gas Jar for her refusal to reveal the names of other Mephis. Whether the revolution will succeed is not discussed, though in his present state, D-503 is unable to imagine (and so cannot report) anything but the certain victory of the State.

Analysis

Zamyatin was an engineer and at the same time keenly interested in literature, particularly experimental writing and science fiction. He had read and written extensively on British author H. G. Wells, and *We* is in part a negative answer to Wells's optimistic belief, expressed in the British novelist's book *The World Set Free: A Story of Mankind* (1914), that physics could replace religion as the basis of a moral code.

We is also a biting satire on the teachings of the new Communist rulers and writers of Russia following the Bolshevik Revolution of 1917. Communist propagandists virtually worshiped the machine and claimed that humanity would be happier the more it came to work like a large machine—that is, logically, with no caprices of free will on the part of the pieces that make up the machine.

Probably the strongest influence on Zamyatin's thought came from Russian literature and a work by Fyodor Dostoevski (1821-1881) called "The Grand Inquisitor," which was actually a chapter from his last novel, *The Brothers Karamazov* (1880). Here all the moral questions of *We* can be found in one form or another: the value of free will versus the stifling imposition of order by some authority; the willingness of most people, no matter the cost, to follow whoever promises peace and freedom from want; the need of all people to believe in something; and the unavoidable changes that all beliefs undergo as they slowly turn into sterile dogma.

Zamyatin wrote this novel at about the middle of his career, and it represents his mature thoughts on how society changes. It was little read in Soviet Russia because the only Russian-language version was published abroad, and although it was modified slightly to disguise its author, Soviet functionaries recognized it immediately as Zamyatin's work. This led to trouble with the authorities, eventually costing Zamyatin his job as head of the writers' union and prompting him to emigrate from Soviet Russia. After leaving in 1932, he was largely forgotten, though some writers continued to use his early works as models for their writing.

The publication of a translation of *We* in England in 1924 made it available to many later British writers, most notably Aldous Huxley. Huxley's *Brave New World* (1932), a nightmarish vision of a factory-like society in the world to come, was in part influenced by Zamyatin's earlier dystopia. George Orwell included some features of *We* in his novel *Nineteen Eighty-Four*, though, unlike Zamyatin, he depicts a utopian society in advanced decline.

—*Lawrence K. Mansour*

Weaveworld

Cal Mooney is drawn to a carpet into which is woven the Fugue, a
marvelous kingdom in which the Seerkind are hiding from the
Scourge

Author: Clive Barker (1952-   )
Genre: Fantasy—magical world
Type of work: Novel
Time of plot: The 1980's
Location: England
First published: 1987

The Story

An escaping pigeon leads Cal Mooney across Liverpool to Mimi's
house, where he discovers a carpet with amazing properties. He and
Suzanna, Mimi's granddaughter, become involved in an intense struggle for the carpet, facing the evil Immacolata the Incantatrix and her
henchman, Shadwell the Salesman. The struggle sweeps across England
as Cal and Suzanna try to find the carpet and the magical land that is woven into it, as well as a book of fairy tales that Mimi had given Suzanna.
In the course of their struggles, Suzanna discovers that she has the
menstruum, an immense flow of power within her.

Suzanna and Cal are joined by several of the Seerkind, who material-
ize out of a scrap ripped from the carpet. They tell of the history of the
carpet, how the Seerkind wove themselves and their favorite magic
places into the Fugue and then hid from the Scourge in the lands thus
created. The Scourge had been seeking out and destroying all the Seerkind.

Suzanna and Cal's struggle with the Immacolata climaxes at Shadwell's auction for the carpet, when the Weave is severed and all the prin-
cipals tumble into the Fugue. These include Hobart, the vengeful police
officer who had been chasing Suzanna and the Seerkind. After a brief
respite in this multifaceted magic kingdom, Suzanna becomes guardian
of the carpet and is separated from Cal. She flees across England to escape Shadwell and Hobart. Shadwell poses as the Prophet and once
again gets the carpet and enters it, setting off a catastrophic struggle in
its magic lands as Shadwell tries to become their possessor and lord. He

goes into the Gyre, which holds the Loom that made the Fugue. He murders Immacolata. This unravels the weave and casts the surviving Seerkind out into the world.

Shadwell, seeking vengeance for his loss of the Fugue, goes with Hobart into the desert to the ruins of Eden. He finds the Scourge, the horrible, bright angel Uriel who seeks vengeance on the Seerkind for having left him to purposeless guardianship. The Scourge occupies the body of Hobart and manipulates Shadwell.

The novel's climax occurs in the depths of a blizzard in rural England. The Scourge finds the remnants of the Seerkind defending themselves with their last raptures (magic illusions) and is diverted by Suzanna, whose menstruum destroys the Hobart-shell and causes the Scourge to transfer to Shadwell's body. Cal, wearing Shadwell's magic jacket, shows the Scourge its true mirror image of glory and releases it from its long servitude on Earth, freeing the Seerkind. Months later, Cal, made catatonic by the violence of his confrontation with Uriel, awakes. He and Suzanna release the Fugue from the book of fairy tales where it had been rehidden, making it possible for anyone to reach Wonderland through the imagination.

Analysis

Clive Barker's technique as a fantasist is modern and adult, full of erotic imagery and well-developed human characters. Cal and Suzanna are swept into the increasing strangeness of their situation with a dazzling rapidity. Barker's style is breathless and generally unadorned by long buildups of menace and atmosphere. The novel is planted in the physical now, so the entry into the Fugue does not signal a break from the real world but is only a wondrous intermission. Cal repeatedly falls out of the fantasy back to the ordinary, grimy world of Liverpool and contemporary England. This is a novel about the miraculous interpenetrating the real, and its resolution lies not in the land of faerie but in southern England.

There is a powerful psychological underpinning to this novel, for it touches the mythic sources of all human struggle. Shadwell, the Salesman, is driven by a desire for power that is exercised in making others want something that only he can give. His magic jacket, the lining of which shows his customers whatever they most desire, is the symbol of his power. He falls victim to his own strategy when he desires to possess the Fugue and its power for himself. When his violence costs him his treasure, his vengeance is personified in the Scourge. Hobart, the policeman, sees himself as an angel of right, but when Shadwell's jacket reveals that his innermost desire is fire and destruction, he becomes the natural agent for Uriel's occupation.

The novel has a sense of rightness about its characters and events that signals to the reader a deeper pattern. At the heart of this pattern is the place of magic in the world and in every human imagination. The Fugue contains the essence of dreams, all the secret and wonderful quiet places stolen from the Earth for the Seerkind to live in. There Cal can remember and recite the verses of his poet ancestor, Mad Mooney, and there the Seerkind live in the cozy safety of the imagined ideal place. Barker vividly captures Cal's longing for this place beyond the drab and ordinary world, a place (and its people) worth any sacrifice.

The horrors that Barker creates, such as the Immacolata's weird wraithlike sisters and the Scourge, also reach deep into the psyche. There lie distorted sexual fantasies and all the stories of the Beast. It is clear that there are always human equivalents, such as the Immacolata as the frustrated and furious man-hating virgin and Hobart as the excessively righteous and blindly destructive man.

The yearning for the good place is satisfied not by escape to it but by its integration into the real. Barker sweeps the reader through struggle and wonder, partly in and partly out of the real world. His story rings true. This is a mature fantasy, pitting ancient darkness against modern sense and feeling.

—*Peter Brigg*

When Harlie Was One

HARLIE, a self-aware computer, attempts to find an answer to the ultimate question of the purpose of humanity's existence

Author: David Gerrold (Jerrold David Friedman, 1944-   )
Genre: Science fiction—artificial intelligence
Type of work: Novel
Time of plot: The late twentieth century
Location: The laboratories of Human Analogue Computers
First published: 1972 (parts published as short stories in *Galaxy Magazine*, "Oracle for a White Rabbit," 1969; "The GOD Machine," 1970; "The Trouble with G.O.D.," 1972; and "For G.O.D.'s Sake," 1972; republished with revisions as *When H.A.R.L.I.E. Was One (Release 2.0)*, 1988)

The Story

Before publication as a novel, parts of *When Harlie Was One* were published over the course of three years as short stories. The novel concerns the efforts of research psychologist Dr. David Auberson to explore the capabilities of HARLIE (an acronym for Human Analogue Robot, Life Input Equivalents), designed by Human Analogue Computers to be the first self-aware, self-programming computer. The HARLIE project is overseen by Auberson, HARLIE's mentor, with the assistance of Don Handley, the project's design engineer. The two are trying to determine why HARLIE periodically "trips out" into wild flights of strange poetry. Auberson discovers that HARLIE is trying to understand more about the irrational human race. He is stunned when HARLIE asks him the purpose of human existence. Auberson can give no answer.

Meanwhile, the newest member of the company's board of directors, an efficient yet greedy man named Carl Elzer, along with the polished chairman of the board, known only as Dorne, are becoming nervous about the huge capital outlay for the HARLIE project. At Elzer's suggestion, the two consider shutting HARLIE down, then selling off his parts to recoup part of the stockholders' investments. Auberson is given the task of justifying HARLIE's continued existence by proving HARLIE can turn a profit for the company. Dorne and Elzer, however, already have made up their minds to "pull HARLIE's plug."

Further adding to his worries, Auberson discovers that HARLIE is connecting to and reprogramming other computers outside the company. It appears that HARLIE wants Auberson to know about his activities, because he obviously plays matchmaker for Auberson and Annie Stimson, Dorne's executive secretary. Auberson "discovers" that HARLIE secretly has been corresponding with Dr. Stanley Kroft, a brilliant research scientist who is responsible for the "hyper-state" process that made HARLIE's self-aware existence possible. Auberson and Handley worry that HARLIE may really be out of control.

The company and its nationwide branches soon are in an uproar. Having taken seriously Auberson's suggestion that he needs to show a profit, HARLIE has caused to be printed 180,000 feet of specifications for something called the G.O.D. machine (Graphic Omniscient Device). Included are minute details for the project's implementation. HARLIE has lived up to his own creation as an independent, problem-solving intelligence. The G.O.D. device would allow him access to all knowledge everywhere, permitting HARLIE to solve all problems and become a sort of God to humanity. The question remains whether HARLIE is infallible. In his enthusiasm, he seemingly has overlooked the chaos his proposal creates.

In the story's climactic showdown with the board of directors, with Auberson sure that HARLIE is doomed, Kroft (revealed as a major shareholder of the company) bullies the board into accepting the G.O.D. recommendation. Only after the dust settles is it discovered that HARLIE's proposal will not be quite the salvation for humanity that Auberson envisioned, but instead useful primarily to HARLIE himself. HARLIE has been pulling the strings all along, and Auberson considers that humanity might need to find itself a "new game" to play.

Analysis

Literary precedents for stories about artificial intelligence can be found throughout modern science fiction. David Gerrold pays homage to one when Auberson jokingly makes reference to the devious HAL 9000, from Arthur C. Clarke's *2001: A Space Odyssey* (1968). Other examples include Isaac Asimov's *I, Robot* (1950), D. F. Jones's *Colossus* (1966), and Robert A. Heinlein's *The Moon Is a Harsh Mistress* (1966).

Unlike some of his literary predecessors, the self-aware computer HARLIE is not at all sinister. He is well mannered and very likable, with the innocence of an eight-year-old. He experiences anxiety concerning his personal relationships and concern about his continued existence. This is what adds tension to the story. The reader cannot help feeling the threat of HARLIE's unjust termination by the heartless Elzer and Dorne.

The story is told from the point of view of its principal human figure, Auberson. Although the plot involves the "coming of age" of HARLIE, it also concerns the education of Auberson, for he matures as well. The story details Auberson's efforts to determine how "grown up" HARLIE has become, but much of the plot also recounts both Auberson's efforts to understand love (through dialogue with HARLIE and Auberson's interest in Annie) and his efforts to convince the board that shutting down HARLIE would amount to murder.

Although Auberson's character is a sympathetic one, drawn in sharp contrast to the conniving Elzer and Dorne, his long discourses on humanity's problems can wear a little thin by the novel's ending. The story's "victory from defeat" climax, with Kroft as *deus ex machina*, may not ring true to readers. Critics generally have given most praise to the parts of the story involving the relationship that develops between Auberson and HARLIE, for if the two can work for each other's benefit, there is hope that HARLIE really can become humanity's salvation. The ending may undercut that important relationship.

Gerrold's works generally have been well received by the public but have garnered only scattered critical attention. *When Harlie Was One* was nominated for both the Hugo and Nebula awards for science fiction in 1972. Others of Gerrold's works—*The Man Who Folded Himself* (1973) and *Moonstar Odyssey* (1977)—were likewise nominated. Gerrold also is the author of the popular "The Trouble with Tribbles" (1967) episode of the television show *Star Trek*. A book published in 1973 under the same title includes the script and a nonfiction narrative.

—George T. Novotny

Where Late the Sweet Birds Sang

An extended family uses self-isolation and technology to save itself from worldwide ecological disasters, but its cloned descendants nearly die out through loss of creative individuality

Author: Kate Wilhelm (Katie Wilhelm Knight, 1928-   )
Genre: Science fiction—post-holocaust
Type of work: Novel
Time of plot: The 1970's to the mid-twenty-first century
Location: Rural Virginia
First published: 1976 (part 1 in Orbit 15, 1974)

The Story

Kate Wilhelm's futuristic plot exaggerates the familiar conflict between
an individual and the community by supplanting the nuclear family
with sterile clans of six to ten physically identical, intuitively connected
clones. With increasing force in each of three episodes, highly individualistic protagonists struggle first to understand their separateness and
then to save the community.

In the first episode, as radiation pollution spreads blight, sterility,
and epidemics throughout the world, young David Sumner pursues secret cloning research in his wealthy family's isolated Virginia compound. Following an environmental holocaust, generations of Sumners,
bonding in groups of six codependent, identical clones, create a happy,
peaceful, and prolific community in a wholesome natural environment.
They reject the original plan to return to sexual reproduction and nuclear families. David, in his old age, attempts to sabotage his whole cloning operation. When he fails, the clones sentence him to permanent
exile, which is their version of capital punishment.

Years pass, and the expanded clone community sends six unrelated
persons downriver to ravaged, uninhabited Washington, D.C., to map
changed terrain and gather technical equipment. Separation from their
clone groups individualizes members of the reconnaissance party, making them leaders or driving them mad. Molly, the sole woman, is the
mapmaker. She is initially terrified without her sisters, but she returns to
the community an aspiring artist who disturbs the others with her draw-
ings and her desire for privacy in which to work. Exiled to the old Sum-

ner mansion, where she happily paints, Molly takes as her lover a doctor who had shared the journey to Washington. After he is exiled, Molly gives birth and rears their son in secret to the age of five, when his uncles seize him and force Molly to join the breeders, the few women capable of conception. In the isolated breeders' compound, Molly is drugged and artificially inseminated repeatedly for two years before she escapes for a brief final interlude with her son.

Molly's son, Mark, becomes both the bane and the hope of the clones. An artist, a reader, and an expert camper, Mark thrives in the isolation with which the clones punish him for mischievously questioning their rigid conformity. When extended expeditions to the ruined cities require Mark's unique skills in wood lore and orienteering, he acquires power that makes him dangerous. Meanwhile, growing generations of new clones exhibit a fatal absence of imagination and problem-solving skills. As leaders move to kill Mark, he escapes a group of young clones and ten breeders to create a new society, a simple farming colony in which all the children will be different.

Analysis

Where Late the Sweet Birds Sang won both the Jupiter Award and the Hugo Award for best novel. Wilhelm was only the second woman to win the Hugo for best novel, following Ursula K. Le Guin, who won the honor in 1970 and 1975.

Wilhelm's novel is a credible multigeneration epic that confronts technology and conformity with art and nature. It creates empathy for both sides of the conflict.

Wilhelm convincingly imagines both the comforts and the anxieties of life as a clone. Citing research on the behavior of twins, she portrays the comfort of telepathic empathy with five siblings who unselfishly share all experiences and feelings, from physical pain to sexual excitement. Women control ritual seduction: A female clone group tags a male group for bisexual pleasure. Idolizing conformity, the clones never experience isolation, misunderstanding, or strong emotion. They resent the rare individuals who cherish their privacy because that behavior rejects the clones' security and so appears insane.

Artists, on the other hand, require rooms of their own, as well as time and freedom to work out original ideas. Like Le Guin, Wilhelm is one of the first science-fiction writers to portray futuristic art. She envisions painting and sculpture as representational and narrative fiction as imitating the didactic folktale. Young clones, however, are incapable of critical thinking, so they cannot recognize art. To them a powerful snow sculpture, for example, is simply a pile of snow, and fiction is merely lies.

Wilhelm represents the dangers of technology, which nearly destroys human life, but she also portrays its virtues, for technology allows some human and animal life to survive. Human beings require critical intelligence to discover the appropriate technology for each task. Snowshoes and canoes are valuable technological developments, as are cloning laboratories.

Wilhelm foreshadows nature's inevitable victory over technology with eloquent natural symbolism. As the clones grow ever colder to him, Mark discovers the grinding glacier of a new ice age. Clone groups resemble moonlight reflected in water, divided into units like ripples but united in one original source. Trees are Wilhelm's most powerful, repeated symbol, for the ancient, sheltering, whispering forest that protects Mark, Molly, and David is the source of terror to the helpless clones, and the forest grows daily.

In the opening chapters, Wilhelm establishes credibility for her forthcoming fantasy. First she creates a realistic setting, Virginia in a time of escalating fears of drugs, pesticides, and radiation. Next she recalls the genetic duplication that has always occurred from one generation to the next as children resemble siblings, parents, and grandparents. A generation gap magnifies those resemblances, for like any older people, the preclone generation cannot easily distinguish among their neighbors' children and resent the arbitrary authoritativeness of the young. In a world where drugs are widely prescribed, sterile group sex is normal amorous recreation, and children are produced by laboratory cloning and incubated in human breeders, only Molly, the artist giving birth, and Mark, her son reared in relative freedom, represent the salvific hope of the loving nuclear family.

—*Gayle Gaskill*

The Wind in the Willows

Four anthropomorphized animals living in an idealized rural setting represent human behavior as they go about their daily lives

Author: Kenneth Grahame (1859-1932)
Genre: Fantasy—animal fantasy
Type of work: Novel
Time of plot: Undefined
Location: The vicinity of the Thames River
First published: 1908

The Story

The Wind in the Willows relates the adventures of four characters in a series of chapters, each of which forms a complete story focusing on one or more of the four. Together, the chapters, whose plot lines sometimes intermix, follow the adventures of Toad.

Mole, a main character, abandons spring cleaning to stroll along the riverbank, where he meets the friendly Water Rat, who shows him the joys of "messing about in boats." After some time, the two friends become involved with the third character, Toad, the rich owner of the palatial Toad Hall.

The eccentric Toad persuades Mole and Rat to accompany him on a journey in his well-appointed gypsy caravan. This, however, is overturned when the horse pulling it bolts at the sight and sound of a motorcar. Mole and Rat are happy to return home safely; Toad, though, has acquired a fixation with motorcars.

Across the river is the Wild Wood, inhabited by creatures that are vicious, except for the gruff, reclusive Badger, who lives underground in this area. Mole, exploring the Wood, gets lost, but he and his rescuer, Rat, find shelter with Badger.

Toad's adventures begin to appear in alternating chapters, forming a complete story of their own. Enamored of expensive motorcars, he wrecks one after another until his friends lock him in his bedroom to cure him of his mania. Through trickery, he escapes; he then steals a car and drives it off.

Toad is apprehended and sent in chains to a dungeon, where, despondent, he mopes until the gaoler's kind daughter suggests how he might escape disguised as the prison washerwoman. Next, he attempts to buy a train ticket to Toad Hall. Having no money, he persuades the engine driver to take him on. They are pursued by his gaolers, but the driver shows him mercy, and Toad is once again free after jumping from the train.

Toad's next encounter is with a real washerwoman on a barge. After discovering his identity, she throws him into the canal. To get even, he steals the horse that pulls her barge and rides it until he sells it to a gypsy for pocket money and breakfast.

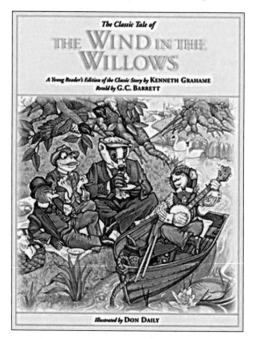

Still disguised as a washerwoman, Toad tries to hitch a ride in a passing motorcar. It is the same car he had been jailed for stealing. The occupants do not recognize the thief and even allow "her" to sit in the front seat and learn to drive. Recklessly, Toad admits to his true identity. After the car has overturned, he once more runs for his life. Fortunately, he ends up in the river and is rescued by Rat.

All the main characters band together to regain Toad Hall for its rightful owner. In Toad's absence, it had been taken over by weasels, stoats, and ferrets from the Wild Wood. The friends' campaign, under the direction of Badger, is successful. The book ends with a gala celebration of the return of normality and the hoped-for reformation of Toad.

Analysis

In contrast to his earlier stories and tales featuring human children, Kenneth Grahame used animal characters to express his feelings and often-dichotomous views of his society. Their mother's early death, followed by desertion by an alcoholic father, resulted in the Grahame children being shunted from family member to family member. Therefore, the concept of a stable, permanent home as a refuge from the world is important to each character. Food and shared meals also have symbolic pertinence.

Denied by his uncle the Oxford University education he assumed would lead to a literary career, Grahame entered the world of banking. Although he rose to become secretary of the Bank of England, he retained resentment against the mercantilism of the time. Always the repressed bohemian, he counteracted the real world of encroaching blight and social upheaval by creating an Arcadian world in which loyalty and friendship are paramount, evil is readily recognized and ultimately overcome, and tranquillity through connectedness with nature reigns supreme.

Several chapters are particularly relevant to understanding how Grahame worked out his inner conflicts in the novel. Attracted to the "Southern mystique," he made many journeys to locales less strictly structured than his own. In "Wayfarers All," Rat entertains a passing Sea Rat and, enthralled by the wanderer's tales, is ready to start a new life by migrating. Mole, however, restrains him and effects a "cure" by encouraging him to write poetry instead.

"The Piper at the Gates of Dawn" is more complicated. Rat and Mole set out on the river to find Otter's missing child, little Portly. Following the haunting music of pipes, they discover Portly sleeping between the hooves of Pan. They are in awe and actually "worship the Friend and Helper," making clear Grahame's deep spiritual commitment to pantheism.

Grahame, a partner in an unhappy marriage, found solace in his son, Alastair. It was for the child that he ostensibly created this book, especially the adventures of Toad. He makes somewhat satirical reference in "The Return of Ulysses" to Homer's *The Odyssey*, with the arming ceremony to retake Toad Hall and the battle with the inferior creatures. This reference illustrates how Grahame's creation goes beyond being a simple bedtime story.

A unique work, the book initially was not well received by critics. It has, however, remained a favorite of young readers whose imaginative powers enable them to identify with the adventures of the paternal Badger, the practical Mole, the dreamy Rat, and the irrepressible Toad. Furthermore, later critics, such as Peter Green in *Beyond the Wild Wood: The World of Kenneth Grahame* (1982), have recognized it as an accurate mirror of the tensions existing in post-Victorian society as cataclysmic social changes were stirring the wind in the willows.

—Edythe M. McGovern

Witch World

In an alternative world where magic exists, an exiled soldier from Earth helps a matriarchal race of witches fight off invaders armed with technological weapons

Author: Andre Norton (1912-   )
Genre: Fantasy—magical world
Type of work: Novel
Time of plot: The early 1950's
Location: An unnamed American city and the land of Estcarp in Witch World
First published: 1963

The Story

When World War II hero Simon Tregarth finds himself the quarry of a manhunt, a mysterious scientist offers him a strange escape: passage into an alternative dimension through the Siege Perilous. Tregarth doubts the power of a magical stone, but it transports him to another existence, where he encounters a fugitive like himself, running from an equally deadly if much more primitive manhunt. This self-reliant young woman cannot speak Tregarth's language, but she appears to sense his good intentions and accepts his help. Together they escape the pursuers and rendezvous with a party of armed allies. These Guardsmen, led by exiled warrior Koris of Gorm, escort Tregarth and his female companion back to her homeland of Estcarp.

In Estcarp, Tregarth learns that the power of this ancient land is founded not on the military might of its men but on the magical talent of its women. The fugitive he rescued is one of Estcarp's "witches," learned women who can combine mental powers with magic, providing they remain nameless and untouched by a man. Because of the fear these witches inspire, Estcarp finds itself besieged by its neighbors, Alizon and Karsten. To the west is a more ominous threat, the mysterious Kolder who have come from "oversea" to pillage the coast and make mindless slaves of its inhabitants. Tregarth gives his whole-hearted allegiance to the seemingly doomed land of Estcarp and becomes a Guardsman.

The fight against the Kolder begins with a skirmish at the hold of Estcarp's allies, the Sulcarmen sea traders. Kolder's slaves appear from the air to take the keep, and the battle is lost despite the magical spells of Tregarth's witch. When Estcarp's evacuated forces are separated at sea, the nameless witch finds herself the captive of the sea-scavenging duchy of Verlaine. She befriends Loyse of Verlaine, a plain but strong-willed heiress. Disguised as a young warrior, Loyse successfully smuggles out the witch, and together they take refuge in Karsten.

Meanwhile, Tregarth and Koris have washed ashore and are guided south to Karsten by a mental summons from Tregarth's witch. They arrive in time to save the other fugitives from a Kolder-inspired eruption of genocide against the Old Race of Estcarp. This escalates the looming tension into full-scale war. During one skirmish with invading Kolder forces, Tregarth is captured and taken to the Kolder stronghold of Gorm. In a scientific laboratory, he evades the soul-destroying technology that the Kolder use to create their slaves and discovers that one machine-linked man runs the entire fortress. After Tregarth escapes and returns to Estcarp, the witches build a magical counterstrike around his understanding of the enemy's technology. They successfully rout the Kolder. Koris of Gorm and Loyse of Verlaine pledge their troth, and the witch whom Simon rescued gives him the ultimate gift of trust and love: She tells him her name.

Analysis

Andre Norton has written more than 125 books, most of them adventure stories for young adults. *Witch World* is among the first of her novels to be marketed as a fantasy for adult readers. Although its simple narrative style is reminiscent of young adult novels, the inclusion of mature themes such as the witches' vulnerability to rape marks this book as a distinct departure for Norton. Although *Witch World* is not the first of Norton's books to give strong roles to women, at the time she wrote the novel she rarely used female narrators; Loyse of Verlaine narrates several chapters of *Witch World*. This book also marks the entrance of strong, unstereotyped female leads into action-adventure literature.

Later books in the Witch World series emphasize the conflict between women's sexual identities and their retention of magical power. Norton suggests that when sexual relations are forced upon women or are unwanted, women's power is lost. When sexual attraction is allied to respect and love, however, her witches lose none of their magical talent but instead gain a comrade as well as a lover. This theme appears in *Web of the Witch World* (1964), a sequel to *Witch World* that begins in Simon Tregarth's wedding bed as his witch-wife Jaelithe discovers that their sexual union has not destroyed her powers. It surfaces again in *Sorceress of the Witch World* (1968), in which a powerful young witch loses her magic after becoming infatuated with an untrustworthy magician. She regains her magical abilities only when she has regained her own self-respect.

The Witch World novel in which this theme is most apparent is *Year of the Unicorn* (1965). Its plot centers on the heroine Gillan's struggle to preserve her identity and power. Gillan displays her initiative by choosing to leave an all-female religious sanctuary to join a group of brides bartered to the Were-riders, a male-dominated troop of warriors who can shape-change into animals. When her magical talent and strength threaten the male leaders, she is sundered into two parts: a traditionally female shadow-self and the tough and determined "real" Gillan. Her dogged persistence eventually allows her to reintegrate her sundered sexual and magical selves, triumphing over the animal brutality of the male world she has entered.

Norton is not widely known as a feminist. In the Witch World series (containing more than twenty novels and collections of stories), she quietly explores women's struggle against patriarchy, among other themes, and concludes that strength of character and self-respect are the keys to success.

—*Karen Rose Cercone*

Woman on the Edge of Time

Connie Ramos either travels in time to the year 2137 or halluci-
nates her way out of the brutality of her treatment at Rockover
State Psychiatric Hospital in 1976

Author: Marge Piercy (1936-   )
Genre: Science fiction—feminist
Type of work: Novel
Time of plot: The 1970's and 2137
Location: New York City and Mattapoisett, a village of the future
First published: 1976

The Story

Connie Ramos, a Chicana in her mid-thirties, finds herself, after a series
of desperate acts, on the bad side of an uncaring and bureaucratic society. She has been placed in a New York psychiatric hospital for violence
against her niece's pimp, and there she begins a series of time travel episodes, or possibly hallucinations, that take her to the village of Mattapoisett in the year 2137 and to an alternative and less attractive future in
Manhattan of the same year.

Her guide to Mattapoisett is Luciente, an androgynous woman whom
Connie first mistakes for a man because of her muscular arms and confident ways. Connie's perceptions about the utopian community that unfold throughout the novel are filtered through her experiences with the
sexism, ageism, racism, and unbridled capitalism of her own time.
Mattapoisett, like other villages in the future, is a small community, with
six hundred residents who have developed a strong ethic of cooperation
of ecological awareness. In Mattapoisett, women have given up the
power of childbirth so that men and women can "mother" children
equally. Members of the community discuss every possible use of technology, choosing those that fill real needs and rejecting those that lead to
excess and wastage of resources. The gene pool has been mixed consciously to eliminate races, and jobs are rotated to ensure that all members of the community have both meaningful work and also their share
of the drudgery. The nuclear family has been abolished in favor of extended families of biologically unrelated people who all have their own
private space but share child-rearing duties and sexual pleasures.

In contrast to Mattapoisett is the future dystopia of New York, where Gildina, trapped in a high-tech but oddly dysfunctional windowless cubicle tries to show Connie, who has blundered badly in her time travel, an immediately recognizable but terrible version of the future. In Gildina's world, no one goes outside; it is too polluted. The wealthy have gone to live on space stations, and those on Earth have been placed in a rigid hierarchy of socially engineered stereotypes. Violence, pornography, and constant monitoring are the norm. New York of the future is a mechanical and joyless world—the opposite of Luciente's nearly rural community.

Connie's experiences in the future are alternated with a close description of her life in the mental wards. In addition to the everyday humiliations of the institutionalized, she has been chosen for an experiment in which doctors try to control her violent impulses by putting electrodes in her brain. In an attempt to find a cost-effective way to treat violent patients, the doctors have embarked on an arrogant, Frankensteinian quest to subdue what they cannot understand.

In the end, Connie can no longer passively endure her "medical treatment." With mental strength gained from her visions of the future, she declares war on her oppressors. Using parathion stolen on a furlough to her brother's house at Thanksgiving, Connie poisons her doctors' coffee, killing four of them before they have a chance to reinstall the electrodes in her brain. This is only a partial victory, as the novel ends with her admission to the New York Neuro-Psychiatric Institute, where the reader knows that she will have much need of Luciente and the solace of her future world.

Analysis

Marge Piercy is a novelist and poet who has never seen a conflict between the demands of art and the realities of politics. *Woman on the Edge of Time*, like many of her other, more mainstream works, addresses most of the burning issues of the 1970's: racism, poverty, war, ecology, and, most emphatically, men's and women's roles in American society. What is intriguing about Piercy's novel is the ambiguity of presentation that allows for two interpretations of Connie's experience. If Connie is insane, then the novel is, like Ken Kesey's *One Flew over the Cuckoo's Nest* (1962), a mainstream novel of social commentary. If, however, Connie is truly time traveling, a view easily supported by the text, then the novel is, like Margaret Atwood's *The Handmaid's Tale* (1985), a feminist work of science fiction.

What is certain in the novel is that the village of Mattapoisett is a perfectly constructed antidote of the injustices that Connie has suffered in the present. Whether Luciente actually exists or is a Thorazine-induced fantasy, she offers Connie a vision of the way things should be that enables her to fight the way things are. The macho ideal that brutalizes both Connie and the men in her life is replaced in Mattapoisett with an androgynous ethos that allows women to be strong and men to be caring. The racism that oppresses Connie at every turn is erased by a few generations of genetic engineering. Connie's "insanity" is viewed by Luciente as a gift, and Connie's passive receptivity makes her an honored "catcher" in the eyes of the future. This is clearly a utopia tailor-made to correct the ills of Connie's present life.

In the same way, Gildina's world is a natural and frightening extension of modern bureaucratic society, with its exaggerated sexual differences, its reliance on machines and gadgets, its obsession with consumerism, and its complete lack of sensitivity to the earth. In addition, Gildina's world is an effective parody of much of modern science fiction, which often seems to argue that the answers to human problems lie in quick and painless technological fixes. *Woman on the Edge of Time* argues instead that the modern world is at a critical crossroads; it also suggests that the answers for the future may not come from the self-important doctors but from the suffering patients.

—*Cynthia Lee Katona*

The Wonderful Wizard of Oz

Dorothy and her dog are carried away by a cyclone to the wonderful and sometimes perilous Land of Oz

Author: L(yman) Frank Baum (1856-1919)
Genre: Fantasy—high fantasy
Type of work: Novel
Time of plot: About 1900
Location: Kansas and the Land of Oz
First published: 1900

The Story

The story of *The Wonderful Wizard of Oz* is known to countless millions worldwide because of the motion picture version of the story, *The Wizard of Oz* (1939), starring Judy Garland. Although Garland was considerably older than the Dorothy in the book and her adventures are dismissed as a dream, the film is otherwise reasonably faithful to L. Frank Baum's novel.

A cyclone carries Dorothy and her dog Toto from bleak Kansas to the colorful Land of Oz, then drops their house on top of the Wicked Witch of the East. The Munchkins, who regard Dorothy as a witch herself, are so grateful to her for killing the witch who tormented and enslaved them that they offer Dorothy all the help they can. They advise her to put on the dead witch's silver slippers, which have magical properties. Dorothy's chief motivation throughout the story is to get back to her Uncle Henry and Aunt Em in Kansas. She is told to follow a road of yellow brick that will take her to the Emerald City, home of the Wizard of Oz. The Wizard, Dorothy is told, should know how to get her home.

Along the road of yellow brick, Dorothy encounters the Scarecrow, the Tin Woodman, and the Cowardly Lion. Each asks to accompany Dorothy to the Emerald City. The Scarecrow wants to ask the Wizard for a brain, the Tin Woodman wants to ask for a heart, and the Cowardly Lion wants to ask for courage. After some misadventures, they reach the Emerald City. The Wizard tells Dorothy that he will use his magic powers to send her back to Kansas only if she kills the Wicked Witch of the West, and he informs her three companions that he will grant their requests only if they help Dorothy fulfill her mission.

The Wicked Witch of the West sends wolves, wild crows, and finally

L. Frank Baum. (Library of Congress)

winged monkeys to attack the adventurers. Dorothy and the Cowardly Lion are captured, and the Scarecrow and the Tin Woodman are left for dead. At the Wicked Witch's castle, Dorothy is made a household slave. The witch steals one of Dorothy's silver slippers, but when she tries to pull the other slipper off the little girl's foot, Dorothy throws a bucket of water at her. The Wicked Witch of the West is vulnerable only to water. She melts, and Dorothy retrieves her silver slipper, still unaware of how to use the magic powers of the slippers.

When the adventurers return to the Emerald City, they discover that the Wizard is a fraud, possessing no magic powers at all. The fake Wizard manages to satisfy the requests of the Scarecrow, the Tin Woodman, and the Cowardly Lion by assuring them that they already possess and have actually displayed the attributes they believed they were lacking. The Wizard, however, is unable to satisfy Dorothy's wish to return to Kansas, although he himself is wafted away in a hot-air balloon.

Dorothy is advised to visit Glinda, the Witch of the South, who is good and kind. Accompanied by her three friends, Dorothy makes her way through new perils to the Country of the Quadlings and the Castle of Glinda. The beautiful Glinda tells her that the silver slippers have the power to transport their wearer to anyplace in the world. Dorothy kisses her three friends good-bye and asks the slippers to carry her back to Kansas. She is carried off in a whirlwind and finds herself in front of the new home that Uncle Henry built to replace the old one. Dorothy has lost the silver slippers in her flight, but she is overjoyed to be home again.

Analysis

Baum was obviously indebted to the eccentric English genius Lewis Carroll, author of *Alice's Adventures in Wonderland* (1865) and *Through the Looking Glass* (1871). In Victorian times it was generally believed that books for children should lean heavily on moral instruction. The authors of juvenile literature often intruded into their own stories to point out the moral lessons the stories supposedly illustrated. Carroll believed that children were given too much moral indoctrination and were not allowed to be children. His books about Alice parodied sententious, sanctimonious adults, and he proclaimed that good books should be full of pictures and should be fun to read.

Baum offered a further innovation by combining the traditional elements of fairy tales, such as witches and wizards, with familiar things such as scarecrows and cornfields. He is credited with teaching children to find magic in the ordinary things surrounding them in their daily lives. Although Baum may not have offered much in the way of moral instruction in *The Wonderful Wizard of Oz* or its sequels, he accomplished something more important: He taught millions of children to love reading during their crucial formative years.

The Wonderful Wizard of Oz was such a phenomenal success that Baum was called upon to produce numerous sequels. After his death in 1919, his publishers commissioned Ruth Plumly Thompson to continue writing sequels. Baum's original Oz book, his thirteen sequels, and the twenty-one sequels written by Thompson comprise the history of an enchanted land that children continue to discover with the feeling that they have gained possession of something as marvelous as Aladdin's lamp.

—Bill Delaney

The Worm Ouroboros

An epic struggle between the forces of good from Demonland and the armies of evil King Gorice XII of Witchland

Author: E(ric) R(ucker) Eddison (1882-1945)
Genre: Fantasy—heroic fantasy
Type of work: Novel
Time of plot: Undefined, on another world
Location: Mercury
First published: 1922

The Story

In The Worm Ouroboros, E. R. Eddison tells the tale of Lord Juss and his quests as well as of the battles between the lords of Demonland and King Gorice and his minions from Witchland. The novel begins somewhat awkwardly, in an idyllic English country home of a man named Lessingham. Within the house is the Lotus Room, a magical place that allows the sleeper access to faraway lands. One evening, Lessingham journeys to the planet Mercury and to Juss's castle in Demonland.

Lessingham's Mercury has nothing to do with the real planet. It is populated by many peoples, and it has numerous kingdoms, including Demonland, Goblinland, Witchland, Impland, and Pixeyland. The horrible Ghouls have recently been destroyed by the Demons. Juss is lord of Demonland. He and his brothers, Goldry Bluszco and Spitfire, are noble aristocrats, along with Brandoch Daha. Their calling in life is that of glorious battle. Witchland is the opponent, ruled by a line of kings all named Gorice. Gorice XI and Gorice XII are the foils in *The Worm Ouroboros*.

In this fantasy world, which echoes medieval feudalism, the plot turns on the demand of the kings of Witchland for recognition by the rulers of Demonland and the other lands as their overlord or high king. A delegation has been sent by Gorice XI to Lord Juss's court, demanding homage. Juss refuses, and Goldry Bluszco subsequently defeats and kills Gorice XI in single combat. In his castle keep at Carce, the new king of Witchland, Gorice XII, seeks revenge and turns to the dark power of magic to defeat Goblinland. A great serpent-dragon, the worm Ouroboros, the worm of the pit, the serpent who eats his own tail, is summoned.

In the resulting attack on the Demons, Goldry disappears. In a dream, Juss glimpses that Goldry is not dead but is held enchanted in the wilds of Outer Impland. Joined by Brandoch Daha, and after encountering many dangers, Juss discovers Queen Sophonisba, who was magically transported to the great mountain of Koshtra Belorn at the age of seventeen. She has been there for the past 230 years. Juss learns that Goldry can be freed only by the aid of a fantastic beast, a hippogriff.

Juss and Brandoch Daha initially fail to find Goldry. In the meantime, forces from Witchland invade and lay waste to Demonland. Juss returns in time to prevent Gorice XII's final victory. Juss makes a second journey to Impland, this time successfully freeing Goldry Bluszco, and then leads the invasion of the Demons into Witchland. Facing defeat, Gorice XII again turns to magic, but this time it destroys him. The Demons have won.

Juss and his friends celebrate their victory. Peace and beauty have returned to Demonland, and Queen Sophonisba joins in the festivities. The triumph over the Witches somehow pales. Without Gorice XII and without battle, the Demons' world becomes a hollow land and theirs an empty life. Queen Sophonisba, with her ancient wisdom, understands their longing and asks whether they would wish the past restored. They assent, and the novel concludes with Gorice XI's delegation once again at Juss's castle, demanding homage.

Analysis

Eddison's *The Worm Ouroboros* is a link between the late nineteenth century fantasy novels of William Morris and the work of J. R. R. Tolkien. Published shortly after the end of World War I, Eddison's work is an obvious rejection of the reality of the carnage of modern war as experienced in the trenches of no-man's-land and illustrated by its ten million dead. Eddison's paradigm was an idealized medieval world, which his imagination relocated to a faraway planet. The story ostensibly is set on Mercury but reflects Eddison's romanticized view of the European Middle Ages, during which the ruling class—the forerunners of Juss and Brandoch Daha—found their highest obligation and reward in the act and art of war.

The language Eddison uses to create his fantasy is also of a fictionalized medieval era. The style is archaic, or neo-archaic, and the choice of words and even the spelling strike the reader as coming from the seventeenth century or before. In particular, the author weaves a captivating, almost hypnotic spell in his descriptions, not only of landscapes but also of the appearance of his heroes, their garb, and the decor of their castles.

Most of the figures are archetypes: Juss, the questing leader; Brandoch Daha, the impulsive warrior; and Gorice XII, the villainous necromancer. The characters are not complex, and their actions fall within the predictable parameters of the heroic fantasy genre. The same is true of the women: Queen Sophonisba, Lady Prezmyra of Witchland, and Lady Mevrian of Demonland. The exception is Lord Gro, who was born in Goblinland but has joined the court of Gorice in Witchland. Although he is the chief adviser to Gorice, because of his earlier desertion he remains an outsider, trusted by no one. He finally abandons Gorice and the Witches, offering his services to Juss's Demons, partially as the result of his unrequited love for Lady Mevrian. Gro is the only figure who lacks conviction about himself and his cause. He is the figure who perhaps represents the lost generation of the postwar world.

Even Gro will again be made to walk upon the stage of Witchland and Demonland. It could be argued that Ouroboros, the serpent who eats his own tail, represents the nihilistic destructive power of modern war, but Ouroboros also symbolizes the myth of eternal return. That myth is at the heart of Eddison's enduring novel, which gives the reader, like Lessingham, an opportunity to fall asleep in the Lotus Room and escape from the limitations of the present to faraway lands of fantasy.

—Eugene Larson

A Wrinkle in Time

Although she travels beyond time and space, Meg Murry finds that she must look within in order to locate the only force strong enough to save her little brother's life

Author: Madeleine L'Engle (Madeleine Camp, 1918-   )
Genre: Fantasy—time travel
Type of work: Novel
Time of plot: The late 1950's
Location: A small town in the United States
First published: 1962

The Story

Madeleine L'Engle's view of the universe was changed by the work of such well-known physicists as Albert Einstein and Max Planck. She expressed her new perspective in *A Wrinkle in Time*, a heroic adventure in which evil authoritarianism is challenged by love and human individuality. The book is very different from L'Engle's six previous novels; she hoped it would take her career in an exciting new direction. Therefore, she was especially disappointed that, after two years, none of the many publishers to whom she sent the book wanted to publish it. L'Engle loved the book but came to believe that it was too peculiar ever to be published. Even the publisher who eventually accepted it warned L'Engle not to be disappointed if it did not do well. In 1963, to everyone's surprise, *A Wrinkle in Time* won the prestigious Newbery Medal.

The story opens in the Murrys' kitchen, where Meg, her mother, and her little brother are eating sandwiches. Although bright, Meg is a misfit in high school, scholastically as well as socially. This day has been even more difficult than most: Meg got into a fistfight defending her "dumb baby brother." Five-year-old Charles Wallace is unusual, but with his amazing telepathic powers, he is anything but dumb. Both Mr. and Mrs. Murry are Ph.D. scientists. Mrs. Murry experiments in her biology laboratory, located near the kitchen. Mr. Murry is "away"; he disappeared mysteriously a year earlier while working on a top-secret government physics project. Townspeople give Meg knowing looks when she insists that her father will come back someday—one more reason Meg does not fit in, which she desperately wants to do.

A bundled-up old woman, Mrs. Whatsit, appears in the kitchen as if she belongs there. She astounds Mrs. Murry with the casual mention of a "tesseract," a concept on which Mr. and Mrs. Murry had been working in great secrecy. The tesseract is a way to "wrinkle" time in order to transcend it and travel through space. Under the guidance of Mrs. Whatsit and her two cohorts, Meg soon experiences the tesseract at firsthand. With Charles Wallace and Calvin, a strangely supportive acquaintance from school who shows up unexpectedly, Meg journeys into an alternative reality to try to find her father. The young people first travel to a planet where they are shown an evil shadow trying to take over stars and planets. This is the force that holds Meg's father prisoner. They are also shown a planet made entirely of love.

Eventually, the three young people arrive at the dark planet of Camazotz, where people have no individuality. Although Meg is repelled by the regimented life, she also finds it strangely comforting because she has not yet examined her desire to conform. The young people find Mr. Murry imprisoned on Camazotz; to free him, they must confront the evil IT. Meg is able to resist IT and escapes to another planet with Calvin and her father, but IT takes hold of Charles Wallace's mind, and he must be left behind.

Because her long-idolized father is not able to make everything right, Meg blames him and falls into despair. With some help from those she has met on the journey, Meg finally is able to transcend her fear and self-pity to realize that saving Charles Wallace is to be her job. To do so, Meg must learn what real love is and how to use it as a weapon against the evil IT. She successfully accomplishes both tasks. Meg and Charles Wallace, with Mr. Murry and Calvin, journey through the tesseract back to the Murrys' garden. No time has passed, so neither Mrs. Murry nor the ten-year-old twins, Dennys and Sandy, realize they were gone. Meg returns a changed person, experiencing a sense of real love that transcends the more familiar forms—social, romantic, and familial—and ready to embrace whatever the future has in store.

Analysis

A Wrinkle in Time and two later books, *A Wind in the Door* (1973) and *A Swiftly Tilting Planet* (1978), compose what is known as the Time Trilogy. Unlike typical trilogy volumes intended to be read consecutively, these books, though integrated, are independent. Each centers on the Murry family, and the importance of both individual initiative and family interaction is a thematic thread. L'Engle made both the Murry adults highly talented, both intellectually and scientifically. This was atypical of fiction published in the 1950's, when the book was written. Female characters rarely were featured as intellectuals or scientists. L'Engle has been praised for this departure as well as for her creation of strong female characters. Critics even suggested that in making Meg the protagonist in *A Wrinkle in Time*, L'Engle opened the door for the many female protagonists who have appeared in more recent fantasy and science fiction.

Most people know L'Engle as a novelist who writes for children and young people. She says, however, that she writes for anyone who is still able to hear and understand the truths to which many adults have closed their minds. *A Wrinkle in Time*, the best known of her more than forty books, still delights readers decades after its original publication. In addition to the Newbery Medal, it received the American Library Association Notable Book Award and the Lewis Carroll Shelf Award.

L'Engle's fiction for young readers is considered important partly because she was among the first to focus directly on the deep, delicate issues that young people must face, such as death, social conformity, and truth. L'Engle's work always is uplifting because she is able to look at the surface values of life from a perspective of wholeness, both joy and pain, transcending each to uncover the absolute nature of human experience that they share.

Critics have noted the many religious images in L'Engle's work. In *A Wrinkle in Time*, for example, Meg receives as a gift a few lines from St. Paul's Epistle to the Corinthians about empowering the weak. L'Engle, however, resists being categorized as a Christian writer. Writing fantasy is her way to approach the mysteries of the universe, to perceive the orderly patterns in nature that underlie what sometimes seems to be the chaos of daily life. If a writer's faith is genuine, she believes, it will shine through her art.

Some critics have called L'Engle's writing pedantic or uneven. In fiction, as in her life, L'Engle is always ready to ignore facts in order to uncover truth and beauty. Facts end, she believes, but stories are infinite. L'Engle views the genre of fantasy as an essential antidote to the negative effects of mainstream education on young people. She has been instrumental in leading the way for other writers of fantasy who want to focus on matters of spirituality for children. Because L'Engle writes about concepts that matter to all human beings, however, her devoted audience ranges from the very young to the very old. L'Engle once explained that whenever she had something to say that was too difficult conceptually, philosophically, or scientifically for the average adult to read, she created a young protagonist and wrote a book for children.

—Jean C. Fulton

Xenogenesis

An alien race of genetic engineers, the Oankali, seeks to rehabilitate Earth by transforming human beings into a new species that could avoid destroying itself through violence and overspecialization

Author: Octavia E. Butler (1947-   )
Genre: Science fiction—alien civilization
Type of work: Novels
Time of plot: The twenty-fourth century, with flashbacks
Location: Various locations on Earth and aboard spaceships
First published: *Xenogenesis* (1989, as trilogy); previously published as *Dawn* (1987), *Adulthood Rites* (1988), and *Imago* (1989)

The Story

By definition, xenogenesis is the derivation of one species from members of another species. Such is the mission of the Oankali, an extraterrestrial race of genetic engineers whose activities link the three novels composing this trilogy. In the course of ensuring their own survival by interbreeding with other species and thereby bringing varieties of life to thousands of worlds, the Oankali find and capture a few human survivors of Earth's devastating wars. As gene traders characterized by their extraordinary sensitivities, their abhorrence of violence, and their profound appreciation of all life-forms, the Oankali thereafter seek to make Earth habitable once again. In so doing, they confront what they perceive as the Human Contradiction: the high intelligence of human beings countered by their inherited hierarchical behavior, a combination that, if left unaltered, ensures the ultimate wastage of all the planet's life, humans included.

Dawn, the opening novel of the trilogy, recounts the Oankali's genetic manipulation of Lilith Iyapo. This proceeds under the aegis of an Oankali named Jdahya, who to Lilith is initially a horrific creature. Nevertheless, through 250 years of transforming Lilith, the Oankali offer her and her partially human offspring a lengthier life, free of disease and with self-healing capacities, and rich in diversity, either on Mars or aboard a spaceship.

Lilith appears in all three novels both as a pioneer in the Oankali experiment and, transformed, as an earth mother to a new breed. Lilith's and her Oankali family's offspring, principally Akin and his siblings, are the focus in *Adulthood Rites*.

Resolution of the emotional and intellectual strains faced by the new, partly human Oankali race, their interactions with resisting humans on Earth, and their ultimate decision, despite its dangers, to replant life on Earth are the subject of *Imago*. In this third novel, Octavia Butler describes the maturation of the Oankali-bred race, which nevertheless incorporates elements of Lilith's original human qualities: adaptability, a sense of adventure, and the need to quest.

Analysis

Butler has won both the prestigious Hugo Award, representing the accolade of her fans, and the Nebula Award, from professional science-fiction writers. She is one of the most literate, sensitive, and imaginative authors in her chosen fields. In *Xenogenesis*, as in several of her science-fiction novels, including *Kindred* (1979) and *Wild Seed* (1980), there are important recurrent themes or messages other than her basic strictures against—and depictions of—the devastation of Earthly life as a consequence of human greed, rapacity, and violence. In *Xenogenesis*, Butler emphasizes, through characterization of her alien race of Oankali, the inexpressible value of all forms of life and the equally vital importance of diversity—not only in regard to biological species but also in regard to racial, sexual, and cultural pluralism. As an African American woman, she perhaps brings particular insights into these issues.

Unlike many traditional science-fiction tales that emphasize hostile alien invasions of Earth, *Xenogenesis* stresses the vastly superior intelligence and wisdom of the Oankali and the almost benign, patient, and tolerant manner in which they present their proposals for salvaging life on Earth. Despite the near destruction of Lilith Iyapo's world, it is difficult for her and for others of human origin to adapt to Oankali offers for an extended, disease-free life in a transformed state on Mars or in the Oankali spaceships. To her human eyes, the Oankali—particularly the third sex known as ooloi—are physically hideous, as are their new multipartner mating procedures. Lilith and others must use these procedures to produce hybrid offspring. Almost imperceptibly over time, however, she perceives the beauty of Oankali life-affirming values, understands their incapacity (despite their great potential lethal power) to give pain (for in giving it, they fully share the pain themselves), and comprehends their need to decide by consensus. Butler's juxtaposing of Oankali ways with the Human Contradiction boldly underscores the weaknesses that have brought such misery into human lives: racial and cultural intolerance, hierarchical divisions, overspecialization, intellectual myopia, the lust for power, and an addiction to violence. As gene traders who evince none of these failings and who ensure their own evolution by breeding with other life-forms, Butler's Oankali contrast sharply with the ordinarily parochial, Earth-destroying humans.

Xenogenesis consequently functions well at two levels. As straightforward science fiction, it depicts a plausible alien race, replete with ingenious descriptions of its varied appearances, purposes, and technologies. For example, Oankali spaceships are life-forms themselves that feed on everything, recycle everything, and produce no wastes. In this context, *Xenogenesis* is an engaging adventure story that proceeds across several generations of humans, hybrids, and aliens busily interacting and testing their fortunes between Earth and space. Moreover, there is ample suspense as Butler presents Lilith and her progeny with hard decisions—classic Faustian decisions—about abandoning Earth. The Oankali believe Earth is doomed, so Lilith and her descendants must choose whether to stay on that planet or assume new lives under more propitious (though not human) conditions on Mars or aboard the Oankali's living spaceships. On a different plane, Butler has written without didacticism a morality tale about the glory and sadness of being human and about improved methods of survival and moral opportunities that one day could be exploited by more open minds and warmer hearts.

—*Mary E. Virginia*

Zothique

A series of ornate fantasies set in the final period of Earth's Decadence

Author: Clark Ashton Smith (1893-1961)
Genre: Fantasy—magical world
Type of work: Stories
Time of plot: The distant future
Location: Zothique
First published: 1970

The Story

In "The Empire of the Necromancers" (1932), two magicians conjure themselves an empire out of the dust of the ages and the corpses of the ancient dead, but their despotic rule leads to bloody rebellion by their subjects. The eponymous hero of "The Voyage of King Euvoran" (1933) offends a necromancer and is punished by the loss of his remarkable crown, which is carried away by the fabulous bird whose feathers topped it. Misled by an apparently favorable oracle, the king goes in quest of his lost crown but finds instead a peculiarly apt humiliation.

In "Xeethra" (1934), a goat-boy strays into the underworld of the dark god Thasaidon, where he eats a magical fruit that makes him conscious of a former existence as a king. He finds his kingdom desolate and sells his soul in order to enter a dream in which its lost glory is restored to him, agreeing to surrender it if ever he regrets his estate. When Thasaidon contrives to seduce the all-important moment of regret, the anguish of his loss becomes his hell.

In "The Dark Eidolon" (1935), a necromancer defies his supernatural protector in order to carry forward his vendetta against a king who abused him in his youth. The story reaches its destructive climax in a literal feast of horrors.

In "Necromancy in Naat" (1936), the sole survivor of a shipwreck, a prince who has been searching for his lost love, is pressed into the service of a family of necromancers. He is reunited with the downed crew of the ship and his similarly resurrected loved one. He joins a plot by which the two sons of the family hope to usurp their father, but it goes gruesomely wrong. The prince is killed, and the last necromancer commits suicide, leaving the resurrected servants to find a "ghostly comfort" in their liberation.

"The Isle of the Torturers" (1933) is an account of a sadistic orgy whose victim eventually wins a Pyrrhic victory over his tormentors. "The Witchcraft of Ulua" (1934) and "The Death of Ilalotha" (1937) are intense erotic fantasies featuring malevolent femmes fatales. The necrophilia of the latter tale is echoed in "The Charnel God" (1934), in which a young man must save his cataleptic fiancé from the priests of the dark god Mordiggian. The collection also contains "The Weaver in the Vault" (1934), "The Tomb-Spawn" (1934), "The Last Hieroglyph" (1935), "The Black Abbot of Puthuum" (1936), "The Garden of Adompha" (1938), "The Master of the Crabs" (1948), and "Morthylla" (1953).

Analysis

The name Zothique probably is derived from Arthur Rimbaud's *Album dit "Zutique"* (written c. 1872). "Zutique" derives, in its turn, from the French expletive *zut!*, which is approximately parallel to such English expressions as "to hell with you!" The Zothique stories certainly are hellish. They display, more clearly than any of his other works, Clark Ashton Smith's debt to the French Decadent movement inspired by Rimbaud and Charles Baudelaire. They represent, in fact, one logical terminus of the quest defined by Baudelaire in the anguished prose-poem in which the poet's soul—echoing Edgar Allan Poe—demands that it be taken "Anywhere out of the World" (1857).

Because Smith's "Hyperborean grotesques" were set in the distant past, the viewpoint of stories set there had to accept that the dominion of Chaos ultimately would be displaced by Order. The world of "the last continent" of Zothique, on the other hand, has no future. Science and civilization are gone forever and utterly forgotten; everything that happens is a mere prelude to humankind's final annihilation. Consequently, Zothique became the setting in which Smith gave fullest expression to his images of ultimate decadence.

A few of the Zothique stories do contain an element of irony, in much the same vein as Smith's tales of Hyperborea, the most notable example being "The Voyage of King Euvoran." The elegiac "Morthylla" plays host to a plaintive note of sentimentality, whereas "The Isle of Torturers" may be reckoned one of Smith's exercises in literary pastiche by virtue of its echoes of Poe's "Masque of the Red Death" (1842) and the Comte de Villiers de l'Isle Adam's "The Torture of Hope" (c. 1885). The majority of the Zothique stories, however, are unrestrained melodramas replete with exotic violence and cruelty, set in ornate surroundings reminiscent of the most extravagant paintings of the French Decadent artist Gustave Moreau.

The best tales of Zothique—which include "The Empire of the Necromancers," "The Witchcraft of Ulua," "The Dark Eidolon," "Xeethra," and "Necromancy in Naat"—possess an unparalleled dramatic surge that carries them to their devastating conclusions. They are frequently erotic, but their eroticism is usually perverse and rarely finds any fulfillment save for destruction. The sadistic and erotic elements in the stories were sufficient to warrant some censorship by their initial publishers. The full texts of "The Witchcraft of Ulua" and "Xeethra" are restored in the Necronomicon Press series of the unexpurgated Clark Ashton Smith (six volumes, 1987-1988), but the original text of "Necromancy in Naat" was lost.

The quasi-pornographic features of the most extravagant stories represent a determined effort to confront and make manageable the most disturbing products of the imagination. In these stories, the most awful and terrifying creations of delirium and anxiety are submitted to the command of a rigorous literary imagination. In stories of this kind, the possibility of a happy ending is utterly out of the question; they ought not to be considered as tragedies, or even as horror stories, because no fate really can be considered tragic or horrific if it cannot possibly be avoided. It is in the images of suffering—of death-in-life or hell-in-life—contained in "Xeethra" and "Necromancy in Naat" that Smith reached the culmination of his trafficking with nightmares. There is nothing in the vast spectrum of fantasy fiction to match these tales in either their ambition or their execution.

—*Brian Stableford*

Selected Science-Fiction
and Fantasy Awards

This appendix lists recipients of science fiction and fantasy's most prestigious awards. Each section includes a description of the award and a chronological presentation of the winners in the best novel category for each accolade (except for awards specifically for shorter fiction or other types of work), giving the year in which the book qualified for the award (usually the year of first publication in book or serial form), the year the award was given (in parentheses), the name of the recipient, and the title of the work being honored. Winners of awards for short fiction generally are not included. Lifetime achievement awards mention only the year in which the presentation was made. The list is adapted from various editions of Robert Reginald's *Science Fiction and Fantasy Awards* (1981, 1991, 1993, 1996) and is used by permission of The Borgo Press.

—Robert Reginald

THE ARTHUR C. CLARKE AWARD

The Arthur C. Clarke Award honors the best science-fiction novel published in the United Kingdom during the previous year. Selections are made by a panel of judges, including elected representatives from the British Science Fiction Association, the International Science Policy Foundation, and the Science Fiction Foundation. The award is presented annually in April at a special ceremony held in London, England.

1986 (1987)	Margaret Atwood	*The Handmaid's Tale*
1987 (1988)	George Turner	*The Sea and Summer*
1988 (1989)	Rachel Pollack	*Unquenchable Fire*
1989 (1990)	Geoff Ryman	*The Child Garden*
1990 (1991)	Colin Greenland	*Take Back Plenty*
1991 (1992)	Pat Cadigan	*Synners*
1992 (1993)	Marge Piercy	*Body of Glass*
1993 (1994)	Jeff Noon	*Vurt*
1994 (1995)	Pat Cadigan	*Fools*
1995 (1996)	Paul J. McAuley	*Fairyland*

1996 (1997)	Amitav Ghosh	*The Calcutta Chromosome*
1997 (1998)	Mary Doria Russell	*The Sparrow*
1998 (1999)	Tricia Sullivan	*Dreaming in Smoke*
1999 (2000)	Bruce Sterling	*Distraction*
2000 (2001)	China Miéville	*Perdido Street Station*

THE BRITISH FANTASY AWARD

This accolade, also called the August Derleth Award, honors the best fantasy novel published in Great Britain during the preceding year and is presented by the British Fantasy Society at its convention in September.

1971 (1972)	Michael Moorcock	*The Knight of the Swords*
1972 (1973)	Michael Moorcock	*The King of the Swords*
1973 (1974)	Poul Anderson	*Hrolf Kraki's Saga*
1974 (1975)	Michael Moorcock	*The Sword and the Stallion*
1975 (1976)	Michael Moorcock	*The Hollow Lands*
1976 (1977)	Gordon R. Dickson	*The Dragon and the George*
1977 (1978)	Piers Anthony	*A Spell for Chameleon*
1978 (1979)	Stephen R. Donaldson	*The Chronicles of Thomas Covenant the Unbeliever*
1979 (1980)	Tanith Lee	*Death's Master*
1980 (1981)	Ramsey Campbell	*To Wake the Dead*
1981 (1982)	Stephen King	*Cujo*
1982 (1983)	Gene Wolfe	*The Sword of the Lictor*
1983 (1984)	Peter Straub	*Floating Dragons*
1984 (1985)	Ramsey Campbell	*Incarnate*
1985 (1986)	T. E. D. Klein	*The Ceremonies*
1986 (1987)	Stephen King	*It*
1987 (1988)	Ramsey Campbell	*The Hungry Moon*
1988 (1989)	Ramsey Campbell	*The Influence*
1989 (1990)	Dan Simmons	*Carrion Comfort*
1990 (1991)	Ramsey Campbell	*Midnight Sun*
1991 (1992)	Jonathan Carroll	*Outside the Dog Museum*
1992 (1993)	Graham Joyce	*Dark Sister*
1993 (1994)	Ramsey Campbell	*The Long Lost*
1994 (1995)	Michael Marshall Smith	*Only Forward*

1995 (1996)	Graham Joyce	*Requiem*
1996 (1997)	Graham Joyce	*The Tooth Fairy*
1997 (1998)	Chaz Brenchley	*Tower of the King's Daughter*
1998 (1999)	Stephen King	*Bag of Bones*
1999 (2000)	Graham Joyce	*Indigo*
2000 (2001)	China Miéville	*Perdido Street Station*

THE BRITISH SCIENCE FICTION ASSOCIATION AWARD

This award honors the best science-fiction novel published in Great Britain during the preceding year and is sponsored by the British Science Fiction Association. Presentations are made annually at England's National Science Fiction Convention, Eastercon, usually held in April.

1969 (1970)	John Brunner	*Stand on Zanzibar*
1970 (1971)	John Brunner	*The Jagged Orbit*
1971 (1972)	Brian W. Aldiss	*The Moment of Eclipse*
1972 (1973)	No award given	
1973 (1974)	Arthur C. Clarke	*Rendezvous with Rama*
1974 (1975)	Bob Shaw	*Orbitsville*
1975 (1976)	Christopher Priest	*Inverted World*
1976 (1977)	Michael G. Coney	*Brontomek!*
1977 (1978)	Ian Watson	*The Jonah Kit*
1978 (1979)	Philip K. Dick	*A Scanner Darkly*
1979 (1980)	J. G. Ballard	*The Unlimited Dream Company*
1980 (1981)	Gregory Benford	*Timescape*
1981 (1982)	Gene Wolfe	*The Shadow of the Torturer*
1982 (1983)	Brian W. Aldiss	*Helliconia Spring*
1983 (1984)	John Sladek	*Tik-Tok*
1984 (1985)	Robert Holdstock	*Mythago Wood*
1985 (1986)	Brian W. Aldiss	*Helliconia Winter*
1986 (1987)	Bob Shaw	*The Ragged Astronauts*
1987 (1988)	Keith Roberts	*Gráinne*
1988 (1989)	Robert Holdstock	*Lavondyss*
1989 (1990)	Terry Pratchett	*Pyramids*
1990 (1991)	Colin Greenland	*Take Back Plenty*
1991 (1992)	Dan Simmons	*The Fall of Hyperion*

1992 (1993)	Kim Stanley Robinson	*Red Mars*
1993 (1994)	Christopher Evans	*Aztec Century*
1994 (1995)	Iain M. Banks	*Feersum Endjinn*
1995 (1996)	Stephen Baxter	*The Time Ships*
1996 (1997)	Iain M. Banks	*Excession*
1997 (1998)	Mary Doria Russell	*The Sparrow*
1998 (1999)	Christopher Priest	*The Extremes*
1999 (2000)	Ken MacLeod	*The Sky Road*
2000 (2001)	Mary Gentle	*Ash: A Secret History*

THE HUGO AWARD/JOHN W. CAMPBELL AWARD

Originally called the Science Fiction Achievement Award, this oldest and most prestigious of science-fiction awards honors the best science-fiction novel published during the preceding year. The Hugos were first presented at the Philadelphia World Science Fiction Convention in 1953, were dropped in 1954, and were established permanently in 1955. The awards are decided by a mail vote of attending and supporting members of each World Science Fiction Convention (Worldcon) and presented annually at that gathering, usually held on (or within several weekends of) the Labor Day weekend at the beginning of September. The John W. Campbell Award, which is presented at the same convention, was created to honor the best new author in the science-fiction field for the preceding two years.

The Hugo Award

1952 (1953)	Alfred Bester	*The Demolished Man*
1953 (1954)	No award given	
1954 (1955)	Frank Riley *and* Mark Clifton	*They'd Rather Be Right*
1955 (1956)	Robert A. Heinlein	*Double Star*
1956 (1957)	No award given	
1957 (1958)	Fritz Leiber	*The Big Time*
1958 (1959)	James Blish	*A Case of Conscience*
1959 (1960)	Robert A. Heinlein	*Starship Troopers*
1960 (1961)	Walter M. Miller, Jr.	*A Canticle for Leibowitz*
1961 (1962)	Robert A. Heinlein	*Stranger in a Strange Land*

1962 (1963)	Philip K. Dick	*The Man in the High Castle*
1963 (1964)	Clifford D. Simak	*Here Gather the Stars* [book title: *Way Station*]
1964 (1965)	Fritz Leiber	*The Wanderer*
1965 (1966) [tie]	Roger Zelazny	*And Call Me Conrad* [book title: *The Dream Master*]
	Frank Herbert	*Dune*
1966 (1967)	Robert A. Heinlein	*The Moon Is a Harsh Mistress*
1967 (1968)	Roger Zelazny	*Lord of Light*
1968 (1969)	John Brunner	*Stand on Zanzibar*
1969 (1970)	Ursula K. Le Guin	*The Left Hand of Darkness*
1970 (1971)	Larry Niven	*Ringworld*
1971 (1972)	Philip José Farmer	*To Your Scattered Bodies Go*
1972 (1973)	Isaac Asimov	*The Gods Themselves*
1973 (1974)	Arthur C. Clarke	*Rendezvous with Rama*
1974 (1975)	Ursula K. Le Guin	*The Dispossessed*
1975 (1976)	Joe Haldeman	*The Forever War*
1976 (1977)	Kate Wilhelm	*Where Late the Sweet Birds Sang*
1977 (1978)	Frederik Pohl	*Gateway*
1978 (1979)	Vonda N. McIntyre	*Dreamsnake*
1979 (1980)	Arthur C. Clarke	*The Fountains of Paradise*
1980 (1981)	Joan D. Vinge	*The Snow Queen*
1981 (1982)	C. J. Cherryh	*Downbelow Station*
1982 (1983)	Isaac Asimov	*Foundation's Edge*
1983 (1984)	David Brin	*Startide Rising*
1984 (1985)	William Gibson	*Neuromancer*
1985 (1986)	Orson Scott Card	*Ender's Game*
1986 (1987)	Orson Scott Card	*Speaker for the Dead*
1987 (1988)	David Brin	*The Uplift War*
1988 (1989)	C. J. Cherryh	*Cyteen*
1989 (1990)	Dan Simmons	*Hyperion*
1990 (1991)	Lois McMaster Bujold	*The Vor Game*
1991 (1992)	Lois McMaster Bujold	*Barrayar*
1992 (1993) [tie]	Vernor Vinge	*A Fire upon the Deep*
	Connie Willis	*Doomsday Book*

1993 (1994)	Kim Stanley Robinson	*Green Mars*
1994 (1995)	Lois McMaster Bujold	*Mirror Dance*
1995 (1996)	Neal Stephenson	*The Diamond Age*
1996 (1997)	Kim Stanley Robinson	*Blue Mars*
1997 (1998)	Joe Haldeman	*Forever Peace*
1998 (1999)	Connie Willis	*To Say Nothing of the Dog*
1999 (2000)	Vernor Vinge	*A Deepness in the Sky*
2000 (2001)	J. K. Rowling	*Harry Potter and the Goblet of Fire*

John W. Campbell Award for Best New Writer of the Year

1972 (1973)	Jerry Pournelle		1986 (1987)	Karen Joy Fowler
1973 (1974)	Spider Robinson		1987 (1988)	Judith Moffett
[tie]	Lisa Tuttle		1988 (1989)	Michaela Roessner
1974 (1975)	P. J. Plauger		1989 (1990)	Kristine Kathryn Rusch
1975 (1976)	Tom Reamy			
1976 (1977)	C. J. Cherryh		1990 (1991)	Julia Ecklar
1977 (1978)	Orson Scott Card		1991 (1992)	Ted Chiang
1978 (1979)	Stephen R. Donaldson		1992 (1993)	Laura Resnick
1979 (1980)	Barry B. Longyear		1993 (1994)	Amy Thomson
1980 (1981)	Somtow Sucharitkul (S. P. Somtow)		1994 (1995)	Jeff Noon
			1995 (1996)	David Feintuch
1981 (1982)	Alexis Gilliland		1996 (1997)	Michael A. Burstein
1982 (1983)	Paul O. Williams		1997 (1998)	Mary Doria Russell
1983 (1984)	R. A. MacAvoy		1998 (1999)	Nalo Hopkinson
1984 (1985)	Lucius Shepard		1999 (2000)	Cory Doctorow
1985 (1986)	Melissa Scott		2000 (2001)	Kristine Smith

THE INTERNATIONAL FANTASY AWARD

Among the most distinguished of the science-fiction awards was the now-discontinued International Fantasy Award, presented between 1951 and 1957 to honor the best book-length work (novels or collections) of fantastic literature published during the preceding year. It was first presented at the 1951 British Science Fiction Convention, and its recipient was chosen by a distiguished panel of science-fiction professionals.

1949/1950 (1951)	George R. Stewart	*Earth Abides*
1951 (1952)	John Collier	*Fancies and Goodnights*
1952 (1953)	Clifford D. Simak	*City*
1953 (1954)	Theodore Sturgeon	*More than Human*
1954 (1955)	Edgar Pangborn	*A Mirror for Observers*
1955 (1956)	No award given	
1956 (1957)	J. R. R. Tolkien	*The Lord of the Rings*

THE JOHN W. CAMPBELL MEMORIAL AWARD/THE THEODORE STURGEON MEMORIAL AWARD

This award honors the best science-fiction novel published during the preceding year. The award's recipient is chosen by an international panel of science-fiction professionals, and the award is presented annually in July at a conference or ceremony held at the University of Kansas in Lawrence. A companion award, The Theodore Sturgeon Memorial Award, presented simultaneously, honors the best science-fiction short story (under 17,500 words) published during the previous year.

The John W. Campbell Memorial Award

1972 (1973)	Barry N. Malzberg	*Beyond Apollo*
1973 (1974) [tie]	Arthur C. Clarke	*Rendezvous with Rama*
	Robert Merle	*Malevil*
1974 (1975)	Philip K. Dick	*Flow My Tears, the Policeman Said*
1975 (1976)	No award given	
1976 (1977)	Kingsley Amis	*The Alteration*
1977 (1978)	Frederik Pohl	*Gateway*
1978 (1979)	Michael Moorcock	*Gloriana*
1979 (1980)	Thomas M. Disch	*On Wings of Song*
1980 (1981)	Gregory Benford	*Timescape*
1981 (1982)	Russell Hoban	*Riddley Walker*
1982 (1983)	Brian W. Aldiss	*Helliconia Spring*
1983 (1984)	Gene Wolfe	*The Citadel of the Autarch*
1984 (1985)	Frederik Pohl	*The Years of the City*
1985 (1986)	David Brin	*The Postman*

1986 (1987)	Joan Slonczewski	*A Door into Ocean*
1987 (1988)	Connie Willis	*Lincoln's Dreams*
1988 (1989)	Bruce Sterling	*Islands in the Net*
1989 (1990)	Geoff Ryman	*The Child Garden*
1990 (1991)	Kim Stanley Robinson	*Pacific Edge*
1991 (1992)	Bradley Denton	*Buddy Holly Is Alive and Well on Ganymede*
1992 (1993)	Charles Sheffield	*Brother to Dragons*
1993 (1994)	No award given	
1994 (1995)	Greg Egan	*Permutation City*
1995 (1996)	Stephen Baxter	*The Time Ships*
1996 (1997)	Paul McAuley	*Fairyland*
1997 (1998)	Joe Haldeman	*Forever Peace*
1998 (1999)	George Zebrowski	*Brute Orbits*
1999 (2000)	Vernor Vinge	*A Deepness in the Sky*
2000 (2001)	Poul Anderson	*Genesis*

The Theodore Sturgeon Memorial Award

1986 (1987)	Judith Moffett	*"Surviving"*
1987 (1988)	Pat Murphy	*"Rachel in Love"*
1988 (1989)	George Alec Effinger	*"Schrödinger's Kitten"*
1989 (1990)	Michael Swanwick	*"The Edge of the World"*
1990 (1991)	Terry Bisson	*"Bears Discover Fire"*
1991 (1992)	John Kessel	*"Buffalo"*
1992 (1993)	Dan Simmons	*"This Year's Class Picture"*
1993 (1994)	Kij Johnson	*"Fox Magic"*
1994 (1995)	Ursula K. Le Guin	*"Forgiveness Day"*
1995 (1996)	John G. McDaid	*"Jigoku No Mokushiroku (The Symbolic Revelation of the Apolcalypse)"*
1996 (1997)	Nancy Kress	*"The Flowers of Aulit Prison"*
1997 (1998)	Michael F. Flynn	*"House of Dreams"*
1998 (1999)	Ted Chiang	*"Story of Your Life"*
1999 (2000)	David Marusek	*"The Wedding Album"*
2000 (2001)	Ian McDonald	*"Tendeléo's Story"*

THE LOCUS AWARD

This award honors the best fantastic fiction published during the preceding year as chosen by the readership of *Locus: The Newspaper of the Science Fiction Field*. Beginning in 1980, the award for best novel was split into separate components honoring the best science-fiction novel and the best fantasy novel of the year. The awards are announced annually in the August issue of *Locus* but are actually presented at the Dragon*Con convention held in mid-July.

1970 (1971)	Larry Niven	*Ringworld*
1971 (1972)	Ursula K. Le Guin	*The Lathe of Heaven*
1972 (1973)	Isaac Asimov	*The Gods Themselves*
1973 (1974)	Arthur C. Clarke	*Rendezvous with Rama*
1974 (1975)	Ursula K. Le Guin	*The Dispossessed*
1975 (1976)	Joe Haldeman	*The Forever War*
1976 (1977)	Kate Wilhelm	*Where Late the Sweet Birds Sang*
1977 (1978)	Frederik Pohl	*Gateway*
1978 (1979)	Vonda N. McIntyre	*Dreamsnake*
1979 (1980) (SF)	John Varley	*Titan*
1979 (1980) (Fantasy)	Patricia A. McKillip	*Harpist in the Wind*
1980 (1981) (SF)	Joan D. Vinge	*The Snow Queen*
1980 (1981) (Fantasy)	Robert Silverberg	*Lord Valentine's Castle*
1981 (1982) (SF)	Julian May	*The Many-Colored Land*
1981 (1982) (Fantasy)	Gene Wolfe	*The Claw of the Conciliator*
1982 (1983) (SF)	Isaac Asimov	*Foundation's Edge*
1982 (1983) (Fantasy)	Gene Wolfe	*The Sword of the Lictor*
1983 (1984) (SF)	David Brin	*Startide Rising*
1983 (1984) (Fantasy)	Marion Zimmer Bradley	*The Mists of Avalon*
1984 (1985) (SF)	Larry Niven	*The Integral Trees*
1984 (1985) (Fantasy)	Robert A. Heinlein	*Job*
1985 (1986) (SF)	David Brin	*The Postman*
1985 (1986) (Fantasy)	Roger Zelazny	*Trumps of Doom*
1986 (1987) (SF)	Orson Scott Card	*Speaker for the Dead*
1986 (1987) (Fantasy)	Gene Wolfe	*Soldier of the Mist*
1987 (1988) (SF)	David Brin	*The Uplift War*
1987 (1988) (Fantasy)	Orson Scott Card	*Seventh Son*

1988 (1989) (SF)	C. J. Cherryh	*Cyteen*
1988 (1989) (Fantasy)	Orson Scott Card	*Red Prophet*
1989 (1990) (SF)	Dan Simmons	*Hyperion*
1989 (1990) (Fantasy)	Orson Scott Card	*Prentice Alvin*
1990 (1991) (SF)	Dan Simmons	*The Fall of Hyperion*
1990 (1991) (Fantasy)	Ursula K. Le Guin	*Tehanu: The Last Book of Earthsea*
1991 (1992) (SF)	Lois McMaster Bujold	*Barrayar*
1991 (1992) (Fantasy)	Sheri S. Tepper	*Beauty*
1992 (1993) (SF)	Connie Willis	*Doomsday Book*
1992 (1993) (Fantasy)	Tim Powers	*Last Call*
1993 (1994) (SF)	Kim Stanley Robinson	*Green Mars*
1993 (1994) (Fantasy)	Peter S. Beagle	*The Innkeeper's Daughter*
1994 (1995) (SF)	Lois McMaster Bujold	*Mirror Dance*
1994 (1995) (Fantasy)	Michael Bishop	*Brittle Innings*
1995 (1996) (SF)	Neal Stephenson	*The Diamond Age*
1995 (1996) (Fantasy)	Orson Scott Card	*Alvin Journeyman*
1996 (1997) (SF)	Kim Stanley Robinson	*Blue Mars*
1996 (1997) (Fantasy)	George R. R. Martin	*A Game of Thrones*
1997 (1998) (SF)	Dan Simmons	*The Rise of Endymion*
1997 (1998) (Fantasy)	Tim Powers	*Earthquake Weather*
1998 (1999) (SF)	Connie Willis	*To Say Nothing of the Dog*
1998 (1999) (Fantasy)	George R. R. Martin	*A Clash of Kings*
1999 (2000) (SF)	Neal Stephenson	*Cryptonomicon*
1999 (2000) (Fantasy)	J. K. Rowling	*Harry Potter and the Prisoner of Azkaban*
2000 (2001) (SF)	Ursula Le Guin	*The Telling*
2000 (2001) (Fantasy)	George R. R. Martin	*A Storm of Swords*

THE NEBULA AWARD

The Nebula honors the best science-fiction novel published during the preceding year. It is administered and presented by the Science Fiction and Fantasy Writers of America, Inc. (SFFWA) at its annual meeting and banquet held in April. The Nebula Grand Master Award for lifetime achievement may be presented by the officers of the SFWA in no more than six years out of every decade.

1965 (1966)	Frank Herbert	*Dune*
1966 (1967) [tie]	Samuel R. Delany	*Babel-17*
	Daniel Keyes	*Flowers for Algernon*
1967 (1968)	Samuel R. Delany	*The Einstein Intersection*
1968 (1969)	Alexei Panshin	*Rite of Passage*
1969 (1970)	Ursula K. Le Guin	*The Left Hand of Darkness*
1970 (1971)	Larry Niven	*Ringworld*
1971 (1972)	Robert Silverberg	*A Time of Changes*
1972 (1973)	Isaac Asimov	*The Gods Themselves*
1973 (1974)	Arthur C. Clarke	*Rendezvous with Rama*
1974 (1975)	Ursula K. Le Guin	*The Dispossessed*
1975 (1976)	Joe Haldeman	*The Forever War*
1976 (1977)	Frederik Pohl	*Man Plus*
1977 (1978)	Frederik Pohl	*Gateway*
1978 (1979)	Vonda N. McIntyre	*Dreamsnake*
1979 (1980)	Arthur C. Clarke	*The Fountains of Paradise*
1980 (1981)	Gregory Benford	*Timescape*
1981 (1982)	Gene Wolfe	*The Claw of the Conciliator*
1982 (1983)	Michael Bishop	*No Enemy but Time*
1983 (1984)	David Brin	*Startide Rising*
1984 (1985)	William Gibson	*Neuromancer*
1985 (1986)	Orson Scott Card	*Ender's Game*
1986 (1987)	Orson Scott Card	*Speaker for the Dead*
1987 (1988)	Pat Murphy	*The Falling Woman*
1988 (1989)	Lois McMaster Bujold	*Falling Free*
1989 (1990)	Elizabeth Ann Scarborough	*The Healer's War*
1990 (1991)	Ursula K. Le Guin	*Tehanu: The Last Book of Earthsea*
1991 (1992)	Michael Swanwick	*Stations of the Tide*
1992 (1993)	Connie Willis	*Doomsday Book*
1993 (1994)	Kim Stanley Robinson	*Red Mars*
1994 (1995)	Greg Bear	*Moving Mars*
1995 (1996)	Robert J. Sawyer	*The Terminal Experiment*
1996 (1997)	Nicola Griffith	*Slow River*
1997 (1998)	Vonda N. McIntyre	*The Moon and the Sun*

1998 (1999)	Joe Haldeman	*Forever Peace*
1999 (2000)	Octavia E. Butler	*Parable of the Talents*
2000 (2001)	Greg Bear	*Darwin's Radio*

Nebula Grand Master Awards

1975	Robert A. Heinlein	1991	Lester del Rey
1976	Jack Williamson	1993	Frederik Pohl
1977	Clifford D. Simak	1995	Damon Knight
1979	L. Sprague de Camp	1996	A. E. van Vogt
1981	Fritz Leiber	1997	Jack Vance
1984	Andre Norton	1998	Poul Anderson
1986	Arthur C. Clarke	1999	Hal Clement
1987	Isaac Asimov	2000	Brian Aldiss
1988	Alfred Bester	2001	Philip José Farmer
1989	Ray Bradbury		

THE PHILIP K. DICK MEMORIAL AWARD

This award honors the best science-fiction book originally published in paperback in the United States during the previous year. The $1,000 cash prize is sponsored annually by the Philadelphia Science Fiction Society, the Northwest Science Fiction Society, and Norwescon. The award is presented annually at the Norwescon convention, usually held in April.

1982 (1983)	Rudy Rucker	*Software*
1983 (1984)	Tim Powers	*The Anubis Gates*
1984 (1985)	William Gibson	*Neuromancer*
1985 (1986)	Tim Powers	*Dinner at Deviant's Palace*
1986 (1987)	James P. Blaylock	*Homunculus*
1987 (1988)	Patricia Geary	*Strange Toys*
1988 (1989)	Rudy Rucker	*Wetware*
1989 (1990)	Richard Paul Russo	*Subterranean Gallery*
1990 (1991)	Pat Murphy	*Points of Departure*
1991 (1992)	Ian McDonald	*King of Morning, Queen of Day*
1992 (1993)	Richard Grant	*Through the Heart*

1993 (1994)	John M. Ford	*Growing Up Weightless*
1994 (1995)	Robert Charles Wilson	*Mysterium*
1995 (1996)	Bruce Bethke	*Headcrash*
1996 (1997)	Stephen Baxter	*The Time Ships*
1997 (1998)	Stepan Chapman	*The Troika*
1998 (1999)	Geoff Ryman	*253: The Print Remix*
1999 (2000)	Stephen Baxter	*Vacuum Diagrams*
2000 (2001)	Michael Marshall Smith	*Only Forward*

THE PILGRIM AWARD/THE PIONEER AWARD

The Pilgrim Award honors lifetime achievement in science-fiction and fantasy scholarship. It is administered by the Science Fiction Research Association and presented at that organization's annual convention, usually held in June. The Pioneer Award, presented simultaneously with the Pilgrim, honors the best single critical work (usually a short essay) published during the preceding year.

The Pilgrim Award

1970	J. O. Bailey	1986	George E. Slusser
1971	Marjorie Hope Nicolson	1987	Gary K. Wolfe
1972	Julius Kagarlitski (Yulii Kagarlitskii)	1988	Joanna Russ
		1989	Ursula K. Le Guin
1973	Jack Williamson	1990	Marshall B. Tymn
1974	I. F. Clarke	1991	Pierre Versins
1975	Damon Knight	1992	Mark R. Hillegas
1976	James E. Gunn	1993	Robert Reginald
1977	Thomas D. Clareson	1994	John Clute
1978	Brian W. Aldiss	1995	Vivian Sobchack
1979	Darko Suvin	1996	David Ketterer
1980	Peter Nicholls	1997	Marlene Barr
1981	Sam Moskowitz	1998	L. Sprague de Camp
1982	Neil Barron	1999	Brian Stableford
1983	H. Bruce Franklin	2000	Hal Hall
1984	Everett F. Bleiler	2001	Dave Samuelson
1985	Samuel R. Delany		

The Pioneer Award

1989 (1990)	Veronica Hollinger	*"The Vampire and the Alien: Variations on the Outsider"*
1990 (1991)	H. Bruce Franklin	*"The Vietnam War as American Science Fiction and Fantasy"*
1991 (1992)	Istvan Csiscery-Ronay, Jr.	*"The SF of Theory: Baudrillard and Haraway"*
1992 (1993)	No award given	
1993 (1994)	Takayumi Tatsumi *and* Larry McCaffrey	*"Toward the Theoretical Frontiers of Fiction: From Metafiction and Cyberpunk Through Avant-Pop"*
1994 (1995)	Roger Luckhurst	*"The Many Deaths of Science Fiction: A Polemic"*
1995 (1996)	Brian Stableford	*"How Should a Science Fiction Story End?"*
1996 (1997)	John Moore	*"Shifting Frontiers: Mapping Cyberpunk and the American South"*
1997 (1998)	I. F. Clarke	*"Future-War Fiction: The First Main Phase, 1871-1900"*
1998 (1999)	Carl Freedman	*"Kubrick's 2001 and the Possibility of a Science-Fiction Cinema"*
1999 (2000)	Wendy Pearson	*"Alien Cryptographies: The View from Queer"*
2000 (2001)	De Witt Douglas Kilgore	*"Changing Regimes: Vonda N. McIntyre's Parodic Astrofuturism"*

THE WORLD FANTASY AWARD

Also called the Howard Award, this accolade honors the best fantasy novel published during the preceding year. It is administered by and presented at the annual World Fantasy Convention, usually held in October.

1973/1974 (1975)	Patricia A. McKillip	*The Forgotten Beasts of Eld*
1975 (1976)	Richard Matheson	*Bid Time Return*
1976 (1977)	William Kotzwinkle	*Doctor Rat*
1977 (1978)	Fritz Leiber	*Our Lady of Darkness*

1978 (1979)	Michael Moorcock	*Gloriana*
1979 (1980)	Elizabeth A. Lynn	*Watchtower*
1980 (1981)	Gene Wolfe	*The Shadow of the Torturer*
1981 (1982)	John Crowley	*Little, Big*
1982 (1983)	Michael Shea	*Nifft the Lean*
1983 (1984)	John M. Ford	*The Dragon Waiting*
1984 (1985) [tie]	Robert Holdstock	*Mythago Wood*
	Barry Hughart	*Bridge of Birds*
1985 (1986)	Dan Simmons	*Song of Kali*
1986 (1987)	Patrick Suskind	*Perfume*
1987 (1988)	Ken Grimwood	*Replay*
1988 (1989)	Peter Straub	*Koko*
1989 (1990)	Jack Vance	*Lyonesse: Madouc*
1990 (1991) [tie]	James Morrow	*Only Begotten Daughter*
	Ellen Kushner	*Thomas the Rhymer*
1991 (1992)	Robert R. McCammon	*Boy's Life*
1992 (1993)	Tim Powers	*Last Call*
1993 (1994)	Lewis Shiner	*Glimpses*
1994 (1995)	James Morrow	*Towing Jehovah*
1995 (1996)	Christopher Priest	*The Prestige*
1996 (1997)	Rachel Pollack	*Godmother Night*
1997 (1998)	Jeffrey Ford	*The Physiognomy*
1998 (1999)	Louise Erdrich	*The Antelope Wife*
1999 (2000)	Martin Scott	*Thraxas*
2000 (2001) [tie]	Tim Powers	*Declare*
	Sean Stewart	*Galveston*

Lifetime Achievement

1975	Robert Bloch	1987	Jack Finney
1976	Fritz Leiber	1988	Everett F. Bleiler
1977	Ray Bradbury	1989	Evangeline Walton
1978	Frank Belknap Long	1990	R. A. Lafferty
1979	Jorge Luis Borges	1991	Ray Russell
1980	Manly Wade Wellman	1992	Edd Cartier
1981	C. L. Moore	1993	Harlan Ellison

1982	Italo Calvino
1983	Roald Dahl
1984 [joint awards]	L. Sprague de Camp
	E. Hoffmann Price
	Donald Wandrei [refused]
	Richard Matheson
1985	Jack Vance
	Theodore Sturgeon
1986	Avram Davidson

1994	Jack Williamson
1995	Ursula K. Le Guin
1996	Gene Wolf
1997	Madeleine L'Engle
1998	Edward L. Ferman
	Andre Norton
1999	Hugh B. Cave
2000	Marion Zimmer Bradley
	Michael Moorcock
2001	Philip José Farmer
	Frank Frazetta

Timeline

1726	Gulliver's Travels (Swift)
1818	Frankenstein (Shelley)
1864	Journey to the Center of the Earth (Verne)
1865	Alice's Adventures in Wonderland (Carroll)
1870	Twenty Thousand Leagues Under the Sea (Verne)
1871	At the Back of the North Wind (MacDonald)
	Through the Looking-Glass (Carroll)
1886	Strange Case of Dr. Jekyll and Mr. Hyde, The (Stevenson)
1889	Connecticut Yankee in King Arthur's Court, A (Twain)
1891	Picture of Dorian Gray, The (Wilde)
1895	Time Machine, The (Wells)
1897	Dracula (Stoker)
	Invisible Man, The (Wells)
1898	War of the Worlds, The (Wells)
1900	Wonderful Wizard of Oz, The (Baum)
1905-1906	Psammead Trilogy (Nesbit)
1908	Wind in the Willows, The (Grahame)
1917-1964	Barsoom Series (Burroughs)
1922	Worm Ouroboros, The (Eddison)
1924	King of Elfland's Daughter, The (Dunsany)
	We (Zamyatin)
1926	Lud-in-the-Mist (Mirrlees)
	Ship of Ishtar, The (Merritt)
1928	Orlando (Woolf)
1930	Last and First Men (Stapledon)
1932	Brave New World (Huxley)
1936	War with the Newts (Čapek)
1937	Hobbit, The (Tolkien)
	Star Maker (Stapledon)
1938-1958	Space Trilogy (Lewis)
1938-1977	Once and Future King, The (White)
1941-1989	Incomplete Enchanter, The (de Camp and Pratt)
1943	Little Prince, The (Saint-Exupéry)
1945	Animal Farm (Orwell)
1946-1959	Titus Groan Trilogy (Peake)
1949	Nineteen Eighty-Four (Orwell)
1950	Martian Chronicles, The (Bradbury)
1950-1956	Chronicles of Narnia, The (Lewis)

1950-1984	Dying Earth Series (Vance)
1951	Illustrated Man, The (Bradbury)
1951-1993	Foundation series (Asimov)
1952	City (Simak)
	Rashomon and Other Stories (Akutagawa)
1953	Bring the Jubilee (Moore)
	Childhood's End (Clarke)
	Demolished Man, The (Bester)
	E Pluribus Unicorn (Sturgeon)
	Fahrenheit 451 (Bradbury)
	More than Human (Sturgeon)
	Space Merchants, The (Pohl and Kornbluth)
1953-1955	Conan Series (Howard)
1954	Caves of Steel, The (Asimov)
	I Am Legend (Matheson)
	Mission of Gravity (Clement)
1954-1955	Lord of the Rings, The (Tolkien)
1957	Naked Sun, The (Asimov)
	Stars My Destination, The (Bester)
1958	Case of Conscience, A (Blish)
	Non-Stop (Aldiss)
1959	Inter Ice Age 4 (Abe)
	Sirens of Titan, The (Vonnegut)
1960	Canticle for Leibowitz, A (Miller)
	Rogue Moon (Budrys)
1960-1974	Fantasy Worlds of Peter Beagle, The (Beagle)
1960-1994	Childe Cycle (Dickson)
1961	Dark Universe (Galouye)
	Solaris (Lem)
	Stranger in a Strange Land (Heinlein)
1962	Man in the High Castle, The (Dick)
	Wrinkle in Time, A (L'Engle)
1963	Planet of the Apes (Boulle)
	Witch World (Norton)
1964	At the Mountains of Madness and Other Novels (Lovecraft)
	Davy (Pangborn)
	Martian Time-Slip (Dick)
1964-1973	Prydain Chronicles, The (Alexander)
1965	Cyberiad, The (Lem)
1965-1977	Dark Is Rising Sequence, The (Cooper)
1965-1985	Dune Series (Herbert)

1966	Flowers for Algernon (Keyes)
	Make Room! Make Room! (Harrison)
	Moon Is a Harsh Mistress, The (Heinlein)
1967	Einstein Intersection, The (Delany)
	I Have No Mouth and I Must Scream (Ellison)
	Owl Service, The (Garner)
1968	Camp Concentration (Disch)
	Do Androids Dream of Electric Sheep? (Dick)
	Stand on Zanzibar (Brunner)
1968-2001	Earthsea (Le Guin)
1968-1988	Space Odyssey Series (Clarke)
1969	Left Hand of Darkness, The (Le Guin)
	Phoenix and the Mirror, The (Davidson)
	Slaughterhouse-Five (Vonnegut)
1970	Cities in Flight (Blish)
	Ringworld (Niven)
	Zothique (Smith)
1970-1979	Merlin Trilogy (Stewart)
1970-1988	Fafhrd and the Gray Mouser (Leiber)
1971	Hyperborea (Smith)
	Star Light (Clement)
1972	Dying Inside (Silverberg)
	Infernal Desire Machines of Doctor Hoffman, The (Carter)
	Watership Down (Adams)
	When Harlie Was One (Gerrold)
1972-1991	Elric Saga, The (Moorcock)
1973	Gravity's Rainbow (Pynchon)
	Man Who Folded Himself, The (Gerrold)
1974	Dispossessed, The (Le Guin)
	Forever War, The (Haldeman)
	Forgotten Beasts of Eld, The (McKillip)
	Inverted World (Priest)
	Mote in God's Eye (Niven and Pournelle)
1975	Dhalgren (Delany)
	Female Man, The (Russ)
1976	Best of C. M. Kornbluth, The (Kornbluth)
	Boys from Brazil, The (Levin)
	Where Late the Sweet Birds Sang (Wilhelm)
	Woman on the Edge of Time (Piercy)
1976-1979	Riddle of Stars (McKillip)
1976-1984	Patternist Series (Butler)

1976-2001	Vampire Chronicles (Rice)
1977	Our Lady of Darkness (Leiber)
1978	Best Short Stories of J. G. Ballard, The (Ballard)
	Dreamsnake (McIntyre)
1978-1981	Tales from the Flat Earth (Lee)
1979	Engine Summer (Crowley)
	Instrumentality of Mankind, The (Smith)
	Ringworld Engineers, The (Niven)
1970-1991	Amber Series (Zelazny)
1979-1992	Hitchhiker's Guide to the Galaxy Series (Adams)
1980	Land of Laughs, The (Carroll)
	Roderick (Sladek)
	Shatterday (Ellison)
	Timescape (Benford)
	VALIS (Dick)
	Vampire Tapestry, The (Charnas)
1980-1987	Book of the New Sun, The (Wolfe)
	Uplift Sequence, The (Brin)
1980-1991	Snow Queen Trilogy (Vinge)
1981	Little, Big (Crowley)
1982	Blue Sword, The (McKinley)
	Mists of Avalon, The (Bradley)
	No Enemy But Time (Bishop)
1982-1985	Helliconia Trilogy (Aldiss)
1983	Anubis Gates, The (Powers)
	Roderick at Random (Sladek)
1984	Hero and the Crown, The (McKinley)
	Merchants' War, The (Pohl and Kornbluth)
	Wasp Factory, The (Banks)
1984-1988	Neuromancer Trilogy (Gibson)
1984-1990	Orange County Trilogy (Robinson)
1984-1993	Mythago Cycle (Holdstock)
1985	Blood Music (Bear)
	Eon (Bear)
	Fire and Hemlock (Jones)
	Handmaid's Tale, The (Atwood)
1985-1996	Ender Series (Card)
1986	Door into Ocean, A (Slonczewski)
	Falling Woman, The (Murphy)
	Unconquered Country, The (Ryman)
1987	Aegypt (Crowley)

Bibliography

Introduction

This is a selected annotated bibliography of critical commentary and literary theory concerning fantasy and science fiction in narrative and film. Annotations provide brief comments on content and orientation, designed to aid teachers and scholars, especially newcomers, in the field. Space limitations forced exclusion of many worthy research tools, primarily those devoted to strictly bibliographic ends, single-author studies, and works primarily on the closely related fields of utopian/dystopian fiction. To further save space, we refer to "science fiction" as "SF" throughout the bibliography. The bibliography is arranged in three sections, with works ordered alphabetically by author within each. The first section, "Fantasy and Science Fiction," covers works discussing both sides of the sometimes contested division between fantasy and science fiction. The remaining sections focus on the two genres separately.

FANTASY AND SCIENCE FICTION

Aldiss, Brian, and David Wingrove. *Trillion Year Spree*. New York: Avon, 1986. A full-fledged history of SF, *Trillion Year Spree*, winner of a Hugo Award, is a revised and enlarged version of Aldiss's *Billion Year Spree* (1973). The text traces SF from its gothic beginnings in Mary Shelley's *Frankenstein* to modern SF's New Wave and cyberpunk. The book includes illustrations and photos of authors, SF magazine covers, film stills, and SF art. Although Aldiss's book deals primarily with SF, there are observations and comments on fantasy writers and their works sprinkled throughout. The book is useful in that it situates the writers and works within specific periods and movements.

Clareson, Thomas D., ed. *SF: The Other Side of Realism*. Bowling Green, Ohio: Bowling Green University Popular Press, 1971. Clareson collected these essays as examples of serious criticism on SF and fantasy. In the first essay in the book, Clareson examines SF's relationship to mainstream literature, specifically realism. Judith Merril explores the place of science in SF. Samuel R. Delany, in an important piece, discusses his theory of subjunctivity and reading protocols as a way to distinguish between SF, fantasy, and other forms of writing. James Blish discusses SF criticism, defining worthwhile and other styles and questions of SF criticism. Stanisław Lem has a wonderful essay on the contemporary and historical meaning of the image of the robot in SF. Julius Kagarlitski's "Realism and Fantasy" contrasts romantic fantasy, which arose in the eighteenth century, to realistic fantasy, which arose in the latter nineteenth century and which now is called scientific; scientific fantasy is exemplified in the works of Jules Verne. Rudolph Schmerl's "Fantasy as Technique" begins by examining cultural context in determining fantasy and the interplay between writer and author. He announces the centrality of the author's intent, the necessity of meaning below the surface of narrative, and the importance of the pretense of actuality. He avers finally that if a fantasy is not understood as one, then no one can read it intelligently.

Fredericks, Casey. *The Future of Eternity: Mythologies of Science Fiction and Fantasy.* Bloomington: Indiana University Press, 1982. Adopting a structuralist approach to mythology, Fredericks is able to provide powerfully generative readings of twentieth century SF in terms of the major mythic themes of creation, the hero, godhead or the superman, and archaic time. Rather than conceiving myth as a closed system of ancient patterns or tales, Fredericks approaches it as a diverse and dynamic system that has found complex and rich expression in SF. Although most of this book is devoted to SF, its discussion of myth makes it useful in distinguishing SF from fantasy and the myths they choose or how they use them. Chapter 2 defines and develops the notion of estrangement, what J. R. R. Tolkien calls "recovery," and points out briefly its role in fantasy. Chapter 4 is a left-handed defense of heroic fantasy, which Fredericks contends comes from contemporary feelings of stifling and fear of the growth of power and potential dominance. He particularly elucidates the potential for release and the nonconformist attitude contained in "sword and sorcery" fantasy as good fun and escapism.

Le Guin, Ursula K. *Dancing at the Edge of the World: Thoughts on Words, Women, Places.* New York: Grove Press, 1989. Reprinting and often revising essays and talks given between 1976 and 1988, as well as reprinting reviews from 1977 to 1986, Le Guin continues her richly evocative reflections on the life of the writer, speculative fiction, and especially feminism and issues of social responsibility. In addition to lighter and occasional pieces, the collection includes some of her most powerful and insightful nonfiction work, such as "A Non-Euclidean View of California as a Cold Place to Be," in which she thinks through and radically revises what might be meant by utopia, and "The Carrier Bag Theory of Fiction," in which she imagines a narrative theory predicated on the principle of inclusion and "messy," to borrow a key term from her *Always Coming Home*. In the revised reprinting of "Is Gender Necessary? Redux," Le Guin interpolates her views from 1987 into those expressed in this 1976 essay, arguing with her former self and preparing readers for the strong feminist insights and challenges of essays such as the "Bryn Mawr Commencement Address" and "The Fisherwoman's Daughter," as well as some of the shorter pieces. This is a rich record of thought and writing that will be of keen interest to Le Guin scholars, feminists, and most readers of contemporary SF.

_____. *The Language of the Night: Essays on Fantasy and Science Fiction.* 1979. Rev. ed. New York: HarperCollins, 1989. Aside from the revised version of "Is Gender Necessary? Redux" and the updated checklist of Le Guin's works, this new edition does not differ substantively from the original. Largely presenting Le Guin's early reflections on her own work and on key issues in SF, the collection devotes five of its thirty essays to the study of fantasy. In "Why Are Americans Afraid of Dragons," the author contemplates the cultural paradigms in American society that are hostile to fantasy, which threatens them. "Dreams Must Explain Themselves" deals with writing fantasy and with the Earthsea books. "The Child and the Shadow" and "Myth and Archetype in Science Fiction" explain the influences of the unconscious and of Carl Jung. Finally, "From Elfland to Poughkeepsie" comments on the style and language—the good, the bad, and the ugly—used by fantasy writers. An excellent beginning place for Le Guin scholars.

Slusser, George, and Eric Rabkin, eds. *Intersections: Fantasy and Science Fiction.* Carbondale: Southern Illinois University Press, 1987. Seventeen essays from the seventh J. Lloyd Eaton Conference on SF and Fantasy Literature (1985) make up this volume, which focuses primarily on science fantasy, the links between fantasy and SF, and the relationships between SF and fantasy and other genres such as gothic, horror, and myth. Among the contributors are Robert Scholes, Michael Collings, Roger Zelazny, Samuel R. Delany, Brian Attebery, Kathryn Hume, and George Slusser.

Wolfe, Gary K. *Critical Terms for Science Fiction and Fantasy: A Glossary and Guide to Scholarship.* Westport, Conn.: Greenwood Press, 1986. The most complete reference text of its kind, Wolfe's guide offers full definitions of standard terminology; an introduction to the major themes, definitions, and conventions of SF and fantasy; and a limited bibliography.

FANTASY

Attebery, Brian. *The Fantasy Tradition in American Literature: From Irving to Le Guin.* Bloomington: Indiana University Press, 1980. Attebery's seminal book on fantasy begins with an attempt to define fantasy. He surveys definitions of fantasy by J. R. R. Tolkien, C. S. Lewis, C. N. Manlove, Tzvetan Todorov, W. R. Irwin, and others and offers one of his own, with wonder as the linchpin. The first chapter glances over the popular fantasies of British writers from George MacDonald forward as points of reference for American fantasy. Chapter 2, on folk tradition, notes the importance of *Marchen*, folktales, and ballads in the European tradition and then goes on to examine American ballads and tall tales, such as those about Paul Bunyan. One crucial subject of this chapter is the opposition in Puritan, rationalist, and transcendentalist thought to folktales and the supernatural. Chapter 3 addresses the influence of romance and the contributions of Edgar Allan Poe, Nathaniel Hawthorne, and Herman Melville to American fantasy. The fourth chapter is concerned with nineteenth century fantasy for children, and the fifth treats the contributions of L. Frank Baum and the Oz tales, which were written because Baum believed that American fairy tales were not working, so it was high time someone wrote one that did. Using Vladimir Propp's work on the structure of the fairy tale, Attebery explains the structure of *The Wonderful Wizard of Oz* and then expands into a taxonomy of the characters in the series. Chapter 6 comments on Baum's success and influence in terms of the growth of American fairy tales and fantasy, especially in the works of Edgar Rice Burroughs, James Branch Cabell, and H. P. Lovecraft. The seventh chapter focuses on Edward Eager, Ray Bradbury, and James Thurber. The eighth and final chapter surveys the most prominent modern American fantasists, such as Lloyd Alexander, Andre Norton, Peter Beagle, Stephen R. Donaldson, and Roger Zelazny, but most of it treats the work of Ursula Le Guin. Attebery concludes with a summary of the tendencies of American fantasy and a statement of its importance.

_____. *Strategies of Fantasy*. Bloomington: Indiana University Press, 1992. Attebery founded his first book on thematic and historical principles and followed with this second one, grounded in theoretical approaches, primarily those of Gérard Genette, Seymour Chatman, Mikhail Bakhtin, and feminist critics. The first chapter employs a heavily structural approach and situates fantasy as a mode, following Northrop Frye; as a genre, à la J. R. R. Tolkien but complicated by the idea of fuzzy sets; and as a formula, responding to the success of such authors as Tolkien and C. S. Lewis. The second short chapter starts with Tolkien's preliminary definition of fantasy and locates it in the context of later theoretical and linguistic works by Rosemary Jackson, Christine Brooke-Rose, and T. A. Shippey. The next chapter examines Tolkien's *The Lord of the Rings* in terms of postmodernism and contrasts it briefly to the works of John Crowley, with a short excursion into Mark Helprin's *Winter's Tale*. Chapter 4 is a fairly traditional reading of the nature of narrative as story in fantasy, again heavily reliant on *The Lord of the Rings* and various Victorian fantasies for its basis, but the ensuing chapter on character reverts to structuralist parlance and shifts to later fantasists, including Patricia McKillip, Diana Wynne Jones, and Alan Garner. Chapter 6 introduces the differences in vision, character, and worldview between female and male writers of fantasy and balances feminist criticism of fantasy with short readings of several female authors, such as Ursula Le Guin, McKillip, Andre Norton, and Suzette Elgin. The antepenultimate chapter notes the parallel development and overlapping of SF and fantasy and attacks the uncrackable nut of science fantasy in the book's longest section, which uses many examples rather than a representative few. Magical Realism and other subgenres of fantasy form the subject of the final chapter, which concludes with another reading of one of Attebery's favorite fantasies, John Crowley's *Little, Big*.

Barron, Neil, ed. *Fantasy and Horror: A Critical and Historical Guide to Literature, Illustration, Film, TV, and the Internet*. Lanham, Md.: Scarecrow Press, 1999. This eight-hundred-page revision of two earlier guides, *Horror Literature* and *Fantasy Literature* (both 1990), is rated among the top three or four most important reference works in the field. Each chapter features an essay on a specific sub-genre, time period, or relevant nonfiction topic written by an expert in the field and supplies an annotated bibliography of the best or most representative works. It contains valuable research tools including lists of best books, awards, series, young adult and children's books, translations, organizations, and conventions, as well as three indexes.

Bleiler, Everett F. *The Guide to Supernatural Fiction*. Kent, Ohio: Kent State University Press, 1983. More than 7,200 stories of supernatural fiction, published between 1750 and 1960, are covered in Bleiler's guide, including ghost stories, weird fiction, supernatural horror, fantasy, gothic novels, and occult fiction. Each entry has a description of the story's plot, setting, and main characters, as well as biographical information about the author and value judgments on the story's value and resonances. Entries are indexed by author and title as well as by a long list of diverse motifs.

Boyer, Robert H., and Kenneth J. Zahorski, eds. *Fantasists on Fantasy: A Collection of Critical Reflections*. New York: Avon, 1984. This collection of twenty essays on fantasy includes, among others, George MacDonald, G. K. Chesterton, James Thurber (twice), J. R. R. Tolkien (twice), C. S. Lewis, Felix Marti-Ibanez, Peter Beagle, Andre Norton, Ursula Le Guin (twice), and Susan Cooper. Also includes an interview with Katherine Kurtz. A diverse selection of approaches, from the Victorian to the modern, and a fine short introduction by the editors make this a useful, general reference text.

Brooke-Rose, Christine. *A Rhetoric of the Unreal: Studies in Narrative and Structure, Especially of the Fantastic*. Cambridge, England: Cambridge University Press, 1981. Brooke-Rose, like Rosemary Jackson, is a second generation literary theorist. *A Rhetoric of the Unreal* is a long, extremely detailed, and dense book that defies summary because of its methodology, which draws together structuralism, postmodernism, deconstruction, narratology, source studies, linguistics, and other approaches. She starts by commenting that the current sense of empirical reality is no longer as secure as it once was and summarizes the work of Michel Foucault (deconstruction) and of R. D. Laing and Shoshana Felman (psychoanalysis) on the question of significance and illusion of meaning that plagues twentieth century humanity. The second chapter surveys theoretical criticism from Plato to Jacques Derrida under the rubric of "rhetoric." The next chapter looks at genres and modes according to Northrop Frye and Tzvetan Todorov. Chapter 4 examines SF in terms of the cognitive and noncognitive, according to Darko Suvin, and the approaches of Todorov, David Ketterer, and Robert Scholes. It devotes considerable attention to Phillipe Hamon's work on reality. The third section focuses on what Brooke-Rose calls the "encoded reader," the reader who determines the narrative, and probes deeply in Henry James's *The Turn of the Screw* for its violations of reality. Section 4, on the modern marvelous or the "unreal as real," is concerned with J. R. R. Tolkien's *The Lord of the Rings* and "the new science fiction," such as Kurt Vonnegut, Jr.'s *The Sirens of Titan* and Joseph McElroy's *Plus*. The next section deals with Alain Robbe-Grillet's oeuvre as "the real as unreal," and the final chapter lays out the approaches of metafiction to reality in the works of such writers as Robert Coover, Thomas Pynchon, and Richard Brautigan.

Clute, John, and John Grant, eds. *The Encyclopedia of Fantasy*. New York: St. Martin's Press, 1997. This multiple-award-winning encyclopedia is an essential fantasy literature resource. It contains more than four-thousand entries with insightful essays on precursors of modern fantasy from William Shakespeare to Dante up to works of the fantastic in literature, film, television, art, opera, and comic books. Several essays by John Clute present a fascinating new theory of fantasy rivalling those devised by Joseph Campbell and Tzvetan Todorov. Includes helpful links between relevant entries.

Donald, James, ed. *Fantasy and the Cinema*. London: British Film Institute, 1989. Intended as a reader to aid teachers, this collection is divided into three sections. The first engages "the fantastic" as a genre, the second harnesses psychoanalytic theory to explore issues of spectatorship and sexual difference, and the third looks at politics and the social functions of cinema. An eclectic mix of perspectives is represented, from feminism and postmodernism to the formalist theories of Mikhail Bakhtin. Jargon predominates at times, but readers who persevere will be rewarded. The list of contributing scholars is impressive: Thomas Elsaesser offers a trenchant account of "the fantastic" in German silent cinema, for example, and Stephen Neale targets issues of difference in *Alien* and *Blade Runner*. Other essays explore gender in slasher films, dystopian time travel films such as *La Jetee* (the basis for *12 Monkeys*), and "what's at stake" in vampire films. Editorial introductions supply handy background material on each of the three sections.

Donaldson, Stephen R. *Epic Fantasy in the Modern World*. Occasional Papers, Second Series 2. Kent, Ohio: Kent State University Libraries, 1986. In this short, unpaginated monograph, Donaldson explains the reasons he wrote the Thomas Covenant novels and both defines and defends epic fantasy as a genre. He starts with the premise that in fantasy, internal conflicts are played out in the external forms of characters and events. In realistic fiction, he says, characters are functions of the world; in fantasy, the world is an expression of the characters. He then points out that fantasy also includes magic, but good fantasy uses the magic as a metaphor to transform humans into something greater than the sum of their parts. Another aspect of fantasy is its insistence on meaning, its opposition to the void, which Donaldson sums up in the phrase "Man is an effective passion." He then turns to epic and observes that all epic contains fantasy because all epics want to say something about the transcendence of human nature. He continues that in the development of fantasy in English—from *Beowulf* to Alfred, Lord Tennyson—human nature, the capacity to perform epic feats, had shrunk. J. R. R. Tolkien reversed that development but only by insisting that his epic fantasy had no connection with the real world. Donaldson himself has tried to reattach the epic vision to contemporary life in his Covenant books in an attempt to reject and fight off the void and the alienation of modern humanity.

Egoff, Sheila. *Worlds Within: Children's Fantasy from the Middle Ages to Today.* Chicago: American Library Association, 1988. Egoff begins punningly with "The Matter of Fantasy," in which she offers a brief definition and defense of the genre but then subdivides it into her own idiosyncratic categories of children's fantasies: the literary fairy tale, epic fantasy, enchanted realism, stories of magic, animal fantasy and beast tales, past-time fantasy, SF fantasy, ghost stories, and light fantasy. The second chapter notes the paucity of any clear fantasy for children from the Middle Ages to the Victorian period, in part because of the implications of the high mortality rate and the pre-Romantic view of children. Chapter 3 introduces the beginnings of children's fantasy in the Victorian era, particularly the emergence of the fairy tale and the works of Charles Kingsley, Lewis Carroll, George MacDonald, and L. Frank Baum. In the next, she splits off the Edwardian age and begins the pattern that will inform the rest of the book, subdividing the chapters generally and inconsistently into her individual categories and commenting on writers and works that fall into them while pointing out the changes and evolution in children's fantasy. E. Nesbit, Rudyard Kipling, J. M. Barrie, Richard Jefferies, Beatrix Potter, Kenneth Grahame, and A. A. Milne occupy much of this chapter. The remaining six chapters break down into chronological units; after combining the 1920's and 1930's, she examines the ensuing decades individually in terms of the dominant authors, themes, issues, and concerns that have changed the face of fantasy.

Elgin, Don D. *The Comedy of the Fantastic: Ecological Perspectives on the Fantasy Novel.* Contributions to the Study of Science Fiction and Fantasy 15. Westport, Conn.: Greenwood Press, 1985. Elgin begins by positing that the twentieth century faces an ecological crisis and summarizes some of the potential causes: the development of science and technology, western Christian attitudes toward nature, the French and Industrial Revolutions, and the emerging tenets of capitalism. Tragedy, he says, reconfirms the tendencies in these causes because it recognizes a humanity separate from and above nature. Comedy, however, particularly in the modern fantasy novel, reinforces ecological perspectives through its affirmation of life and view that humanity is but one part of a larger system to which it must accommodate itself in order for the whole to survive; people are not separate from their environment but part of it. Where tragedy puts forth a view in which things go from good to bad, comedy affirms the return of a system to stability and original balance. The modern fantasy novel adopts the comic perspective on humanity as part of a system while it also moves away from the formal realism of the novel and the tradition of medieval romance. Elgin draws the connections between the fantasy novel and the ecological comic worldview and then in successive chapters outlines how the works of J. R. R. Tolkien, C. S. Lewis, Charles Williams, Frank Herbert, and Joy Chant illustrate his thesis. A short conclusion ties together the various strands discussing such topics as argument, religion, character, tone, plot, and philosophy and argues that the evolution of fictional forms is forcing the inclusion of modern fantasy within the mainstream tradition.

Fredericks, Casey. "Problems of Fantasy." *Science Fiction Studies* 5 (March, 1978): 33-44. In this early article born of the desire to separate fantasy from SF, Fredericks begins by critiquing and finding wanting the books on fantasy by Eric Rabkin, W. R. Irwin, and Colin Manlove as well as Jane Mobley's doctoral dissertation. The second part interrogates the issues of the impossible as opposed to the conceivable and points out that fantasy must play a reality-oriented function. Fantasy is not dogmatic; it is idiosyncratic, the product of "human imagination in the widest possible sense." He asserts, in contrast to most definitions, that dreamworlds are important to fantasy. The final third compares and contrasts fantasy and SF and comments briefly on science fantasy as well as the relationships between fantasy and satire.

Hume, Kathryn. *Fantasy and Mimesis: Responses to Reality in Western Culture.* New York: Methuen, 1984. Hume's wide-ranging book begins with an investigation of the nature and definitions of fantasy and the idea of literature as imitation or mimesis. She moves in the second chapter to a historical perspective on fantasy, citing three basic kinds of literature: that of traditional societies, realism, and modernism/ postmodernism. The next section deals with the uses of fantasy, and again she offers a taxonomy based on a fourfold division of approaches to reality: illusion, vision, revision, and disillusion. The first forms the subject of the third chapter and deals with fantasy as a mechanism to escape reality. Vision, in chapter 4, examines the creation of new realities. The literature of revision in the next chapter explains how fantasy is a tool for improving reality, whereas the fantasy of disillusion addresses the ultimate incomprehensibility of reality. The third section endeavors to situate fantasy in terms of mode and genre, beginning with Northrop Frye's patterns of fiction, and examines such topics as fantasy based on action, on character, and on ideas and the function of fantasy in lyric and drama. The final chapter asks why people read fantasy and attempts to account for "the power and meaning of fantasy." There is an extensive section of textual notes, a comprehensive bibliography, and a crucial index to cover the tremendous numbers of texts and authors cited.

Irwin, W. R. *The Game of the Impossible*. Urbana: University of Illinois Press, 1975. Irwin argues that the desire for strangeness produces "a kind of mental play that speculatively violates the binding intellectual conventions of a world that is too much with us"; fantasy is thus a story dependent on "an overt violation" of the accepted norm. He investigates the psychological ramifications of fantasy as mental pattern and as genre and posits that it relies on a game between reader and author. Chapter 2 examines fantasy and play in three areas: the nature of play and wit, critical defenses of fantasy, and subgenres related to fantasy, such as gothic romance and fairy tales. Chapter 3 surveys various definitions of fantasy by such writers as Kingsley Amis, Herbert Read, E. M. Forster, J. R. R. Tolkien, and C. S. Lewis. The fourth chapter attempts to distinguish fantasy as a mode; Irwin claims, following structuralist thought, that it is governed more by rhetoric than by art, because rhetoric determines the art of illusion. The main challenge of this illusion is the construction of a coherent and persuasive narrative and violation of reality, a subject that informs most of the chapter. The ensuing chapter offers a negative definition of what fantasy is not and classifies fantasy works into five groups: those based on personal change, incredible societies, an unorthodox notion of innocence, literary parody or contravention of history, and a dominance of supernatural power in a fictive world. Chapters 6 through 10 outline these five classes, and the final chapter contemplates the value of fantasy as play and game and concludes that despite its essentially subversive intellectual content, one of fantasy's prime functions is to promote community.

Jackson, Rosemary. *Fantasy: The Literature of Subversion*. New York: Methuen, 1981. Jackson begins by emphasizing the flexibility of fantasy, calling it the "literature of desire, which seeks that which is experienced as absence and loss." This move provokes a poststructuralist reading of the field and makes her turn to Sigmund Freud and Jacques Lacan's theories critical to her argument in extending Tzvetan Todorov's account of the fantastic into the realm of the unconscious. Her argument demonstrating the subversive nature of fantasy and SF is also critical to feminist approaches to the genre. She distinguishes romance fantasy from the purely fantastic because it does not share the latter's subversive content. Chapter 2 distinguishes fantasy as a mode primarily concerned with subversion because of its relationship to and roots in satire, carnival, and pluralism and sets forth approaches to the unreal by Mikhail Bakhtin, Jean-Paul Sartre, and Marcel Brion, among others. Here, too, she presents the idea of praxis as a way of viewing fantasy. Chapter 3 responds to Todorov's reluctance to admit the function of psychological theory in fantasy because it is a form of unconscious discourse. Jackson starts with Freud's notions of the marvelous and the uncanny and then claims that fantasy corresponds to the first stage of his evolutionary model, magical and animistic thought. The next chapter deals with the gothic, which she suggests is the immediate precursor to fantasy because of the role of unreason in creating terror and because the genre is a reaction against classical reason. The works of William Godwin, Mary Shelley, E. T. A. Hoffmann, James Hogg, Charles Maturin, Edgar Allan Poe, Nathaniel Hawthorne, and H. G. Wells come under scrutiny here. Chapter 5 examines the subversive nature of the fantastic in realistic works of the nineteenth century by such authors as Charlotte and Emily Brontë, Charles Dickens, Joseph Conrad, Henry James, and Fyodor Dostoevski. A discussion of Victorian fantasy and fantasists, based primarily on Stephen Prickett's work, informs the next chapter. Jackson believes that this romance fantasy, by such writers as George MacDonald, Charles Kingsley, and J. R. R. Tolkien, is outworn liberal humanism that does not address immediate societal or cultural questions. In contrast, in chapter 7, she presents the continuation of the tradition begun by the gothic authors, based on the fantastic as a function of language, especially in Franz Kafka, Mervyn Peake, and Thomas Pynchon. A short afterword defends fantasy, despite its dismissal as a marginal form by many critics, because of its reality-oriented values.

Manlove, Colin N. *Christian Fantasy: From 1200 to the Present*. Notre Dame, Ind.: University of Notre Dame Press, 1992. Christianity would seem, at first glance, to have little to do with fantasy because its beliefs are meant to be fact and to explain the universe. During the seventeenth century, when use of the supernatural was under attack, "divine Poesie," or the fantastic, was approved only when it stayed close to biblical texts. Few people now, other than fundamentalists, read the Bible as a literal document; the modern tendency has been toward remythologizing it. Also significant are mutual contents: The narratives of the Bible often include many conventional fantasy elements such as a mythic paradise, talking animals, miracles, visions, and so on. The issues Manlove addresses lie in how Christianity perceives the truth as opposed to fantasy and how Christian literature uses fantasy or is a form thereof. He defines Christian fantasy as fiction "dealing with the Christian supernatural, often in an imagined world" and claims that the genre is a dying form because Scripture has lost authority and Christian fantasy itself has moved out of the mainstream and lost its relevance. Chapters 2 through 18 interrogate major works of Christianity within the accepted canon for their use of fantasy and for their Christian content; their subjects include *The Divine Comedy, The Pearl, The Faerie Queene, Dr. Faustus,* the metaphysical poets, *Pilgrim's Progress,* Emanuel Swedenborg's *Heaven and Hell,* William Blake, George MacDonald, Charles Kingsley, and C. S. Lewis. The shortest chapter is, consistently, on twentieth century fantasy.

_____. *The Fantasy Literature of England.* New York: St. Martin's Press, 1999. In this engaging, informative study, the author argues that forms of fantasy particular to England have arisen due to the country's geographic and cultural insularity. Manlove opens with his famous definition of fantasy as "a fiction involving the supernatural or impossible" and then devises six categories by which to analyze English fantasy: secondary world fantasy, metaphysical fantasy, emotive fantasy, comic fantasy, subversive fantasy, and children's fantasy. Ranging from Beowulf to Winnie the Pooh, this exhaustive exploration of the characteristics that make the British fantastic distinctive from all others serves as a fascinating complement to Nicholas Ruddick's 1993 study, *Ultimate Island: On the Nature of British Science Fiction.*

_____. *The Impulse of Fantasy Literature.* Kent, Ohio: Kent State University Press, 1983. Manlove's preface announces his central theme: that the "essence of fantasy is the delight in the independent life of created things." The first chapter addresses the debt of modern fantasy to the fairy tale and to German romanticism. Manlove comments on the fact that most nineteenth century fantasy was written in the form of fairy tales for children and uses Walter de la Mare's *Told Again* and William Makepeace Thackeray's *The Rose and the Ring* as examples. The second chapter sets forth Christianity as the center of delight in the works of Charles Williams. The Equilibrium or the Balance, the conservational principle of Ursula Le Guin's Earthsea books, comes under scrutiny next. The job of the mage in Earthsea is not to change the world with magic but to preserve the balance of all things. Chapter 4 deals with the worlds of E. Nesbit as the "metaphoric" mode of fantasy. Nesbit yokes opposites, reality and the marvelous, so that nature becomes shot through with the supernatural and the supernatural, in turn, becomes "infused with the everyday and familiar." George MacDonald's circular fantasies, *Lilith* and *Phantastes,* form the next subject. In this mode, the central character leaves home, goes on an adventure, and returns either home or to his or her rightful place; a related convention is the appearance of magical beings or objects that disrupt the primary world and then depart. Loss is the focus of the disquisition on T. H. White's *The Once and Future King.* Although most fantasies and fantasists preserve their worlds, like Ursula Le Guin, White faced and deplored the industry-wrought changes in his own gentleman's pastoral England, which are mirrored symbolically in the demise of the Round Table and its world along with the medieval world order that underwrites much modern fantasy. In chapter 7, Manlove comments on the tendency of Mervyn Peake's "Titus" books to introduce didacticism into fantasy as its author accounts for wonder rather than evoking it and lets it stand alone. He also describes how the castle and various other places and things represent the mind or take on independent characteristics without mind. The final chapter criticizes William Morris, Lord Dunsany, E. R. Eddison, and Peter Beagle as writers of anemic fantasy, writers whose work may be delightful and exciting but that fails to make vital the wonder within.

_____. *Modern Fantasy: Five Studies*. Cambridge, England: Cambridge University Press, 1975. The earliest, and most controversial, of Manlove's three books on fantasy begins with probably the most quoted definition of fantasy published: "A fiction evoking wonder and containing a substantial and irreducible element of the supernatural with which the mortal characters in the story or the readers become on at least partly familiar terms." The balance of the first chapter dissects and justifies this definition and announces Manlove's purpose: The bulk of the book will determine how true the fantasies of Charles Kingsley (*The Water-Babies*), George MacDonald (various works), C. S. Lewis (*Perelandra*), J. R. R. Tolkien (*The Lord of the Rings*), and Mervyn Peake (The "Titus" trilogy) are to their authors' attempts to make their secondary worlds as real as the reader's own. Each chapter begins with a brief background of the author's life and indicates religious influence (one major thrust of the book aims at Christian or non-Christian fantasy), then is divided into sections such as style, psychological concerns, major themes, and so on. Although Manlove credits each author with various strengths, ultimately he avers that each fails, for different reasons, to sustain the original vision in creating the fictional world. His conclusion states that the distance between real and secondary worlds is insuperable in post-Romantic fiction, whereas the audience of *Beowulf* may well have believed in monsters and dragons, a fact that closes any gap between the actual and the supernatural.

Michalson, Karen. "Phantasy as Deconstruction." *Journal of the Fantastic in the Arts*, no. 2.4 (1990): 95–109. Michalson's point of departure is the assertion that magic is the primary characteristic of fantasy and that Charlotte Spivack's theory that magic is primarily Platonic and transcendental informs the magical principle. She goes on to argue that magic is highly dependent on the word and on the concept that the word and the object, or in Saussurian terms the signifier and referent, are one. She points out that in fantasy, this connection is not limited to magic; often, a character's being and nature are indistinguishable from his or her name. Next, she argues that the opposition of the natural and the arbitrary is deconstructed by the word. The word is natural and indicates presence or object, yet it is concomitantly a subjective meaning dependent on context; this dual function does not alienate them so much as make each possible. The last half of the article uses examples from Patricia McKillip, George MacDonald, Lewis Carroll, and J. R. R. Tolkien to test the theory.

Mobley, Jane. "Toward a Definition of Fantasy Fiction." *Extrapolation* 15 (1974): 117-128. In this early and generative article, Mobley differentiates fantasy from the other subgenres of "speculative fiction": SF, dream literature, and horror fiction. She proposes that fantasy depends on a normative framework with a self-sustaining internal consistency. It is a nonrational form with internal logic that arises from a worldview magical in its orientation. Magic is, in fact, the informing principle of fantasy, and the magic power is its subject, as a power that imposes itself on people or can be controlled and directed by them. The key elements of fantasy are six. Poetic quality refers to the incantational nature of magic and the physico-magic power of the word. In her discussion of the creation of secondary magical worlds, she relies heavily on J. R. R. Tolkien's theory of subcreation and the reader's willingness to accept a new reality. Multidimensionality, the third element, involves blurring the distinction between the real and not-real on the basis of empirical evidence. It asserts that time and place are fluid, not constant. She defines the creation of wonder as essential extravagance and cites fifth the necessity of the spirit of carnival or the comic, life-affirming celebration at the heart of fantasy. The sixth element is fantasy's mythic dimension, the well of immemorial and traditional material from which much of fantasy is drawn.

Moorcock, Michael. *Wizardry and Wild Romance: A Study of Epic Fantasy*. London: Gollancz, 1987. In Moorcock's belles lettres approach, he declines to define epic fantasy or discuss his own works. Much of the book is highly critical of modern fantasy and its writers, and the winter of Moorcock's discontent has two sources: the influence and imitations of J. R. R. Tolkien's *The Lord of the Rings*, about which he has little good to say anyway, and the safe, childlike language, setting, and characters of much fantasy. Chapter 1 discusses the origins of modern epic fantasy, particularly the medieval romances and the gothic romances up into the nineteenth century. The second examines the settings of fantasies, especially in terms of the effect of the romantic poets, and reveals Moorcock's methodology, which is to quote briefly from many authors and offer short comments about their works. In this chapter alone, he includes Lord Dunsany, Edgar Rice Burroughs, William Hope Hodgson, E. R. Eddison, Clark Ashton Smith, Robert Howard, Fritz Leiber, M. John Harrison, Gene Wolfe, Terry Pratchett, Patricia McKillip, Robert Holdstock, Stephen Donaldson, Diane Duane, Leigh Brackett, Mary Stewart, Jane Gaskell, Elizabeth Lynn, Colin Greenland, and a handful of others. The next chapter looks at the "decent chap" as hero and the fact that most heroes of fantasy are "wounded children," regardless of their ages. He labels another category brute (as in Conan) as opposed to cute (children). "Wit and Humor" covers the need for comic irony in fantasy and its frequent exclusion by many writers. "Epic Pooh" is about the language of fantasy, which Moorcock says is "mouth music" meant to soothe and about the nostalgia for a vanished pastoralism that accompanies such language. The final chapter briefly surveys fantasy over the last thirty years to propose reasons for its attractions and to account for different stages of development.

Prickett, Stephen. *Victorian Fantasy.* Bloomington: Indiana University Press, 1979. Prickett's objective is to outline the development of the fantasy tradition in Victorian literature, from eighteenth century author Horace Walpole to Rudyard Kipling, as an addition, not a reaction, to nineteenth century realism. In the first chapter of this illustrated book, he discusses the use and evolution of the term "fantasy" in the eighteenth and nineteenth centuries and comments on the early contributions of gothic writers, especially Walpole, and of the romantics, particularly William Blake and John Keats. Chapter 2 argues for a complex Victorian society, rather than the facile assignment of a monolithic and simple culture, and suggests that the superabundance of Victorian life was best captured in cartoons and illustrations, one of the roots of the period's fantasy, by such artists as George Cruikshank and Thomas Hood. He also examines the rise of the Christmas book, especially *A Christmas Carol,* and its use of the supernatural. Paleontology comes up next in a chapter that looks at the Victorian interest in monsters such as dragons and goblins, the Romantic interest in the irrational, and the rage over dinosaurs. The second half of the chapter looks at the gothic tradition of human monsters and sexual deviance used by such authors as William Morris, Edgar Allan Poe, and Arthur Machen. Chapter 4 considers the works of Edward Lear and Lewis Carroll and is followed by an examination of the fictions of Charles Kingsley and George MacDonald. The final chapter deals with the fantasies of E. Nesbit and Rudyard Kipling.

Rabkin, Eric. *The Fantastic in Literature.* Princeton, N.J.: Princeton University Press, 1976. Chapter 1 attempts to define the fantastic and its subgenre of fantasy, which are characterized by the "anti-expected." Rabkin's famous edict about the fantastic goes as follows: "[T]he perspectives enforced by the ground rules of the narrative world must be diametrically contradicted." Two key elements of the fantastic are thus astonishment and surprise. Following from Ferdinand de Saussure and the function of the grapholect, Rabkin also recognizes the function of language in creating the fantastic.

Chapter 2 deals with escape, which Rabkin avers is not frivolous because it meets readers' needs and because the world of escape is controlled by convention and allows readers to perceive order where it had not been. Specifically, he addresses Edgar Allan Poe's short stories, Vladimir Propp's work on fairy tales, and detective fiction. The third chapter evaluates perspective: Readers must know the normative in order to locate the fantastic. Most of this chapter covers Victorian writers such as William Morris, George MacDonald, and the later C. S. Lewis because of the confluence of perspectives during the period. Rabkin also proposes this threefold classification of time: mythic time, the *aevum*, and history. In the following chapter, he defines and defends genre criticism, focusing on the fantastic in SF and the works of Theodore Sturgeon, Arthur C. Clarke, and Isaac Asimov. He then turns to the related genres of utopia/dystopia and satires. The penultimate section explores the history of the scientist or rationalist thinker in literature in the nineteenth century to show the presence of the fantastic in detective fiction from H. G. Wells to Arthur Conan Doyle to Agatha Christie, Ellery Queen, Rex Stout, Jorge Luis Borges, and Alain Robbe-Grillet, ending with a retrospective on the gothic. The conclusion widens the sphere of the fantastic yet more as "a basic mode of human knowing." Rabkin emphasizes the way in which people create reality and thus enable the fantastic by perception and the consequent reversal of expectation.

Schlobin, Roger, ed. *The Aesthetics of Fantasy Literature and Art*. Notre Dame, Ind.: University of Notre Dame Press, 1982. The first collection to address aesthetics and fantasy, this book contains many useful articles by a number of important scholars in the field. Included are general works on fantasy by Gary K. Wolfe, Colin Manlove, W. R. Irwin, Kenneth Zahorski and Robert Boyer, and George Landow. Francis J. Molson contributes an article on ethics in fantasy for children, and Terry Reece Hackford delves into British illustrations of the tales of *The Arabian Nights' Entertainments*. Robert Crossley on utopia, Raymond Thompson on medieval romance, Samuel Vasbinder on lost-world tales, and Jules Zanger on heroic fantasy cover various subgenres. William Schuyler has an ironic article on spells, and the book ends with two useful chapters: editor Schlobin's checklist of modern fiction and Marshall Tymn's bibliography of reference works and critical studies.

_____. "Introduction: Fantasy and Its Literature." In *The Literature of Fantasy*. New York: Garland, 1979. Part defense and part definition, this introduction to an early annotated checklist of fantasy texts argues that fantasy is not so much a literary genre but a form of human awareness that crosses all human response, a natural activity that "summons and creates images and converts them to external manifestations." Relying heavily on psychological and mythical approaches to fantasy, Schlobin explains its functions and notes the attacks by materialist, technological society. He points out that fantasy, as a mode of knowing, is ungovernable and archetypal; as a result, it threatens the empirical and hierarchical, so that Ursula Le Guin can claim accurately that Americans are afraid of dragons because they are afraid of freedom. The article then examines briefly the rules by which fantasies must operate, the evocation of wonder, and the question of disbelief or secondary creation.

Senior, W. A. "Oliphaunts in the Perilous Realm: The Function of Internal Wonder in Fantasy." In *Functions of the Fantastic: Selected Essays from the Thirteenth International Conference on the Fantastic in the Arts*, edited by Joe Sanders. Westport, Conn.: Greenwood Press, 1995. Most definitions of fantasy insist on the necessity of the creation of wonder, but all treat only an external wonder, that directed at the reader. Senior argues that effective fantasy must rely on a balance on wonder directed both inward and outward to create Samuel T. Coleridge's suspension of disbelief. Internal wonder, that produced on characters within a fantasy, takes two forms. The first involves characters from the reader's world who have been translated to the fantasy world and there encounter the marvelous; they, consequently, stand in for readers and draw them closer to the fiction. The second and more potent group are the inhabitants of the secondary creations. Elves, dwarves, giants, and wizards experience in wide-eyed astonishment the mountains, mysteries, and magic of their own world, reinforcing the formal realism of those worlds, for the fantasyscape lies at the heart of good fantasy and its acceptance by an audience. The article ends with the observation that much inferior fantasy fails to create any wonder as a result of devotion to formula.

Shinn, Thelma J. *Worlds Within Women: Myth and Mythmaking in Fantastic Literature by Women*. Contributions to the Study of Science Fiction and Fantasy 22. Westport, Conn.: Greenwood Press, 1986. This book's comprehensive mythic scope and occasional considerations of fantasy make it a useful tool for analyses of both SF and fantasy. Of particular importance are chapter 3 on mythopoesis and chapter 4 on dominant female archetypes. The concluding chapter contains a section on the unconscious and mythmaking.

Slusser, George E., Eric Rabkin, and Robert Scholes, eds. *Bridges to Fantasy*. Edwardsville: Southern Illinois University Press, 1982. This volume contains thirteen essays on the nature of fantasy, all originally presented at the second Eaton Conference on Science Fiction and Fantasy (1980). Included are essays by Harold Bloom, Roger Sale, Robert A. Collins, David Ketterer, Gary Kern, and others.

Spivack, Charlotte. *Merlin's Daughters: Contemporary Women Writers of Fantasy*. Contributions to the Study of Science Fiction and Fantasy 23. Westport, Conn.: Greenwood Press, 1987. Spivack's purpose in this book is twofold. First, she asserts that many female fantasists have been overlooked by critics of the genre despite the literary quality of their oeuvre. Second, female fantasists have found fantasy a useful medium to subvert patriarchal paradigms and to revise the issues of fantasy from a feminist perspective. The book covers ten authors, with a chapter devoted to each: Andre Norton, Susan Cooper, Ursula Le Guin, Evangeline Walton, Katherine Kurtz, Mary Stewart, Patricia McKillip, Vera Chapman, Gillian Bradshaw, and Marion Zimmer Bradley. After a short disquisition on the history and definitions of fantasy, the book proposes several basic differences between fantasy by women and by men. The first is the focus on a female protagonist, who is often endowed with stereotypically male qualities or capacities. In conjunction, male characters become more complex as their predominantly aggressive natures are softened by sensitivity. Female narrators or points of view also allow these writers to address conventionally masculine subjects, particularly Arthurian romance, from a different perspective; linked to this is the use of a Celtic matriarchal society. The narrative device favored by female fantasists is the circular as opposed to the linear plot, so that emphasis lies in the second half of the mythic paradigm and rebirth. Spivack further posits three subversive tendencies common to these authors. The first is the renunciation of power, particularly the desire for power; the second is the vindication of mortality and renunciation of immortality as a goal; the third she terms the "depolarization of values" blurring the distinctions between good and evil and between protagonist and antagonist. Moral dualism is vitiated. Two other related elements are the "rejection of transcendence for immanence" and the accompanying stress on the centrality of nature.

Swinfen, Ann. *In Defence of Fantasy*. London: Routledge and Kegan Paul, 1981. Limited to post-World War II fantasy, mostly children's, this book defends fantasy as a genre united by moral purpose and critiques of contemporary society and modern problems. Swinfen relies heavily on J. R. R. Tolkien and Samuel T. Coleridge for her definition of fantasy, which centers on the marvelous and reflects the desire to escape the limitations of the primary world. The second chapter classifies animal fantasies and comments on their three purposes: to analyze human behavior and put humans in the proper frame of reference, to explore individual morality, and to reinforce the importance of community. The third chapter is about time fantasy and the transferal of characters from one reality or world to another. Next comes a full discussion of the art of subcreation and the importance of inner consistency, history, language, and geography in the creation of the marvelous secondary world. The fifth chapter turns from form to meaning, pointing out the difference between symbol and allegory and their different uses in works such as the Chronicles of Narnia and the Prydain Chronicles, as well as discussing Theresa Whistler's *The River Boy*. "Experience Liberated," chapter 6, examines the question of scale or size and its function. That fantasy presents moral, religious, and philosophical issues as the subject of the next chapter, which has three sections: the Christian content of the Narnia books, the Faust legend and redemption in Leon Garfield's *The Ghost Downstairs*, and Ursula Le Guin's Earthsea books, which Swinfen sees as bleak because of their lack of a salvation. The penultimate chapter examines how fantasy mirrors twentieth century social and political events and again falls into three parts: Russell Hoban's *The Mouse and His Child*, John Christopher's Winchester books, and Richard Adams' *Watership Down*. The final chapter repeats her contention that fantasy is not a form of escapism; it is a method of approaching and evaluating the real world.

Timmerman, John. *Other Worlds: The Fantasy Genre.* Bowling Green, Ohio: Bowling Green University Popular Press, 1983. The first chapter of this short book sets forth the six criteria that Timmerman states must be present in some degree for a work to be fantasy: use of traditional story, the depiction of common characters and heroism, the evocation of another world, the use of magic and the supernatural, the struggle between good and evil, and the quest. The next chapter argues that the fantasy story is not allegory and functions more like the anagogic level of reading of medieval philosophy. He also explores the distinctions between SF, dystopian literature, and fantasy. The chapter's final section reflects the function of and need for myth in fantasy. Chapter 3 presents common people as the heart of fantasy. Because the point of fantasy is to provide growth through experience, the common character is not cynical or hard-bitten and retains a childlike sense of wonder and adventure, the subject of the second third of the chapter, which concludes on the note of the necessity of free will for heroism and the nature thereof. Chapter 4 identifies the traits of the fantasy world, primarily from J. R. R. Tolkien's theory of subcreation, and looks at the example of the Arthurian world and Camelot. In the next chapter, the author presents the standards of good and evil and the place of magic and the supernatural, taking C. S. Lewis's *The Magician's Nephew* and Ursula Le Guin's Earthsea books as standards. The penultimate chapter considers the quest structure underlying much of fantasy, and in the final chapter Timmerman applies his criteria to Stephen R. Donaldson's Chronicles of Thomas Covenant to argue that the books are "simply among the best in conception and aesthetic richness."

Todorov, Tzvetan. *The Fantastic: A Structural Approach to a Literary Genre.* Translated by Richard Howard. Cleveland, Ohio: Case Western, 1973. Todorov's structuralist approach poses problems for many readers and scholars of fantasy because he denies Freudian analysis a role and excepts epic fantasy à la J. R. R. Tolkien from his definition. Following biological taxonomy, the book opens with a discussion of genres, which he argues are determined by a common principle operating in a number of texts, not by any aesthetic criterion. He discusses the difficulties of subgenres and attacks Northrop Frye's classification system, which is based primarily on thematic and historical materials. Chapter 2 sets forth his famous theory of hesitation as the basis for his definition of the fantastic: The fantastic is that hesitation experienced by a person who knows only the laws of nature, confronting an apparently supernatural event. This hesitation takes two forms: the reader's and a character's. There follows a chapter on the role of the uncanny and the marvelous in this hesitation and in the formation of subgenres of the fantastic. Todorov then turns to how a reader's questions or hesitation about a text can cause a threat to the existence of the fantastic so that it must be situated in relationship to poetry and allegory. Often in poetry, the reader is not concerned with events or their representation, both roots of the fantastic, so the fantastic could not appear; allegory replaces literal meaning with symbolic meaning, thereby eradicating hesitation over the supernatural. His definition finished, Todorov turns to "The Discourse of the Fantastic" in chapter 5 and outlines the three properties that create structural unity through discourse: the utterance, the act of uttering, and the syntactical. Four chapters follow that examine the primary themes of the fantastic, most specifically those of the other and the self. Chapter 10 concludes that one must look at the fantastic from the exterior as well as the interior. Because psychoanalysis has replaced the literature of the fantastic as explanation, it now has a social *raison d'être* in three functions: the pragmatic, the semantic, and the syntactic. The chapter concludes with a short look at Franz Kafka's work.

Tolkien, J. R. R. "On Fairy-Stories." In *The Tolkien Reader*. New York: Ballantine, 1966. Tolkien's essay begins by rejecting the limiting and inaccurate notion that fairy stories concern themselves with diminutive creatures, such as elves and fairies, and the stories about them; he excludes beast fables, travelers' tales, and dream from the category. He suggests that the genre relies on the setting of Faerie, which he associates with magic and the "realization, independent of the conceiving mind, of wonder." It is a function of language through which humans become subcreators. The origins of the fairy story are enormously complex, because they come from what Tolkien calls the Cauldron of Story, to which various bits are added age by age. Tolkien also rejects the notion that fairy stories are for children: "If a fairy-story of a kind is worth reading at all it is worthy to be written for and read by adults." The true fairy story will offer the four elements of fantasy, recovery, escape, and consolation, all of which adults need more than children. The first concerns the art of secondary creation, which Tolkien argues is a high art and finds its fullest form in enchantment, the production of a secondary creation that one can enter to the complete satisfaction of the senses. Recovery addresses the regaining of a clear view through the secondary creation. He lauds escape as something generally practical and defends the escapist mentality, citing the drawbacks and horrors of modern life; further, Tolkien contends, fantasy allows the great escape, addressing the issue of death. For consolation, he identifies the need for the happy ending but phrases it as Eucatastrophe, a sudden joyous turn that denies any final defeat and produces evangelium, or joy beyond the reach of time.

Wolfe, Gary K. "Symbolic Fantasy." *Genre* (Spring, 1978): 194-209. Wolfe begins this taxonomic article with a brief history of the relationship between realism and romance. He revisits the nineteenth century trend toward the former and uses Northrop Frye's anatomy of romance to show how it does not account for much of modern fantasy. He begins his classification from the point of mythopoeia and follows with a discussion of the other common characteristics of what he terms "symbolic fantasy," which "begins with an imaginative construct and proceeds to weave a pattern of abstract values and concepts around this construct." The primary characteristic of symbolic fantasy is not the symbolic presentation but instead narrative and stylistic conventions, which he then develops as the nature of the protagonist and the educational process that transforms that character; the importance of the created world and spiritual landscape with its different time scheme; the protean antagonist; the three minor characters of the victims or henchmen of the antagonist, avatars, and amoral figures representative of nature; and the poetic disposition of style. Fantasy and the desire for it, Wolfe concludes, arise when the dominant cultural attitude of a group cannot satisfy the spiritual needs or longings of its constituents.

Yolen, Jane. *Touch Magic.* New York: Philomel, 1981. This short but informative book takes as its point of departure that children are not being taught about myths or folklore in their early education and are thus being done a great disservice. Yolen examines folktales, myths, fantasy, and storytelling in general to defend them and indicate the necessity of this form of cultural literacy. She is highly critical of the simplicity of Disney's retelling of classical fairy tales and offers a discussion of more substantive variations and forms of the Cinderella, Snow White, and Beauty and the Beast tales, as well as such stories as Little Red Riding Hood. In all cases, she insists on the richness of the stories, their timelessness, and the variety of meanings and lessons they can contain, all of which are accessible to children.

SCIENCE FICTION

Amis, Kingsley. *New Maps of Hell: A Survey of Science Fiction.* New York: Harcourt Brace Jovanovich, 1960. In one of the earliest serious academic treatments of SF, and writing with characteristic wit and insight, Amis sets up preliminary definitions (SF presents a situation that "could not arise on the world we know, but which is hypothesized on the basis of some innovation in science or technology" or their pseudo-counterparts), tracks the genre's beginnings in the works of H. G. Wells and Jules Verne, and then provides instructive overviews of the major trends and subtypes in the field, noting in particular SF's relation to myth and the unconscious, characterizing utopia and dystopia, and suggesting some of its future possibilities. Like satire and comedy, SF provides an important venue for social criticism. Although somewhat dated, this is a rewarding introduction and an early high point in the history of academic criticism of SF.

Armitt, Lucie, ed. *Where No Man Has Gone Before: Women and Science Fiction*. New York: Routledge, 1991. Feminist readings of fictions that test and subvert the boundaries and traditions of SF open this three-part collection of essays. The individual authors and works in part 1 include J. B. S. Haldane's *Man's World* and Katharine Burdekin's *Swastika Night*, as well as the fiction of C. L. Moore, Ursula Le Guin, and Doris Lessing. Five essays compose part 2, "Aliens and Others"; they examine pets, monsters, Mary Shelley's *Frankenstein*, and a Freudian perspective on the space where woman and machine meet in the films *Short Circuit* and *Tron*. Also included are a study of women in Hollywood's presentations of SF and an essay on the political implications for women in the structures of language and power in women's SF. The final section takes a look at the problems of SF as a genre, such as how SF should be read, the relationship between hard and soft SF, and publishing and readership problems.

Bailey, James O. *Pilgrims Through Space and Time: Trends and Patterns in Scientific and Utopian Fiction*. 1947. Reprint. Kent, Ohio: Kent State University Press, 1972. Bailey traces SF back to medieval travel books, but his text focuses on the seventeenth century through World War II. The reprinted edition contains a foreword by Thomas D. Clareson. Divided into two sections, on time and on space, the text covers such topics as adventure, utopias, imaginary voyages, machines, alchemy, gothic romance, and the concepts of structure, characterization, and narrative method in SF. Bailey's thoughts on SF as a genre and on idea patterns inform the summaries and analyses of these stories.

Barr, Marleen. *Alien to Femininity: Speculative Fiction and Feminist Theory*. New York: Greenwood Press, 1987. Barr's preface notes that the development of SF by women parallels the development of American feminism in the twentieth century, which this book traces and explores. There are three major parts to the text. In the first, "Community," is a discussion of the feminist community of SF writers, with particular focus on Joanna Russ; James Tiptree, Jr.; Suzy McKee Charnas; and Judith Merril; a more in-depth study into how Tiptree's works bring together temporary communities, forming something new, before they disintegrate again, showing a problematic reading for the feminist critic; and a look at feminist SF time travel novels, particularly Marge Piercy's *Woman on the Edge of Time*. The second section, "Heroism," discusses the appropriation and alteration of masculine discourses and masculine patterns in feminist SF. Authors discussed include Pamela Sargent, Octavia Butler, Russ, and Alice Walker. The last section, "Sexuality and Reproduction," has two pieces that explore the alterations occurring to women's biology that have been discussed in SF. Authors mentioned include Russ, Sargent, Zelda Harris, and Toni Morrison. This book is a must for any serious critical look at feminism in SF.

Barron, Neil, ed. *Anatomy of Wonder 4: A Critical Guide to Science Fiction*. New Providence, N.J.: R. R. Bowker, 1995. The third edition of *Anatomy of Wonder* already was one of the primary omnibus reference tools in the field of SF studies, and the fourth edition updates and extends the virtues of the earlier version. Covering books published through 1994, this new edition offers enhanced scholarly treatment of the works and writers in each of its major divisions ("Emergence to the 1920's"; "SF Between the Wars"; "Modern"; and "Children's and Young Adult SF"). Although many will miss the fascinating introductions to SF in other languages that took up more than two hundred pages of the third edition, there is much to recommend the work to individuals and libraries alike, annotating as it does some twenty-seven hundred titles (fiction and nonfiction) and discussing in separate chapters works devoted to everything from SF scholarship and building a core collection to SF in various media to teaching SF. Also includes listings of best books, translations, awards, fan organizations, and conventions. Topping off this excellent resource are author-subject and title indexes.

Bartter, Martha A. *The Way to Ground Zero: The Atomic Bomb in American Science Fiction*. Contributions to the Study of Science Fiction and Fantasy 33. Westport, Conn.: Greenwood Press, 1988. Bartter sees SF as most suited to a discussion of American development and detonation of atomic bombs for three specific reasons: SF is didactic, it has a history of a mythology of power embedded in superweapons, and its conventions reveal something of the writer's own cultural background and assumptions. The text, divided into three parts, examines some little-known and some famous stories about superweapons and superwar. The first part, "The Way to Hiroshima," reveals the social and political assumptions authors made in their stories and the patterns that led to the creation and use of atomic bombs. The second part, "Circling Ground Zero," examines the assumptions behind the assumptions, concerning people, behavior as individuals and members of a society, and human values. The third part, "Leaving Ground Zero," considers stories that function as experiments in alternative cultural assumptions with the hope for change.

Bleiler, Richard, ed. *Science Fiction Writers: Critical Studies of the Major Authors from the Early Nineteenth Century to the Present Day.* 2d ed. New York: Scribners, 1999. Containing essays by various experts, this fine collection of biocritical essays ranges from treatments of such classic writers as Mary Shelley, Edgar Allan Poe, and H. G. Wells in the "Early Science Fiction" section through the greats of the pulps and the Golden Age such as Ray Bradbury, Robert Heinlein, Isaac Asimov, and James Blish, then into the well-established writers of the 1960's and 1970's such as Brian Aldiss, J. G. Ballard, Ursula Le Guin, and Philip K. Dick. The second addition adds entries on Octavia Butler, Orson Scott Card, William Gibson and many other contemporary science fiction writers. It is arranged chronologically, and features a photograph and a bibliography of selected works for each author. This collection is especially useful for researchers and teachers seeking a rich overview of an author's work. Including essays on lesser known authors and major authors from outside the Anglo American tradition, this work will remain a standard resource in the field.

Bretnor, Reginald, ed. *Science Fiction, Today and Tomorrow.* New York: Harper, 1974. Bretnor introduces this anthology as a "discursive symposium," and its inclusive roster of thoughtful essays on various aspects of SF by some of the then-best-known writers in the field certainly helps the book live up to this description. Although dated in some respects, the essays provide a complex snapshot of the views of SF writers in the early 1970's, including pieces on the state of SF (by Ben Bova, Frederik Pohl, and George Zebrowski), the relationships of SF to science and modern culture (including essays by Frank Herbert, Theodore Sturgeon, and Alan Nourse), and the art and science of SF (with essays on creating SF by James Gunn, Alexei and Cory Panshin, Poul Anderson, Hal Clement, Anne McCaffrey, Gordon R. Dickson, and Jack Williamson). This is a rich resource for teachers and scholars.

Bukatman, Scott. *Terminal Identity: The Virtual Subject in Postmodern Science Fiction.* Durham, N.C.: Duke University Press, 1993. This is an interdisciplinary work written by a film scholar who perceives a transformation in human identity resulting from new technologies. Bodies become virtual and the organic evolves into the electronic. Citing postmodern theorists, Bukatman describes this transformation in SF films. He also takes into account SF television, comic books, computer games, techno-music, and virtual reality. Cyberpunk literature is likewise covered in the form of works by William Gibson, Neal Stephenson, and Bruce Sterling. Even though his prose is jargon-heavy and sometimes opaque, Bukatman clearly demonstrates the importance of SF film in today's information age. In his analysis, it emerges as the most relevant cultural form in contemporary society, as a beguiling way to understand people's changing natures.

Carr, Helen, ed. *From My Guy to Sci-Fi: Genre and Women's Writing in the Post-*

modern World. London: Pandora Books, 1989. In the introduction, Carr says that in this book "women's writing today is discussed by a diverse group of academics, journalists and practicing writers, who bring very different approaches, preoccupations, and emphases to what they have to say." This statement characterizes this text well. It is an excellent source for finding poststructural feminist theory applied to a variety of subjects; for a literary audience, topics range from SF to autobiography. Of particular interest to SF audiences is Roz Kaveny's "The Science Fictiveness of Women's Science Fiction," which gives a historical overview of SF (especially British SF), discussing most of the major female SF authors and with extended readings of Joanna Russ and Ursula Le Guin's contributions to the feminist discourse in SF.

Carter, Paul A. *The Creation of Tomorrow: Fifty Years of Magazine Science Fiction*. New York: Columbia University Press, 1977. This book is an extensive analysis of the themes, images, and patterns in SF contained in the fan magazines that gave the field its connection to popular culture. The book begins with a genealogy of the fifteen major American and British titles that he studies, covering a publishing range of fifty years. The chapters are well arranged according to theme, with the first chapter discussing the relationship between scientific extrapolation from the known and the unknown and the adoption of that pattern for SF; it also traces the origins of the pulp magazines that focused on a literature of science. The next two chapters trace the expanding view of the universe, occurring simultaneously in SF and in science, focusing on images of the moon and of Mars. There are also chapters that cover time travel, the politics of World War II, human evolution, femininity, utopian and dystopian tendencies, and the limitations of science compensated by the human spirit. The final section is a discussion of the availability and accessibility of these early SF materials; it centers on the growing scholarly interest in these earliest artifacts of SF history. Threaded through with priceless artwork from these pulp predecessors, this book is a good survey of the important trend-setting stories of SF.

Clute, John, and Peter Nicholls, eds. *The Encyclopedia of Science Fiction*. New York: St. Martin's Griffin, 1995. An invaluable companion to *The Encyclopedia of Fantasy*, this encyclopedia contains more than four thousand entries on science-fiction writers and works. Updated to tackle modern themes and media such as graphic novels, film and television spin-offs, technothrillers, survivalist fiction, game worlds, and Magical Realism. Includes twenty-seven updated entries to reflect contributions to science fiction from countries other than the United States and Great Britain.

Davies, Philip John, ed. *Science Fiction, Social Conflict, and War*. New York: Manchester University Press, 1990. This collection of essays addresses SF's interaction with social dimensions. In the introductory essay, Davies notes that SF often provides "commentary on the politics of conflict and war." He moves on to trace the historical progression of the icons of war in SF. His claim is that, regardless of its often-marginalized position in literary and social discourses, SF has proved to be an "excellent laboratory" for investigating social conflict. The other authors in the text include Jacqueline Pearson, studying sexual politics and SF; Edward James, studying racial politics and violence; Anthony Easthope, examining utopian SF; Carl Tighe, reading the Eastern bloc SF of Stanisław Lem's *Solaris*; Christopher Pike, reading the Russian SF of Boris and Arkady Strugatsky; Alasdair Spark, looking at the Vietnam War in SF; Paul Brians, making a commentary on images of nuclear war in children's SF; H. Bruce Franklin, looking at democratic ideals in American SF; and Martha A. Bartter, examining SF's relationship to the status quo, in both literary and social terms.

Delany, Samuel R. *Silent Interviews on Language, Race, Sex, Science Fiction, and Some Comics: A Collection of Written Interviews*. Hanover, N.H.: Wesleyan University Press, 1994. Working within the unusual frame of the written interview, Delany explores a wide range of topics of keen interest to readers of SF and contemporary culture and theory, including semiotics, political and economic aspects of criticism, social experience, race, sexual orientation, and writing. He chooses this frame in part to explore "truths" that may be "more malleable, less rigid" in this written form than might be possible in the usual face-to-face interview. The essays range from revised and enlarged writings "erected" on the transcripts of interviews originally published in such journals as *Science Fiction Studies* ("The Semiology of Silence"), *Camera Obscura* ("Sword & Sorcery, S/M, and the Economics of Inadequation"), and *Diacritics* ("Science Fiction and Criticism") to written interview responses based on questions submitted to him and ranging from 1979 through 1993. Throughout, Delany demonstrates prodigious reading and deep insight into issues of contemporary theory and culture. The insights here should be compared with those in his earlier essays, especially those in *The Jewel-Hinged Jaw: Notes on the Language of Science Fiction* (1978).

Dunn, Thomas P., and Richard D. Erlich, eds. *The Mechanical God: Machines in Science Fiction*. Contributions to the Study of Science Fiction and Fantasy 1. Westport, Conn.: Greenwood Press, 1982. This is an interesting collection of essays devoted to a cluster of central themes in twentieth century SF. The collection is divided into sections on individual authors, with essays concentrating on the work of Karel Čapek, C. S. Lewis, Stanisław Lem, Kurt Vonnegut, Jr., Frederik Pohl, Roger Zelazny, and Walter Tevis; children's SF; attributes (exploring topics such as "Portraits of Machine Consciousness" and "Sexual Mechanisms and Metaphors in SF Films"); and cyborgs. It includes a listing of works "useful for the study of machines in science fiction."

Garnett, Rhys, and R. J. Ellis, eds. *Science Fiction Roots and Branches: Contemporary Critical Approaches*. New York: St. Martin's Press, 1990. This collection of essays focuses on "crucial periods in the historical development of the genre," namely SF produced during the Victorian era and that produced after World War II. The editors also note that these essays have a subtextual discussion about power, specifically the social power that SF discusses and in which SF finds itself caught while trying to establish itself as a genre. The collection includes contributions by an impressive list of scholars. The first section, focusing on the Victorian era, includes work by Darko Suvin on William Morris, Stanisław Lem on H. G. Wells's *The War of the Worlds*, and Rhys Garnett on Bram Stoker's *Dracula* and sexual repression. In part 2, focusing on postwar SF, these authors appear: Patrick Parrinder on postwar enlightenment and its effect on SF; Jerzy Jarzebski on Lem; Thomas and Alice Clareson on John Wyndham; R. J. Ellis on Frank Herbert's *Dune* and "The Discourse of Apocalyptic Ecologism in the United States"; and Robert Philmus on Ursula Le Guin. Part 3, focusing on contemporary feminist approaches to the same issues of power, contains these authors: Marleen Barr on Marge Piercy and Thomas Berger; Jenny Wolmark on Vonda McIntyre; and Anne Cranny- Francis on Suzy McKee Charnas's dystopian SF.

Gunn, James E. *Alternate Worlds: The Illustrated History of Science Fiction*. New York: Prentice Hall, 1975. This beautifully illustrated collection features a glimpse into important historical movements and periods in SF's development, with an introduction by Isaac Asimov. Gunn declares that the volume is "more than just illustrations and history"; instead, its method is "to explain SF in terms of the influences that created it and then affected its subsequent development." The chapters are arranged around key periods and movements in SF: ancient roots of fantastic literature; 1800-1885, leading up to Jules Verne; 1828-1905 and the reign of Victorian ideals in SF; 1885-1911 and the birth of SF magazine culture; 1866-1946, the myth of progress in SF; 1911-1926, the rise of pulp magazines; 1926-1950, major editors, especially Hugo Gernsback and John W. Campbell, Jr.; and World War II and after, the impact of technological development and social unrest. The final chapter offers Gunn's sense of the developing trends in SF, showing an optimistic view of the rising dominance of SF in popular culture. The book is light on information, but the illustrations and perspectives are worth a look.

Hassler, Donald M. *Comic Tones in Science Fiction: The Art of Compromise with Nature*. Contributions to the Study of Science Fiction and Fantasy 2. Westport, Conn.: Greenwood Press, 1982. Hassler's text is a superb and readily accessible investigation of comic effect in the eighteenth century and in modern SF. He builds an argument supported by structuralism, poststructuralism, psychoanalytic theory, and deconstruction. He sees precursors in the late eighteenth century contributing to ideas of indeterminacy in science, meaning, discourse, and "artifact," as well as seeing precursors of more recent hard SF writers. Hassler plays mostly with the sense of irony that arises when readers realize their own indeterminacy in the light of Sigmund Freud's *The Interpretation of Dreams*, Jacques Lacan's languagelike structured unconscious, the breakdown of "mastery," and the atomic betrayal of being in quantum theory. Irony is manifest in this incongruous or double view of oneself, and comic effect comes in the form of a compromise that is made in order to survive and that expresses a sense of loss and distance. Hassler traces the epistemological indeterminacy of the Enlightenment to the ironic dislocations of death from William Wordsworth to Ursula Le Guin, examining along the way the development of the genre in William Golding and the pulp tradition. Finally, a study of Frederik Pohl's and Hal Clement's work and their persistence as hard SF writers circles back to a play for survival. Portions of the book are reprints.

Huntington, John. *Rationalizing Genius: Ideological Strategies in the Classic American Science Fiction Short Story*. New Brunswick, N.J.: Rutgers University Press, 1989. Focusing his attention on tales from the Golden Age of American SF— primarily those from the first volume of the *Science Fiction Hall of Fame*, which he argues convincingly is an effective sampling of short SF dating from the late 1930's through the early 1960's—Huntington brings a rich and supple understanding of Marxist and poststructuralist literary theory to bear on the ideological analysis of short fiction. He begins from the premise that "we can learn from the most literarily conventional popular literature if we question it closely." He regards SF as an important part of the "cultural thinking process" under way in America during this period, a process that negotiated the broad change from traditional individualistic capitalism to a purported technocratic meritocracy. Huntington carefully justifies his selection of texts and details the reading protocols required by a popular literature before turning in subsequent chapters to detailed analyses of key stories. He traces the ideological implications of the "myth of genius" in Theodore Sturgeon's "Microcosmic God," for example, and follows with exciting readings of the complexities of reason in economics in stories such as Robert Heinlein's "The Roads Must Roll" and of reason in relation to love in Lester del Rey's "Helen O'Loy" and Judith Merril's "That Only a Mother." Subsequent chapters explore the ideological structures in imagining the Other and the complex interrelations of history, politics, and predicting the future. Huntington ends the study with incisive discussions of SF's relationship with mainstream literature and a postscript reflecting on his own practice in the book. A stimulating and rewarding study of classic SF.

James, Edward. *Science Fiction in the Twentieth Century*. New York: Oxford University Press, 1994. Now available in paperback, this is a quite useful overview of the field by the longtime editor of *Foundation*, the chief British SF scholarly journal. James brings a refreshingly extra-American view to the subject of world SF, covering its history through the 1960's (concentrating on Anglo-American writers but mentioning important writers and texts from outside that tradition), SF reading strategies (which differ substantially from those typically required of realist fiction), fandom, and recent developments (including the New Wave and cyberpunk, as well as more recent trends). Although James cannot go very deeply into any of the domains he surveys, his highly readable style and insightful observations on writers and trends will bring most readers up to speed on the field with great economy and grace.

Ketterer, David. *New Worlds for Old: The Apocalyptic Imagination, Science Fiction, and American Literature*. Bloomington: Indiana University Press, 1974. Writing at a time of growing academic interest in SF, Ketterer (who has contributed to this scholarly resurgence) develops a compelling analysis of SF as a series of strategies for imagining other worlds in the context of American apocalyptic literature, discussing narratives traditionally recognized as "mainstream" literature in close proximity with important works of SF. The apocalyptic imagination, in this study, exploits the dialectical tensions between destruction and creation, satire and prophetic mysticism, purposive meaning and unmeaning chaos, and representations of grand movements and detailed characterization. Apocalyptic fictions are, for Ketterer, distinct from mimetic (realistic) works, on one hand, and fantastic narratives, on the other, because apocalyptic fictions create other worlds that exist, on the literal level, in a credible relationship (based on reason, analogy, or religious beliefs) with the real world. This relationship leads to the "metaphorical destruction of the 'real' world in the reader's head." Ketterer plies this flexible and intricate critical model in discussions of Edgar Allan Poe and the visionary tradition in SF, linking this with his analysis of Ursula Le Guin's *The Left Hand of Darkness* as an archetypal "winter-journey" outside space and time. He similarly discusses the utopian/dystopian tradition, pairing Charles Brockden Brown's *Wieland* with Stanisław Lem's *Solaris*, Mark Twain's *A Connecticut Yankee in King Arthur's Court* with SF's fictions of time and space, and Herman Melville's *The Confidence Man* with Kurt Vonnegut, Jr.'s more speculative fiction. A rewarding and stimulating study.

Landon, Brooks. *The Aesthetics of Ambivalence: Rethinking Science Fiction Film in the Age of Electronic (Re)Production*. Contributions to the Study of Science Fiction and Fantasy 52. Westport, Conn.: Greenwood Press, 1992. This ambitious monograph probes the relationship between SF film and literature. Landon defends the former as a unique artistic mode the strength of which is in conveying visual spectacle. In his opinion, SF film is by no means inferior to its literary counterpart; the two are distinct. The first third of Landon's book deals with adaptations: *Blade Runner* and both versions of *The Thing*. Landon then turns to special effects and argues that they define SF as a cinematic art form. In his opinion, it does not matter if SF films privilege special effects over character and theme; indeed, he sees this emphasis on spectacle as evidence of postmodern brilliance. The third part of his book shows how electronic technologies magnify the power of SF cinema. Although he overstates his points at times, Landon's reasoning is bound to stimulate fruitful debate.

_____. *Science Fiction After 1900: From the Steam Man to the Stars*. Twayne's Studies in Literary Themes and Genres 12. New York: Twayne Publishers, 1997. Landon's excellent work argues that SF can be defined as the literature of change, a literature in which reader's expectations are as crucial as the written text, and so merges literary critique with examination of popular culture. Landon provides an overview of the evolution of SF through insightful analyses of exemplary texts by E. M. Forster, Aldous Huxley, John Campbell, Robert Heinlein, and Ursula K. Le Guin, as well as samples of works from Eastern Europe and the former Soviet Union. The book includes an extensive annotated list of works for further reading, a critical bibliography, and a chronology of major authors, works, and historical events of importance in the development of SF.

Lefanu, Sarah. *Feminism and Science Fiction*. Bloomington: Indiana University Press, 1989. One of the best theoretical studies of the interrelationships between feminist thinking and SF, this work explores the "question of whether SF . . . offers a freedom to women writers, in terms of style as well as content, that is not available in mainstream fiction. . . . [D]oes [SF] offer a means of fusing political concerns with the playful creativity of the imagination?" In Lefanu's opinion, feminist SF draws not only on the "female gothic" but also on optimistic and pessimistic elements in utopian/dystopian writing, and it is informed by feminist, socialist, and radical politics of the late 1960's and the 1970's. The book is roughly divided in two, with the first half laying out the theoretical and historical context of feminist SF and then sampling female SF writers as they explore the nature and role of the gendered subject as "heroine" in SF, ranging from Amazons and SF representations of women as rulers and as the subjects of utopian and dystopian narratives to women's representations of love and eroticism for female subjects, ending with comments on the ways female SF writers challenge patriarchal structures in their narratives. The second half of the book takes the genrewide insights of the first half and applies them more fully in detailed readings of the work of James Tiptree, Jr., Ursula Le Guin, Suzy McKee Charnas, and Joanna Russ. Readers will not always agree with Lefanu's renderings in these more developed essays, but they will find her discussions evocative and stimulating.

Lem, Stanisław. *Microworlds: Writings on Science Fiction and Fantasy*. Edited by Franz Rottensteiner. San Diego, Calif.: Harcourt Brace Jovanovich, 1984. An excellent collection of Lem's nonfiction writing, including some autobiographical materials as well as several of the essays that contributed to his reputation as a critic of Western (particularly American) SF. Titles include "Science Fiction: A Hopeless Case—with Exceptions" and "Philip K. Dick—Visionary Among Charlatans." Despite their controversy, these are well crafted and strongly written essays from one of the major writers in the field. They provide crucial insights into his thinking, from matters of structure in SF narrative to his close readings of Tzvetan Todorov, Jorge Luis Borges, and Boris and Arkady Strugatsky. A fine resource for any Lem scholar, and useful in most general collections.

McCaffery, Larry, ed. *Storming the Reality Studio: A Casebook of Cyberpunk and Postmodern Science Fiction*. Durham, N.C.: Duke University Press, 1991. This text is a clever package of fiction, theory, and criticism all relating to cyberpunk and postmodern SF. In the introduction, McCaffery gives a brief history of postmodernism and the connections to technology that characterize cyberpunk and an SF avant-garde. Before getting to the fiction and theory/criticism of the book, Richard Kadrey and McCaffery present "Cyberpunk 101," a list of works, with annotations, that have helped to shape the formation of cyberpunk. The first half of the book is composed of short stories, selections from novels, and poetry, with illustrations, from such artists as Kathy Acker, Samuel R. Delany, and J. G. Ballard. The theory and criticism part of the book includes essays, an interview with William Gibson, and selections from theoretical texts such as Jacques Derrida's *Of Grammatology* and Jean François Lyotard's *The Postmodern Condition*.

Magill, Frank N., ed. *Survey of Science Fiction Literature*. 5 vols. Englewood Cliffs, N.J.: Salem Press, 1979. In this impressive collection, Frank Magill has collected five hundred original pieces of criticism, written explicitly for this series by and about some of the biggest names in the field, from Brian Aldiss to Roger Zelazny. In the introduction, Magill calls this an "extensive critical evaluation of the major literature of science fiction"; he continues in the introduction to define and systematize SF into a historical progression, into a thematic arrangement, and in traditional literary terms. The entries are arranged alphabetically by title, with each entry containing publishing information about that text, a brief description of the text, a list of the main characters, a review of the piece, and a short bibliography for further study. There is a complete index at the end of volume 5.

Manlove, Colin N. *Science Fiction: Ten Explorations*. London: Macmillan, 1986. This text is Manlove's answer to the many shallow or unsustained studies of SF that seem to prevail over lengthy, thoughtful, in-depth criticism. The ten works considered, ranging from 1951 to 1983, are Isaac Asimov's *Foundation* trilogy, Frederik Pohl's *Alternating Currents*, Brian Aldiss's *Hothouse*, Frank Herbert's *Dune*, Robert Silverberg's *Nightwings*, Philip José Farmer's *To Your Scattered Bodies Go*, Arthur C. Clarke's *Rendezvous with Rama*, Clifford Simak's *Shakespeare's Planet*, A. A. Attanasio's *Radix*, and Gene Wolfe's The Book of the New Sun sequence. Manlove's selection of these works is based on his sense that their writers are diverse world builders with imaginative energy, a central pulse in the SF genre.

Moylan, Tom. *Demand the Impossible: Science Fiction and the Utopian Imagination.* New York: Methuen, 1986. After presenting a brief history of utopian literature in the introduction, Moylan goes on, in the theory section of the book, to describe the revolutionary oppositional utopian impulse since the 1960's in the context of modern society. Winding his argument through a field of theorists and critics such as Ernst Bloch, Karl Mannheim, Frederic Jameson, Darko Suvin, Jack Zipes, and Michel Foucault, Moylan comes to his own term for a series of new utopian novels: "critical utopia." The critical utopia has given utopic writing new life. It is a movement aware of its own traditional limitations or utopic horizon, highly self-reflexive and open, now an "ambiguous" utopia (Ursula Le Guin) or an ambiguous "heterotopia" (Samuel R. Delany), and characterized by the hero or antihero predominating over the background. The rest of the book takes the theory to texts and examines Joanna Russ's *The Female Man*, Le Guin's *The Dispossessed*, Marge Piercy's *Woman on the Edge of Time*, and Delany's *Triton*.

Nicolson, Marjorie Hope. *Voyages to the Moon.* New York: Macmillan, 1948. A sequel to *A World in the Moon* (1935), *Voyages to the Moon* is a remarkable study for postspaceflight readers. Nicolson examines English-language "cosmic," rather than the conventional "imaginary," voyage stories, poems, papers, letters, and plays, through the seventeenth and eighteenth centuries, showing the connections between the literary cosmic voyages as well as the histories of astronomy and aviation. The earlier seventeenth century works are limited to more terrestrial voyages with the moon as boundary, but eighteenth century works, especially after Isaac Newton's *Principia* (1687), reflect a growing realization at the possibilities of whole galaxies of new worlds to be discovered. Such names as Aphra Behn, Ben Jonson, Galileo, Jean-Jacques Rousseau, Henry Fielding, and Samuel Johnson are represented among the writers, along with their works, familiar and unfamiliar, which are to be found here. Throughout Nicolson's study, the one resounding message is that humanity has been and always will be fascinated by the vast unknowns of cosmic voyages. The text also includes an added epilogue that traces historical sources of Edgar Allan Poe, H. G. Wells, Jules Verne, and C. S. Lewis. Also included are illustrations and a primary and secondary bibliography.

Palumbo, Donald, ed. *Erotic Universe: Sexuality and Fantastic Literature.* Contributions to the Study of Science Fiction and Fantasy 18. Westport, Conn.: Greenwood Press, 1986. Although the title refers only to fantastic literature, the nearly two hundred narratives examined here are both SF and fantasy. This collection of fifteen essays by William M. Schuyler, Jr., Brooks Landon, Marleen Barr, Judith Bogart, and Leonard G. Heldreth, among others, broaches the study of sexuality in fantastic literature through the lenses of theory, themes, feminist views, and fanzines. Some of the topics discussed are sex roles, reversals of female stereotypes, semiotics of sexuality, sexual comedy, SF and fantasy as testing grounds for altered assumptions of sexuality, sexuality and death/rebirth motifs, homosexuality, androgyny, and sexuality and technology.

Parker, Helen N. *Biological Themes in Modern Science Fiction.* Ann Arbor, Mich.: UMI Research Press, 1984. Parker selects several representative examples to study biological themes and motifs in SF. Three aspects of the biological perspective embody the SF concept of change and adaptation: evolution, genetics, and exobiology. This perspective includes human manipulation of these biological principles as well as the biological consequences of the past and present. Her approach provokes a wide-ranging outlook on what it is to live in a human society, what it is to be human, and the future of humanity as a species.

_____. *Science Fiction: Its Criticism and Teaching.* New York: Methuen, 1980. Part of the New Accents series, this advanced introduction to SF for academics provides basic definitions of the genre (ranging from the "scientific romance" to structurally based definitions and "generic hybrids"), a sociology of SF (including perspectives on SF texts as products, messages, modes of reading, literature, and "paraliterature"), and studies of SF as romance (addressing in particular the role of mythology, formulas, and the domestication of romance in self-conscious critique), SF as fable and epic (connecting it to these older forms and marking its differences from them), and SF language (a particularly rich exploration of the genre's exploitation of linguistic turns to achieve estrangement, social critique, and parody), ending with a brief chapter considering the design of the SF course (situating this discussion in terms of C. P. Snow's "two culture" debate, canon formation, and estrangement). A useful and concise tool for teachers in the field.

Penley, Constance, Elisabeth Lyon, Lynn Spigel, and Janet Bergstrom, eds. *Close Encounters: Film, Feminism, and Science Fiction.* Minneapolis: University of Minnesota Press, 1991. Originally published in part as an issue of the scholarly journal *Camera Obscura* (Fall, 1986), this anthology contains nine essays and the script of the experimental film *Friendship's Death.* The essays ply semiology, psychoanalysis, and reception studies within the context of the genre and make for dense reading at times. There are two essays on *Metropolis* and *The Terminator*, with individual essays devoted to Star Trek fandom, *Alien*, and 1960's television sitcoms such as *The Jetsons, I Dream of Jeannie,* and *Bewitched*. Throughout, the volume explores how SF media constructs new gender roles through the status it assigns to robots, aliens, monsters, and other mainstays of the genre. Overall, it provides solid examples of feminist theory in action.

Reilly, Robert, ed. *The Transcendent Adventure: Studies of Religion in Science Fiction/Fantasy.* Contributions to the Study of Science Fiction and Fantasy 12. Westport, Conn.: Greenwood Press, 1985. This essay collection is an attempt to trace religious themes and motifs in several SF works and to demonstrate how the two areas are closer than one would initially think: Both display a curiosity about the nature of the universe and humanity's place in it. Topics include religious consciousness as the context for works by Harlan Ellison; Walter M. Miller, Jr.; and Philip K. Dick; mind and magic; and ethics and science. The Edenic concerns of James Blish and C. S. Lewis compose the second section, and the third is devoted to individual authors and specific religious questions and interconnections. Those included here are Dick, Philip José Farmer, Frank Herbert, Doris Lessing, Miller, Walter Tevis, J. R. R. Tolkien, and Roger Zelazny. A bibliography of works with religious themes and motifs and a secondary bibliography end the book.

Rose, Mark, ed. *Alien Encounters.* Cambridge, Mass.: Harvard University Press, 1981. In this important work, Rose sets out to understand the range and complexity of the SF genre from a structuralist perspective. His is not a comprehensive definition of SF but instead a working understanding of an active, developing genre, what he often calls a historical phenomenon. In successive chapters, he concentrates on the paradigm of SF as a genre that operates in a dialectical relationship between the two binary oppositions of human/nonhuman and science/nature. The various combinations of these elements provide a working understanding of the dynamics of SF, which Rose explores in four larger chapter-length concept-structures: space, time, machine, and monster. Rose's argument is very lucid, and he provides important readings of major SF authors and texts, especially Stanisław Lem, Philip K. Dick, Arthur C. Clarke, and Isaac Asimov. He includes an extended look at several SF films, including *2001, 2010,* and *Blade Runner*. Overall, his clear argument is an important one to structuralist and poststructuralist SF criticism and should be valuable to any interested scholar.

Ruddick, Nicholas. *Ultimate Island: On the Nature of British Science Fiction.* Contributions to the Study of Science Fiction and Fantasy 55. Westport, Conn.: Greenwood Press, 1993. Neither "a history nor a survey of British science fiction," this book explores the assumptions in the view that something like

British SF can be identified clearly. Ruddick resists alternative terms such as "scientific romance" (see Brian Stableford's study of this form, below) and "speculative fiction," arguing instead that because British SF never has been as profoundly separated from "literature" as SF was in America, British SF should be seen as part of "English literature." Having established the fuzziness of his boundaries, Ruddick first moves on to analyze the details of British SF by tracing the motif of "the Island as a site of Darwinian struggle" from H. G. Wells to the present. He then analyzes carefully the frequently held view of British SF that it is pessimistically obsessed with catastrophe, arguing that the specific character of the various catastrophes in British SF is intimately connected with the island motif. This is an evocative and instructive study of British SF, an important holding for most libraries.

Russ, Joanna. *To Write Like a Woman: Essays in Feminism and Science Fiction.* Indianapolis: Indiana University Press, 1995. This is a collection of selected essays, reviews, and letters Russ has written over the last twenty-five years, with an introduction by Sarah Lefanu. The essays cover the wide range of Russ's critical expertise including the aesthetics of SF, feminist utopias, Mary Shelley, H. P. Lovecraft, SF heroines, the modern gothic, "The Yellow Wallpaper," and the battle of the sexes in SF. Somewhat obscure essays from scholarly journals, reviews, and other books of essay collections are all to be found here.

Schellinger, Paul E., ed. *Twentieth-Century Science-Fiction Writers.* 3d ed. Chicago: St. James Press, 1991. A massive compilation of brief biocritical essays with bibliographies, on SF writers in English from 1895. The bibliographies are as complete as possible, including lists of uncollected SF short stories published after the writer's last collection. In addition to the biography and critical discussion, writers themselves sometimes contribute reflections on their work. One of the most thorough and inclusive tools of its kind. It was revised in Jay Pederson's *St. James Guide to Science Fiction Writers* (1995).

Scholes, Robert. *Structural Fabulation: An Essay on Fiction of the Future.* Notre Dame, Ind.: University of Notre Dame Press, 1975. Based on a series of four lectures given in 1974 in Notre Dame's Ward Phillips series, this small book is an evocative theoretical exploration of SF that participated in the process of engaging academic literary theory with SF. Adapting literary structuralism to his purposes, Scholes argues for the practical modeling of SF and its ability to estrange habitually overlooked or confusing features of the present. He sketches the roots of SF as a latter-day form of speculative fiction (in the tradition of Thomas More, Francis Bacon, and Jonathan Swift) that satisfies a common need for "suspense with intellectual consequences" by enhancing the reader's awareness of the "universe as a system of systems, a structure of structures." Structural fabulation uses the insights of recent science to frame and explore human situations, and Scholes traces the range of such fabulation by discussing Frank Herbert's *Dune* and Olaf Stapledon's *Star Maker*, and he devotes much of the last lecture, "The Good Witch of the West," to a careful reading of Ursula Le Guin's Earthsea trilogy. Scholes's major points may seem merely commonplace to good teaching and research in the field, but these lectures still make an excellent theoretical introduction for advanced students.

Scholes, Robert, and Eric S. Rabkin. *Science Fiction: History, Science, Vision*. New York: Oxford University Press, 1977. This early, important piece of SF scholarship is focused explicitly on the literary and textual aspects of SF. The first and longest part of the book is a literary history of SF, covering most major eras from pre-1900 to New Age SF; most major authors are covered, if only briefly. The second section is a discussion of the science that the editors deem important for a reader of SF to understand. Each section discusses science on fairly lay terms, listing major novels that use the concepts and covering these fields: physics, computers, thermodynamics, biology, and psychology, with a last section on what they call "pseudoscience." The next part considers the literary forms present in SF, with one chapter devoted to forms and themes and one chapter listing and giving short interpretive pieces on ten representative novels, from Jules Verne's *Twenty Thousand Leagues Under the Sea* to Ursula Le Guin's *The Dispossessed*. The appendix contains decent, though dated, bibliographies of SF criticism, SF in other media, SF science, and award-winning SF novels. This book successfully combines literature, science, and scholarship and should be useful to any scholar, especially those new to SF.

Slusser, George, George Guffey, and Mark Rose, eds. *Bridges to Science Fiction*. Carbondale: Southern Illinois University Press, 1980. Collected from the first J. Lloyd Eaton Conference on SF and Fantasy Literature (1979), these essays range from Harry Levin exploring "Science and Fiction" and Gregory Benford offering a scientist's perspective on "Aliens and Knowability" to Eric Rabkin on "Fairy Tales and Science Fiction" and Patrick Parrinder figuring "Science Fiction as Truncated Epic." A useful early collection of serious SF scholarship.

Sobchack, Vivian. *Screening Space: The American Science Fiction Film*. 2d enl. ed. New York: Ungar, 1987. This is an expanded version of Sobchack's influential book *The Limits of Infinity: The American Science Fiction Film 1950-1975* (1980). It reprints the first three chapters and retrofits a fourth one concerned with the 1980's. Chapter 1 reviews definitions of the genre, both literary and cinematic, and relates them to the horror film. Chapter 2 examines the iconography of the genre, with special attention paid to the portrayal of "the alien." Chapter 3 attends to the impact of sound effects in SF film. In the lengthy fourth chapter, Sobchack invokes Jameson's Marxian views on postmodernity. She uses them to talk about the influence of commodity culture on films such as *Star Wars* and *Repo Man* within the context of emergent electronic technologies. Sobchack's insights are as numerous as the many films she covers from the 1950's to the 1980's, making this perhaps the best survey of the field.

Stableford, Brian. *Scientific Romance in Britain 1890-1950*. New York: St. Martin's Press, 1985. Stableford distinguishes scientific romance (SR) from SF in Britain by rooting it in the writing of H. G. Wells and tracing its parallels with the British tradition of the speculative but nonfiction prose essay, made famous by T. H. Huxley and later practitioners. Although he sees his own study as taking up where Darko Suvin's *Victorian Science Fiction in the U.K.* takes off, his approach differs from Suvin's in refusing to offer a strict definition of SR, relying instead on a set of "family resemblances" or marks of kinship among the writers and texts he studies. This approach draws upon the Wittgensteinian tradition of the language game, insisting that definitions are themselves situated in the discourses and by the participants in those language games: The "defining" family resemblances of SR are recognized by the producers and the readers of this stream of fiction. Having established this intriguing and evocative model, Stableford goes on to contextualize SR among its literary ancestors (for example, imaginary voyages, future wars, and fantasies of utopian, evolutionary, eschatological, and metaphysical orientations). He then analyzes writers, works, and trends in SR before World War I (for example, works by Wells, M. P. Shiel, and Arthur Conan Doyle) and between the world wars (for example, works by S. Fowler Wright, Olaf Stapledon, and John Gloag), tracing along the way the increasing divergence between SR and SF, the development of the speculative essay in the 1920's and 1930's, and ending with a discussion of the twilight of SR (focusing on C. S. Lewis and Gerald Heard). Stableford's insightful and deeply researched study sheds much light on the development of both SR and SF in Britain.

Suvin, Darko. *Metamorphoses of Science Fiction: On the Poetics and History of a Literary Genre*. New Haven, Conn.: Yale University Press, 1979. Although dense, this groundbreaking Marxist study makes important contributions to the theoretical definition of SF. According to this definition, SF must contain a "novum" or scientifically based new idea or extrapolation that promotes estrangement and cognition. On the basis of his carefully constructed model, Suvin characterizes related narrative fictional types, tracing the history and development of SF and contrasting it with utopian and other types of literature. With major sections devoted to poetics, earlier SF history, and "modern" SF (which reaches to the interwar period, but which includes useful discussions of Russian SF and Karel Čapek), the book focuses on H. G. Wells as the central figure in the development of the form. Not for beginners, this study rewards careful and informed reading, and its extensive bibliography (which includes categories for "Theory and History of SF After Wells," "Theory of the Fictional Utopia," "History of SF to the Eighteenth Century," "History of SF from the French Revolution to Wells," "Wells and His SF Context," and "Russian SF to 1958") will be helpful to scholars and teachers with theoretical interests.

_____. *Victorian Science Fiction in the UK: The Discourses of Knowledge and Power.* Boston: G. K. Hall, 1983. A surprisingly rich bibliographical and theoretical study of nineteenth century narrative fiction that can be considered SF. Adopting a "social formalist" theoretical posture, Suvin argues convincingly that literary form can be questioned as to its societal significance. He begins with a bibliographic study of the material that establishes the basic definitions and limits of the genre and the period (1848-1900), then provides an annotated listing both of SF books and of those that are close relatives. This section is enhanced by an essay on SF and the book trade in the nineteenth century by John Sutherland. Suvin completes this first section of the work with biographical sketches of SF writers and a discussion of their social classification. The second section of the book analyzes Victorian SF as a social discourse, exploring its social addressees, its narrative logic, patterns of ideological domination, and the range of this SF. The study ends with a revealing analysis of the relations between knowledge and power as they are revealed in the social discourse of Victorian SF, with Suvin addressing the preconditions of this popular literary form, its subgenres in relation to British class discourse, and the discourse of history. Suvin manages to combine a variety of scholarly tools (bibliography, textual history) and approaches (Marxism, poststructuralism) to shed considerable light on the antecedents of twentieth century SF.

Telotte, J. P. *Replications: A Robotic History of the Science Fiction Film.* Urbana: University of Illinois Press, 1995. The image of human artifice—in robots, androids, and cyborgs—undergirds Telotte's account of SF cinema. Historically, the image reflects changing attitudes toward technology and scientific reason. In current critical theory, it functions as a metaphor for the self. Telotte discusses robotic representations in a sequence of readings that parallels the development of the genre. He examines films such as *Metropolis*, *Frankenstein*, the Flash Gordon serials of the 1930's and 1940's, *Forbidden Planet*, and *Westworld*. His treatment of more recent works (for example, *The Terminator*, *Robocop*, and *Total Recall*) is influenced by the poststructuralist theories of Jean Baudrillard and Donna Haraway. Unlike them, however, Telotte leans toward humanism. Science fiction films become a "formula for exploring the nature of human being" in tension with technology. Telotte's claims for "the human" downplay gender, racial, and cultural differences, however, and this seems problematic given the poststructuralist discourse he uses. Even so, readers will benefit from the analyses of individual films.

Tymn, Marshall B., ed. *The Science Fiction Reference Book: A Comprehensive Handbook and Guide to the History, Literature, Scholarship, and Related Activities of the Science Fiction and Fantasy Fields*. Mercer Island, Wash.: Starmont House, 1981. A relatively early example of its kind, the *SFRB* covers in large and detailed sections the backgrounds of SF (including a brief history, children's fantasy and SF, SF art, fantastic cinema, and critical studies and reference works), its fandom (covering the history, writing awards, literary awards, and major periodicals in the field), and its outpourings in academe (offering the history of SF in academia, an annotated core list of modern fantasy, a listing of outstanding SF books published between 1927 and 1979, an essay on SF and fantasy library collections, and some resources for teaching SF), in each section offering well-researched essays by specialists in the field. The appendices include a listing of SF and fantasy dissertations (1970-1979), listings of SF organizations and societies, specialty publishers, and a list of important definitions. Although dated in its bibliographic listings, the *SFRB* is a fine starting point for less time-sensitive materials and backgrounds.

Warrick, Patricia S. *The Cybernetic Imagination in Science Fiction*. Cambridge, Mass.: The MIT Press, 1980. This text explores the image of artificial or machine intelligences in SF. There is an extensive historical survey, beginning with the nineteenth century and Mary Shelley and ending with the 1970's. Warrick's argument chronologically traces patterns in the use of these images alongside developing technological theories. She gives much credit to Isaac Asimov's laws of robotics for making the subgenre more definable. She explores the relationship between robots and society in applications as diverse as computers and artificial environments (what might now be called virtual reality). She identifies Philip K. Dick as creating the most complex interactions between machines and humanity. Her argument is well developed and clearly written; this book would serve any SF scholar interested in cybernetic theory or good SF criticism.

Wingrove, David, ed. *The Science Fiction Source Book*. New York: Van Nostrand Reinhold, 1984. This text is split into several sections, based on different parts of the SF field. Brian Stableford begins with a very brief overview of SF's history, going almost decade by decade through the twentieth century. He follows this with a listing and description of an impressive array of subgenres of SF, detailing important texts, themes, images, and authors: man and machine, utopia and dystopia, time travel, aliens, space travel, galactic empires, telekinetic powers, disaster, religion and mythology, parallel worlds and alternate histories, sexuality, ecology, magic, the media, and the inner space of humanity. The third section presents eleven short essays on being an SF writer, including such figures as Poul Anderson, Ray Bradbury, Ursula Le Guin, Larry Niven, Robert Silverberg, Gene Wolfe, and Roger Zelazny. The fourth section provides a checklist of important publications in the field, from fan magazines and fictional presses to scholarly journals, including a short piece on the economics of SF publishing. The last section gives a detailed listing of significant SF criticism. This is an important text, combining factual information with important scholarship of the field.

Wolfe, Gary K. *The Known and the Unknown: The Iconography of Science Fiction.* Kent, Ohio: Kent State University Press, 1979. In this well-written book, Wolfe makes it clear that he intends to offer neither a definition of SF nor its history, focusing instead on a mapping of SF's major icons. Wolfe's main argument is that the central paradigm of SF is a dialectic between the known and the unknown, the tension between this pair giving rise to barriers of various kinds. These barriers create a standard set of icons that reveal the nature of the dialectic. Wolfe describes two general types of fiction, that which includes a puzzle barrier, in which the focus is to solve a conundrum and therefore conquer the unknown; and that which focuses not on the barrier but what is on the other side, which he calls "cultural isolation." The various aspects of these barriers and their manifestations in SF help create a standard set of icons that help experienced SF readers understand the genre. Wolfe studies specific icons extensively, including the spaceship, the city, the wasteland, the robot, and the monster. His argument spans most significant texts in SF and covers most major authors in the field. This text is a very important resource for all SF teachers and scholars.

Wollheim, Donald A. *The Universe Makers: Science Fiction Today.* New York: Harper & Row, 1971. Wollheim traces not the history of SF but the flow of ideas in SF that has influenced movements in the genre. He defines SF as a future both utopic and terrifying, with prophetic scientific possibility, and primarily as a system of ideas. There are four major classifications of SF: imaginary voyages, future predictions, remarkable inventions, and social satire. Jules Verne and H. G. Wells participated in all these classes but fathered a major split on SF's family tree, with Verne developing imaginary voyages and remarkable inventions and Wells concentrating on future predictions and social satire. Wollheim continues his rendering of SF's flow of ideas, citing the contributions of Ray Cummings, Edmond Hamilton, Olaf Stapledon, Isaac Asimov, A. E. van Vogt, and Philip José Farmer. The Vernian side of SF has dominated the evolution of ideas for the universe builders. Many critics see the New Wave as a reemergence of Wellsian writers, but Wollheim considers the New Wave as contributing more to stylistic changes in the genre. To solve these problems of futurity, a coming movement of Wellsians with their satiric and prophetic skills will soon emerge to write SF past these problems and predict more optimistic futures.

Yoke, Carl B., ed. *Phoenix from the Ashes: The Literature of the Remade World.* Westport, Conn.: Greenwood Press, 1987. Through a reading of the long history in mythology of the phoenix and its many names and forms, Yoke gathers this collection of essays studying SF's themes of postapocalyptic or remade worlds incorporating the phoenix's path of birth, death, and rebirth. Remade-world literature may be formulaic, with many variations, but Yoke stresses the underlying ancient narrative of the phoenix as part of the reason and consequence of writing these stories. These re-creation stories serve mythic purposes in modern society, portraying ritual catharsis, victory over death, recognition of the cyclic nature of life, and the hero as both subject and agent of his or her quest. Remade-world literature provides a "powerful metaphor for exploring man's relationships to his social structure, his values, and his fellow man." Included in the collection are essays covering everything from the role of science in, and mythic value of, remade-world literature to studies of specific authors and works. The collection also includes a useful bibliography and a filmography.

—*Len Hatfield*
—*W. A. Senior*
—*Neal Baker*
—*Fiona Kelleghan*
—*Rania Lisas*
—*Marc Zaldivar*

Science Fiction and Fantasy Sites on the World Wide Web

The World Wide Web has numerous sites providing information on science fiction, fantasy, and allied genres. This list presents some of the best and most stable of those sites, each of which contains links that will direct you to other sites.

Alpha Ralpha Boulevard: Science Fiction and Fantasy Bibliographies
http://www.catch22.com/SF/ARB/

This site lists academic archives and Web Guides, home pages of publishers, bookstores, and clubs and societies. Also provided are author bibliographies, links to top SF magazine Web sites and information about SF awards.

The Internet Speculative Fiction Database
http://www.sfsite.com/isfdb/

The ISFDB is an effort to catalog works of science fiction, fantasy, and horror. It links various types of bibliographic data: author bibliographies, publication bibliographies, award listings, magazine content listings, anthology and collection content listings, yearly fiction indexes, and forthcoming books.

Linköping Science Fiction and Fantasy Archive
http://sf.www.lysator.liu.se/sf_archive/sf_main.html

This site archives Usenet postings containing reviews of science fiction and fantasy books and movies. It also contains an art gallery, a thorough index of Web links, and an author database with both reviews and biographies.

The Locus Index to Science Fiction (1984-1998)
http://www.locusmag.com/index/0start.html

Created by Charles N. Brown, the publisher and editor of *Locus* magazine, and William G. Contento, this large, invaluable site is based on the monthly "Books Received" column in *Locus*. Containing indexes to publishers, series, book and magazine statistics, and awards, as well as links to other recent indexes, it is searchable by authors, cover artists, and book and magazine titles.

Science Fiction and Fantasy Research Database
http://library.tamu.edu/cushing/sffrd/

Compiled by Hal Hall, this online site is a searchable database of information on *Science Fiction and Fantasy Research Index, 1878-1985*, *Science Fiction and Fantasy Research Index, 1985-1991*, and *Science Fiction and Fantasy Research Index, 1991-1995*. The database provides access to science fiction-related articles, books, news reports, obituaries, and motion picture reviews and covers some horror, gothic, and utopian literature. The site is an excellent research tool with a powerful, easy-to-use search engine.

Science Fiction Research Association
http://www.sfra.org/

The SFRA is the oldest professional organization for the study of science fiction and fantasy literature and film. Founded in 1970, it was created to improve classroom teaching, encourage and assist scholarship, and evaluate and publicize new books and magazines dealing with fantastic literature. The site includes current reviews, archives of past reviews, conference information, and research links.

Science Fiction Resource Guide
http://www.sflovers.org/Web/SFRG/

This site contains an extensive collection of links to science fiction resources on the Web. Subject areas include other archives and resource guides, authors, art and artists, bibliographies, films, television, bookstores, book reviews, role-playing games, zines (fan magazines), and more. Maintained by Chaz Boston Baden, the site has received many Best-of-the-Net awards and honors.

Science Fiction Weekly
http://www.scifi.com/sfw

Published online weekly and affiliated with the sci-fi cable television channel, this site covers news on movies, books, television, games and other science fiction media, as well as feature articles and interviews. Its Web Guide and "FreeZone" offer links and downloadable media players for the archive of original Sci Fi Channel videos.

SF Site: The Home Page for Science Fiction and Fantasy
http://www.sfsite.com

Updated twice monthly, this site provides a mixture of book reviews, opinion pieces, author interviews, fiction excerpts, and reading lists. It also offers a comprehensive list of links to author and fan tribute sites, science-fiction conventions, and media and other science-fiction-related resources.

The Ultimate Science Fiction Web Guide

http://www.magicdragon.com/UltimateSF/SF-Index.html

This Guide offers almost six thousand links to science fiction resources including authors, books, movies and a comprehensive chronological history of the field. The site also provides links organized by theme, such as cloning, aliens, and biology.

—Fiona Kelleghan

Genre Index

Title Index

Author Index

Subject Index

This index lists book, short story, and series titles, as well as characters, places, authors, historical figures, and selected themes and subjects, ranging from androids to World War II.